THE DEVIL'S CHAIN

THE DEVIL'S CHAIN

PROSTITUTION AND SOCIAL CONTROL IN PARTITIONED POLAND

KEELY STAUTER-HALSTED

CORNELL UNIVERSITY PRESS
Ithaca and London

Cornell University Press gratefully acknowledges receipt of a subvention from the Stefan and Lucy Hejna Endowment for Polish Studies at the University of Illinois at Chicago, which aided in the publication of this book.

Copyright © 2015 by Cornell University

First published 2015 by Cornell University Press

Printed in the United States of America

Library of Congress Cataloging-in-Publication Data

Stauter-Halsted, Keely, 1960– author.
    The devil's chain : prostitution and social control in partitioned Poland / Keely Stauter-Halsted.
        pages cm
    Includes bibliographical references and index.
    ISBN 978-0-8014-5419-6 (cloth : alk. paper)
    1. Prostitution—Poland—History—19th century.
    2. Prostitution—Poland—History—20th century. 3. Sex—
    Social aspects—Poland—History—19th century. 4. Sex—
    Social aspects—Poland—History—20th century.
    5. Poland—History—1864–1918. I. Title.
        HQ217.7.A5S73 2015
        306.7409438—dc23   2015021725

Cornell University Press strives to use environmentally responsible suppliers and materials to the fullest extent possible in the publishing of its books. Such materials include vegetable-based, low-VOC inks and acid-free papers that are recycled, totally chlorine-free, or partly composed of nonwood fibers. For further information, visit our website at www.cornellpress.cornell.edu.

Cloth printing   10 9 8 7 6 5 4 3 2 1

Contents

ACKNOWLEDGMENTS

We often think of research and writing as solitary tasks. Yet this book like many of its kind is the product of years of collaborative interactions with colleagues and friends across the globe. From the moment Nathan Wood and I picked up a police registry in Cracow's National Archive and spotted Larry Wolff's name on it, to conversations with Leslie Moch on commutes between Ann Arbor and East Lansing as we fantasized about what this research might become, this book has benefited from the wisdom and kindness of colleagues the world over. My friends in the Gender Studies consortium at MSU were receptive to the idea from the beginning even while pushing me into more broadly comparative frameworks. Kirsten Fermaglich and Ethan Segal weighed in on the Jewish dimensions of the sex trafficking chapters, as did Ken Waltzer, whose close readings have always inspired the highest standard of scholarship. Lisa Fine taught me about parallel patterns of behavior among single women in North America and in Eastern Europe. Erika Windler and I spent lovely afternoons in various cafés reading each other's chapters and realizing the profound overlap between nineteenth-century Brazilian and Polish history. John Waller served as a sounding board for my early ideas about eugenics and the growing power of the medical profession in the nineteenth century. Lewis Siegelbaum has been an engaging conversational partner on any number of topics, including those surrounding this project. His friendship and that of other MSU colleagues, like David Bailey, Peter Beattie, Walter Hawthorne, and Mark Kornbluh, are among the lasting benefits of my time in East Lansing.

Farther afield, Robert Blobaum guided me to Polish scholarship that overlapped with my own and put me in touch with academics at Polish institutions. Arista Cirtautas invited me to speak at the University of Virginia when the project was in its infancy, challenging me to articulate my conception of personal agency among the women who were the subjects of my book. She remained willing to puzzle through conceptual issues in many late-night phone conversations and conference dinners as the work unfolded. Antony Polonsky offered encouragement and an enormous list of bibliographical leads that expanded the project's dimensions. Nathan Wood's vast knowledge of Polish newspapers and archives, his collegial connections, and his ability to conjure up turn-of-the-century conditions made it a joy to work with him and to compare notes on our overlapping projects. A series of road shows with Nancy Wingfield, including the "Sex in the City" Conference in L'viv, helped establish prostitution as a historical topic with some cachet in East Central Europe; researching in tandem during Vienna archival trips encouraged us both to appreciate the continuities and distinctions of the sex trade in the Habsburg space. Tara Zahra invited me to present a draft of what was then a single chapter on sex trafficking at University of Chicago's European History Colloquium, prompting me to think more seriously about the migration elements of any trafficking story. Similarly, Patrice Dabrowski's invitation to present my work at the University of Vienna's doctoral seminar on Austrian Galicia helped clarify some of the multicultural dimensions of my story. Beth Holmgren was kind enough to bring me in to speak at Duke in the finishing stages of the project, and her students offered useful iterations of the book's potential significance.

Since arriving at the University of Illinois at Chicago, I have found similarly warm and supportive colleagues who have from the beginning found value and excitement in this book. The Department of History abounds with Polish and East European specialists and I've been blessed with the collegial support of Gosia Fidelis, Jonathan Daly, and Marina Mogilner, in addition to my colleagues in the Department of Slavic and Baltic Studies. The Jewish Studies team, including Sam Fleischacker, Richard Levy, Ralph Keen, Robert Johnston, and Elizabeth Loentz, offered productive insights as I sought to situate my argument in the larger context of nineteenth-century anti-Semitism. Marina Mogilner has been particularly receptive in thinking through the eugenics piece. My graduate students—Melissa Hibbard, Jenni Marlow, Michał Wilczewski, and Tiffany Wilson—have provided constant opportunities to talk through the manuscript's many quandaries and at times offered much-needed concrete assistance. Melissa helped me navigate the world of social work and charity activists; Jenni inspired me to think about housekeepers in a more complex way; Michał assisted in depicting the importance of the war and in his tenacious search through Polish archives and libraries for suitable images to accompany the manuscript; and Tiffany stepped in to edit footnotes in the latter stages of preparation. Anna Szawara, our Polish Studies assistant, saved me from much embarrassment through her meticulous proofreading of the Polish-language citations. My undergraduate students at UIC have also shaped this project through their animated discussions in several spicy senior seminars. Finally, two conscientious anonymous readers for Cornell University Press improved the final product enormously, helping me sharpen the argument in important ways. Roger Haydon has been a joy to work with at the press, his low-key demeanor and dry wit reducing the anxiety that typically accompanies the final stages of producing a manuscript.

On the other side of the Atlantic, research for this book has brought me closer to colleagues in Poland and the rest of Central Europe. Krzysztof Zamorski of the Historical Institute at Jagiellonian University in Cracow has helped at every stage of the project, sharing his understanding of the intricacies of Polish archives and helping to conceptualize the narrative during our annual lunches. Adam Walaszek offered his encyclopedic knowledge of migration literature, parts of his personal library, and much welcome hospitality. Dobrochna Kałwa served as a guide to existing research on gender and social history in the Polish lands, and a sounding board for all things crazy about Polish life. Martin Pollack shared his archival finds with me. Dietland Hüchter in Leipzig helped bring me into a wider circle of scholars researching trafficking. Above all, Jolanta Sikorska-Kulesza was more generous than I could have imagined about Polish collections touching on the prostitution question. Her recommendation of a research assistant was invaluable. I only hope my own results serve as the complement Jolanta was seeking to parallel her work on registered prostitution in the nineteenth-century Polish Kingdom.

I am pleased to acknowledge the help and support of several European libraries and archives, including the rich collections at the Jagiellonian University Library in Cracow, the National Library in Warsaw, and the University of Warsaw Library. The archivists at the National Archive in Cracow and at the Academy of Sciences Archive in Cracow were consistently resourceful, patient, and accommodating to the needs of a foreign researcher conducting marathon raids on their collections, as was the staff at Poznań's efficiently run National Archive and the Central Archives of Historical Records (AGAD) in Warsaw. The warmth and generosity of the archivists at Warsaw's Medical Library (Biblioteka Lekarska Warszawska) may be unsurpassed in the East European archival context. The staff's graciousness in obtaining digital photographs for the manuscript virtually overnight was much appreciated, and I am enormously grateful for their overall goodwill during two very intense research stints. In Vienna, I benefitted from the massive collections at the Austrian State Archives and the rich concentration of police records on trafficking (*Mädchenhandel*) housed at the Central Police Department Archive, as well as the published material available in the Austrian National Library. Back home, the librarians at UIC's Daley Library have been gracious and efficient in processing my often bizarre interlibrary loan requests and have amazed me at the speed and finesse with which they are able to fill them. I have received generous research funding from the Department of History and the Jewish Studies Program at Michigan State University, as well as from the research budget of the Stefan and Lucy Hejna Endowment for Polish Studies at UIC. This steady stream of short-term travel support permitted the regular research visits to European collections without which it would have been impossible to accomplish a book of this scope and detail.

Even as the book was researched via collegial connections the world over and its results have been presented in public arenas, the writing itself has mainly been accomplished in isolation. In my case, the splendid isolation was the cozy nest of our family home. Though a large part of the manuscript was written in various coffee shops around Ann Arbor (including the first chapter, which was started the morning our son, now graduated from college, took his SAT exam), my fondest memories will always be composing yet another new draft chapter in my cozy Chicago study, surrounded by a gaggle of high school girls (and increasing numbers of adolescent boys), our son home from college, and my husband busy with some new project in the next room. Though I am sure they have all long since tired of me waxing on at school functions about my research on ladies of the night, my family has remained incredibly patient and supportive throughout. No one could ever be more encouraging or more adept at solving problems—both logistical and interpretive—than my husband, Dave Halsted. Without him, this book's contribution to larger historical questions would have been comparatively meager. His willingness to read multiple drafts, his problem-solving skills, his generosity in encouraging my research trips during periods when most "normal" families would be attending family reunions or celebrating holidays, and his bravery in being left alone with small children even during dance recitals and school plays is a debt I can probably never repay. So thanks to my son Chris (especially for his final close edit of the manuscript), to my daughter Caroline for her charm and good cheer, and most of all to Dave, to whom this book is appropriately dedicated.

THE DEVIL'S CHAIN

Introduction
Reforming the National Body

> I cannot imagine in all of Europe a town as
> unrestrained as Warsaw. . . . Such female figures as
> one sees in the darkness of Warsaw, such legions, such
> impudence in accosting passersby, these things do not
> exist anywhere else. A country is its customs!
>
> —Bolesław Prus, "Nim słońce wejdzie" (Before the
> sun rises)

In January 1883 an angry exchange of letters in Warsaw's popular press drew attention to the epidemic of streetwalkers polluting public spaces in the former capital. Residents complained that every other house had become a brothel and that the cacophony of singing, dancing, and brawling was disrupting their otherwise orderly lives.[1] Anxiety about open sexuality on city streets soon spilled over into fears of innocence violated as high-profile trafficking trials called attention to the mass kidnapping of innocent virgins.[2] By the early years of the twentieth century, gang-related sexual violence burst onto the public stage with the bloody Alfonse Pogrom of 1905 that left dozens of casualties in a ruined Warsaw vice district.[3] Even during the waning days of World War I, when the empires occupying Polish territory lay in ruins and the nation's fortunes were finally on the ascent, concern about a spike in prostitution and climbing rates of venereal infection gripped the population with renewed force. Experts warned that Poland was

---

1. See, for example, the exchanges in *Kurier Poranny,* January 9, 1883, 2; and *Kurier Warszawski,* no. 345 (1883): 3.

2. "Z tajemnic społeczeństwa: Handlarz dziewcząt," *Gazeta Narodowa,* July 9, 1892, 2; "Handlarze dziewcząt," *Gazeta Narodowa,* October 19, 1892, 2.

3. "Kilka słów w kwestyi prostytucyi z powodu ostatnich pogromów," *Nowe Słowo* 4 (October 15, 1905): 391–95; "Krwawy dramat," *Słowo,* May 25, 1905, 3; "Precz prostytucją i nierządem," *Czystość* 1 (June 20, 1905): 5–6.

"on the verge of a new and dangerous calamity" at the very moment of her political rebirth. Syphilis raged through city and country alike, felling huge portions of the population and sapping the strength of future generations.[4] In all, the forty years between the 1880s and the founding years of the Polish Second Republic witnessed an unprecedented outpouring of public concern around the problem of prostitution. Again and again, contemporaries pointed to commercial sex as a grave danger to the Polish nation. Long a fixture of urban life, prostitution took on new meaning in these years as the focus of reforming zeal and the key to national self-preservation.

What accounted for the sudden interest in venal sex across the lands of partitioned Poland? How can we understand the panic about sexuality, disease, and intimate violence among Polish-speaking observers? What elements did this panic and the response to it share across the political boundaries of Austrian, Prussian, and Russian Poland, with their very different legal and regulatory structures and distinct approaches to issues of gender, migration, health care, and social control? *The Devil's Chain* explores the life world of prostitution in the Polish provinces as a prism through which to assess Poland's difficult transition to modernity in the context of its struggling movement for political independence. Beginning with the moment of public alarm in the 1880s when journalists and civil servants set out to address the burgeoning sex industry, the narrative encompasses the crest of anxiety about prostitution following the 1905 Revolution and traces the course of the white slavery scare that extended through the early years of the twentieth century. The incidence of paid sex peaked during the long years of total war from 1914 to 1921, when widows and abandoned women resorted to sex work to survive foreign occupation and military conflict. Prostitution reform was again in the air during the interwar Second Republic, but two decades of economic crisis and political chaos ushered in only limited adjustments to the system of police regulation inherited from previous administrations.

Looking at prostitution in the Polish lands highlights broad patterns of multiclass contact under conditions of imperial subjugation. As such, this study is intentionally situated at the crux of a cross-border dialogue encompassing all three portions of the divided Polish state. It seeks to trace an increasingly urgent conversation about a problem plaguing "Polish" society as a whole. I argue that an emerging national elite consisting of educated writers, journalists, social workers, university lecturers, students, scientists,

---

4. Emil Wyrobek, *Choroby weneryczne: Ich skutki i znaczenie w życiu jednostki i społeczeństwa, tudzież osoby leczenia i zapogiegania* (Cracow, 1916), 64–65. Please note that all translations from foreign documents are my own unless otherwise indicated.

legal experts, and medical professionals engaged in an ongoing discussion about the causes and consequences of commercial sex. The premise of this debate, conducted everywhere from daily newspapers to specialized medical journals, lecture halls, and associational meetings, was that the incidence of public sex in the Polish lands had reached near crisis proportions and that the solution to the burgeoning rates of prostitution lay at the heart of Polish hopes for national renewal. Variable censorship laws across the three partitions combined with permeable borders and relatively rapid train communications to facilitate a conversation that spanned the Polish-speaking territories from Poznań to Lublin. We hear from muckraking journalists in Lwów, welfare activists in Cracow, feminists in Warsaw, venereal experts in Łódź, and legal specialists in Poznań, in conversation with one another, each publishing in professional journals and daily presses across imperial boundaries. Stricter censorship laws in the Polish-speaking provinces of the German Empire kept the prostitution debate out of the daily press there, but physicians and legal experts nonetheless managed to take part in cross-border debates by publishing in the more permissive intellectual environment of Austrian Galicia or post-1905 Warsaw.

For the most part, the interlocutors who appear in this book conducted their discussions in Polish, though they clearly had access to literature on prostitution reform, scientific developments, and social-work innovations in Western languages and in Russian. The community they referenced—the population they sought to improve—was "Poland," by which they meant the people of the former Polish Commonwealth [*Rzeczpospolita*] before its late eighteenth-century dismemberment. Many of the women they discussed were native Polish speakers, but a substantial minority functioned primarily in Yiddish. Still others were recorded on police registries as Ruthenian speakers (usually noted as Greek Catholics or Russian Orthodox by rite), or as Germans, Lithuanians, Czechs, Hungarians, Roma, or any number of other minorities inhabiting the towns and cities of former Polish territory. The focus of reformers' efforts was not always ethnically defined. Agendas and programs were instead addressed at resolving a problem besetting the nation or the *naród*, attacking "*Polska*," or even the "*lud*," or folk. Distinctions became clearer when reformers turned to their occasional characterization of prostitution and especially of international trafficking as a "Jewish problem," an epithet that did not go unchallenged in contemporary debates.

The pages that follow explore the broader meanings behind the prostitution debate in the half century leading up to Poland's renewed political independence. I argue that discussion of prostitution and its attendant disorders—sexual deviancy, alcoholism, child abuse, vagrancy, venereal disease, and other related problems—provided a perfect backdrop for mapping out alternative visions of the nation's future. Public discussion of the flourishing sex industry helped shape larger negotiations about modernizing the Polish national body in preparation for political independence. By charting solutions to the prostitution dilemma Polish actors allowed commercial sex to stand in for a whole host of calamities the country had suffered since the late eighteenth-century collapse of the Republic. Prostitution became a symbol of the malevolent rule of three occupying powers and of the crushing need to reform nearly every aspect of Polish social practices. Beginning in the 1880s and continuing into the founding years of the Second Polish Republic, residents of the Polish territories struggled to ameliorate the conditions of the local and international sex trade and to reduce the incidence of young women turning to paid sex. *The Devil's Chain* traces a new conversation about sexuality, gender propriety, and social class that was conducted through the idiom of prostitution. This book is about how Polish commentators introduced gender and sexuality into the national conversation and how that changed the configuration of modern Poland.

The book begins with an exploration of the drama that unfolded over the problem of paid sex during the last decades of imperial rule in the Polish lands. Prostitution lay at the juncture of mass and elite culture.[5] The sale of sex permeated visits to the opera and the symphony, colored the atmosphere at local restaurants and pubs, and crept into the bourgeois home by way of underpaid housekeepers who moonlighted as registered prostitutes. City life brought rural migrants and working girls into contact with elite students, officials, and garrisoned soldiers, transforming urban centers into the sites of conflicting social codes. Prostitution in all its permutations was practiced at the interstices of this social upheaval, bringing together sharply divergent social classes in what had long been a radically stratified society. Since rhetoric about the vanquished nation coursed through nearly every public discussion of social ills or future promise, reforming actors were explicitly preoccupied with their country's political independence while implicitly navigating the landmines of sexual modernity.

At the heart of the reform discussion was a debate about the women who practiced paid sex, a social group that existed at the very margins of fin de

---

5. As Timothy Gilfoyle has observed, "commercial sex" is a particularly useful category of analysis for the historian because it "functioned at the nexus of social relations in community life." Timothy J. Gilfoyle, "Prostitutes in the Archives: Problems and Possibilities in Documenting the History of Sexuality," *American Archivist* 57, no. 3 (1994): 514–27.

siècle Polish society. *The Devil's Chain* explores the lives of the impoverished women who turned to the streets and the social milieu that shaped their limited choices, mapping the contingent circumstances that drove them to the practice. Prostitution lay at the center of vital concerns plaguing Poland's lower classes, including issues of morality, gender roles, family and reproductive life, and the ways poor women understood and manipulated the administrative systems within which prostitutes were legally bound. Viewed as an unfortunate and often dangerous option, prostitution nonetheless served as an important temporary expedient for a certain subset of needy women. Understanding sex work as a tool for survival allows us to highlight the ways in which Poland's wider social classes experienced the heightened sexual tensions of the late nineteenth century.[6] The women who served as the mainstay of garrisoned solders and who facilitated the sexual induction of gymnasium and university students also had very real lives. They made difficult decisions about their own fates and experienced a variety of outcomes as a result of their participation in the sex trade. The focus here, then, is on prostitution as an economic "weapon of the weak," a potential escape route from inherited poverty for women whose voices are rarely found in the historical record.[7]

Women who turn to commercial sex—or to any of a number of other seemingly unsavory practices—often appear in the historical record as passive victims of their own fate. Historians and other scholars present them as "duped" or forced into particular behaviors. They are subjected to the will of powerful, wealthy, or cunning handlers. Moreover, even the most liberal-minded and generous contemporary social commentators frequently perceived poor and uneducated girls as being easily led astray. The social distance that remained from Poland's feudal past continued to inform their judgment about sexual impropriety. Yet, as we will see, sometimes it was elite power brokers who were duped by clever lower-class women, many of whom changed jobs to avoid unwanted sexual advances or migrated to new communities seeking a fresh start. This book argues that many poor women found ways to exercise limited agency in times of personal hardship, material shortage, or family crisis. Selling sex was but one among a range of difficult options available to them.

---

6. On the historiography of broader sexuality studies in the east-central European context, see Matti Bunzl, "Desiderata for a History of Austrian Sexualities," *Austrian History Yearbook* 38 (2007): 48–57.

7. On strategies of opposition among relatively powerless, politically subordinate population groups, see James C. Scott, *Weapons of the Weak: Everyday Forms of Peasant Resistance* (New Haven, CT, 2008).

To a great extent, legal and medical authorities imposed the "prostitute" label onto lower-class women. As a category, it was not always embraced among practitioners of paid sex. A high proportion of the young women inscribed onto police registries in urban centers across east-central Europe did not self-identify as professional prostitutes. Instead, many turned to public sex during periods of unemployment or in order to supplement substandard wages. Selling sex temporarily or part time was not necessarily considered a major step among working women. Nonetheless, social activists, vice squads, and elite public opinion often wrongly branded such strategic sexual behavior as comprising a permanent moral downfall from which its actor could not recover. This book is explicitly focused on these lower-class streetwalkers and brothel residents rather than the elite courtesans who served as companions to local military officers or wealthy aristocrats. This latter type of sexual encounter was less ubiquitous in the impoverished Polish lands than in Western Europe and, in any case, represents a social cohort distinct from the milieu addressed in this book. I mean to examine here the category of inexpensive public women of lowly social background who were unskilled and only minimally educated. It is these women—defined both by what they did and by their social origin—who represent a rising class of ambitious individuals intent on constructing their own future in a modernizing Polish society.

The Devil's Chain also explores the figures at the edges of the sex trade, who formed a vital component of Poland's modernizing processes. Often driven to their roles as sexual mediators by economic structures that allowed little room for maneuver, the pimps, procurers, madams, and traffickers who inhabited this liminal terrain typically traded in other wares besides women. Those who helped guide women into the local sex trade also functioned as smugglers, migration agents, or employment recruiters. Some of them worked as night watchmen in tenement apartment houses; others were "knife men" who belonged to urban gangs. Regardless, it was relatively easy for a homeless or needy young woman to find her way to a place of prostitution through contact with one of these urban mediators. A disproportionate number of the madams, procurers, and long-distance traffickers who facilitated the transition into professional sex work were Jews, a fact that fed notions of anti-Semitism and assumptions about Jewish victimization of Christian girls. In particular, international migration agents who assisted single, young women in gaining passage abroad were often characterized as traffickers in human goods, an accusation that detracted from the personal agency of the women who frequently elected voluntarily to leave their homes. Viewing migration agents and local procurers in their own social context helps deconstruct the difficult but important relationship between procurer and prostitute, showing the limits on individual agency afforded Poland's marginal classes.

Finally, and perhaps most centrally, the narrative turns to the fin de siècle social activists who took on the prostitution problem as part of their larger agenda. Educated Poles sought to apply social control and reform to nearly every aspect of the nation's life in the late nineteenth century. Part of a larger emphasis on working at the base of society, programs to improve the country's economic and cultural conditions after a century of failed uprisings encompassed a wide range of efforts to assist impoverished young women. A broad range of actors, including journalists, women's rights activists, charity workers, physicians, and religious figures, focused their disciplining energies on everything from education and agriculture to industrial development and urban planning. Prostitution also came under their critical lens. Social activists wondered publicly how morally challenged young women, variously depicted as dirty, diseased, psychologically unstable, genetically flawed, or physically degenerate, could be integrated into a nation that was beginning the process of democratizing and expanding its political suffrage. The new multiclass Polish nation would need to integrate and elevate individuals from the dregs of society if it was to fulfill the hope of a democratic future. Two generations after peasant emancipation, the young women turning tricks on city streets were invariably migrants from the impoverished countryside or daughters of the urban poor. Only recently considered part of the political nation, the peasantry had yet to gain equal footing with their former lords. It would be several generations before those of peasant background would find common cause with their social betters. For all of these reasons, the study of commercial sex in this period gives us insight into the shifting status of the public woman from reviled outsider to pitied insider, from the focus of efforts to castigate and isolate her to the object of the reformers' gaze.

Concern about commercial sex brought activists and reformers together to fashion a "shadow state" of public actors operating largely outside imperial institutions. The prostitution debate reveals a detailed and complex record of social visions about how to remedy the existence of an impoverished, sexually debauched female subculture within Polish society. Those involved in these discussions constructed their agendas according to varying prescriptions for how a "modern" society such as Poland should respond to and treat social ills. Competing institutions of social control—moral, religious, medical, administrative, legal, pedagogical, and others—asserted themselves in the absence of and at times as a substitute for centralizing state apparatuses. This "shadow state" operated behind the scenes and away from the gaze of imperial overlords, providing an opportunity for Poles to experiment with social transformation agendas even before taking active roles in official administrative hierarchies.

In particular, physicians throughout Europe and North America became newly aware of the dangers of contagious diseases and especially of venereal contaminations during the nineteenth century. They also became increasingly professionalized and tasked with the responsibility for public health dangers. By the end of the century, progressive doctors had become preoccupied with the overall degeneration of the "species" and many viewed inherited ailments as a direct danger to the national corpus, a sentiment that helped drive the growth of an active eugenics movement on Polish territory. Relying on images of the female body, references to unrestrained sexuality and metaphors of disease, medical commentators manipulated the direction of national reform, shaping it into a scientific, rational model of social organization. The preoccupation with the strength of the national body led some reformers to pursue a eugenic solution to the prostitution danger, a scientific trajectory that distorted efforts to direct the debate toward more economic, pragmatic programs for helping potential sex workers. As eugenics initiatives turned to discussion of inherited sexual deviance, prostitution reform took on a more fatalistic, deterministic aspect. This distortion in the Poles' efforts to rationalize national sexuality would stymie the success of reform legislation during the early years of Polish statehood.

Prostitution was a grave concern to residents of the Polish lands at the turn of the century. It was a favorite theme of the novelist and newspaper columnist Bolesław Prus (born Aleksander Głowacki), who filled Warsaw's daily press with commentary on the hardships suffered by working-class women. It preoccupied the young Janusz Korczak (born Henryk Goldszmit), pediatrician and children's author, who penned tirades about child labor and the sexual abuse of minors. Prostitution appeared in the work of Aleksander Świętochowski, the philosopher best known for his advocacy of the program of scientific modernity known as Warsaw Positivism, and in addition was a persistent focus for feminist advocates such a Eliza Orzeszkowa, Maria Turzyma, Izabela Moszczeńska, and Paulina Kuczalska-Reinschmit, all of whom railed against a social practice that made lower-class women the playthings of bourgeois males and led to the contamination of innocent wives and children. Finally, of course, commercial sex was a research interest for a whole generation of physicians who lambasted the imperial governments for failing to control venereal infections.

Prostitution as a public policy was less of a direct concern to the thousands of women who appeared for their twice-weekly checkups at police stations across the Polish lands. These women were more concerned with making their way in a hostile urban environment. Nonetheless, they too expressed their complaints about arbitrary police roundups, harsh medical exams, and the volatility of employment for unskilled workers. Each of these actors saw the regulation apparatus as a broken system that no longer served its intended function. All were hostile to a process that had been introduced by the ruling empires and that was blamed for much of what was wrong in Polish society. In a political context where open criticism of the ruling powers was nearly impossible, activists turned to debate about prostitution reform as a foil for discussing any number of other problems—including the limitations of public education, relations between the sexes, female emancipation, migration, rural poverty, and the dangers of the great city.

The Polish Case in International Context

The system of police-regulated prostitution, introduced across Europe in the early nineteenth century, was never subjected to such searing social criticism as in the years leading up to the Great War. Everywhere in Europe and the Americas, social activists, politicians, religious leaders, and the medical community portrayed commercial sex as the bogeyman responsible for a whole host of social ills. Swelling urban centers with their overcrowded working-class neighborhoods brought commercial sex and other forms of sexual "deviance" to the public's attention.[8] European metropolises featured unabashed sex workers lining city streets, filling venereal wards of local hospitals, and staffing the cafés and watering holes in otherwise upstanding urban neighborhoods. Thousands of public women were inscribed on police registries from Paris to Berlin, Hamburg to Budapest; others operated clandestinely, away from the prying eye of state authorities. The Jack the Ripper murders of the late 1880s and the sex trafficking cases that followed helped rivet Europe's collective imagination on commercial sex and its dangerous milieu.[9] Meanwhile, pundits filled newspaper columns with sensational

---

8. On the preoccupation with sexual deviance in Vienna, see Harry Oosterhuis, *Stepchildren of Nature: Krafft-Ebing, Psychiatry, and the Making of Sexual Identity* (Chicago, 2000).

9. On the 1888 Jack the Ripper case, see Judith K. Walkowitz, *City of Dreadful Delight: Narratives of Sexual Danger in Late-Victorian London* (Chicago, 1992). Richard J. Evans highlights the sensational murder trial of the Berlin pimp Heinze and his wife that helped bring commercial sex to the attention of the German imperial public, in "Prostitution, State, and Society in Imperial Germany," *Past and Present* 70 (February 1976): 119 ff. Edward J. Bristow surveyed the panic among the Jewish community over white slavery in *Prostitution and Prejudice: The Jewish Fight against White Slavery, 1870–1939* (Oxford, 1983).

reports and scholars researched the causes, implications, and cures for rampant public sex, releasing an unprecedented array of studies on the ubiquitous sex workers haunting Europe's urban centers.[10]

Everywhere the problem of paid sex was understood in the context of wider social problems and existing paradigms of progress.[11] Recent historiography has reflected many of these perspectives, addressing varying aspects of the world the prostitute inhabited. Much of this scholarship has been shaped by available documentation and by the priorities of reformers and other contemporary social actors. North American scholars, for example, have tended to focus on the abolitionists who set out to eliminate commercial sex in much the same way (and often led by the same crusading individuals) as they worked to abolish the enslavement of Africans.[12] In Britain, charitable societies struggled to "save" fallen women, few of whom were interested in rescue. Historians have captured this philanthropic crusade in their work.[13] Concerns about prostitution in the newly unified states of Italy and Germany have led researchers to focus on the

10. An early such report was "The Maiden Tribute of Modern Babylon," a series of newspaper articles on child prostitution and kidnapping that appeared in the *Pall Mall Gazette* in July 1885. Written by the crusading editor W. T. Stead, the sensational reports were widely translated and became a model for journalists of boulevard presses across Europe. See Deborah Gorham, "The 'Maiden Tribute of Modern Babylon' Re-examined: Child Prostitution and the Idea of Childhood in Late Victorian England," *Victorian Studies* 21, no. 3 (1978): 353–79. Among the encyclopedic studies conducted at the turn of the century are Abraham Flexner, *The Regulation of Prostitution in Europe* (New York, 1914); Josef Schrank, *Die Prostitution in Wien in historischer, administrativer und hygienischer Beziehung*, 2 vols. (Vienna, 1886); Schrank, *Der Mädchenhandel und seine Bekämpfung* (Vienna, 1904); and Iwan Bloch, *Die Prostitution* (Berlin, 1912).

11. The French historian Alain Corbin, author of perhaps the most influential study of nineteenth-century prostitution, observed that the "nature of the sources created by the social system [in each country] has its effect on the historian's view" of prostitution, a situation that helps explain why British and American scholars study the antiprostitution abolition movement whereas French scholars examine the machinery of the police regulation system itself. Alain Corbin, *Women for Hire: Prostitution and Sexuality in France after 1850,* trans. Alan Sheridan (Cambridge, MA, 1990), ix.

12. Mark Connelly, *The Response to Prostitution in the Progressive Era* (Chapel Hill, 1980); David Pivar, *Purity Crusade: Sexual Morality and Social Control, 1868–1900* (Westport, CT, 1973); and Roland Wagner, "Virtue against Vice: A Study of Moral Reformers and Prostitutes in the Progressive Era" (PhD diss., University of Wisconsin, 1971). Timothy J. Gilfoyle's *City of Eros: New York City, Prostitution, and the Commercialization of Sex, 1790–1920* (New York, 1992) takes a slightly different tack, showing the colorful history of prostitution as a central component of New York City's economic life before the reformers forced the trade underground.

13. Frances Finnegan, *Poverty and Prostitution: A Study of Victorian Prostitutes in York* (Cambridge, 1979); and Linda Mahood, *The Magdalenes: Prostitution in the Nineteenth Century* (New York, 1990).

role of the state, national unity, the modernization of the police system, and the strength of the military in these settings.[14] The Russian imperial bureaucracy set out to categorize and control its emerging female subclass in the aftermath of peasant emancipation, providing documentation for scholars to trace the evolution of the liberal state through reform efforts.[15] Meanwhile, social activists in Latin America concerned themselves with the position of the family, with questions of honor, and with damage to the nation engendered by rampant indulgence in commercialized sex, encouraging a nationalist focus on prostitution studies in the region.[16] Finally, historians of European colonies in Africa and Asia have approached the battle with prostitution through the prism of colonial relations, nationalism, race, and class tensions.[17] In each of these settings, the historical record reflects the interests of the actors who guided the reform efforts and who often shaped the movement in their own particular interests. Historians who take on the prostitution question typically leaven their narratives with local concerns and priorities. This book, preoccupied as it is with questions of national subjectivity, modernization, social tensions, and imperialism, is no exception.

Sources for Accessing the World of Paid Sex

Research on the history of prostitution is hampered by an unusual dearth of documentation, particularly in the East European space. Scholars of modern Poland have faced challenges with access to sources, especially those distributed among the capitals of the imperial states that administered Polish

14. Mary Gibson, *Prostitution and the State in Italy, 1860–1915* (Columbus, OH, 1999); and Evans, "Prostitution, State, and Society in Imperial Germany." German activists also conducted morality crusades along the pattern of their American sisters. See Marion Kaplan, "Prostitution, Morality Crusades, and Feminism: German-Jewish Feminists and the Campaign against White Slavery," *Women's Studies International Forum* 5, no. 6 (1982): 619–27.

15. See Laurie Bernstein, *Sonia's Daughters: Prostitutes and Their Regulation in Imperial Russia* (Berkeley, CA, 1995); and Laura Engelstein, *The Keys to Happiness: Sex and the Search for Modernity in Fin-de-Siècle Russia* (Ithaca, NY, 1992).

16. Donna J. Guy, *Sex and Danger in Buenos Aires: Prostitution, Family, and Nation in Argentina* (Lincoln, NB, 1991); and L. C. Soares, *Prostitution in Nineteenth-Century Rio de Janeiro* (London, 1988).

17. Phillippa Levine, *Prostitution, Race, and Politics: Policing Venereal Disease in the British Empire* (New York, 2003); Elizabeth B. Van Heyningen, "The Social Evil in the Cape Colony, 1868–1902: Prostitution and the Contagious Diseases Acts," *Journal of Southern African Studies* 10 (April 1984): 170–97; Gail Hershatter, *Dangerous Pleasures: Prostitution and Modernity in Twentieth-Century Shanghai* (Berkeley, CA, 1997); and Luise White, *The Comforts of Home: Prostitution in Colonial Nairobi* (Chicago, 1990). Ann Laura Stoler looks at race and class relations among concubines in settler families within a colonial context in *Carnal Knowledge and Imperial Power: Race and the Intimate in Colonial Rule* (Berkeley, CA, 2002).

territory. Apart from Jolanta Sikorska-Kulesza's *Zło tolerowane,* which examines the mechanics of regulated prostitution in the Russian Congress Kingdom of Poland, little of a comprehensive nature exists. For the interwar Polish Second Republic, Marzena Lipska-Toumi has accomplished an effective legal history of changes in the regulation system.[18] For the most part, however, practitioners of commercial sex were mostly unlettered; they did not leave written exposés testifying to their motivations or experiences. Their voices can be heard only through mediated testimonials like court transcripts, reports of investigative journalists, comments on police blotters, or reflections of social workers. Interviews with women returning from being "trafficked" abroad or who corresponded with diplomatic officials about their plight provide one perspective on the international trade, but even these documents tend to follow a formulaic script as migrants sought to gain the sympathies of consular personnel and aid workers. Nonetheless, Austrian archives—especially the Central Police Headquarters in Vienna—contain a rich diplomatic correspondence touching on the missing women from across the imperial landscape, many suspected of having been trafficked abroad. Detailed depictions of accused traffickers and their travels between Eastern Europe and Latin America or the Middle East are also housed in Austrian police archives.

Police registries and medical reports are foundational for re-creating the contours of the lives of inscribed women. Most major towns in Polish territory have retained lists of registered women, which include detailed demographic data on their social origins, educational level, marital status, religion, native language, birthplace, and the profession of their fathers. Registries also record medical updates and hospital stays for regulated women, changes of address, and any legal penalties imposed on them. Reports from the directors of rescue shelters offer surprisingly frank insights, characterizing the "wild and uncivilized" behavior of the women who came to their doors and recounting their recidivist behavior. Documents from Polish charitable societies devoted to rescuing vulnerable women are limited to annual reports and transcriptions of meetings, although the Austrian Society for the Protection of Women, founded in 1906, conducted some fruitful interviews with women returning from abroad. Reports from international congresses devoted to trafficking offer valuable material about shifting governmental policies on the sex trade.

---

18. Jolanta Sikorska-Kulesza, *Zło tolerowane: Prostytucja w Królestwie Polskim w XIX wieku* (Warsaw, 2004); and Marszena Lipska-Toumi, *Prawo polskie wobec zjawiska prostytucji w latach 1918–1939* (Lublin, 2014).

Beyond this, the research of contemporary experts in the new fields of psychiatry, criminology, medical anthropology, sexology, and syphilology helps chart perceptions about the causes of sexual deviance and biological degeneracy and reflects efforts to pinpoint a cure for venereal diseases. Several classic studies of the prostitution problem circulated throughout the European medical community in the late nineteenth century and were standard fare among Polish specialists. Scientific discoveries related to prostitution and its attendant diseases also appeared in the professional organs of the influential Warsaw Medical Society, *Pamiętnik Towarzystwa Lekarskiego Warszawskiego* (Proceedings of the Warsaw Medical Society) and *Kronika Lekarska* (Medical Chronical), as well as the more scientific *Medycyna*. In the provincial capital of Lwów, *Przegląd Hygieniczny* (Hygienic Review) focused on the increasing anxiety about public hygiene in urban centers across Europe, including the epidemic-like spread of sexual ailments. Warsaw's long-running *Gazeta Lekarska* (Medical Gazette) (1866–1921) and *Tygodnik Lekarski* (Medical Weekly) in Lwów also aired debates on the treatment of venereal disorders and discussions of the mechanics of regulated prostitution.[19]

Regular newspaper reports on prostitution, white slavery, and sexual violence published in all three Polish partitions serve as a guide to the level of public interest in the topic and reflect the degree to which the reigning powers were willing to permit open coverage. The latter years of the nineteenth century saw the growth of several reform-minded publications in the Polish space read mainly by urban professional classes and intelligentsia. Warsaw's *Przegląd Tygodniowy* (Weekly Review) appealed to educated Poles to "work at the base of society" through its critique of social issues. It was here that writers such as Aleksander Świętochowski and Bolesław Prus addressed the women's question and examined issues of public hygiene and education among the poor. Several other weeklies joined *Przegląd* at the turn of the century, including *Prawda* (The Truth), *Ogniwo* (The Link), and *Głos* (The Voice). These were among the first publications to take a close look at the gritty side of city life reflected in the growing rates of homeless children, bloody knife fights, and open prostitution. The readership of these weeklies never grew beyond a few thousand subscribers, yet their combined audience comprised some of the most influential social actors in the Polish Kingdom (the portion of Polish territory allotted to Russian at the 1815 Congress

---

19. These publications printed lectures and research reports from well-known physicians both in the Polish lands and abroad, helping medical specialists stay informed about the exciting developments in their fields. Zenon Kmiecik, *Prasa warszawska w latach 1886–1904* (Wrocław, 1989), 196; and Jerzy Jarowiecki, *Dzieje prasy polskiej we Lwowie do 1945 roku* (Cracow, 2008), 126.

of Vienna), including Warsaw city administrators, school teachers, lawyers, members of the medical community, writers, and university students. Discussions about the problem of commercial sex radiated out from these papers and helped shape public opinion across the kingdom and beyond. Each of these papers printed correspondence and reports from journalists in other sections of divided Poland, helping to promote a cross-partition debate about matters of broader Polish interest. Although most of these leading journals were published in Warsaw, copies regularly found their way to Galicia and Poznań.[20]

Spinoffs of these reform-minded periodicals, among them journals focused on women's issues, soon gained audiences throughout the Polish lands. In 1895, Paulina Reinschmidt-Kuczalska founded the fortnightly *Ster* (The Helm) in Lwów. The paper folded after only two years, but the same subject matter was addressed in Maria Turzyma-Wiśniewska's more widely circulated Cracow-based *Nowe Słowo* (The New Word, 1902–1907) and the Warsaw monthly *Ster*, published from 1907 to 1914. These papers were intended mainly for activists in the budding Polish equal rights movement. As such, they helped foster a wider social agenda among protofeminists focused on the needs of impoverished lower-class women, especially the desperate rural women flooding to Poland's urban centers. In addition to polemics about civic equality, they aired concerns about alcoholism and venereal diseases, the paucity of jobs for unskilled women, and the dangers of white slavery. The women writing for these nascent feminist periodicals were often hard-hitting in their representation of the conditions of life and employment restrictions for poor women, demonstrating in a series of grueling articles the virtual impossibility of single women working in unskilled jobs to support themselves. *Nowe Słowo* was particularly aggressive in its discussion of social problems touching poor women, among them the turn to prostitution. Finally, periodicals intended for housekeepers, such as the Lublin-based Catholic *Pracownica Polska* (The Polish Female Worker) and

---

20. *Przegląd Tygodniowy* reached 2,500 subscribers in 1896, mainly in the city of Warsaw. *Prawda*, which peaked at 1,400 weekly issues, was careful to include reports from correspondents in Lwów, Cracow, and Poznań and to reprint articles from liberal Galician journals like Cracow's *Nowa Reforma* and Poznań's *Dziennik Poznański*. *Głos* reached a peak of 1,850 weekly issues in 1904 and collapsed in severe deficit the following year. *Ogniwo*'s radical socialist content was popular among readers in Lithuania, Podola, and Kiev, as well as factory towns across the Polish Kingdom; a certain number of copies made their way to readers in Galicia and Poznań. The paper's subscriptions peaked at 2,300 in 1904. Kmiecik, *Prasa warszawska*, 8–9, 47, 56–58, 89–91; and Jerzy Łojek, ed., *Prasa polska w latach 1864–1918* (Warsaw, 1976), 111–12.

Przyjaciel Sług (The Servant's Friend), which served as the organ of the Galician Housekeepers Society, are a particularly rich source of material on the white slavery panic and related migration anxiety.[21]

The cusp of the twentieth century also saw the proliferation of daily papers intended for an increasingly broad readership, many of which supplied colorful reporting on issues of prostitution as a way of capturing audience share.[22] Despite the challenge of gaining publishing permission from tsarist authorities, several commercially successful ventures began appealing to urban workers, craftsmen, and impoverished intellectuals in Warsaw during this period. Newspapers like *Kurier Warszawski* (Warsaw Courier), *Kurier Codzienny* (The Daily Courier), and later *Kurier Poranny* (Morning Courier) circulated vivid depictions of daily life in the former capital city along with letters from local residents angry at the moral decline of city streets. Warsaw's first morning paper, *Kurier Poranny*, increased its circulation dramatically by capitalizing on local scandals and trafficking trials, often telegraphed from other parts of Europe. Wide publication of Bolesław Prus's socially satirical column in these presses helped boost their popularity. All told, the three main Warsaw dailies sold over fifty thousand copies each day in the early years of the twentieth century through postal subscriptions, urban kiosks, and hundreds of newspaper boys hawking them on city streets. The tradition of shared readership within households and neighborhoods and the distribution of papers within cafés and coffeehouses meant that as many as five separate readers had access to each individual issue, giving the majority of adult readers in this town of 750,000 access to a daily paper.[23]

But it was in the much smaller city of Cracow that the boulevard press reached its zenith in the Polish lands. Here papers such as *Nowiny dla Wszystkich* (The News for All) and *Ilustrowany Kurier Codzienny* (Illustrated Daily Courier) achieved record circulation rates in the years preceding World War I. These publications attracted readers from the lowest social levels by keeping their prices well below that of the mainstream dailies, while featuring colorful reporting, scandal mongering, and captivating illustrations. *Nowiny* reached daily circulation levels of forty thousand papers on weekdays and sixty thousand on Sundays within two years of its 1910 inauguration, clearly

---

21. Łojek, *Prasa polska*, 74, 84, 142; and Jerzy Myśliński, *Studia nad polską prasą społeczno-polityczną w zachodniej Galicji, 1905–1914* (Łódź, 1970), 206–7.

22. As the largest metropolitan area in the Polish lands, Warsaw was also home to a vibrant and thriving periodical press. Whereas only 18 periodicals circulated in the former capital in 1864, by 1904 some 111 weekly, monthly, and daily publications were circulating. Kmiecik, *Prasa warszawska*, 10.

23. The most successful of these were *Kurier Warszawski* with a circulation of 33,000 in 1909 and *Kurier Poranny* with 24,000. Kmiecik, *Prasa warszawska*, 8–42; and Łojek, *Prasa polska*, 111–12.

reaching beyond the social elite in this town of barely 140,000 people. Both papers covered stories of child prostitution, infanticide, sex trafficking, and other sensational issues.[24]

The post-1905 reduction of censorship in both Russian Poland and Habsburg Galicia marked a period of openness in the discussion of sex scandals, public women, and sexual deviance. In particular, two new journals were launched during these heady days, both focused on commercial sex and its implications. *Czystość* (Purity), initially released as a supplement to Cracow's *Nowe Słowo*, addressed the nationalist implications of declining public morality. *Świat Płciowy* (Sexual World), produced in Lwów's bawdier social atmosphere, was a muckraking journal focused on the varied dimensions of the early twentieth-century revolutionary in sexual mores, though it was able to stay afloat for only two years, from 1905 to 1907.

Original trial proceedings for white slavery cases are unavailable, but court transcripts were republished in the daily press, especially Cracow's *Nowa Reforma* (New Reform) and Lwów's *Gazeta Narodowa* (National Gazette), both of which remained the journals of record for Galician liberal democrats despite relatively low circulation rates of around two thousand a day. In addition, reports of charitable societies such as the League for the Defense of Women and the Society for Combatting Traffic in Women offer information about members, transcripts of meetings, and speeches articulating organizational goals. Buried on the inside pages of such bulletins one finds a tally of the limited successes such societies had in placing needy women in shelters, educational facilities, or convents. Finally, pamphlets and polemical monographs promoting reform solutions for transforming or eliminating regulated prostitution are useful sources for understanding contemporary attitudes.

Chapter Outline

The Devil's Chain examines the genesis of the panic that erupted in all three partitions of the divided Polish territories. It analyses prostitution as a lower-class weapon of the weak. Finally, it assesses social responses to the "problem" of regulated prostitution, exploring the wide range of solutions proposed by community activists—doctors, philanthropists, feminist leaders, Roman

---

24. Myśliński, *Studia nad polską prasą*, 96–103. On Cracow's turn-of-the-century boulevard press, see also Nathaniel D. Wood, "Becoming a 'Great City': Metropolitan Imaginations and Apprehensions in Cracow's Popular Press, 1900–1914," *Austrian History Yearbook* 33 (2002): 105–29; "Sex Scandals, Sexual Violence, and the Word on the Street: The Kolasówna Lustmord in Cracow's Popular Press, 1905–1906," *Journal of the History of Sexuality* 20, no. 2 (2011): 243–69; and *Becoming Metropolitan: Urban Selfhood and the Making of Modern Cracow* (DeKalb, IL, 2010).

Catholic and Jewish aid organizers, socialist sympathizers, and journalists. Each of these associations and individuals emphasized the preoccupations of their constituents, yet each was also at some level concerned with the status of the Polish *naród* and the social flaws that public sex exposed in the Polish nation. The narrative begins in chapter 1 with the explosion of popular interest in prostitution across the Polish lands during the waning years of the nineteenth century. Fundamental shifts in town life brought commercial sex to the attention of the wider public. The closing of bordellos released enterprising prostitutes onto city streets, while the expansion of military garrisons and institutions of higher education led to an influx of prospective clients to city centers, increasing the gender imbalance in most Polish towns.

Chapter 2 grapples with the role paid sex played in the lives of its practitioners. Here we contrast literary images of passive "fallen women" tricked or coerced into a life of prostitution with more practical understandings of the uses to which working-class women put their sexual labor. The chapter emphasizes the permeable boundary separating the world of "honest" female employment and the practice of prostitution, addressing the socioeconomic context of the turn to paid sex. Lacking support networks, regular incomes, or nearby family, young women on their own slipped into and out of sex work during times of need, giving prostitution a greater significance at all levels of Polish society than has previously been acknowledged. Nowhere was the presence of prostitutes more troubling to middle- and upper-class Poles than in the intimate space of their homes, the subject of chapter 3. Here I explore the myriad ways urban residents interacted with the world of prostitution. Commercial sex was woven into the fabric of everyday life in fin de siècle Poland as poor females supplemented their wages with part-time sex work and lower-class families hired out their wives and daughters. Women flowed on and off police registries in times of financial stress, a situation that prompted police across Polish territory to expand the categories of women they were legally permitted to register as sex workers. Broadening legal definitions of commercial sex, I argue, helped link poverty with immorality in the popular consciousness and worked to permanently brand a whole class of female workers.

Even more frightening to the Polish public than intimate interactions with prostitutes in their homes was the prospect of international traffickers whisking away their innocent daughters. Chapters 4 through 6 analyze the white slavery panic that coursed through Europe and the Americas at the cusp of the twentieth century, looking closely at the way the panic played out in the Polish context. Chapter 4 explores the uses to which Polish reformers put scenarios of innocent Christian girls abducted by Jewish traffickers. White slavery offered local activists and private charities the ammunition to fight tolerated domestic prostitution, on the one hand, and to intervene in the lives of migrating women, on the other. Chapter 5 reads the popular understanding of trafficking against a backdrop of migration scandals that played out in all three empires. By portraying migrating young women as passive "victims" of traffickers, advocates effectively ignored the very real economic problems driving them to leave their homes. The rhetoric surrounding the white slavery scare camouflaged the agenda of a whole cohort of ambitious young women who left Polish shores in search of better fortunes.

Chapter 6 considers migration facilitators in the context of East European Jewish cultural practices, including the tradition of ritual marriage. The Polish narrative of white slavery, the chapter proposes, made it possible to attribute primary causality to Jewish ringleaders. Anxiety about white slavery was manifested in an anti-Semitism that was ultimately tied to tropes of hygiene in women's bodies and purity in the Polish nation. This chapter also emphasizes that perceptions of a "devil's chain" of traffickers, procurers, madams, and pimps, leading ultimately to the imperial state itself, informed the way many contemporaries approached the prostitution conundrum. More than just a series of individual decisions or personal tragedies, prostitution comprised a system of connected links, beginning with the imperial state that ostensibly relied on houses of assignation to cultivate a tranquil subject population and ending with the much maligned prostitute herself. When reformers proposed solutions to this vexing social problem, they invariably addressed a whole host of moral, economic, and political issues they saw as needing correction. The "devil's chain" of the prostitution business had to be broken for Poland and the Poles to modernize and reemerge as a sovereign state.

The Warsaw pimp riots of May 1905 brought the problem of paid sex out into the open as never before. The burst of organizational energy that followed the so-called Alfonse Pogrom forms the focus of chapter 7. Here the narrative shifts away from a direct examination of the world of paid sex and turns to social reactions to it. Part of the much more widespread Revolution of 1905 in the Russian Empire, the events in Warsaw sent shockwaves through Polish society. Commentators from across the Polish lands viewed the attacks on old-town brothels as a call to arms, an invitation to impose reforming zeal on a practice that had grown out of control and that threatened to jeopardize Poland's national reputation. The chapter thus traces the rising power of private charity in imperial Poland during this period. Aid agencies stepped in to offer assistance to marginalized women and to serve as a partial substitute for the social welfare work of the absent Polish state. These societies also provided space for bourgeois women to operate publically in the name of assisting their less fortunate sisters. Finally, I argue that the failure of the philanthropic efforts to "solve" the prostitution problem and the intransigence of many of its practitioners helped fuel a renewed cynicism about the permanence of the sex trade and prompted activists to turn to other, more militant solutions for the problems of sexual immorality and disease.

Chapters 8 through 10 address the evolution of this more hardened scientific reform direction during the years preceding the outbreak of the Great War. In a trajectory similar to that of charity workers, physicians initially approached the prostitution problem with an air of optimism. Over time, however, the seemingly limitless supply of women suspected of selling sex and an awareness of the dangerous diseases they communicated prompted a rising tide of cynicism. In addressing these new medical needs, physicians in the Polish lands effectively leveraged the panic over prostitution to expand their powers in unprecedented ways, carving out a new status for themselves as the moral conscience of a damaged nation. The heightened power of medicine in engaging with social problems like prostitution meant a new scientific basis for morality campaigns in the period leading up to the rebirth of the Polish state. As patriotic despair was inscribed onto medical frustration, a peculiar form of eugenics evolved that emphasized social pathologies rather than ethnic or racial purity. Chapter 9 traces the rise of the eugenics initiative and its unique focus, stressing the links with West European eugenics ideas and the efforts to script a new national body through the image of the prostitute.

Concerns about biological inheritance and national degeneration prompted discussions about the future of the independent Polish state, the subject of chapter 10. Here we examine attempts to reform the system of tolerated prostitution in the new Polish state. The changing perception of prostitution as an economic technique rather than a moral failing transformed the discussion about regulation into a debate about the future of the Polish nation and its people. Prostitution reform in the 1920s and 1930s became one of many means for engaging broader social issues in the new Polish Republic. Yet despite energetic action by physicians, social activists, feminists, socialists, and others, the political chaos of interwar Poland prevented significant reform prior to the country's collapse in 1939. In the end, through a half century of discussion and negotiation on the subject of prostitution reform, the image of the prostitute was leveraged by a variety of organizations and agencies often in ways that furthered their broader agendas and enhanced the associations through which they acted. In this sense, depictions of sex workers in the Polish space—from unredeemable sinner to fallen angel, desperate waif, or transmitter of disease—tell us as much about early twentieth-century social activism as they do about the shifting status of the prostitute herself. Prostitution became normalized in the 1920s as an economically driven choice that was regulated primarily by the medical community rather than via law enforcement organs. Yet even here, discussions of the "problem" of paid sex continued to be marshaled behind any number of larger reform projects. Once lower-class women were integrated conceptually into the body of the Polish nation, they became a constant focus of efforts to shape and mold them in the image of elite reformers. By the early years of the Second Republic, women selling sex on Polish streets were "merely" poor, desperate, and possibly diseased. They were no longer permanently cast out of the moral universe of the larger nation, but rather represented a potential part of the national project as a whole.

Chapter 1

Out of the Shadows

> Let prostitution flourish so long as it does not show
> itself on the streets.
>
> —Karol Radek, "Z badań nad prostytucyą"

A quiet panic unfolded on the streets of central
Warsaw. The winter of 1883 brought a tangible new threat as residents of
the historic Old Town (*starówka*) neighborhood faced a plague of aggressive,
morally abrasive harlots invading their peaceful terrain. Locals wrote frantic
letters to city papers complaining of the "evening wanderings of women of
ill repute . . . contaminating principal streets, and reaching quarters that until
now have been the quietest and most peaceful." They recounted the public scandals streetwalkers created by "shamelessly accosting male pedestrians
and subjecting decent women to unpleasant . . . scenes."[1] No matter how
strenuously readers objected to the prostitutes' activities, "nothing seemed
to change" and residents' "voices cried out in vain" for a remedy. The epidemic of visible public women created an "utter hell" for those living amidst
them. As one older gentleman described it, the string of brothels emitted "a
cacophony of out-of-tune pianos, accompanying clarinets, bass, violins, . . . and
guests drinking, dancing, shouting, and singing in hoarse voices." Worse yet,
he complained, "quarrels break out" regularly, spilling over onto city streets.
The nightly disturbances kept the neighborhood awake until the wee hours

---

1. Letter signed by "Residents of Żurawia, Krucza, and Wspólna Streets," "W sprawie
przyzwoitości publicznej," *Kurier Poranny*, January 9, 1883, 2.

of the morning, making residents increasingly anxious and sleep deprived.[2] Warsaw's urban elite was convinced that it was losing control to the forces of crime, immorality, and sexual impropriety.

Nor was the problem limited to residential districts. By the early 1880s, Warsaw's elegant Saxon Park also enjoyed an "infamous reputation" as a "great Warsaw salon of love" and a site for women of "ruined morals" to conduct their scandalous business, a place "orderly women did not go" lest they be mistaken for prostitutes. Brothels and streetwalkers made their appearance in the suburbs as well, along Marszałkowska Street and Jerożolimska Boulevard.[3] The daily newspaper, Niwa Polska, confided to its readers in 1898 that "barely a day goes by when we do not receive some sort of letter from a distressed parent with grown daughters at home complaining bitterly about the worsening situation" in these residential neighborhoods. Sexual debauchery was on display, the paper noted, "even in the very stately buildings where honest families live[d]."[4] By the turn of the new century, journalists and readers alike agreed that "open demoralization on the streets of Warsaw [had] reached a frightening scope."[5] As Kurier Codzienny portrayed it, "Barely does dusk descend than these open, shameless ones appear on the streets, not embarrassed by anything or anyone. It is enough to look at what is happening on such busy places as Krakowskie Przedmieście [a key shopping street] . . . near the hotel Europejski, or on Nowy Świat near the intersection of Aleje Jerożolimska . . . to confirm the public decline that is presented here in all of its abomination, bringing with it unlimited moral harm."[6] Journalistic exposés elicited a stream of letters from impassioned Warsaw residents, who reported that the "evening moths reigned freely and openly practiced their public scandal not only on the streets we named [in our report] but in all parts of town as well." The situation, they averred, was causing "enormous grief" and had reached "drastic" proportions.[7]

---

2. This self-proclaimed "nervous retiree" described the nineteen new houses of prostitution recently established in the streets surrounding ulica Freta in the center of Warsaw's Old Town. "Jeszcze z ulicy Freta," Kurier Warszawski, no. 345 (1883): 3. See also "Przeciw nietoperzom nocnym," Kurier Poranny, January 14, 1883, 4.

3. Przegląd Tygodniowy 40 (1900), cited in Stanisław Milewski, Ciemne sprawy dawnych warszawiaków (Warsaw, 1982), 110–12.

4. Milewski, Ciemne sprawy, 111.

5. "Z chwili," Kurier Codzienny, September 27, 1901, 2.

6. Ibid.

7. "Z chwili," Kurier Codzienny, October 1, 1901, 2.

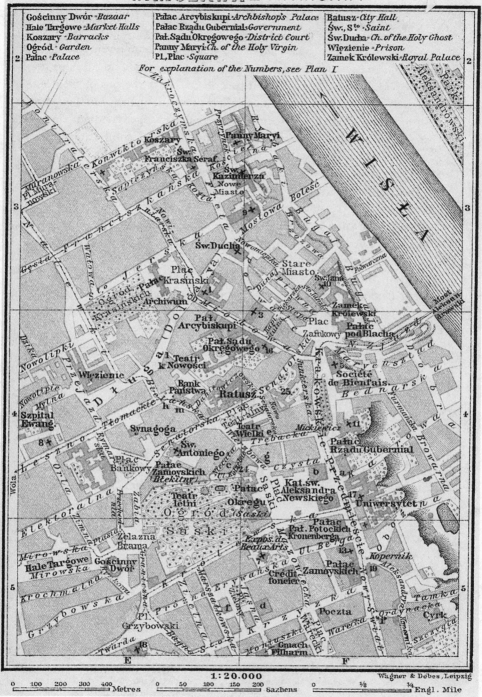

FIGURE 1.1 Warsaw City Center Map, 1914.

Courtesy of discusmedia.com. Areas frequented by prostitutes included the Ogród Saski (Saxon Park), Stare Miasto (Old Town), and the main shopping street of Krakowskie Przedmieście.

A Moral Panic

And yet what was really so new about the situation these observers described? Had commercial sex not been a part of the urban landscape across Europe for centuries? Did "moral" city residents not always decry the sins of their less virtuous neighbors, even while living cheek by jowl among them? In short, was the "panic" of middle-class Varsovians a reflection of changed conditions in the urban sex trade or merely a novel way of expressing the discomfort onlookers experienced when faced with moral improprieties? This chapter addresses the explosion of information about and reactions to open prostitution in Poland's city centers between the early 1880s and the first years of the new century. It considers some of the shifts in town life that brought commercial sex to the attention of journalists and their urban readership. Finally, it suggests the ways commentators may have used prostitution as a foil for discussing issues at the center of shifts in gender and class alignments in Polish society.

Certainly, the sale of sex by poor women to their social betters was a long-standing phenomenon in nearly every society. In modern Europe, the practice was driven partially by late marriage among middle- and upper-class males. The Victorian-era sexual double standard mandating chaste brides and sexually experienced grooms combined with the limited range of economic opportunities available to females made prostitution an integral part of European society. The socioeconomic transformation wrought by nineteenth-century industrialization and the dramatic growth of cities brought new conditions for the sale of sex. By the late nineteenth century, an expanding bourgeoisie took possession of large city centers across the Continent. Town walls came down. Wide arterial roads and broad, open parks replaced them. More important, the centers of larger urban enclaves now featured fashionable shops, cafés, restaurants, and businesses. Soon thousands of female migrants from smaller towns and surrounding villages flooded into this vibrant, bustling atmosphere, attracted by economic opportunity and the glamour of the great city. It was in this context, as Alain Corbin has observed, that "the prostitute emerged from the shadows." In earlier times, her activities were hidden within brothels and military garrisons on the outskirts of town. By the last quarter of the century, she "sought the light . . . she dared to show herself; she circulated tirelessly." The prostitute was "on show" along the wide boulevards frequented by bourgeois males. She had become "woman as spectacle."[8]

---

8. Corbin notes that the transfer of prostitutes away from ghettos and brothels outside of town and toward the city center "appears to have been a general phenomenon in the larger cities" during France's Second Empire from 1852 to 1870. Alain Corbin, *Women for Hire*, 204–6.

These newspaper correspondents were reacting partially to the new openness that characterized prostitution in the large towns of east-central Europe. As municipalities across Polish territory—from Warsaw and Łódź in the Russian Kingdom, to Cracow and Lwów in Galicia, and Poznań in Germany—grew in size they featured an increasingly visible sex trade. By the turn of the twentieth century, Warsaw had swelled to three-quarters of a million inhabitants and Cracow had doubled from 1870 to 1910, partially by incorporating surrounding suburban communities. Łódź experienced a population explosion as the textile industry took off, doubling every ten years throughout the nineteenth century. In 1806, the town had only 767 residents; by 1905 it boasted 344,000 mostly industrial laborers.[9] The demographics of many Polish cities help account for an increased demand for prostitution. Both Warsaw and Cracow were garrison towns where thousands of conscripts were separated from their families.[10]

Despite the relatively slow pace of industrial development, young men and women flocked to large population centers throughout the Polish lands in search of seasonal jobs, high culture, education, and entertainment.[11] An expanded rail network brought easy access to urban centers from nearby provincial towns during the latter half of the nineteenth century.[12] Peasant emancipation followed by massive migration out of the countryside and a dearth of employment opportunities for unskilled women created a dramatic upsurge in lower-class reliance on prostitution as a means of subsistence.[13]

---

9. By 1910, Vienna reached a population of 2,031,000, Budapest 880,000, Warsaw 771,000, Prague 640,000, and Cracow 150,000. See Paul Robert Magocsi, *Historical Atlas of Central Europe* (Toronto, 2002), 93, 96; and Nathaniel Wood, "Urban Self-Identification in East Central Europe before the Great War: The Case of Cracow," *East Central Europe* 33, nos. 1–2 (2006): 12–13.

10. Over thirty thousand soldiers were permanently stationed in Warsaw in the 1880s. Cracow was home to over six thousand soldiers in 1900. Jolanta Sikorska-Kulesza, "Prostitution in Congress Poland," *Acta Poloniae Historica* 83 (2001): 128–29; and Kazimierz Kumaniecki, *Tymczasowe wyniki spisu ludności w Krakowie z 31 grudnia 1910 roku* (Cracow, 1912), 28, 31.

11. Tomasz Gąsowski has demonstrated that the dramatic growth of large cities (with populations over ten thousand) in Galicia during the last half century of the partitioned period was due largely to migration from small and medium-sized towns, which correspondingly shrunk in size. Contrary to contemporary assumptions, only about one-third of the in-migration to Galician cities came directly from the countryside. "Urbanizacja Galicji w dobie autonomicznej," *Studia historyczne* 28, no. 2 (1985): 223–43.

12. Prostitutes registered in Cracow during the period 1879–1911 mainly originated in villages and small towns in Galicia that were served by railway lines. Some 65 percent of registered prostitutes fell into this category, whereas the remainder were longtime residents of Cracow itself (8 percent) or its suburbs (3 percent), or migrated from elsewhere in the Habsburg Monarchy (21 percent) or abroad (4 percent). Michał Baczkowski, "Prostytucja w Krakowie na przełomie XIX i XX w." *Studia Historyczne* 43, no. 4 (2000): 595–97.

13. Polish-speaking peasants in the Habsburg Monarchy were released from serfdom in 1848. Those in the Romanov Empire were emancipated in 1861. Peasants in Prussian Poland achieved their personal freedom gradually beginning in 1806. See Stefan Kieniewicz, *The Emancipation of the Polish Peasantry* (Chicago, 1969).

As Łódź and other textile producing centers exploded in size, economic crises brought on by low-paying factory work and seasonal unemployment forced new waves of women into prostitution. At the same time, Warsaw's population of single males and institutions of higher education offered abundant opportunity for open and aggressive prostitutes to ply their trade.[14] The growing professional class in Cracow offered similarly willing clients for desperate women flocking in from surrounding towns and villages. Lwów's emergence as the capital of a burgeoning Galician provincial government after 1867 and its position as a trading crossroads guaranteed a lively brothel scene. Cracow and Lwów drew the sons of gentry along with ambitious peasants to their vernacular-language high schools and universities. Each of these settings offered a steady clientele for commercial sex workers. In many respects, then, the anxiety surrounding the incidence of prostitution in Polish cities had its roots in very real socioeconomic causes.

Certainly, conditions in late nineteenth-century Polish towns created a situation favorable for the expanding sex trade, as did the growth of large cities elsewhere in Europe. Yet it was not the increased numbers alone that troubled our interlocutors. Rather, the "moral panic" reflected in the columns of Poland's popular newspapers stemmed from a sense of unease about the changed *meanings* of prostitution. Long discretely hidden behind the walls of noble estates, in remote army garrisons or brothels in darkened alleyways, the prostitute's physical emergence from the shadows allowed her to be inspected and analyzed by those with whom she came into contact. Journalists and physicians, academics and jurists, could shine a light on her every detail, interrogating her behavior and scrutinizing her demeanor. She could be used as a foil for discussing any number of social problems her presence touch on.

The prostitute became, in late nineteenth-century Poland, a sort of "folk devil" in Stanley Cohen's reckoning, a scapegoat that could be substituted for the real problems and conditions causing social turmoil.[15] According to Cohen, "societies appear subject every now and then to periods of moral panic. A condition, episode, person or group of persons emerges to become identified as threat to societal values and interests; its nature is presented in

---

14. Jolanta Sikorska-Kulesza notes that some fifty-nine thousand single males above the age of fifteen resided in Warsaw in 1882, along with thirty thousand garisoned soldiers stationed within Warsaw and an aditional seventy-nine thousand in a garison outside of town. "Miasto--przestrzeń niebezpieczna dla kobiet (Prostytucja w Królestwie Polskim w drugiej połowie XIX wieku)," *Polskie Towarzystwo Historyczne Przełomy w Historii. XVI Powszechny Zjazd Historyków Polskich: Pamiętniki* 3, no. 4 (1999): 341–49.

15. Stanley Cohen, *Folk Devils and Moral Panics: The Creation of the Mods and Rockers* (London, 1972), 9.

a stylized stereotypical fashion by the mass media; the moral barricades are manned by editors, bishops and politicians." Moral panics, according to Jeffrey Weeks, have the effect of "crystalliz[ing] widespread fears and anxieties." It is not uncommon, Weeks points out, for "sexuality [to have] a peculiar centrality in such panics." For this reason, he emphasizes, "sexual 'deviants' [such as prostitutes] have been omnipresent scapegoats."[16] Prostitutes, defined by medical and juridical experts elsewhere in Europe during this same historical moment as "sexual deviants" and "born criminals," became a way to discuss publicly issues of female sexuality, changing gender roles, cross-class liaisons, and other socially sensitive issues. Venting about the prostitution menace became a way for Poland's intellectual elite along with its middle-class readers to navigate the newly visible underclass of poor women moving into bourgeois public spaces. The "moral panic" in late nineteenth-century Polish cities may tell us less about the practice of selling sex itself than it does about the anxieties among those who observed it.

Expressions of unease about illicit sexual behavior such as those in the pages of Polish papers highlight the extent to which analyses of sexual proclivities spilled over from the pages of professional journals during the last quarter of the nineteenth century into everyday conversations among broader social strata. It was via panicked letters and sensational reportage in this period that scientific discourses on sexuality came into contact with popular understandings. Outbreaks of moral panic like the one reflected in the Warsaw press, as Scott Specter has argued, "brought the public to an awareness of the new 'type of person' defined by medical, juridical, and criminological discourses."[17] Whereas physicians and criminologists had circulated research on prostitution in specialized publications for much of the century, it was not until later that the general public in east-central Europe began to have access to information about the world of commercial sex. In the period around the turn of the century, newspaper editors also "discovered" sexual themes as a way to increase readership and sell papers.[18] Readers of the popular press and nonspecialist reporters alike developed their own

16. Jeffrey Weeks, *Sex, Politics, and Society: The Regulation of Sexuality since 1800* (London 1981), 14–15.

17. Scott Spector, "Where Personal Fate Turns to Public Affair: Homosexual Scandal and Social Order in Vienna, 1900–1910," *Austrian History Yearbook* 38 (2007): 17.

18. See, for example, the work of Nathaniel Wood on sex scandals, prostitution, and Jack the Ripper themes in the early twentieth-century Cracovian boulevard press. "Urban Self-Identification," esp. 23–24; "Becoming a 'Great City,'" 105–29; and "Becoming Metropolitan: Cracow's Popular Press and the Representation of Modern Urban Life, 1900–1915" (PhD diss., Indiana University, 2004), esp. 172.

understandings of the causality behind phenomena such as commercial sex and suggested remedies for alleviating the "problem" of rampant prostitution. As shifts in the prostitution dynamic brought the sex trade closer to mainstream Polish society, observers of all kinds increasingly employed the image of the prostitute both metaphorically and literally in order to position themselves on a wide range of issues.

The Peculiar Institution of Tolerated Prostitution

The system of police-regulated prostitution that bore the brunt of social criticism in this period had been in place for nearly a century, yet it was satisfactory to almost no one. Prior to the late eighteenth-century partitions of the Polish Lithuanian Commonwealth, commercial sex had been tolerated within closed brothels but only minimally regulated. Dozens of public houses thrived in relative peace on the outskirts of central Warsaw beginning with its establishment as the national capital in the sixteenth century, as they did in other chief Polish cities and market towns.[19] Most cities in the Commonwealth levied taxes on prostitutes and brothel keepers alike. Morals police began conducting sanitary inspections in public houses and hospitalizing women with signs of infection in the fifteenth century.[20] The first hospital devoted entirely to the treatment of venereal diseases, St. Sebastian's, was founded in Cracow in 1528, and in 1591 the court preacher, Piotr Skarga, helped sponsor a similar hospital, St. Lazarus, in Warsaw.[21] Polish army garrisons staffed their own brothels beginning in the eighteenth century.

After the Commonwealth was partitioned, most of the divided state adopted a version of "tolerated" or police-regulated prostitution modeled on Napoleon's reforms.[22] The system established commercial sex in a legal twilight zone, neither officially sanctioned nor prohibited, but "tolerated" by the authorities so long as women selling sex registered with the police and

---

19. For an overview of regulated prostitution in the Polish Republic, see Sikorska-Kulesza, *Zło tolerowane*, 9–10.

20. Zaleski, *Z dziejów prostytucji w Warszawie*, 3–11.

21. Several reasonably reliable surveys of prostitution in the Polish lands were written in the interwar period, among them Józef Macko, *Prostytucja* (Warsaw, 1927); Wacław Zaleski, *Z dziejów prostytucji w Warszawie* (Warsaw, 1923); and Rząśnicki, *Prostytucja a proletarjat* (Warsaw, 1920). These texts tend to be critical of foreign powers for introducing prostitution and venereal diseases during periods of army occupation.

22. On the system of police regulation in the Congress Kingdom, see Sikorska-Kulesza, *Zło tolerowane*; "Prostitution in Congress Poland"; and "Miasto-przestrzeń niebezpieczna dla kobiet," 341–49. Michał Baczkowski provides insights into the police-run system in Austrian Galicia in "Prostytucja w Krakowie," 593–607.

(at least in the early period) limited their activities to licensed public houses. Police regulation required all women engaging in commercial sex to inscribe their names on the municipal police registry, to report for twice-weekly gynecological examinations, and to maintain a booklet or "passport" documenting their medical checks and hospital stays. The Prussians first codified the system in 1802 as part of their effort to protect the health of their soldiers and officials stationed in Warsaw. As long as public women were registered, prostitution was decriminalized; harsh penalties were imposed only for the crime of procurement and for knowingly contaminating clients.[23]

The Prussian system was extended virtually unchanged to the lands comprising the Duchy of Warsaw during the period 1807–1815, and to Congress Poland from 1815 to 1830, though most accounts portray its enforcement as increasingly loose. Police during this period were reported as having "maintained a supremely neutral attitude toward prostitution." The medical supervision process lacked an enforcement wing and "depended on the will of the prostitute" to appear at the police station and register her activities. Although those who did not submit to formal registration were theoretically subject to flogging or incarceration, few records indicate that women were punished in any way for avoiding registration. Indeed, during the Napoleonic Wars when Russian armies passed through Polish territory regularly, prostitution was rampant in the military encampments and venereal diseases climbed at "alarming rates." Neither local authorities nor military leaders appear to have taken any action to stem the tide of prostitution and Warsaw's Ujazdowski military hospital was full of Polish and Russian soldiers out of commission with venereal diseases. Reports submitted to Grand Duke Constantine in the early nineteenth century describe public women who prowled around neighborhoods near military encampments with impunity. Łazienki Park after dark reportedly crawled with prostitutes and soldiers seeking their services.[24] Overall, some thirty-nine licensed brothels operated in Warsaw between 1821 and 1830, along with twenty-two illegal public houses, employing over two hundred registered prostitutes a year in addition to innumerable unregistered "illegal" prostitutes. Russian imperial authorities

---

23. One in every five residents of Warsaw during the Prussian occupation was a soldier, whereas some one thousand Prussian bureaucrats lived among the sixty thousand Polish civilians. Prostitution was treated in widely divergent ways throughout the Prussian state at the time, ranging from absolute prohibition to tolerance or complete legalization. Sikorska-Kulesza, *Zło tolerowane*, 34–40; and Macko, *Prostytucja*.

24. Report by General Kuruta to Grand Duke Constantine, *Wojenne istoriczeskij Wiestnik,* ed. Izmiestjew (1811), cited in Zaleski, *Z dziejów prostytucji w Warszawie,* 15–17; and Macko, *Prostytucja*, 38–39.

maintained these facilities partially to keep their soldiers occupied and at least theoretically free of disease. The brothels were kept under heavy police surveillance at all times out of concern they might be used as sites for hatching political conspiracies.[25] Sexual diseases grew rampant in this period, with the medical facility at St. Lazarus treating close to four thousand patients for venereal diseases in 1840 alone.[26]

European-wide concern about issues of public health in urban centers prompted the establishment of more rigorous measures to control and regulate prostitution in the 1840s. Governor General Iwan Paskiewicz extended the apparatus for registering and supervising prostitutes to all thirty-two districts of the Congress Kingdom, though the majority of those under medical control continued to be registered in Warsaw. Paskiewicz sent representatives abroad to study the organization of West European public health systems, examining especially the system Alexander Parent-Duchatelet devised in Paris to isolate prostitutes from mainstream society.[27] The resulting 1843 regulations represented a continuation of the Prussian-based system of 1802 but were now applied to municipalities throughout the kingdom. Police-medical committees, comprising local police chiefs, hospital directors, representatives of civilian governments, and a public health inspector became known as the Polish Model and were introduced in St. Petersburg, Moscow, and Riga, cities that had not previously used a system of prostitution control.[28] In most municipalities, prostitutes were permitted to live either in licensed brothels or operate independently out of their own apartments.[29]

Similar regulations applied to the residents of Austrian Galicia, where prostitution was first administered according to the civic code of 1859 (revised in 1876 and 1885).[30] Here too all women selling sex were mandated to enter their names on the police registry, to appear for a medical examination twice weekly, and to inform authorities of their changes of address. Once a

---

25. Constantine issued some 282 reports regarding the supervision of Warsaw's brothels between 1815 and 1830. Małgorzata Karpińska, *Złodzieje, agenci, policyjni strażnicy . . . Przestępstwa pospolite Warszawie 1815–1830* (Warsaw, 1999), 53–58.

26. Jolanta Sikorska-Kulesza disputes the notion that police lacked energy in supervising prostitution during the period of Iwan Paskiewicz's governor generalship, noting that some eight-two reports were submitted related to policing brothels, the establishment of new public houses, their opening hours, and the behavior of soldiers in these facilities. *Zło tolerowane*, 42–49.

27. On Parent-Duchatelet's regulationist system in 1939 Paris, see Corbin, *Women for Hire*, esp. 3–29.

28. Sikorska-Kulesza, *Zło tolerowane*, 51–53.

29. Edward Rosset, *Prostytucja i choroby weneryczne w Łodzi* (Łódź, 1931), 10–11.

30. Prostitution was legally banned briefly during the early Habsburg occupation of Galicia under Maria Teresa's Morals Commission, which was eliminated under Joseph II. Thanks to Nancy Wingfield for this information.

woman's name was entered on the registry, her passport was exchanged for a "black" booklet or "booklet of shame," which bore regular stamps testifying to her health.[31] Those found with symptoms of venereal ailment were sent directly to hospital, where they remained until they were free of symptoms. Police-medical committees regulated prostitutes in all Austrian towns larger than ten thousand residents;[32] in smaller municipalities, the local administration was responsible for registering public women, though this was enforced much less rigorously. Police regulations permitted prostitutes to work out of licensed brothels or in their own residences, as long as they maintained a certain distance from educational establishments or religious institutions. Aggressive solicitation or luring men through windows, gates, or on the street was strictly forbidden, as was the wearing of indecent clothing.[33]

Prelude to a Panic

Almost from the first moment after the introduction of government regulations, concerns about rising rates of venereal infection and the seemingly unsolvable problem of unregistered prostitutes made commercial sex the focus of regular commentary among police and medical authorities throughout Polish territory. Warsaw police reports from the 1820s complained of dozens of secret brothels and "rendezvous locations." Authorities fought in vain to prohibit owners of taverns, restaurants, coffee houses, and billiard halls from coercing waitresses to function as prostitutes. Police supervision failed to address the rising numbers of female vagabonds selling sex in parks and near military garrisons, and the regime looked the other way when bordellos were located "brazenly near schools and churches, or facing principal streets with little police supervision."[34] According to the interwar police historian Wacław Zaleski, prostitutes in the 1830s wandered freely along the streets of

---

31. The booklet was dark purple for prostitutes registered in Congress Poland. Unlike in Galicia, no photos were attached to passbooks in Russian Polish towns, only brief descriptions of the individual's appearance. This vagueness allowed practitioners to borrow one another's booklet or to send a substitute to the health inspections when they were visibly ill. Augustyn Wróblewski, *O prostytucji i handlu kobietami* (Warsaw, 1909), 52–53.

32. *Instrukcya dla magistratów miast o 10.000 lub więcej ludności, i miast posiadających załogi wojskowe, względem wykonywania nadzoru nad publicznymi nierządnicom* (Lwów, 1852).

33. After 1906 prostitutes were no longer required to exchange their passports for the security booklets. See "Paszport niewolnicy," *Czystość* 24 (June 12, 1909): 380; "Regulamin zachowania się dla prostytutek" (Lwów, 1888), APKr, DPKr 110, 1221–24; Jan Papée, "O reformie prostytucyi," *Lwowski Tygodnik Lekarski*, no. 8 (1908): 3–4; Macko, *Prostytucja*, 49–50; and Bączkowski, "Prostytucja w Krakowie," 593–94.

34. Cited in Zaleski, *Z dziejów prostytucji w Warszawie*, 18; and Karpińska, *Złodzieje, agenty, policyjni strażnicy*, 58–59.

the capital, "shamelessly accosting young men." Indeed, Governor General Paskiewicz is remembered for having encouraged prostitution and drunkenness, spreading decay and debauchery of every kind "in order to prevent residents of the Polish capital from acting political" after the crushing of the 1830–1831 November Rising.[35]

For those familiar with day-to-day life in the capital, the "most abominable" period for open prostitution began in earnest soon after the defeat of the January Rising in the early 1860s. The collusion between police, brothel keepers, and sex traffickers created a "tragic system" in which "every brothel was also a tavern, and every other establishment was a bar or knajpa with music, and all of this with the doors wide open!" The result was a paradise for police, whom public houses paid generously, offered lavish gifts, and provided access to buffets and free drink. The memory of this period in Warsaw was of unmitigated debauchery. "The oldest generation in Warsaw," Zaleski recounts, "remembers well the evening picture along ulica Trębacka, where people walked from the theater to Krakowskie Przedmieście past six buildings in a row . . . inhabited by public houses." In the evening, passersby could see from the open, unshuttered windows, "prostitutes in low-cut gowns dance with the worse sort of town youth."[36] "Secret," unregistered prostitution also exploded in the 1860s and rates of venereal contamination climbed to unprecedented levels.[37] Nevertheless, concern about the sex trade found voice mainly in professional journals and meetings of scholarly societies; matters connected to sexuality were not yet the stuff of mainstream public discourse.

Instead, heightened anxiety related to commercial sex was expressed in specialized journals devoted to physicians, criminologists, and jurists. Medical experts maintained that the system failed in its efforts to prevent the spread of disease. Criminologists saw regulation as unsystematic in its implementation, allowing thousands of "secret" prostitutes to slip through the legal machinery. Police commissions and medical societies worked to temper some of the most egregious effects of "tolerated" prostitution. In Vienna, the police doctor Nusser set off a vigorous debate within the Viennese medical college with his controversial 1850 lecture, arguing that existing government efforts to reduce prostitution were ineffective and that unregistered prostitutes should be incarcerated in state-run work houses. Nusser's observations prompted the adoption of the May 1852 "Instructions" for supervising

---

35. Zaleski, *Z dziejów prostytucji w Warszawie,* 19–20.
36. Ibid., 28–35.
37. Sikorska-Kulesza, *Zło tolerowane,* 89.

prostitution, which were applied soon thereafter in Galician towns and cities. By the early 1860s, the Society of Warsaw Physicians also took on the issue of secret prostitution, proposing greater police authority to register women who refused to do so voluntarily. Their recommendations resulted in new rules, issued in 1874, strengthening police powers to track women suspected of selling sex.[38] The preoccupation of professional experts was slowly becoming a focus of broader social energies.

The Geography of Sin

Commentators who weighed in during the late nineteenth-century panic used the specter of the streetwalker to test their own conceptual boundaries. They set out to interrogate perceptions of violated limits—geographic, gender, and class—introduced by prostitution's rising visibility. As commercial sex expanded to new, "sacred" parts of town, even residents that had never before dealt firsthand with open sexuality were forced to acknowledge its existence. Rebecka Lennartsson has suggested that regulated women "challenged the class and gender-related boundaries of the urban landscape, making it unsafe and unpredictable."[39] "Fallen women" represented a persistent threat to the social order, threatening the bourgeois desire for hygienic, well-organized town centers. Few complainants during this initial debate in the Polish territories sought to eradicate the prostitute altogether from city life. Instead, they focused on the particular "geography of sin" commercial sex inscribed onto previously "respectable" portions of their city. Citizens of newly corrupted districts sought "a particular limit to open street demoralization" and proposed isolating the practice to "already demoralized streets."[40] "If this harmful activity has to exist on the streets of Warsaw, let it at least be restricted," they agreed.[41] Prostitutes could be exiled to the "periphery of the town" where factories, industrial establishments, and other "useful but noisy" enterprises were located, or their soliciting could be limited to certain hours of the night.[42] Either way, the jarring presence of obvious public women in established neighborhoods was deemed unacceptable.

---

38. Ibid., 90–91. On the varying treatment of prostitution in the Russian law code, see Engelstein, *Keys to Happiness*; and Bernstein, *Sonia's Daughters*.

39. Rebecka Lennartsson, *Malaria Urbana: The Register Girl Anna Johannesdotter and Prostitution in Stockholm around Nineteen Hundred* (PhD diss., Department of Cultural Anthropology and Ethnology, Uppsala University, Stockholm, 2001), 279–81.

40. Antoni Wysłouch, *Ohyda wieku* (Warsaw, 1904), 3.

41. "Z chwili," September 27, 1901, 2.

42. As one newspaper correspondent noted, "anyone who wants or needs to visit them can do this anywhere." "Jeszcze z ulicy Freta," 3.

Yet our journalistic interlocutors were preoccupied with more than just the shocking "visibility" of a practice that had previously been cloaked in secrecy. The open sex trade on city streets touched a nerve in the bourgeois mentality that ran deeper than simple disgust at daily encounters with brazen impropriety. Instead, the invasion of lower-class women selling sex in city centers violated boundaries that were more than physical. The presence of blatant prostitutes, for many of these witnesses, represented a transgression of bourgeois social space, an infringement into sacred territory. One "nervous retiree" on Warsaw's Freta Street depicted the rich tradition of religious, cultural, and charitable institutions in his neighborhood, drawing a stark contrast between Christian, respectable society, on the one hand, and the forces of filth and disease, on the other: "Our forefathers on ulica Freta . . . constructed seven churches and cloisters. . . . The next generation brought educational establishments and places of study here, there is now a women's gymnasium, a facility for the care of children run by the Charitable Society, and a shelter for soldiers' children. Here for centuries religious processions have been conducted, tens of thousands of holy gatherings and numerous ostentatious funerals for stately individuals have been celebrated in these very churches. And yet, in this section of town, as if to profane its holy traditions . . . nineteen houses of prostitution have been opened."[43] The iteration of Warsaw's geography of sin in these urban narratives is placed against a backdrop of the conventional pillars of middle-class respectability—churches, schools, and charitable institutions. The houses of prostitution served as an open affront to the noble lineage of these buildings and their inhabitants. Little conceptual space remains for the prostitute's contaminating presence.

The pairing of figurative and physical boundaries of sin had its origins in the earliest municipal restrictions town governments imposed on the sex trade. In early modern Poland, bordellos were permitted only outside the city walls and near military installations. Prostitutes sighted inside city gates could be beaten by the town hangman, who bore the chief responsibility for keeping city centers clear of unsuitable women.[44] The first officially codified rules about prostitution in the Polish lands reflected this geographical division between sacred and profane parts of town, as did regulations elsewhere in Europe. In early nineteenth-century Warsaw, Prussian administrators strictly prohibited prostitution in the center of town but permitted its

---

43. Ibid.
44. Exceptions were made to this restriction and the executioner always kept a stable of "depraved" women on hand to supply to burghers, their servants, and soldiers in foreign armies. Zaleski, *Z dziejów prostytucji*, 3–6.

open practice in the area where the executioner had traditionally worked.[45] Formal guidelines enshrined within the prostitutes' health booklet explicitly forbade them from renting apartments in the shopping and business streets on which residents complained of their aggressive tactics. The phenomenon of "corner girls," groups of four or five teenagers soliciting passersby at the intersections of main streets, was also strictly prohibited but rarely enforced in the early years of the new century.[46]

Not only did custom and law prohibit prostitution in the "polite" parts of town, so too were bordellos banned near churches, chapels, synagogues, or schools anywhere in the municipality. In the Congress Kingdom and Austrian Galicia, the restriction against prostitutes living within 40 sążen (about 100 yards) of religious and cultural institutions provided a convenient basis for neighbors to object to the opening of new public houses.[47] The rector of Jagiellonian University, for example, based his protest against a brothel on Gregórzecka Street, near the Collegium Medicum, in 1911 on its location near a key facility where students attended lectures and were forced to "constantly walk past this brothel."[48] Although the site was far from the city center, the Cracow police chief was sympathetic to the concerns of the rector and local residents. The neighborhood had only been annexed to the municipality of Cracow the previous year and residents complained that "they did not become annexed to Cracow in order to make a brothel keeper happy."[49]

When the same brothel owner transferred his business to the Jewish district, he immediately incurred the wrath of prospective neighbors, who now complained the establishment was too near a gymnasium. Although the owner, Leon Brand, argued that his enterprise could not harm the school children because "they have no idea what happens in a public house," the police chief nonetheless recommended the brothel be moved again.[50] The proximity of the establishment to an educational establishment may only have been a pretext for banning it, however, since "some of the most important citizens" of the neighborhood also threatened to "administer their own justice" if their formal requests did not hold sway in the governor general's

---

45. Karpińska, *Złodzieje, agenci, policyjni strażnicy,* 60.

46. "Paszport niewolnicy," *Czystość* 5, no. 24 (June 12, 1909): 381–83.

47. This restriction applied both to brothels in the Congress Kingdom and in Galicia. "Paszport niewolnicy," 382–83.

48. Rector of Jagiellonian University to the Police Chief, Cracow, April 5, 1911, APKr, DPKr 110, 1093.

49. Leon Brand to C. K. Namiestnictwo, December 30, 1911, APKr, DPKr 110, 1057–74.

50. Cracow Police Chief to C. K. Rady, szkolnej krajowej in Lwów, November 14, 1911, APKr, DPKr 110, 1057–74.

office. The willingness of Galician authorities to respond to such complaints (and in the case of Mr. Brand, ask him to move his establishment no fewer than three times) reflected the ambivalence with which Polish officialdom viewed prostitution. Although legally tolerated, Poles in positions of authority were nonetheless increasingly eager to discourage the expansion of prostitution's physical manifestations and were disinclined to favor brothel keepers over established citizens in clashes over neighborhood planning.

The task of keeping professional prostitutes hidden from the view of more virtuous townspeople was made more challenging as increasing numbers of them left formal brothels behind, preferring instead to operate independently out of rented apartments in poorer neighborhoods. Ironically, this reduced reliance on brothels was partially the result of police pressure to conceal prostitutes from the public gaze by positioning bordellos away from schools, religious establishments, and shops.[51] As cities expanded and became more crowded, complaints about the "dangerous miasmas and sexual offenses spreading" from the bordellos "to the healthy portions of the population" increased and police were forced to close down the larger urban houses in close proximity to other public institutions. Still, as Lwów Police Chief Łepkowski noted with regret in 1912, having hundreds of prostitutes "living in private residences throughout the city is more harmful to public morality than a bordello because [they] come into contact with innocent women and through their demoralized behavior find new victims."[52] Since prostitutes living in private rooms were forced to locate their own clients, the very effort to protect bourgeois morality from the sight of inner-city brothels contributed to the dispersion of public women in the city streets.

Police struggled to enforce municipal regulations governing the behavior of registered women as the trade boomed in urban centers. The greatest menace appeared to be in Warsaw's inner city, where key shopping areas and neighborhood streets were theoretically off limits from solicitation. Yet the staff of eleven police officers responsible for rounding up women in violation of these restrictions was overwhelmed by the magnitude of the problem. Residents protested against thriving brothels on forbidden streets, clusters of teenaged "corner girls" stationed along Marszałkowska Street and in front

---

51. Correspondence of Lwów Police Chief Łepkowski to the C. K. Ministerstwo Wewnętrzne, August 21 and September 19, 1912, AGAD, CKMSW, sygn. 213. Here, Łepkowski notes that "following the massive growth of the city with its new buildings, public institutions, educational facilities, and schools, the Imperial Central Police Directory has repeatedly . . . sought to eradicate several brothels."

52. Łepkowski to C. K. Ministerstwo Wewnętrzne, August 21, 1912, AGAD, CKMSW, sygn. 213.

of the brewery in broad daylight. "Knajpy" employing only a handful of prostitutes popped up throughout the city in the early 1900s including along the main thoroughfares of the former capital. Despite regulations banning aggressive attempts to attract customers, observers complained that "several hundred if not a thousand" public women performed suggestively in front of courtyard gates each night.[53]

The Transgression of Bourgeois Space: Women and Children

Even more upsetting than the mere presence of streetwalkers in the vicinity of sacred sites was the effect of public women's aggressive behavior on "innocent" passersby, especially young women and children. Thrusting these icons of immorality into the often intimate zones of city streets posed a threat to middle-class efforts to insulate families from the baser elements of city life. In this sense, prostitutes transgressed the moral barriers that separated upstanding bourgeois families, with their formalized gender roles and protective notions of childhood, from dangerous external influences. By far the most common complaint lodged about the expansion of prostitution came from "respectable" citizens outraged that they could not walk the streets with their daughters or wives without being accosted. The Warsaw journalist Bolesław Prus (Aleksander Głowacki) reflected these anxieties in his chronicles of Warsaw life published in various daily newspapers. According to Prus, the prostitutes' "aggression" had "crossed a significant line" by the early 1880s. The streetwalkers' "victims," he argued, were no longer *only* "men of various ages, but also women passersby, who are jostled and insulted."[54] These innocent female "victims" appear to have suffered no more serious damage than a bump on the arm in most cases, yet their exposure to "unclean" elements was nonetheless conceived as a severe affront to bourgeois femininity. Prus repeated one such tale of innocence lost, linking it to an earlier complaint from one of the residents of the Bracka and Żurawia area. There was another sad incident last night," this one connected with a young girl, he notes. "After the theater, Mr. and Mrs. P. were returning home with their daughter to their home on Hoża Street. Right on the corner of Bracka and Żurawia, the daughter fell behind her parents several steps and was attacked by two night bats and one of them even bumped Miss P. in her arm."[55]

---

53. Wróblewski, *O prostytucji*, 53–55.
54. *Nowiny,* January 21, 1883, reprinted in *Kroniki* 6 (Warsaw, 1957): 12–13.
55. *Kurier Poranny,* 1883, reprinted in *Kroniki* 6 (Warsaw, 1957): 13.

FIGURE 1.2   Bolesław Prus (born Aleksander Głowacki), 1897.
Photograph by Antoni Kamieński.

Fortunately, in this case, nothing untoward happened to the girl, whom we can imagine to be of mature age based on her description. Instead, the parents came running, Mr. P. called for the police, and the "bats" quickly disappeared. Nonetheless, Prus suggests that the threat these streetwalkers posed to bourgeois respectability and Victorian virtue mandated a reconsideration of "young ladies taking evening walks . . . in order to prevent similar cases as the one described here from occurring." The presence of prostitutes was used, in this sense, to further restrict the freedom of "respectable" bourgeois women, lest they be harmed by exposure to less virtuous female influences.

Increasingly, the expanded metropolitan geography of sin included deepening anxieties about threats to female innocence. Along "Marszałkowska Street and at the intersection with Próżna" and "on the corner of Zgoda and Marszałkowska" in one of Warsaw's main business districts, respectable burghers found themselves maneuvering around pockets of immoral women while going about their daily affairs. A typical evening at the theater could be ruined when the sexually insulated bourgeois family came face to face with "revolting scenes of shameless harlots" causing them, as one Mr. Str. reported, to whisk their charges to the opposite side of the boulevard in order to "protect the children from a demoralizing view and from the hail of the most abominable words."[56] Life on Chmielna Street, between Nowy Świat and Szpitalna, was no better, according to Mr. Maszyński. "I have no way to smuggle my wife and daughters by that does not pass the gang of street-walkers," he recounted in horror. For Mr. Maszyński and for his neighbor, Mrs. W. N. on St. Aleksander Square, the preeminent concern about open prostitution was that it showed "even honest women and maidens what life was like among such intolerable conditions."[57]

Exposure to poverty and sexual promiscuity was expected to prompt neither pity nor sisterly empathy for the plight of the less fortunate; rather, such scenes posed a risk of moral compromise. Spectators who witnessed these indiscretions feared they would somehow become tainted themselves, along with their innocent children. Mrs. W. N., for example, set out to protect her young daughter from the filth of the city by renting an apartment directly opposite a church. She was horrified, however, when she realized the apartment opened up directly onto a popular area for soliciting sex trade. "Imagine my surprise," she recounts, "while sitting with my daughter in the evening in front of the open window [to discover] what was happening on the sidewalk practically in front of the church. Passersby walking here in the evening treated it as a completely ordinary situation, this open testament to a way of life that should have caused a blush of shame on the face of any honest woman."[58] Not only would any "honest woman" want to "blush with shame" at these sights, so too were the quarrels that broke out among the evening denizens of her street and the "abominable cursing that rained

---

56. "Z chwili," October 1, 1901, 2.
57. Maszyński, letter to the editor, *Kurier Codzienny*, October 6, 1901, 2.
58. "Z chwili," October 1, 1901, 2.

down," a source of profound discomfort. Yet Mrs. W. N.'s primary worry was the visual contact her daughter had with a lifestyle so distant from and yet so threatening to her own.

The challenge these "shameless ones" posed to bourgeois notions of femininity was very real. Depictions of the prostitution "problem" regularly emphasized the alien demeanor of street women and contrasted their behavior to the demure bearing of women in middle-class families. The loud laughs, crass jokes, cynical smiles, "toothless expressions," and generally tawdry appearance of prostitutes helped emphasize their lower-class status and unladylike behavior, features that placed them outside the social circle of most literate observers. Everything about them was anathema to the bourgeois sense of womanhood to which these metropolitan families aspired. Not only were they independent, typically unmarried economic actors—a status that had no clearly defined parallel in "polite" Polish society—but they also displayed "unwomanly" traits in pursuing their livelihoods. Their rough, aggressive approach to prospective customers set them apart from the expected behavior of Victorian-era women, as one Mr. J. noticed. Coming home from a Warsaw theater one night along Nowy Świat, Mr. J. came face to face with a particularly persistent prostitute, who "seized [him] by the pocket of his fur coat, tearing a wide swatch from it." Mr. J. clearly believed the woman, having behaved in an unladylike manner, had forsaken the respect accorded her as a female and he "administered justice to the attacker with his own hand."[59] The willingness to dispense physical retribution on a woman in this manner may well have reflected the social distance separating the prospective client from the lower-class itinerant prostitute and the extent to which the latter's behavior was perceived as outside the realm of acceptable female comportment.

Even more compelling for respectable observers than the damage inflicted on female passersby was the threat prostitutes posed to the innocence of childhood. The "unlimited moral harm" of open prostitution reached its peak when "youth, girls, students, and even children [had to] look around them on the street and through the front windows of their apartments while the night time moths walk back and forth along the pavement." Only occasionally, according to a 1901 complaint, as if to legitimize the world of middle-class virtue, did public women "realize they should maintain decency and turn their attention to the passersby."[60] At other times, protective parents

---

59. "Plaga uliczna," *Kurier Poranny,* January 10, 1883, 3–4.
60. "Z chwili," September 27, 1901, 2.

worried about what might become of their adolescent children if the youths came into direct contact with streetwalkers. As one mother living on the corner of Mokotowska and Wilcza opined, "I have a fifteen-year-old boy in the fourth class. For several days now he has had to leave at eight in the evening to visit a colleague to find out the assignment for class. I was sitting on the balcony and cried out in horror when I noticed that two streetwalkers standing there were clinging to the arm of his jacket. What sorts of ideas and feelings can be inculcated in a boy in the face of such open impertinence I cannot imagine."[61] Again, physical exposure to an "inferior" lifestyle had potentially corrupting effects on unformed children. The possibility that a fifteen-year-old might have experienced sexual "ideas and feelings" apart from his contact with prostitutes seems not to have occurred to these frantic parents. "Danger lurks," the concerned mother concluded, "and we must find the means to eradicate it."[62]

Anxiety about sexually potent prostitutes threatening "innocent" adolescent males or exposing proper young ladies to negative sexual modeling grew partly out of an increased emphasis on childhood as a separate stage of life in Victorian Europe. Middle-class Poles were very much drawn to efforts to distinguish childhood from adulthood by limiting the exposure of adolescents to certain experiences. As Jeffrey Weeks has noted, the "fear of sexual corruption among the young" became an important symbol of social rank in Europe, contributing to increased bourgeois anxieties about sex, including those reflected in Warsaw's prostitution panic.[63] The aggressive, brazen behavior of the streetwalkers was hardly the modeling parents sought in acculturating their offspring into Victorian sensibilities. The challenge to childhood innocence was even greater for Jewish communities. Brothels were often situated in Jewish neighborhoods. Although prostitutes were legally forbidden from conducting business within forty steps of Christian schools or churches in the Congress Kingdom, this restriction did not apply to Jewish houses of worship or *cheders*, perhaps because the latter typically operated out of private homes. Regardless, Jewish school children and those en route to synagogue were increasingly exposed to prostitutes openly marketing themselves. Local police seemed helpless to contain the problem.[64]

Nowhere was this affront to childhood innocence more poignant than in attitudes toward underaged prostitution. The 1906 case of ten- and

---

61. "Z chwili," October 1, 1901, 2.
62. Ibid.
63. Weeks, *Sex, Politics, and Society*, 38–39.
64. Wróblewski, *O prostytucji*, 54.

eleven-year-old Cracow girls commissioned by their parents to sell sex brought concerns about the vulnerabilities of childhood to the fore. The violation of bourgeois morality was particularly acute in this city "known for its great number of churches and the piety of its residents," observers warned. The case presented a clear challenge to contemporary expectations for appropriate models of parenting. "Some of the secrets of this great town" were revealed in the discovery of eleven-year-old Józefa C., who was seemingly coerced into selling sexual favors. During the girl's police interrogation, when it became clear that, "despite her youth [she] had been earning money through prostitution for some time," the popular condemnation was all the greater.[65] The paper revealed that Józefa was but one among a group of girls of a similar age who were occupied in the same business. Even more shocking, the children's parents had reportedly encouraged their daughters to earn money in this manner and the young streetwalkers handed over their profits directly to their elders. Such sanctioning of sexual impropriety in children cut deeply into contemporary notions of the family as a bulwark against harmful influences from the "dregs" of society. When children were manipulated by their own relatives to commit immoral acts, Nowe Słowo argued, "it [was] not difficult to see the destruction of social relations as a whole."[66] The family in this conception was the fundamental component of a stable society. As such, it was intended to protect innocent children, not corrupt them. The class distinctions implicit in this story no doubt encouraged bourgeois readers to redouble their efforts to insulate their own adolescents from base influences. Only a member of the "popular classes" who was "ignorant," in a dire economic situation, and living among the "surrounding scum" of Cracow would turn to such a practice, the article implied. Even so, the ease with which a young girl might be trapped in the world of prostitution may have given pause to parents of teenage girls reading such stories, reinforcing their impulse to sequester their own daughters in the protective environment of their homes.

The Protection of National Public Space

The epidemic of open prostitution on city streets represented a violation not only of bourgeois sexual sensibilities, gender norms, and familial expectations.

---

65. *Nowa Reforma,* September 6, 1906, cited in "Kroniki: Największa ran społecznych," *Nowe Słowo* 5, no. 1 (October 1906): 18–19.

66. "Kroniki: Największa ran społecznych," 19.

At the same time, many Polish observers construed blatant commercial sex as an insult to national public space. A century after the partition of Polish territory and its occupation by Russian, German, and Austrian authorities, members of the Polish-speaking elite continued to assess social problems through the prism of the martyred nation. Visible indications of corruption, demoralization, and poverty such as the throngs of streetwalkers huddled along public thoroughfares troubled positivist-era reformers like Aleksander Świętochowski and Bolesław Prus. They worried, first of all, that the "debauchery" on display in Polish towns served as a sad reminder of the pitiful cultural and economic infrastructure underpinning the Poles' claims for national independence. Positivist intellectuals had argued since the inception of their movement in the 1870s that the nation could only hope to regain its independence if it overcame its cultural backwardness, economic underdevelopment, and weak infrastructure, problems that underlay the turn many poor women took to paid sex.[67]

Second, nationalist activists were concerned that ethical violations of a sexual nature could damage the reputation of the movement's leaders, prompting accusations of hypocrisy and distracting from the public reception of their programs. Świętochowski tacitly acknowledged this danger when recollecting his own brief brush with prostitution as a student in Warsaw's Szkoła Główna during the 1880s. "Whenever the conservatives were unable to escape an attack from the progressive camp in the 1880s," he recalled, "they would throw out the accusation of immorality. And, of course, it existed among us," causing "those who adopted a free life and free thought" to find themselves in a "risky situation," exposed as they were to the potential for public scandal. His own revelations of evenings spent in brothels and red-light districts in the former capital city were enough to lend credibility to such claims.[68]

The third and greatest source of unease among nationalist activists was the damage the visible sex trade might have on Poland's reputation in the eyes of foreign observers. Polish intellectuals knew that a nation without

---

67. On the social-reform movement known as Warsaw Positivism or Organic Work, see Stanislaus A. Blejwas, *Realism in Polish Politics: Warsaw Positivism and National Survival in Nineteenth-Century Poland* (New Haven, CT, 1984); Halina Kozłowska-Sabatowska, *Ideologia pozytywizmu galicyjskiego: 1864–1881* (Warsaw, 1978); Jerzy Rudzki, *Aleksander Świętochowski i Pozytywizm Warszawski* (Warsaw, 1968); and Henryk Markiewicz, *Pozytywizm* (Wrocław, 1950).

68. Świętochowski shares a few brief episodes of "boozing and debauchery" involving a medical student roommate, some tours of Warsaw's red-light district along Bednarska Street, and his own nausea-induced escape from a particularly grotesque brothel scene. Aleksander Świętochowski, *Wspomnienia* (Wrocław, 1966), 26–28.

sovereignty needed the positive opinion of its friends abroad. Those who beheld unsavory street scenes while visiting major cities across Polish territory might be less likely to lend their support to the national cause. Sensing their nation's moral vulnerability in the eyes of strangers, elite writers were quick to point out that conditions on Warsaw's city streets had not yet reached the level of debauchery found in Paris, the true capital of licentious behavior. Some were clearly anxious, however, that if nothing was done to correct the problem, "Warsaw [would] become a town in which immorality [would] begin to approach the levels of Paris."[69] While they were quick to defend themselves against the accusation that Lwów was among the most prostitute-infested towns in all of Europe,[70] Polish journalists were also unabashedly distressed at the level of street prostitution in the nation's former capital. Prus himself commented cynically that "I can't imagine in all of Europe a town as unrestrained as Warsaw . . . such female figures as one sees in the darkness of Warsaw, such legions, such impudence in accosting passersby, such things do not exist anywhere else."[71] Concluding in exasperation, "a country is its customs!" Prus explicitly connected domestic cultural issues such as prostitution with the way the nation would be judged by the international community.

Everywhere commentators lamented the contrast between Warsaw's aspiration as the center of a great nation and its current level of street filth. "Here in Warsaw," began one such story, townsfolk have "pretensions to a great city, to high culture," and yet, "from the streets leading out of the main thoroughfares, one sees throngs of women . . . with unsavory faces." As if to underscore the hypocrisy of great men criticizing tawdry women, the writer notes, "by the light of day, we serious moral people label this prostitution and complain about the decline of virtue."[72] Yet after the sun sets, these same pious critics were not above turning to the pitiful street creatures for their own personal gratification. Foreign visitors to Poland's former capital would no doubt find this level of degeneracy appalling, local observers submitted, and this in turn would affect the martyred nation's international standing. "For those who are looking for the first time at the streets of Warsaw," commented one letter writer, "it will appear to be a great

---

69. Bolesław Prus, "Nim słońce wejdzie," *Kurier Codzienny*, January 11, 1883, 3.

70. Major Wagener's accusation prompted a series of exposes on prostitution in Lwów published during 1906. Wagener's depiction is discussed in detail in "Prostytucja we Lwowie," *Świat Płciowy* 7 (February 1906): 20–21.

71. "Nim słońce wejdzie," 3.

72. "Parę uwag w draźliwej sprawie," *Prawda*, no. 34 (1904): 401.

nest of immorality and nothing more." The image of these street scenes, he worried sardonically, "creates a lovely impression of the level of morality in Warsaw."[73] Prostitution had thus become a serious challenge not only to middle-class respectability but also to Poland's future fortunes. The problem symbolically exposed the nation's inadequacies, self-indulgence, and neglect of its most vulnerable classes.

With increasing frequency, public figures invoked the name of the martyred nation to promote greater attention to issues of illicit sexual activities. Bolesław Prus complained in 1897, for example, that although the Polish lands provided by no means "the smallest quantity of goods for international trafficking in women . . . our country [kraj]" contrasts rather sadly to "Europe," where such problems are openly addressed.[74] Similarly, critiques of a 1903 study of sex trafficking out of the Polish lands focused on the urgent need for social action to combat sexual licentiousness in order to "heal" the wounded nation. "A cultured nation" such as Poland, lamented one reviewer, "possessing so many great minds and hearts," should have "noticed this social wound" earlier and begun "to take action to heal it."[75] By 1905, social purity campaigns mixed moral discourse with national ideology, suggesting that the two were increasingly interdependent. The Warsaw physician and early eugenicist Antoni Wysłouch stressed the close linkage between social purification and nationalism, arguing that reducing prostitution contributed directly to "improving the welfare and health of the nation."[76] Here and elsewhere, the debate about the causes of and solutions to the prostitution "problem" in the Polish-speaking world was couched in a nationalist idiom. As the problem of rampant public sex spread beyond the purview of urban observers and became fodder for broader national debate, the visibility of the prostitute and Polish society's lack of control over her behavior fed a larger concern about Poland's place in the international community. Clearly, those who considered themselves leaders of Polish society would have to take action to correct the problem of visible commercial sex or at minimum force it back into the shadows where it had existed for centuries.

---

73. Maszyński, letter to the editor, 2.

74. "Our country . . . still has no Society for the Protection of Traveling Girls," Prus complained. Bolesław Prus, "Kroniki tygodniowe," *Kurier Codzienny*, January 24, 1897, reprinted in *Kroniki* 15 (Warsaw, 1967): 24–25.

75. "Kroniki" *Nowe Słowo* 5 (March 1, 1903): 114–15.

76. Wysłouch, *Prostytucja i jej skutki* (Poznań, 1905), 37–38.

The Traffic in "Human Flesh"

As much as Polish-speaking commentators chose to perceive the spillover from commercial sex onto the urban pavement as a national problem best tackled by national reformers, the context for discussing prostitution soon grew wider than the boundaries of Polish society. Brief glimpses into the world of international sex trafficking appeared during the moral panic of the 1880s and the imagery employed in these early references helped shape popular conceptions about prostitution. Quiet whispers about innocent girls whisked away into sexual bondage in alien lands came first from the less censored news media of Galicia, feeding bourgeois anxiety about the potential threats to their innocent daughters. In 1885, the conservative Galician newspaper *Czas* announced that members of an accused sex trafficking ring with links to Warsaw, Hamburg, and the interior of Russia had been arrested.[77] Meanwhile, mothers of daughters who had disappeared in "mysterious" ways appealed to Galician authorities for help in locating their children. In 1891 *Kurier Warszawski* and *Tygodnik Ilustrowany* published correspondence from Buenos Aires testifying to the transport of a young woman from Warsaw to Latin America.[78] When twenty-seven accused traffickers were arrested and put on trial in Lwów, journalists in the Galician capital printed a cycle of stories outlining the main components of the way sex trafficking would come to be understood in the Polish imagination.[79]

The Lwów trial (discussed in chapter 4) brought prostitution to the attention of the Polish audience as never before. The case remained in the public eye for several months as the police investigation and deposition of "victims" continued. Just as newspaper coverage of debauched women selling themselves on Warsaw's city streets attracted the attention of the reading public a decade earlier, the 1892 sex trafficking trial provided an opportunity for Galician journalists to explore commercial sex more openly. Acknowledging the traditional reticence of the news media to address the fate of poor women caught up in sex rings, *Gazeta Narodowa,* Lwów's daily Polish-language paper, proclaimed its intent to provide its readers with a full accounting of the trial as it proceeded. Up until now, though, the paper averred, because this practice was "so grievous, so abominable, people [didn't] even want to speak about

---

77. *Czas* 6 (1885), cited in Milewski, *Ciemne sprawy*, 115–18.

78. Milewski, *Ciemne sprawy*, 116. Milewski claims that the Warsaw press was prohibited from publishing information about sex trafficking within the city because it might "frighten the criminals and make the work of the police more difficult."

79. See Keely Stauter-Halsted, "'A Generation of Monsters:' Jews, Prostitution, and Racial Purity in the 1892 L'viv White Slavery Trial," *Austrian History Yearbook* 38 (2007): 25–35.

it and the newspapers [were] silent."[80] The traffickers themselves had hidden in the shadows, the editors claimed, from a society that did not want to be informed about uncomfortable truths. "Up until now, they have known how to hide from justice and conduct their horrible trade, forcing thousands of victims into the most abysmal human misery. Occasionally, a small voice speaks up quietly, a moan escapes from a horrifying human soul, but the noisy excitement of everyday life drowns it out. Society would rather forget about it. Above all, [society, in its] lazy, egoistic calm, protects itself from damaged nerves! Why look into the depths when the smell of putrid depravity emanates from there? The lovely smooth façade suffices."[81] The newspaper promised to break this cycle of silence and "look into this vivisection," revealing to the reader "all that has happened" to these "poor, white lilies." In so doing, the editors acknowledged the occasional murmurings about sex slavery, "the deplorable charge of mothers who had lost their daughters," that had come to the public's attention earlier but failed to catch hold of the readership's imagination.[82]

Part of the reason international trafficking received so little attention may have been tied to the social class of its victims. For the most part, the disappeared women, like the young girls selling sex in Cracow, belonged to the lower ranks of society. The fate of hundreds of poor, sexually compromised women was a nonevent in polite society because, as one reporter suggested, "the disappeared girls belonged to those who existed in poverty or penury; they were creatures of a disinherited world, workers stooping over machines or bleeding their fingers by knitting flowers, or they were day laborers and girls from the peasantry."[83] The social status of the prostitutes—whether they were local streetwalkers on Polish city boulevards or victims of sex trafficking—affected the presentation of their stories. While aggressive, sexually demoralized street women fitted nicely into the paradigm of "dangerous," "otherworldly" representatives of the lower social orders, the image of innocent, hard-working girls trapped into compromising themselves by criminal traffickers or desperate parents challenged conventional notions of sexual complicity and consequently appeared less frequently.

Regardless of whether prostitutes appeared as physically aggressive sexual deviants polluting city streets *or* as impoverished lower-class victims of

---

80. "Z tajemnic społeczeństwa: Handlarz dziewcząt," *Gazeta Narodowa,* July 9, 1892, 2.

81. "Z tajemnic społeczeństwa," 2.

82. The paper alluded to the "cries of mothers" for their missing daughters that had been ignored some seven years previous to the trial. "Handlarze dziewcząt," *Gazeta Narodowa,* October 19, 1892, 2.

83. Ibid.

upper-class greed and social neglect, the popular press and professional experts alike agreed on the need to maintain social distance between these sexual outcasts and respectable circles. Upstanding churchgoing, theater-attending Poles perceived the world of paid sex as fundamentally alien to them and threatening to their way of life. Only by insulating themselves and their families from commercial sex transactions could they hope to protect their own respectability, that of their children, and, ultimately, the reputation of Poland's chief cities. Whether by "closing the windows and tightly sealing the window blinds," as Mrs. N. determined to do, or by "restricting the traffic in shame" to certain key streets, as another correspondent recommended, prostitution needed to be removed from the public landscape.[84] Poland's urban sex workers belonged to "that class of women about whom one does not speak,"[85] and respectable burghers preferred that prostitution itself remain hidden physically from view, that it remain "in the shadows" and dark alleyways, away from polite society.

When these impoverished creatures could be portrayed as crude, abrasive, and sexually promiscuous, their stories were told as if to reinforce bourgeois social values. When those caught up in sex rings could be portrayed as innocent victims, and the "cries and groans" of their mothers could inspire empathy among bourgeois readers, it was far more difficult to distance such tales from everyday middle-class life.[86] Indeed, reporters wondered, "how can one believe such a horrible crime has taken place among us, who sit at the height of civilization?"[87] Polish readers often responded to such stories with shock and disbelief. Audiences had grown accustomed to the depiction of more aggressive prostitutes and were less willing to consider the possible vulnerabilities of poor women. In fact, in 1896, when the Warsaw journal *Niwa* published a series on white slavery, unmasking a ring of Warsaw-based human traffickers, the story was met with sharp protests and accusations that its allegations were pure "*fantazje*."[88]

---

84. "Z chwili," October 1, 1901, 2; P. Maszyński, letter to the editor, *Kurier Codzienny*, October 6, 1901, 2.

85. The phrase is used by a journalist for the Lwów newspaper *Gazeta Narodowa* as an explanation for the lack of public discussion about the disappearance of hundreds of poor Polish girls into Middle Eastern brothels and harems. "Handlarze dziewcząt," 2.

86. Ibid.

87. Ibid.

88. The series was published under the title "Naganiacze" or "Agitators." Cited in Milewski, *Ciemne sprawy*, 90, 115–18.

Information as Social Control

As evidence of the darker side of modern urban life surfaced with increasing frequency and discussions of sexual licentiousness broke onto the pages of the popular press, the Polish public was drawn into competitive fact collecting about the world of the prostitute. This "will to know" was driven, first and foremost, by the intractable problem of the unregistered prostitute and the threat of uncontrolled disease she represented.[89] Whole sections of educated society set out to gain knowledge and classify information about the prostitute. Police constructed an entirely new category of prostitution, that of the "secret" or clandestine sex worker, and established mechanisms for counting and documenting her behavior. Polish-speaking police in Galicia kept a second registry alongside the public or *jawny* record. This was for the so-called clandestine or *tajne* prostitutes. It consisted of names and personal information for women *suspected* of functioning as professional sex workers but who had not voluntarily registered with the police.[90] Experts in all three sections of Polish territory estimated that the number of women functioning as "secret" prostitutes comprised roughly ten times that of those registered on the public record and subject to medical supervision. By carefully recording the names and personal information about every woman brought to the police station for questioning as a suspected prostitute, authorities sought consistently to draw firm legal lines demarcating a strict separation between women selling sex and their more virtuous sisters.

Like the effort to map out a geography of sin in urban areas, the collection of data about prostitutes was part of a larger agenda to protect polite society from direct exposure to depraved women. Professional curiosity and research about the prostitute arose from an ongoing desire to control and order urban surroundings. The first step for many intellectuals and professionals to overcome their panic about uncontrolled sexuality was to study the problem, to document the prostitute's behavior. In the months and years after the initial deluge of information about paid sex, newspapers noted that "the truth is, there is only one area of progress in this matter, and that is statistics." Nonetheless, though, there was a "great hole in our ethics—that

---

89. On the range of public opinion and professional analyses of prostitution in late nineteenth-century Galicia, see Baczkowski, "Prostytucja w Krakowie," 593.

90. See, for example, the elaborate system introduced by Lwów police beginning on March 1, 1906 for registering prostitutes who also maintained legitimate full-time employment and were "screened" by their work in coffee shops or restaurants. These women were known as "discreet" prostitutes and were inscribed in a *third* registry specifically devoted to this category. "Prostytucje we Lwowie," *Świat Płciowy* 2, no. 7 (February 1906): 24–26.

of self-knowledge" and researchers were encouraged to continue producing information about the prostitute's plight.[91] Everywhere publicists complained that journals other than their own failed to uncover the facts of the situation accurately. The Warsaw press criticized Cracow papers, arguing that the "Galician press does not write about it [prostitution]. For them, the question does not exist; they do not want to be irritable." That left the Warsaw papers, which, according to the Galician socialist Karol Radek, "treat important social questions in lyrical feuilletons, [while] their authors themselves [were] guilty" of frequenting the very brothels they criticized.[92] Newspapers in the former capital ostensibly celebrated "illustrious Warsaw," where "there [were] no problems, no misery that require[d] any remedy." But this, argued the medical expert Antoni Wysłouch, was simply not true. "There is misery, horrible misery here about which people are embarrassed to recall and perhaps don't even know exists."[93] Such a situation "must not continue," according to Wysłouch, and the fastest way to a remedy was the compilation of information about the world of prostitution. Yet until the late nineteenth century, most of polite Polish society was content to "let prostitution flourish so long as it [did] not show itself on the streets."[94]

This bid for greater "self knowledge" as a first step to solving ethical problems was soon heeded. The first stage was to collect numbers. Publicists became preoccupied with accurately estimating how many women were active on city streets. Proposals for the number of prostitutes working in Warsaw alone ranged from ten thousand to forty or fifty thousand, out of a total metropolitan population of seven hundred thousand inhabitants in 1900. Everywhere, specialists demanded greater statistical accuracy in calculating the size of the prostitution problem, stressing that research on commercial sex should be approached as analytically as possible, relying on "a deep approach, handled seriously, making use of a wide array of source materials, and vigorous energy."[95] Research documenting the insidious nature

91. B. Lutomski, "Upadłe samobójczyznie," *Głos* 5, no. 7 (1890): 76–77.

92. Karol Radek, "Prostytucya w naszej prasie," *Nowe Słowo* 3, nos. 17–18 (September 15, 1904): 407–11.

93. Wysłouch, *Ohyda wieku*, 11.

94. Radek, "Z badań nad prostytucyą," 536–41.

95. Despite chastising other researchers for their unscientific estimates, the paper was quick to propose its own crude estimate of active prostitutes at approximately one hundred thousand in all of Congress Kingdom. This number was based on the proposal that approximately twenty to twenty-five thousand prostitutes were active in Warsaw, a similar number in Łódź, a total of twenty-five thousand in all the provincial towns together, and an additional twenty to twenty-five thousand in the villages, totaling roughly eighty to one hundred thousand. Stanisław Koszutski, "Na mównicy: Walka z prostytucją," *Głos* 15, no. 25 (June 23, 1900): 386–88.

of prostitution in factories was cited to demonstrate the dangers of clandestine prostitution. One such study, conducted by the German scientist Dr. Alfred Blaschko and cited in the Polish press, argued that "only" 43.4 percent of Berlin factory workers engaged in commercial sex in 1898, whereas the number was as high as 70 percent in 1875.[96] The absence of reliable evidence to support these figures did not prevent Dr. Blaschko from compiling his statistics, nor did it keep Polish journals from reporting them as fact.

Detailed depictions of the prostitute's world soon appeared in publications across Polish territory. Early in 1900, *Głos* published an overview of the police-medical registration system in place throughout the Polish Kingdom. In a thorough exposé that openly discussed flaws in the system of tolerated prostitution and the number of women who slipped out of police control, the paper warned of the dangers of "secret" (unregistered) prostitution.[97] Later that year, *Gazeta Polska* called attention to the implications that easy access to prostitutes had on the health of Warsaw's university students.[98] Thanks partly to the moral panic of the 1880s, the author and others like him had determined that the ongoing practice of university students resorting to prostitute use must not remain masked by polite avoidance or neglect. Polish publicists exchanged accusations of a common unwillingness to speak "openly" about prostitution. They attacked one another for preferring to keep their discussions on the matter "half buried" and for discussing it only "between the lines." According to N. E. Wolski, author of a controversial study of prostitution use among bourgeois males, *Defense of the Family*, the puritanical Victorian tendency to avoid lurid description in assessing social problems was a luxury early twentieth-century Poland could ill afford. "The plague of our times," Wolski advised, "is to defend morality with a closed mouth without allowing things to be called by their names."[99] As if to confirm Wolski's sensitivity to cloaking public concerns under a cover of shame, reviewers of his book quickly chastised him for his too graphic account of the situation he sought to remedy. Arguing that there will always be "questions that the instinct of the ages shields with a cloak of shame," one reviewer proposed removing the debate about regulated prostitution from the public realm and referring it to the purview of "sociologists, moralists, hygienists,

---

96. Review of Dr. Alfred Blaschko, "Prostytucya w XIX wieku," *Nowe Słowo* 2, no. 21 (November 21, 1903): 490–92. Blaschko conducted his research in the factories of Berlin, Dusseldorf, Erfurt, and other German industrial towns.

97. Józef L., "Policja obyczajów," *Głos* 5, no. 30 (1900): 476–77.

98. The *Gazeta Polska* piece was summarized in Bolesław Prus, "Rozpusta czy bieda," *Kurier Codzienny*, October 28, 1900, reprinted in Prus, *Kroniki* (Warsaw, 1968), 16: 505.

99. N. E. Wolski, *Obrona rodziny* (Warsaw, 1907), 5–6.

and educators. The field of discussion should be the special sections of professional journals, monographs, and brochures," the reviewer concluded, not the columns of the popular press. Rather, "in the name of the defense of the family" (a reference to the title of Wolski's book), such things should not be discussed openly.[100]

Within a decade after the initial onslaught of articles and studies produced about Poland's burgeoning sex industry, it was no longer possible to cloak the issue in polite language and professional research. Just as prostitution itself had become a visible component of everyday urban life, impinging on nearly every element of municipal existence, so too had discussions of commercial sex crept out of the safe confines of specialized societies and into everyday discourse. No longer a mere professional subspecialty that could be tempered through stricter controls or more invasive procedures, prostitution had become an urban menace that had imposed itself on the very vocabulary of bourgeois witnesses. Despite the efforts of contemporary correspondents and essayists to remove commercial sex from the map of Polish cities, prostitution and the infrastructure that supported it were very much a part of the urban landscape in the turn-of-the-century Polish lands. Thousands of young women and girls were registered every year on the official police rolls in all parts of the country, and still more worked as "clandestine" or unregistered prostitutes. Brothels dotted the central boulevards, sex workers stalked crowded neighborhoods in search of customers, and pimps and procurers appeared omnipresent after dark. All of this unfolded under the noses of prominent Polish families living on streets where "every other address was a brothel."[101] To make matters worse, venereal diseases were spreading unchecked among university and gymnasium students, in army garrisons, and within middle-class families. VD hospitals and wards were full to overflowing and medical experts cried for more space.[102] Clearly, it was growing difficult for bourgeois Poland to keep these activities at a comfortable distance.

The growing intimacy with which urban Poles experienced the world of the prostitute reinforced bourgeois efforts to define their own social positions

---

100. Wuk, review of *Obrona rodziny*, by N. E. Wolski, *Słowo* 6 (September 9, 1907): 1.

101. Zaleski, *Z dziejów prostytucji*, 37.

102. Dr. Alfred Sokołowski noted, for example, that forty-two thousand residents of Warsaw sought treatment for venereal diseases in 1909, a figure that represented only a small fraction of those actually suffering from these ailments. Sokołowski argued that such diseases were a leading cause of blindness and infertility, and that in certain districts of southwest Poland (Galicia), over 95 percent of the population had been infected since the mid-nineteenth century. *Wielkie klęski społeczne* (Warsaw, 1917), 311–13.

against the background of the ethically deficient lower classes in their midst. Polish speakers sought to reinforce definitions of normality that had been introduced by police, doctors, and legal experts and to confirm boundaries separating bourgeois "respectability" from lower-class sin. Working-class women who violated the prescribed notions of sexual decorum were placed beyond the boundaries of respectability. They were labeled "outsiders" and "deviants," women who did not share membership in the same community of interest the writers enjoyed. Public women challenged nearly every element of iconographic portrayals of bourgeois family life. Neither wives nor mothers, they appeared socially disconnected from larger familial institutions and functioned as independent wage earners engaging in aggressive, unfeminine techniques to ply their trade. Middle-class interlocutors contrasted the "decency and morality" of the bourgeois home with the "danger and pollution" they confronted when entering the public sphere.[103] The prostitute with her tarnished standards of sexual morality was becoming necessary for reinforcing Polish bourgeois values.[104] The prostitute herself served as an invaluable ally in this process of definition and demarcation, threatening the middle-class ideals of public order, morality, and health.[105]

As it turns out, the lives of the women selling sex on Poland's city streets were not so separate from those of their more respectable urban neighbors. Instead, part-time prostitutes were among the household servants, nursemaids, governesses, and wet nurses who migrated from surrounding villages to provide household support for the expanding Polish petit bourgeoisie. Women of ill repute staffed the stores, workshops, factories, cafés, and bars of bustling city centers, turning to prostitution when their insufficient wages ran out. No matter how much bourgeois Poles sought to distance themselves, their families, and their ways of life from the world of the illicit streetwalker, the lives of the two were inextricably linked. Clear distinctions between "respectable" Poland and the disreputable "other" scraping a living on city sidewalks were growing increasingly hazy.

---

103. Weeks, *Sex, Politics, and Society,* 81–88.

104. Ibid., 27–28.

105. In France and Italy, the prostitute was situated in the context of the dangerous, vicious classes who were being described by social investigators. Gibson, *Prostitution and the State in Italy*; and Jill Harsin, *Policing Prostitution in Nineteenth-Century Paris* (Princeton, NJ, 1985).

CHAPTER 2

Into the Abyss

The Turn to Paid Sex

> Girls who were seduced or raped frequently by so-called polite, educated men, slid into the abyss most often, rejected by their families, overwhelmed by shame, and convinced that there was no decent life ahead of them.
>
> —S. Wertensteinowa reporting on her observation of 45 prostitutes sheltered by the Jewish Society for the Protection of Women in 1905. "Z tragizmówżycia"

> A woman who falls into the sphere of prostitution will not emerge from it again because first, society does not allow her to rise up again, and secondly, she herself typically does not want this.
>
> —Józef L., "Policja obyczajów"

On a warm summer evening in 1914 a prostitute in glittering earrings and a golden headband smiled alluringly at a young man on a darkened Warsaw street. The youth found himself both repelled by the streetwalker's "strange, unnatural smile" and yet "intoxicated by the warmth emitting from her body." Against his better instincts, he accompanied her back to her apartment and paid her 1-ruble fee. Rather than demanding sexual favors, however, the young man instead elicited the pitiful story of the harlot's "fall" into prostitution. As reported, the prostitute's tale contained all the iconic elements of the popularly understood transition to paid sex. Growing up in an impoverished artisan family with an alcoholic father, the young woman had been orphaned at an early age and forced to make her way in the world. She worked for a time as a domestic servant and then as a seamstress, but eventually was seduced by an official escorting her home one night. The deed "that the villainous hypocrite committed," she recounted, "shattered" her happiness forever. After a rape, a promised marriage, and abandonment, she found herself once again on the streets, this time with a child to support. She lost her needlework position, wandered from job to job, and finally had to give up her son and resort to the profession "provided for her by society." The root cause of her turn to commercial sex, she stressed, was her initial seduction and subsequent pregnancy. Thereafter, she was treated as "a whore, a degenerate mother!" and forced to take "the only road that remained for [her] . . . the road of filth . . . the alleyways flowing with debauchery."[1]

How accurate is this melodramatic portrayal of the road to paid sex? What actually precipitated the descent into prostitution in fin de siècle Polish society and in what ways did popular assumptions about women who sold sex correspond to the lived reality of brothel residents or streetwalkers? This chapter examines contemporary mythologies about the turn to prostitution and contrasts them with details from the lives of female sex workers. It considers the rhetorical impact of paradigmatic imagery surrounding the prostitute's "fall" and assesses the uses of stereotypical assumptions about poor women in the evolution of Poland's gender dynamic. As with our protagonist, the classic nineteenth-century account characterized women working as prostitutes as passive victims in their own fate. The streetwalker in this case describes her worst sin as her resounding naïveté and trust in people. "Oh, what was I guilty of in this?" she wonders. "Only that I was stupid perhaps, that I didn't know the world and didn't know people! And he, that criminal, took advantage of this and seduced me!" If it had not been for the lecherous official, she proclaims, "I would still be a good, honest girl."[2]

This tale of upper-class seduction and innocence violated contains all the elements implicit in the early twentieth-century prostitution paradigm. First, the moment of transition is depicted as a "fall" similar to the biblical fall from grace. The virtuous young woman nurses her dying mother, toils without complaint at honest work, and then a single incident changes the course of her otherwise exemplary life. Second, the "seduction," which in this case is portrayed as a mixture of rape and a promise of marriage, typically transpires at the hands of a more socially powerful individual—the master of the house where a serving girls is employed, the factory foreman, or a wealthy patron seducing a waitress in a restaurant or café. Prostitutes were portrayed as "unfortunate" girls who were "coerced" by "a pimp pretending to be a fiancé" or "seduced and raped . . . by so-called polite, educated men" and consequently "slid into the abyss" of prostitution.[3] Such unequal power relations inform the third prototypical element in stories of a prostitute's

---

1. Bronisław Topór-Szczygielski, *Kobieta-Ciało. Odysseja kobiety upadłej* (Warsaw, 1914).
2. Ibid.
3. S. Werteinsteinowa, "Z tragizmów życia," *Prawda* 37, no. 13 (1917), quoted in Sikorska-Kulesza, "Prostitution in Congress Poland," 132–33.

"fall"—the almost complete passivity of the "victim" herself. Young women are given little agency to direct their own fortunes in these tales, but instead succumb to forces beyond their control. They are duped by wily procurers pretending to court them, escorted to brothels on the pretense of gaining work as domestics, or appear for waitress or dancing positions only to find themselves servicing customers in other ways. Time and again elite publicists recount the litany of trickery, deception, and coercion used to transform innocent girls into debauched women. In the Polish lands as in imperial Russia, the persistent belief that working-class girls were pulled into prostitution as unwilling participants helped justify medical and police supervision over them as a form of state protection.[4]

Not only is the descent into prostitution typically portrayed—both among Poland's social elite and among its practitioners—as a single, powerless moment. The collapse into the social "muck" is also depicted as permanent. The fourth stereotypical component of the prostitute's biographical journey is the social ostracism "fallen" women ostensibly encountered from those in the "honest" world. As our protagonist despairs, she became "a prostitute! Worse than an animal! A prostitute, whom everyone despises!" Those who turned to paid sex even once believed they could not turn back. Instead, "society" rejected them as outcasts, according to this scenario, and they were banished from "honest" jobs, denied the possibility of legitimate marriage, forced into a lifetime of commercial sex, and fated to suffer a slow death from disease. As one critic of Warsaw's police regulation system noted in 1900, "prostitution is not one of those matters in which society extends a hand with the intention of lifting up its victims, but on the contrary it uses its great power to maintain women on the road to ruin." As a result, the author asserted, the possibility of emerging from the muck of prostitution was extremely low. This was partially because "society [did] not allow her to rise up again, and [partially because] she herself typically [did] not want this."[5] The abolitionist activist Antoni Wysłouch agreed that although the prostitute herself was "not without guilt," the broader public also refused to "lend a hand" and instead repelled prostitutes "with contempt."[6] Wysłouch was not alone in believing that the fate of nearly every woman who turned to prostitution was a violent or miserable death from suicide, murder, chronic alcoholism, diseases like anemia, syphilis, gonorrhea, and tuberculosis, or simply from "traipsing around for years on end without a good night's sleep."[7]

---

4. Laurie Bernstein discusses the patriarchal attitudes of the Russian state that prompted efforts to "protect" and control women engaged in prostitution. Bernstein, *Sonia's Daughters*, 1–12.

5. Józef L., "Policja obyczajów," 476–77.

6. Wysłouch, *Ohyda Wieku*, 18–20.

7. Ibid., 11–17.

FIGURE 2.1 "Man Paying a Prostitute." Anonymous pencil and ink drawing. The National Library in Warsaw (Muzeum Narodowe).

Even the interwar prostitution expert Wacław Zaleski concluded that most sex workers typically ended up in the venereal hospital with their "entire organism destroyed" and were invariably buried anonymously in the public cemetery.[8]

---

8. Wacław Zaleski, *Prostytucja powojenna w Warszawie* (Warsaw, 1927), 115–16.

Finally, our story reveals the classic setting for this paradigmatic fall from grace: the great city. The fifth piece of the prostitution melodrama is the inhospitable context of urban anomy. In the Warsaw tale above, the orphaned girl is thrown out of her apartment by an insensitive landlord and abused by her employer. She is alone in the city and seems to have no confidant to whom she can turn. She is portrayed as the child of an artisan, but her fallen sisters were more typically young women straight from the countryside who migrated to urban centers and struggled to support themselves while seeking factory jobs or positions as serving girls. Torn from their rural support systems and lacking family resources, they were ignorant of the ways of the city, likely to trust strangers and thus find themselves in compromised situations. The metaphor of the "great city" as a corrupting influence on otherwise innocent peasant daughters captures one central aspect of the east European boom in paid sex during the latter part of the nineteenth century: the tremendous growth of urban centers that provided a market for prostitution and the most visible manifestation of sexual commerce. Yet here too reformers and journalists willfully exaggerated the numbers of women engaged in commercial sex, estimating them to include as many as ten thousand in Warsaw during the 1890s and twenty thousand in 1905 Lwów. As one reporter noted archly, this latter figure would imply that "out of twelve women in Lwów between the ages of fifteen and fifty, barely one would be serving in an honest trade and all the rest would be harlots!"[9] This and other prototypical elements of the standard prostitution "story" vastly simplified a complicated nexus of motives, strategy, contingency, and opportunity that greeted poor young women when they left the protection of their families and entered the public stage.

We cannot know whether the chance encounter described above actually occurred or, if it did, whether the conversation unfolded as it was transcribed. Nonetheless, it is clear that either the pamphlet's author or the woman he interviewed believed that certain tropes were essential in constructing a compelling saga of the decline into the netherworld of prostitution. Classic paradigms such as the fall from grace, female victimization, permanent social ostracism, and the transformative power of the great city were woven through narratives of the turn to paid sex that circulated across the Polish lands. Each of these scenarios was rooted in realities of

---

9. "Prostytucya we Lwowie," *Świat Płciowy* 2, no. 6 (January 1906): 35.

lower-class life; each at the same time glossed over elements of the complex circumstances within which poor women operated. The remainder of this chapter looks behind the tidy mask of melodrama and explores the variegated paths through which women came to sell sex and their particular experiences of police-regulated prostitution. Chapter 3 then examines the links between this world and that of bourgeois Poles. Even as simplistic stories stereotyped the long-term removal of immoral girls from polite society, women who practiced venal sex continued to function at all levels of the economy. The banishment of "fallen women" was, in the everyday context of urban east-central Europe, neither permanent nor complete. Instead, the lives of poor women included by necessity a number of strategies for negotiating the often inhospitable terrain of the city. Commercial sex was one of these, but the choice to exchange sex for money or gifts did not necessarily represent a permanent transformation into the status of a professional prostitute.

Rather, sources reveal signs of permeability between, on the one hand, the world of "honest" female employment and "legitimate" family attachments, and on the other hand, the practice of prostitution. Contemporary police reports, prostitution registries, and interviews with women involved in the sex trade point to a complex pattern of impoverished women and girls resorting to prostitution, occasionally even with the knowledge or coercion of their families, as a short-term or part-time measure to alleviate economic stress.[10] Clearly not all downtrodden families made use of the practice, yet it was common enough to be woven tightly into the moral universe and strategic considerations of needy women in both rural and urban settings. The consequences of this widespread resort to prostitution were far-reaching, the most significant among them being the increased tendency of upper-class Poles to equate poverty with sexual impropriety. Beginning in the 1880s and continuing until the outbreak of World War I, government doctors forced all women in certain employment categories to undergo police medical examinations as "secret" prostitutes. This association of particular occupational groups—from household servants to factory workers and service

---

10. Historians of female laborers in the United States have also highlighted a pattern of "occasional" prostitution in turn-of-the-century urban settings. Christine Stansell argues that casual prostitution of "girls or women who turned to prostitution temporarily or episodically to supplement other kinds of livelihoods" was on the rise in the 1850s. *City of Women: Sex and Class in New York, 1789–1860* (Urbana, IL, 1987), 173. Similarly, Kathy Peiss examines women who "slipped in and out of prostitution when unemployed or in need of extra income." *Cheap Amusements: Working Women and Leisure in Turn-of-the-Century New York* (Philadelphia, 1986), 110–11.

personnel—with prostitution effectively reinforced the equation of poverty with sexual immorality in the public consciousness. The implications of this conceptual slippage for the treatment of women in Polish society will be the subject of chapter 3. The focus here is on how these linkages evolved in the popular imagination and how women themselves approached the decision to sell sexual services.

Paid Sex in Country and City

One way to understand the turn to prostitution from the perspective of its practitioners is to consider the situation young women encountered when they arrived in the great city, typically after migrating from smaller towns or nearby villages. Even before poor women got caught up in the whirl of metropolitan life, however, many had experienced prostitution in their rural homes. Contemporary commentary typically assumed that rural–urban migration precipitated the burgeoning sex trade in the Polish lands. Yet the roots of the prostitution "epidemic" lay outside urban enclaves, on the estates and in the garrison towns of provincial Poland. One of the most important sources for assessing the sexual economy of the Polish countryside is the work of Dr. Józef Apolinary Rolle (1829–1894), a Kiev-trained, Polish-speaking physician from the Podlasie region of the eastern Polish lands. Rolle wrote a series of articles published in medical periodicals in Warsaw, Cracow, and Poznań during the 1860s and 1870s, and became one of the first Polish physicians to introduce wider social concerns into the prostitution discussion.[11]

Rolle's work as an estate doctor alerted him to the prevalence of prostitution and rampant venereal disease among impoverished peasant families. In his nearly ten years studying paid "debauchery" in and around the town of Kamieniec, Rolle discovered what he termed a "black page" in the history of the Polish nobility. He painted a picture of provincial gentry who kept stables of peasant girls for the sexual gratification of their guests. Rolle recalls visiting "noble estates where the guest rooms located in the back of the house contained both comfortable bedding and a young girl who gracefully greeted the entering guest." He explains, "the estate girls who served guests were fully prepared to also spend the night with them."[12] Gentry were

---

11. For a rich overview of Rolle's work as it touched on prostitution in Podole, see Jolanta Sikorska-Kulesza, "Prostytucja w XIX wieku na podolu w świetle badań Józef Apolinarego Rolle," *Przegląd Wschodni* 5, no. 3 (1998): 435–42.

12. Józef Rolle, "Materiały do topografii lekarskiej i hygieny Podola. Prostytucja." *Przegląd Lekarski* 8, no. 39 (1869): 313. Reflecting on his interviews with peasant fathers about their daughters "serving" on the local estate, Rolle quotes one man's description of his rather "ugly and difficult" daughter who "fortunately at least" would not be going to serve on the estate.

the primary customers at the brothels that dotted rural hamlets and country roads, each employing a small handful of impoverished women, according to the police doctors who regulated their activities.[13] In all of these ways, Rolle claimed, "the estate was the propagator of prostitution." Under serfdom, he concludes, the gentleman believed that "all animals on his territory belonged to him . . . and this included the wives and daughters of 'his' peasants, who were expected to . . . serve his every need."[14] The practice of employing peasant girls on estates and in rural brothels was an established pattern no doubt familiar to many female migrants in larger cities. The women who served in this capacity were peasant daughters, married women, or unwed mothers on whom rural families relied for support. Their earnings represented an integral part of the village economy, a desperate attempt to keep the household afloat in conditions of dire poverty. The long-standing practice of putting a daughter out to service on the estate was a decision peasant families made reluctantly but out of necessity when other strategies for gaining a livelihood had been exhausted.

Even more tragic than country girls who served the nobility were the young wives of military recruits obliged to sell sex in garrison towns to support their families while their husbands were away. "*Rekrutki*," Rolle noted, "comprise[d] over half the women engaged in rural prostitution, they [were] wives who follow their husbands to the garrison town, usually young and poor." Part of the enormous class of landless laborers formed after emancipation, these families suffered from desperate material conditions in the best of times. After arriving in the garrison where their husbands were stationed, military wives first sold what objects they could at the local taverns, then when they grew hungry, turned to begging and finally to prostitution.[15] From his experience serving as a night guard in 1862, Rolle recalled watching prostitutes emerge from the taverns and wineries at night looking for clients. "I never saw anything more frightening than women of this type, standing outside nearly naked, covered only in rags that disintegrated to the touch, with swollen faces from an excess of alcohol," he recounted. Such

---

13. Józef Rolle, "O prostytucji miejskiej na Podolu," *Pamiętnik Towarzystwa Lekarskiego Warszawskiego* 3, no. 52 (1864): 29, quoted in Sikorska-Kulesza, "Prostytucja w XIX wieku na podolu," 440. Rolle notes that during certain periods, such as carnival or when the army was stationed in the area, the number of prostitutes in the Kamieniec brothel rose from an average of ten women to around fifty.

14. Rolle, "Materiały," 8, no. 38, 307; no. 39, 313.

15. Rolle, "Materiały," 8, no. 39, 315.

women were, he judged, more pitiful than the most miserable prostitute in Paris or London.[16] The rampant use of prostitutes and the attendant spread of venereal diseases on his watch led Rolle to recommend in 1869 that rural industrial establishments such as sugar refineries, textile factories, and cigarette workshops that employed large numbers of women be placed under medical supervision and their female workers checked for signs of venereal disease.[17] Concerned above all with protecting local residents from contamination, Rolle's decision to impose police control on all female laborers nonetheless contributed to a widening sense in Polish elite circles that poor working women were often sexually compromised.

Resort to prostitution among village girls did not diminish in the generations following emancipation from serfdom (1806 in Prussia, 1848 in Austrian Galicia, and 1861 in the Polish Kingdom). Overpopulation in the countryside, primitive agricultural techniques, and harsh indemnities payments to former landlords made it difficult for farm families to feed themselves.[18] According to Russian imperial sources, as late as 1889 some 4.6 percent of the total registered and state-supervised prostitutes operated in rural areas, a figure that is no doubt artificially low given the minimal regulation machinery outside urban areas.[19] The socialist activist Kazimierz Kelles-Krauz observed as late as 1902 that the parceling of large farms and the resulting number of tiny plots meant that peasants could no longer support themselves purely from farming. Instead, he noted, "a large number of village girls have to be rented out for a magically low wage to work on estate lands, where they fall under the absolute authority of estate managers or of the no less brutal owner himself." Here, as in the days of serfdom, the practice of sexual abuse continued, Kelles-Krauz remarked. "Woe to the girl who catches the eye of the estate manager and refuses to do what he wishes." The result of this steady supply of village girls to the manor house was a continuation of patterns of sexual abuse that prevailed under serfdom. "And thus," Kelles-Krauz sums up, "they finish by joining the ranks of rural prostitutes."[20]

16. Rolle, "O prostytucji," 29, 40, quoted in Sikorska-Kulesza, "Prostytucja w XIX wieku," 442.

17. Rolle, "Materiały," 8, no. 40, 321.

18. On conditions among Polish peasants during the first generation after emancipation, see Kieniewicz, *Emancipation of the Polish Peasantry*; Olga Narkiewicz, *The Green Flag: Polish Populist Politics, 1867–1970* (London, 1976); and Inge Blank, "From Serfdom to Citizenship: Polish Folk Culture from the Era of the Partitions to World War I," in *Roots of the Transplanted: Plebian Culture, Class, and Politics in the Life of Labor Migrants,* ed. Dirk Hoerder and Inge Blank (Boulder, CO, 1994), 111–73.

19. A. Dubravskiy, ed., "Prostitutsiya v rossiyskoy imperii po obsiedovaniyu 1-go avgusta 1889 g.," *Statistika Rossyjskoy imperii* 13 (1890), quoted in Sikorska-Kulesza, "Prostitution in Congress Poland," 123, 126.

20. Kelles-Krauz, "Półśrodki," *Nowe Słowo* 1, no. 19 (1902): 455–58.

Unsurprisingly, Polish commentators tended to deemphasize the rural roots of prostitution, stressing instead the corrupting powers of the great city on otherwise virtuous female migrants. This oversight arose partly out of the powerful iconographic significance of the village as a romantic trope in Polish national literature and partly because too close an examination of paid sex in the countryside risked compromising the moral leadership of the estate and the leading role of the gentry in Polish cultural life. Józef Rolle was forbidden even to include material on estate prostitution in his publications printed in the Polish Kingdom. Only in the more liberal press of Galicia, far away from the wealthy families he accused, could he depict details of the sex economy of rural Poland, in which the very men entrusted with protecting and guiding the newly emancipated peasants were responsible for forcing them to sell sex.[21] Nonetheless, the number of registered prostitutes in rural and small-town Poland remained steady, even toward the end of the century as their numbers climbed in major cities. Each of thirty-one moderate-sized towns in the Polish Kingdom recorded ten or more prostitutes on their police rolls in 1889 and eighty others had one prostitute each.[22] Over one hundred smaller towns maintained tolerated houses for their residents. Clearly prostitution was neither limited to large metropolises nor exclusively the result of big-city conditions. Nonetheless, the assumption was widespread that the general atmosphere of social degeneracy characterizing large urban centers was foundational for the thriving sex industry.

Despite long-standing rural precedents in Polish culture, most nineteenth-century journalists and social reformers characterized prostitution as an urban phenomenon. Moralists depicted the eastern European metropolis as the "mother of prostitution." The city's inhuman social relations, dangerously mixed-gender factories, rampant filth, and demoralization drew innocent migrants into a swirl of economic and sexual pressures, according to these assessments. Visitors came face to face with the machinery of prostitution— the brothels, streetwalkers, pimps, and vice police—in metropolitan centers, helping to highlight commercial sex as a feature of the urban landscape.[23] Observers portrayed city life as transformative for residents and resort to prostitution as a survival tactic was part of this transition. The city was the locus of declining family ties. It was where young people migrated alone and established links with other members of their age cohort, sidestepping

21. Sikorska-Kulesza, "Prostytucja w XIX wieku," 438–39.
22. Sikorska-Kulesza, "Prostitution in Congress Poland," 126.
23. Ihnatowicz, E., "Miasto kryminalne," *Miasto-kultura-literatura-XIX wiek* (Gdańsk, 1993), 113–24; and Sikorska-Kulesza, "Miasto-przestrzeń niebezpieczna dla kobiet," 341–49.

the dominant influence of fathers and other male authority figures who
had supervised their activities in the village. Reformers in the United States
were equally insistent that the source of female sexual impropriety lay in
the separation of young women from home and family. As Joanne Meyerowicz argues, the "danger" to an innocent girl in the eyes of turn-of-the-
century reformers began "the moment a girl [left] the protection of home
and mother." Correspondents to Chicago newspapers characterized the city's
single women as "torn from the protective shelter of family and exposed to
the muscle of the city."[24] Polish observers similarly viewed female migrants as
vulnerable without the support of their provincial families. The prevalence
of factory work with its low wages and cycles of unemployment combined
with a large concentration of young adults—especially single males—and
inequities in income helped establish conditions where prostitution flourished. Warsaw in particular, but also industrial centers like Łódź and Poznań,
administrative capitals like Lwów, and the cultural mecca of Cracow, all
boasted features that helped drive the market in prostitution.[25]

The unprecedented expansion and changing demographics of east European cities provided fertile ground for the growth of a visible urban sex trade.
Adrift from family and support networks, recent migrants turned to commercial sex as one of many survival strategies. Contemporary charity groups and
social activists perceived this intermittent turn to paid sex as symptomatic of the
moral decline and degeneracy that characterized industrial centers. For them,
the inhuman forces of metropolitan life—the intense overcrowding, debilitating diseases, unchecked filth and poverty—consumed the innocence and feminine virtue of female migrants, grinding them into savvy sexual actors capable
of negotiating their surroundings by using tools at their disposal.[26] In certain
respects, the emphasis on the great city in contemporary writing about prostitution was not inaccurate. City life provided the opportunity, the anonymity,
and the necessity for many women to turn to paid sex. Yet the resort to prostitution was far from an exclusively urban phenomenon and by wrapping the
discussion in the language of big-city danger, social commentators effectively

---

24. Joanne J. Meyerowicz, *Women Adrift: Independent Wage Earners in Chicago, 1880–1930*
(Chicago, 1988), 43–62.

25. Warsaw boasted over nine hundred registered prostitutes in 1889, and the number of tolerated women in Łódź multiplied fivefold in the period from 1895 to 1910 as the city itself experienced
dramatic growth.

26. For a parallel representation of young women from the countryside corrupted by the great
city in the United States, see Meyerowicz, *Women Adrift*. Here too female migrants appear in contemporary literature as passive innocents ruined by a city that lacked moral standards and placed in
harm's way after leaving behind the protections of home and family.

conflated urbanization with prostitution and modernity with demoralization. In fact, the growth of cities in the Polish lands merely transferred a strategy long employed among lower-class women to a more public arena. Even as moralists, physicians, and other members of the urban elite worried about sexual degeneracy among working-class women, the more common scenario was of thousands of poor female migrants resorting to prostitution for a limited time after first arriving in the city, during periods of extended unemployment, or as a necessary supplement to inadequate wages in poorly paid positions.

Metropolitan Sexual Demography

The preconditions for widespread resort to prostitution in the Polish territories included several factors, some common to the rest of Europe and some unique to eastern Europe.[27] First, cities across Polish territories experienced a population explosion in the last decades of the nineteenth century. The pace of migration from villages and small towns began as a trickle in the 1860s, picking up in the 1880s and continuing through the early years of the new century. In Austrian Galicia alone, close to a half million people migrated from small towns and villages to large cities between 1869 and 1910. By 1910, over half the residents of cities like Cracow and Lwów were not natives but had migrated during their lifetimes.[28] Unlike many local migratory streams in Western Europe, however, east European peasants abandoned the countryside with its abject poverty but lacked assurances of gaining jobs in the city, which often could not accommodate the influx of newcomers. Two generations after emancipation, peasant farms were shrinking as family size grew and inheritance patterns diminished holdings. Indemnities payments to former lords often crushed the possibility of profiting from agriculture. Farm families in some regions were literally starving. For generations males had migrated seasonally to perform agricultural labor in the German lands or traveled overseas "*za chlebem*" ("for bread")[29] Migration to the nearest major

---

27. The urban landscape of east-central Europe has received renewed scholarly attention in recent years. Among the pathbreaking studies highlighting the variegated texture of city life in the region are Maureen Healy, *Vienna and the Fall of the Habsburg Empire: Total War and Everyday Life in World War I* (Cambridge, 2004); Roshanna P. Sylvester, *Tales of Old Odessa: Crime and Civility in a City of Thieves* (DeKalb, IL, 2005); Robert Nemes, *The Once and Future Budapest* (DeKalb, IL, 2005); and Wood, *Becoming Metropolitan*.

28. Gąsowski, "Urbanizacja Galicji w dobie autonomicznej," 223–43.

29. On patterns of peasant migration for work, see Stefan Inglot, *Historia chłopów polskich* (Warsaw, 1972), 262–70; Joseph Obrębski, *The Changing Peasantry of Eastern Europe* (Cambridge, MA, 1976); and Keely Stauter-Halsted, *The Nation in the Village: The Genesis of Peasant National Identity in Austrian Poland, 1848–1914* (Ithaca, NY, 2001), 57–59.

city was but a first step for some. Many would continue on to the factories of Western Europe or the ports of the North Sea. For others, lacking the money to pay the passage or unwilling to leave behind family and language, the city became the primary destination and the hope of rescuing family fortunes. This migratory tradition began in earlier generations when children were sent to work on the estate, to nearby market towns, or to administrative centers. By the end of the nineteenth century, the pattern of traffic from villages and small towns to the growing urban metropolises was well established.[30]

Second, the demographics of Polish cities helped establish the preconditions for a lively sex trade. Unattached males and garrison soldiers created a significant clientele for brothel keepers and pimps. City life in eastern Europe had all the characteristics of a frontier, with a high transient population of single young people passing through its gates. In a one-month period in 1905, for example, over 36,000 men and women made their way to Cracow en route to the United States or Western Europe.[31] Larger towns attracted males serving in the military, enrolling in gymnasium or university, or working in government administration. Despite greater opportunities available to males, women consistently outnumbered men in these boomtowns, a condition that helped account for the resort to sex work. Among the nonmilitary population, there were 116 women for every 100 males in Cracow's 1900 and 1910 censuses.[32] The majority of these female migrants sought work as household servants, a poorly paid profession that encouraged resort to informal prostitution to supplement meager wages.[33] Cities in the Polish lands were the province of the young and unattached, an atmosphere in which families held little sway over the working poor. Some 60 percent of both males and females in Cracow and Warsaw were unmarried in the early 1880s, and over half of all working women were single at the end of

---

30. On internal migration and its relation to transatlantic emigration from east-central Europe, see Annemarie Steidl, Engelbert Stockhammer, and Hermann Zeitlhofer, "Relations among Internal, Continental, and Transatlantic Migration in Late Imperial Austria," *Social Science History* 31, no. 1 (2007): 61–92; and Dirk Hoerder, ed., *Labor Migration in the Atlantic Economies: The European and North American Working Classes during the Period of Industrialization* (Westport, CT, 1985).

31. "Emigracya," *Gazeta Narodowa*, April 5, 1905, 2. The month in question was March 1905. In the first three months of 1905 a total of eighteen thousand came through Cracow bound for the United States, and thirty-one thousand emigrated via Cracow to Germany and Denmark.

32. Kumaniecki, *Tymczasowe wyniki spisu*, 31.

33. Aleksander Świętochowski, "Liberum veto," *Prawda* 2, no. 11 (1882): 130. Demographers have shown that this pattern of female preponderance in short-distance migration streams was common in many parts of the United States, Latin America, and Asia during the late nineteenth century. In the United States, for example, farms were "defeminized" as tenant and small-farm families sent their daughters off in search of work to help support the family. Meyerowicz, *Women Adrift*, 8–15.

the nineteenth century. This demographic created an ideal setting for resort to part-time or temporary sex work. Many jobs required women to remain single, yet paid them lower salaries than males, leaving them to find ways to make do on limited incomes.[34] In addition, the large population of young single men, including high school and university youths, provided potential clientele for urban prostitutes. In 1903, over 80 percent of Warsaw students admitted to making use of prostitutes at some time.[35]

The single females residing in the large fin de siècle Polish cities were mostly newcomers to the urban environs, and those who turned to prostitution were almost entirely migrants from outside city walls, usually from regional towns and villages. Less than 8 percent of the registered prostitutes in Cracow were born in the city during the 1890s and less that 5 percent were natives in the early years of the twentieth century. The majority of the others hailed from smaller towns in Galicia (34 percent) or from the countryside (31 percent).[36] Anecdotal evidence confirms the impression that urban brothels were the province of country girls. The Warsaw police specialist Wacław Zaleski observed in 1923 that "statistics of the registration of Warsaw prostitutes demonstrate that the vast majority of them moved from the countryside, and in the brothels, with the exception of the Jewish locations, one almost never met girls born in Warsaw."[37] Zaleski even went so far as to attribute the absence of aristocratic courtesan "types" in Polish literature to the fundamentally peasant quality of most prostitutes in Polish cities.

Because industrial development was uneven in Poland's urban conglomerations, too few jobs for women were available to accommodate the steady flow of migrants. The industries that employed large numbers of women were prone to regular economic downturns and massive layoffs. Textile centers in Łódź and Białystok and smaller workshops in Warsaw could hardly absorb the migrants flooding into the city each month. Railway connections to Cracow, Lwów, Warsaw, and elsewhere drew thousands of transients each month to cultural

---

34. A one-day survey conducted in 1882, for example, found that some fifty-nine thousand single males over the age of fifteen were living in Warsaw. *Oesterreichische Statistik* (Vienna, 1882), quoted in Lidia Zyblikiewicz, *Kobieta w Krakowie w 1880 r.: Studium demograficzne* (Cracow, 1999), 60; Maria Nietyksza, *Ludność Warszawy na przełomie XIX i XX wieku* (Warsaw, 1971), 97, 238; and Marta Kurkowska, "Birth Control in the Industrial Age: Cracow 1878–1939," *Polish Population Review* 10 (1997): 161–65. On low rates of pay for women relative to men, see Marta Sikorska-Kowalska, *Wizerunek kobiety Łódzkiej przełomu XIX i XX wieku* (Łódź, 2001), 53.

35. A. Annanski, "Zagadnienie prostytucji w świetle higieny społecznej," *Wiedza* (1910): 86, cited in Sikorska-Kulesza, "Miasto-przestrzeń niebezpieczna dla kobiet," 345.

36. Prostitution Registry for Cracow, APKr, DPKr 439–40; and Baczkowski, "Prostytucja w Krakowie," 595.

37. Zaleski, *Z dziejów prostytucji*, 59.

attractions, trade fairs, and the excitement of political life in administrative centers.[38] The fortunes of these migrants once they arrived would be mitigated by the shortage of steady jobs, abysmal working conditions, and the difficulties of finding food and housing. The absence of state agencies to assist migrant workers and transient women meant that poor females easily fell between the social cracks. Prostitution sometimes proved to be the only choice when dreams of life as a factory worker or as a servant for a wealthy family did not materialize.

Jobs for Unskilled Women: Factory Work

The dominant narrative about the "fall" into prostitution in the Polish lands rarely included a critical assessment of the socioeconomic context in which the turn to paid sex played out. Instead, moralists and charity workers portrayed prostitution as the outcome of a moral misstep on the part of otherwise virtuous young women, who may have been coerced into committing sexual indiscretions by someone stronger and more powerful. Social workers such as Ludwika Moriconi, who managed a shelter for "fallen women" outside of Warsaw, insisted that the women in her charge were driven to prostitution because of a fundamental moral failing. It was the inappropriate environment of mixed-sex living quarters and class envy that drove female migrants to prostitution, Moriconi claimed, rather than the abject poverty of women alone in the city. Characterizing her charges as inherently "wild," she held that their "moral misery" made it difficult for them to resist the temptation of the easy life prostitution seemed to offer. Because the hardened women in her shelter lacked the moral foundation of a good home, they struggled to negotiate the challenges of being single and unskilled in an alien environment. Social workers such as Moriconi helped define and depict the background of Poland's prostitutes even while negating the causal link between economic need and the plunge into sexual debauchery. Much of the "misery" Moriconi described was the product of the agonizing adjustment thousands of young women made upon their arrival in the city.

Yet some observers also recognized the east European metropolis as full of challenges for a single female. Those whose work brought them into contact with "fallen women" resisted attributing the turn to commercial sex solely to economic desperation. Nonetheless, a wealth of information about the financial challenges women on their own faced can be teased out of their

---

38. Lwów was an administrative and political center, Przemyśl was a center of trade, and Stanisławów was a district capital. See Gąsowski, "Urbanizacja Galicji," 237–38.

reports, suggesting additional narratives beyond the "fallen woman" trope so common in Polish-language literary accounts. Pani Moriconi stressed the poverty and social neglect from which her charges suffered, noting that most of the three hundred women in her shelter outside Warsaw were driven to prostitution because they were "mired in material misery." These pitiful wretches, she stressed, inhabited a social sphere characterized by "crowded living quarters, several families heaped together, men and women in one room, drunken parents." For Moriconi, "the maintenance of fatal conditions in the home" meant that young women fell into unsatisfactory relations with their employers and became increasingly conscious of "a growing contrast between their own poverty and the conditions of the privileged class." Apart from her destitute family background, the urban prostitute also suffered from a "lack of professional training . . . complete absence of any schooling, illiteracy . . . and a limited supply of employment opportunities relative to demand." Most of the young women raised in such circumstances, Moriconi noted, had no marketable skills whatsoever. "Not only do they not possess a profession," she observed, but "they also do not know how to read, write, sew, cook, and in general have no sense for order and work. As result, they tend to be extremely poorly paid." All of these circumstances helped account for their vulnerability when exposed to persuasive pimps and procurers.[39]

The story of the descent into prostitution is in many respects a migrant's tale. Recent arrivals from smaller towns and villages were far more common than the daughters of factory workers or artisans on the prostitution registries. The feminist newspaper *Nowe Słowo* referred to the "army of women" arriving in the cities every day from surrounding communities. This "epidemic" of independent female job seekers, editors warned, could not be satisfied with the positions available in most Polish cities.[40] Migrants were particularly attracted to the promise of jobs in factories. Textile manufacturers in the booming industrial towns like Łódź hired greater numbers of males than females, yet the majority of recent migrants to Polish cities were women, and of these, large numbers of them were young, unattached, and below the age of twenty.[41] Their initial arrival in the city was often a frightening

---

39. Ludwika Moriconi, "Przyczynek do sprawy prostytucyi u nas," *Przegląd chorób skórnych i werenycznych*, nos. 4–5 (1907): 169–71.

40. "Kronika: Z Warszawy," *Nowe Słowo* 2, no. 1 (January 1, 1903): 13–14.

41. The total number of industrial workers grew steadily in the Polish Kingdom from 130,000 in 1885 to 300,000 in 1905. Much of this new industrial development was in Łódź, where over half the workers were female, and some 60 percent of these were under the age of twenty. Sikorska-Kowalska, *Wizerunek kobiety*, 39.

experience. Most migrants had little money for food or housing and Polish towns in the 1880s offered no shelters for female travelers. According to Moriconi, "it is particularly difficult for girls coming in from the provinces who have no idea what to do with themselves when they arrive. Such girls are usually illiterate, without a guardian of any type, and easily fall into the hands of procurers."[42]

Factory work was a holy grail for female migrants in the late nineteenth century. Women coming from provincial towns or the countryside viewed employment in an industrial enterprise as a symbol of social advancement. Rural women in particular saw the personal independence of a factory job as emblematic of their emancipation. In the 1880s, some 65 percent of all factory workers in Łódź came directly from the countryside, often from among the landless laborers left without resources after the end of serfdom. They relied on a limited network of contacts from their native villages to locate jobs but nonetheless rarely secured employment immediately after arriving. Desperate for a place to sleep and typically lacking a patron to sponsor them, most took much-less appealing positions as domestic servants to alleviate their immediate hunger. Even if they were successful in locating work, female migrants often suffered the vagaries of early industrialization, with its frequent layoffs and lengthy bouts between jobs. Over half of all unemployed factory workers in Łódź were women, and those who were able to sustain employment were paid distinctly less than their male colleagues, adding to the challenge of supporting themselves and sometimes other family members.[43]

Employment in factories and warehouses, although highly sought after, was nonetheless grueling, requiring long hours and uncomfortable working conditions. One informant described the life of a typical female needleworker: The witness had entered the industry as a "seven-year-old girl" and had "killed herself for miserable wages working all day and half the night." Most needleworkers, she explained further, "work twelve hours a day and earn 2 rubles monthly salary for it. The food is a glass of tea and a roll morning and evening, and a dinner worth a złoty or 40 groszen. For such compensation they must often travel to the far end of town, thinly clad, in the frost and rain, and then sit for twelve hours in the dark and damp, and finally return home at night." Some sixteen thousand female workers sustained themselves under such conditions in Warsaw in the 1880s, according

---

42. Moriconi, "Przyczynek do sprawy prostytucji," 171.
43. On pay scales for female factory workers, see Sikorska-Kowalska, *Wizerunek kobiety,* 53.

to a report prepared by female philanthropists.[44] A similar study conducted among female laborers in Lwów during 1903 concluded that on the whole, "female workers do not earn enough to support themselves."[45] In Poznań, meanwhile, women workers complained that "the steady drop in wages [and] the widening poverty among working women" was pushing more and more into the ranks of prostitution.[46]

Even those who were fortunate enough to find salaried posts had to deal with the trauma of daily existence on the shop floor. Factory culture shocked some new employees, who complained of the crude jokes, lewd pictures, and jeering comments to which they were exposed. As Kathy Peiss has argued, the world of work for young laboring women was often an arena of sexual vulnerability. "Wage earning women" in New York, she notes, "were perceived by bosses and male workers to be outside the realm of parental or community protection." Indeed, the same men who would hoot and howl and yell sexual innuendos to female coworkers would act perfectly "respectable" on the street and never consider such behavior outside of the workplace.[47] Worse, according to a letter from an anonymous female worker in Łódź, the collective apartments single males and females shared were the sites of debauched festivities where "everyone was drunk" and occupants engaged in "scandalous" behavior.[48]

Such activities greeted many new employees in industrializing societies, but the challenge for young women was even greater when limited factory positions necessitated moral compromise to keep their jobs. "If a girl is to survive in the factory and not lose those few rubles that she works hard to earn," she had to put up with various forms of exploitation, observed one priest with contacts among the Łódź proletariat. According to Father Marceli Godlewski, at the time a parish priest in Łódź, the real crux of the problem was that the "foreman or vice foreman is the complete master of his subordinates, who can do nothing to oppose him." Young women often had to submit to their bosses' advances or risk losing their positions, Godlewski explained, creating what he termed a "reign of debauchery" in

44. *Kurier Warszawski* (1887), quoted in Prus, *Kroniki* (1953), 10: 28–30.

45. "Położenie lwowskich robotnic chrześcijańskich," *Nowe Słowo* 23 (December 1, 1903): 535–41. The salaries of female industrial workers in Polish cities were considerably lower than those in American industry, where laboring women were often perceived as more assertive and more impudent because of their independent incomes, fancy clothes, and freedom from parental control. Stansell, *City of Women*, 125–27.

46. D. L., letter to the editor, *Nowe Słowo* 2 (January 15, 1903): 36–38.

47. Peiss, *Cheap Amusements,* 50–51.

48. "Głos robotnicy Łódzkiej," *Niwa* 7 (1897): 121–22.

the workplace. "Woe to the poor working girl who does not willingly accept his shameful and impudent propositions," he warned, for "she will certainly be fired. And to whom would the injured one complain, who would support her against the lawlessness? No one, except perhaps God."[49] Because the foreman and the vice foreman could concoct imaginary reasons for dismissing workers from the factory, those who were let go had little recourse to challenge the decision. Instead, women who tried to maintain their virtue and refuse the advances of a foreman might find themselves on the streets.

Such testimonies not only challenge contemporary definitions of prostitution as a full-time profession and reveal details of the sex economy of the factory, but they also expose some of the vulnerabilities working women suffered in attempting to hold onto their positions. The instability of industrial employment helped create a cohort of unemployed, unskilled women for whom prostitution became a strategic option. As Father Godlewski summarized, a recently sacked factory worker might find herself "deprived of work, wandering from factory to factory, searching for wages in order to feed herself and perhaps to help her poor family, who survive on her work. It is a happy thing if she finds a position in a short time, otherwise, she will die from starvation. . . . When she finds a position at another factory, she is slower to be the victim of her supervisor's whim; fear of starving from hunger, or the example of other female workers who slowly become an instrument in the hand of the supervisor, receive better positions and higher pay, lead her also to a heinous existence."[50]

Factory work, by nurturing the notion of trading sex for financial security, helped create an atmosphere in which prostitution was somewhat normalized. The informal banter between male and female coworkers and the sexual harassment that was integral to relationships with factory foremen conditioned laboring women to rely at least occasionally on sexual exchange as a strategic weapon in their arsenal of survival techniques. At the same time, low wages and lack of job security made it all the more likely that a working woman might consciously turn to the sex trade as a way to solve temporary unemployment or to supplement her meager salary. By the early twentieth century, the Polish feminist press concluded that "prostitution accompanied the development of factories and industry" and was associated with "the need for wages among women." As one correspondent to a Warsaw paper

49. Father Marceli Godlewski, "Kilka uwag z powodu listu robotnicy fabrycznej w Łodzi," Niwa 16, no. 9 (1897): 161–62. Godlewski served most of his career at Warsaw's All Saints Church, where he was a parish priest for some thirty years.

50. Ibid., 162.

FIGURE 2.2   Peasant women gathered on the outskirts of Warsaw.
Courtesy of the Cracow Ethnographic Museum (Muzeum Ethnograficzne Kraków).

noted, the low wages, uneven employment, and "fatal working conditions for women forced them to earn money on the side by selling their bodies."[51]

Again, the information social workers and charity groups gathered about the turn to prostitution challenged the prevailing notion that sex work resulted from a failure of will or a lapse in judgment on the part of young women. Instead, anecdotal evidence, local observations, and industry studies indicate that women living on their own in large cities rarely earned enough to support themselves without supplementing their wages. The use of informal or occasional prostitution became for some of them a means to negotiate their new urban environment using the limited resources at their disposal. We cannot know how prevalent such practices were during this period, nor how casually the decision was taken to exchange sex for scarce resources in the context of the urban workplace. We do know that many women who registered on the police rolls as prostitutes noted other occupations as their simultaneous or preferred professions. And we know that social reformers, feminist activists, clergy, liberal intellectuals, and others who worked among the urban poor saw evidence of young women driven to the brink of prostitution primarily out of economic necessity rather than moral failing.

---

51. Błaschko, "Prostytucya w XIX wieku," 490–92.

Authorities in the Polish Kingdom acknowledged the reality of female industrial workers engaging in part-time prostitution in the spring of 1883 when they issued new police-medical regulations mandating that all women "serving in restaurants and working in factories be placed under police surveillance" and inscribed onto the prostitution registry. The new law was the focus of extensive debate in the Warsaw press, partly because it effectively broadened the already expansive powers factory foremen had over their female employees. Exceptions to the new regulation were to be granted only in cases where "the owner of the factory can testify to [a woman's] moral standing." As the journalist Bolesław Prus cynically envisioned, "the impact of this is easy to imagine: From now on, the first good director or vice director of an establishment that employs women can easily obtain relations with his subordinates. Anyone who rejects his advances will not receive a guarantee and will be subject to registration."[52] Such regulations were both a reflection of police administrators' notion that the vast majority of poor, working women were involved in selling sex at some level and the beginnings of the conflation of poverty with immorality. Of the roughly five hundred industrial establishments in Warsaw employing women, only sixty-two testified in the first months after the new rules were implemented to the high moral conduct of the women they supervised, leading at least one reporter to draw conclusions about "the complete absence of moral qualifications among female workers."[53]

Data collected in the early years of the twentieth century brought contemporaries to the same conclusion time and again: survival in the city as an independent woman was virtually impossible among the lower classes without some sort of sexual compromise. Work in feminized branches of employment was poorly paid, making it difficult for workers to survive on their wages alone. The situation required poor women either to marry to help support themselves or to devise some other, alternative means of earning income. Ironically, many jobs for women *required* their recipients remain unmarried, presenting a conundrum difficult to resolve. As one Father Józef Zyskar noted, "work for women is extremely poorly paid. Most branches of industry are completely closed to women, and those that remain can barely keep their workers from starving to death." Because "honest work for women provides such low wages," he believed, the best option for many single women was marriage.[54] He might also have noted that for those who

---

52. Bolesław Prus, "Kroniki," *Nowiny* 42 (1883); Prus, "Kroniki," *Kurier Warszawski* 31 (1883); Prus, "Kroniki," *Nowiny* (1883); reprinted in Prus, *Kroniki* (1957), 14: 31–33.

53. Prus, "Kroniki," *Nowiny* 40 (1883), quoted in Prus, *Kroniki*, 14: 33.

54. Father Józef Zyskar, letter to the editor, *Czystość* 1, no. 4 (August 1, 1905): 27–31.

did not marry and were left to contend with the pitiful wages offered by the feminine trades, part-time prostitution often served as a necessary supplement to their incomes. Indeed, the structure of the urban economy, with its large sectors of female employment at depressed wages, pushed many young women to consider this decision.

Workshops and Pieceworkers

Time and again, economic experts stressed the limited economic opportunities women on their own faced. Dr. Salomea Perlmutter concluded in a 1903 series on female professions in Lwów that the average worker simply did not "earn enough to support even herself." After interviewing fifty-six working women in Lwów from seventeen different professions, Perlmutter concluded that regardless of the type of "difficult, exhausting work in whatever profession" they pursued, most of her subjects experienced prolonged periods of unemployment and severe hunger.[55] The institutionalized abuses and meager compensation doled out to virtually all female laborers in turn-of-the-century Lwów were legendary. For those not fortunate enough to gain employment in a factory, a variety of backbreaking positions from needlework to glove making or cigarette manufacturing were the best that could be expected. Such toil involved workdays ranging from eleven to fourteen hours, with one hour-long dinner break, although in some industries young women were "unofficially" expected to work deep into the night. Overall, Perlmutter concluded, not a single profession surveyed offered conditions for "an individual to feel like a person." Instead, what she referred to as the "horrible, endless Galician poverty" (nędza Galicji) was reflected in the "gray, bleak, desperate situation" of the Lwów female labor force. Conditions both on the job and at home for these girls were "extremely unhygienic," she added. Their "home and workplace" were described as "crowded, humid, and the cause of frequent sicknesses." Girls in such setting suffered from frequent bouts of "anemia, stomach disorders, and tuberculosis." Their tendency toward sickliness was exacerbated by the "thinness of their clothes." And, of course, when such women did contract an illness, they could not afford to visit a doctor or miss a day's work.[56]

---

55. Dr. Salomea Perlmutter, "Położenie lwowskich robotnic chrześcijańskich," *Nowe Słowo* 2, no. 23 (December 1, 1903): 535–41.

56. Dr. Salomea Perlmutter, "Położenie lwowskich robotnic chrześcijańskich," *Nowe Słowo* 2, no. 20 (October 15, 1903): 463–65.

One of the most common nonfactory posts unskilled women procured was that of seamstress or needleworker, a position that appeared frequently on the prostitution registry as a current or previous occupation of a registered sex worker. Needleworkers, partly because of the large number of women who aspired to this profession, suffered from low wages, unhealthy working conditions, and institutionalized abuses.[57] Their career trajectory began early. The lucky ones gained an apprenticeship in a workshop at age eleven or twelve. This completely unpaid training period lasted two years, even though the girls generally gained most of the necessary skills in a matter of months.[58] Only after she had completed her full apprenticeship could the seamstress begin working for pay and then the compensation was typically a starvation wage, if any. The unfortunate employees who could not afford their own apartment or a "corner" in someone else's place boarded with their employer, receiving a single meal per day in lieu of salary. The work itself was strenuous, especially for young girls not yet fully grown. A typical workday lasted from eight in the morning until eight in the evening, but it was not unusual for girls to sit at their work stations until ten or eleven o'clock at night in order to finish their work. Not only were they not compensated for these extra hours, but many seamstresses were also forced to accept work for private individuals in order to make ends meet.[59] The story was the same in Cracow, Lwów, Warsaw, and elsewhere: thousands of young women worked from dawn to dusk as seamstresses for miserable wages. In such situations, Mrs. Moriconi, the director of Warsaw's shelter for fallen women, opined, "it is easy to imagine the turn to prostitution." And, she reminded her readers, a great many women could not even find such pitiful sewing work to begin with.[60]

Pieceworkers had an even more challenging trajectory than those with jobs in small workshops. The thousands of women who cobbled together an existence making hats, gloves, cigarettes, or matches out of their homes did so because in some industries only men had positions in the workshop. Such women worked all night in damp, dark conditions, often taking in laundry to supplement their wages.[61] Women working as glove makers or sewing other items out of their homes unsurprisingly longed for a permanent, stable

57. Bolesław Prus, *Kurier Warszawski*, November 4, 1883, reprinted in Prus, *Kroniki*, 14: 223.

58. Róża Gottliebówna, "Wywiady nad położeniem robotnic w Krakowie: Szwaczki," *Nowe Słowo* 3, no. 10 (May 15, 1904): 217–19.

59. Ibid.

60. Moriconi, "Przyczynek do sprawy prostytucyi," 171.

61. Perlmutter, "Położenie lwowskich robotnic," *Nowe Słowo* 2, nr. 19 (October 1, 1903).

position in a factory. It is no wonder that garment workers were one of the groups from which prostitutes were most commonly recruited, far outranking industrial workers on the prostitution registries. Pieceworkers had no economic cushion for periods of unemployment or low demand. The work was low paid, menial, and extremely lonely.[62] So too was the job of cigarette maker a position that served as a gateway to occasional prostitution. Cigarette rolling was typically performed in small workshop employing a few dozen girls, often of a very young age. Workers received miniscule compensation of between 6 and 15 Austrian Heller per one thousand cigarettes. Whereas such a rate allowed the more experienced employees to earn a living wage, the younger girls suffered. Most workers at these establishments were "not in a position to support themselves" and "ate no dinner at all" during the typical ten-hour workday, according to Dr. Perlmutter's interviews.[63] Workers in Lwów were as young as twelve years old, although the enterprises usually hid their youthful employees from Austrian authorities.

In each of these settings, from country estate to cold and lonely workshop, paid sex presented an alternative or a supplement to grueling labor that was often inconsistently paid and inadequate to support the needs of most female laborers. City life presented the opportunity and sometimes the necessity for poor women to resort to full- or part-time prostitution. Lacking support networks, regular incomes, or nearby family, young women on their own slipped into and out of sex work during times of need. They did so partly as an extension of a survival mechanism established in the village during serfdom, partly because of the moral looseness of factory and workshop settings, and partly because living on their own eliminated many of the constraints imposed on them by their families. At bottom, however, they did so as one of many strategies to exist independently and to make their way in the hostile and unfamiliar environment of the great city. In marked contrast to the stereotypical melodramas circulating about prostitution in turn-of-the-century Polish publications, we have little evidence that all women who turned to prostitution, however briefly, were headed on a one-way trajectory to a life of full-time, permanent sex work. Instead, as we shall see, many registered and secret prostitutes alike maintained a delicate balance between paid sex and legitimate work. They existed in both milieus intermittently or even simultaneously. Indeed, they managed constantly to traverse the porous

---

62. Sikorska-Kowalska, *Wizerunek kobiety*, 37–39. Italian prostitutes were recruited from a similar milieu. See Gibson, *Prostitution and the State in Italy*, 122–24.

63. Dr. Salomea Perlmutter, "Położenie lwowskich robotnic chrześcijańskich," *Nowe Słowo* 14 (July 15, 1903): 319–20.

boundaries separating the world of upper-class, upright Polish speakers and that of sexually compromised working women. None of these truths fit nicely with the narrative of a one-way fall into prostitution as the result of a powerful individual or a single act of sexual weakness. For many, moral weakness was less at the root of the turn to prostitution than was economic need. Nowhere was this pattern of coexistence more discernable than in the field of domestic service. Nowhere, moreover, was the presence of prostitutes more troubling to upper-class Poles than in their bourgeois homes, ostensibly hidden from the filth and decadence of the surrounding city.

CHAPTER 3

Sex and the Bourgeois Family

> With very rare exceptions . . . it is possible to state boldly that all of our serving girls are de facto prostitutes.
>
> —Janusz Bilewski, "Służące a prostytucya."

Social commentators in partitioned Poland identified prostitution as primarily a function of lower-class sexual indiscretions and the weak morals of young women separated from family and home. In so doing, they overlooked the myriad ways paid sex touched the occupants of bourgeois households. In fact, urban residents regularly interacted with the world of prostitution as they navigated their daily existence. They hired part-time prostitutes as domestic servants. They enjoyed the services of poorly paid cashiers, waitresses, bar maids, and shopkeepers, many of whom supplemented their wages through informal prostitution. They tolerated informal prostitution rings operating out of their kitchens and courtyards. In all of these ways, prostitution was intricately woven into the fabric of elite life in Polish cities, yet consistently pushed to the periphery of public dialogue. This chapter explores the permeable boundary between polite society and the underground world of paid sex. It assesses the complex mechanisms lower-class women employed to navigate the slippery sexual terrain of Polish urban life.

The Rigors of Domestic Service

The institution of domestic service lies at the heart of contemporary understandings about the move to prostitution. Nowhere were poor female migrants more exposed to economic vulnerabilities and workplace abuses than in the thousands of households throughout the Polish lands where they were employed as household help. Nowhere were single women and girls as bereft of moral guidance and as prone to illicit activity as in the bourgeois homes of bustling city centers. According to reformers, it was here, far away from the protection of their families and in an atmosphere vibrating with temptation, that most young women experienced the "fall" into a life of prostitution. Police records from cities across Polish territory confirm the widely held belief that the majority of women registered as prostitutes or suspected of selling sex were household servants by profession. In Warsaw, 53 percent of registered prostitutes listed domestic service as their previous or current profession in 1889 and a similar portion of serving girls were inscribed on the registry of "secret" or "clandestine" prostitutes.[1] In 1895 alone, 100 out of the total 192 new prostitutes on Warsaw's city register were domestics.[2] By 1903, nearly 60 percent of Warsaw prostitutes and 66 percent of those active in the sex trade in Lwów were drawn from the ranks of domestic servants.[3] Awareness of the fluid movement between household service and paid sex fed a popular understanding throughout the Polish lands about the morality of serving girls. As the muckraking journalist quoted above concluded, "with very rare exceptions . . . it is possible to state boldly that all of our serving girls are de facto prostitutes."[4] Similar links between domestic help and prostitution existed elsewhere in late nineteenth-century Europe.[5] How can we understand the frequent shift from household servant

---

1. The second most common profession appearing on the police registries was needleworker in a small workshop (14 percent) or seamstress (7 percent). *Komisja Województwa Kaliskiego*, AGAD, sygn. 1697e, in Sikorska-Kulesza, "Prostitution in Congress Poland," 130–31; and Sikorska-Kulesza, "Miasto-przestrzeń niebezpieczna dla kobiet," 346.

2. Wysłouch, *Ohyda Wieku*, 6.

3. Similar fractions were reflected in Lwów police records: 213 of the 366 registered prostitutes functioned as domestic servants before or during their period on the police registry in 1904. Dr. Wł. S-I, "Prostytucya ze szczególnem uwzględnieniem stosunków Lwowskich," *Świat Płciowy* 1, no. 3 (October 1905): 11–15; M., "W sprawie służących," *Ogniwo* 1, 50 (November 22, 1903), 195–96. In contrast, West European metropolises recruited significantly from among household servants, though in slightly reduced percentages: 44 percent of public prostitutes in Petersburg were former domestics, 49 percent in Paris, and 51 percent in Berlin. Rząśnicki, *Prostytucja a proletariat*, 7–10.

4. Janusz Bilewski, "Służące a prostytucya," *Świat Płciowy* 1, no. 3 (October 1905): 33–39. Bilewski was responding to a series of articles published prior to this in Warsaw's *Kurier Codzienny* regarding the close link between household servants and the incidence of prostitution.

5. Alain Corbin theorizes that the frequent transition from domestic servant to venal sex in Paris came about because "the maid, accustomed to free sexual behavior, intoxicated by Monsieur's caresses and compliments, and very often by the approaches of his friends, gave in, when finally sacked and confronted by the prospect of poverty, to the temptation of venal sex." Corbin, *Women for Hire*, 206–10. Laurie Bernstein confirms that 46 percent of Russia's prostitutes noted domestic service as their former occupation. *Sonia's Daughters*, 107.

to streetwalker and what does this liminality tell us about strategies poor women employed as they managed their fortunes in the urban environment?

As east European metropolises experienced unprecedented periods of expansion during the latter years of the nineteenth century, the number of merchant, artisan, and craftsmen households hiring inexpensive assistants exploded. Young women flocked from the countryside and from small provincial towns to urban centers on the assumption that they could secure a position working in a family until a salaried factory post came along. Over thirty thousand women were employed as domestic servants in Warsaw alone during the early 1880s, nearly all unmarried and most recent migrants to the city.[6] By the end of the century that number had reached forty-two thousand in a total population of slightly less than six hundred thousand.[7] Domestic servants were so inexpensive that even less prosperous households could afford live-in maids. Fully half of all craftsmen families in Lwów made use of at least one servant. In Cracow, 40 percent of master craftsmen and seven out of ten petit bourgeois families—from printers and clockmakers to butchers and bakers—could support a servant in 1880.[8] The Polish urban "bourgeoisie," as defined by their ability to hire household help, included a broad range of urban skilled professionals, local and long-distance merchants, government officials, trained professionals, and intellectuals. Most were descendants of petit-gentry families fallen on hard times and had moved to the city to try their hands at trades. The enhancement of social status provided by servants was important to this economically precarious stratum.

Positions as domestics, including cooks, nannies, housecleaners, and personal assistants, were relatively easy for new migrants to land. At the same time, the steady supply of women willing to work for low wages kept rates of compensation low. Abuses at the hands of employers were legendary. Servants could be fired without cause, often leaving them nowhere to turn. Legally mandated minimum salary commitments, a mere fraction of wages paid female factory workers, were frequently violated or withheld.[9] Servants

6. Domestic servants were also recent migrants to many cities in North America. Most household maids in nineteenth-century New York, for example, were recent migrants from Ireland. In 1855, 74 percent of New York domestics were Irish and only 4 percent were native born. See Stansell, *City of Women*, 155–57.

7. According to Maria Nietyksza, 597 women were employed as domestic servants in Warsaw during 1882, and 41,946 in 1897. *Ludność Warszawy na przełomie*, 31, 241, 243.

8. Walentyna Najdus, *Rodzina i domownicy rzemieślnika polskiego w latach 1772–1918 na podstawie materiałów małopolskich* (Warsaw, 1991), 43–44.

9. "Dlaczego służące tak często zmieniają miejsca," *Pracownica Polska* 3 (1909): 11–12. Servants earned the same amount per quarter during the 1880s in Warsaw as a factory worker earned in a two-week period. Sikorska-Kowalska, *Wizerunek kobiety Łódzkiej*, 57–58.

FIGURE 3.1   Women seeking positions as domestic servants and their prospective employers gathered on Cracow's market square.
Courtesy of the Historical Museum of the City of Cracow (Muzeum Historyczne Miasta Krakowa) and Nathaniel Wood.

who nonetheless demanded their full wages risked abuse from the master of the house. Service regulations permitted employers to punish their servants as needed, including whipping them for failure to fulfill their responsibilities. Michalina Każnowska learned this lesson well in April 1906 when she approached her employer to request her earnings from the previous month. Instead of compensation, the "gentleman" hit her in the face and about the head several times, such that she was rendered deaf, then kicked her and threw her barefoot onto the pavement.[10]

Relations between servants and masters were so harsh in certain households that commentators characterized this dynamic as an extension of serfdom. A reporter for a feminist paper in 1902 portrayed servants in the Polish

---

10. The paper reported that the employer had already treated more than one serving girl in a similar way and recommended that the girl proceed to the prosecutor to complain about him." "Co tam słychać w świecie," *Przyjaciel Sług* 4 (April 6, 1902): 62.

Kingdom as "essentially slaves [who are] treated like dogs." Even in the most noble of Polish families, the paper complained, "the single link between the master and the servant is the cane." Official service regulations for Galicia and the Polish Kingdom alike permitted the master and mistress to beat their employee "so long as it does not harm her health." Everywhere, employers were permitted to use corporal punishment to compel serving girls to do their bidding. Reformers complained that Austrian regulations passed in 1857 and revised in 1862 allowed housekeepers to be "beaten with impunity," even while "protections were in place to punish those who abused animals." Indeed, according to section 16 of these regulations, the employer could apply "the most severe means of punishment" in order to "restrain" the behavior of a servant and to "maintain the peace and order of the home."[11]

Societies representing housekeepers lamented the physical abuse and false accusations serving girls bore, as well as their powerlessness at the hands of their employers. Galician critics in 1899 reported a pattern of employers wrongly accusing servants of household theft in order to avoid paying their wages. "Such false accusations come before the police more and more often," noted one Cracow society, "but unfortunately, the serving girls usually just cry and suffer" because they do not know where to turn for help.[12] The workday was not officially restricted and many domestics worked longer than twelve hours per day including Sundays and holidays. "On the basis of these regulations," one report concluded, "a million people in Galicia live in conditions not only similar to serfdom but on the edge of actual slavery as well." Is it any wonder, the study concluded, that the girls who work excessively, are inadequately paid, and are poorly dressed and fed "must work as prostitutes on the side" in order to provide for themselves?[13]

Mistresses were renowned for scolding their servants, accusing them of "being lazy, dishonest, immoral, or impious." Such alleged transgressions could prompt employers to let domestics go without notice.[14] Worse, the lady of the house sometimes became violent when angry and inflicted serious physical damage on her serving girl. One employer in Lwów attacked her maid in 1898 with a butcher's knife, cutting a deep gash above the employee's knee.[15] Some mistresses demanded their maids work from dawn to dusk, up to sixteen

---

11. Kazimiera Bujwidowa, "Idea demokratyczna w wychowaniu," *Nowe Słowo* 6, no. 8 (1907): 180.

12. "Co tam słychać w świecie?" *Przyjaciel Sług* 2, no. 3 (March 5, 1899): 54–55.

13. "Ordynacja służbowa w sejmie galicyjskim," *Nowe Słowo* 6, no. 8 (1907): 186–91.

14. Najdus, *Rodzina i domownicy rzemieślnika*, 44.

15. Róża Weisberg was accused by her servant, Marya Miryło, of attacking her. The "butcher lady" was to be punished for her actions. "Co tam słychać w świecie?" *Przyjaciel Sług* 1, no. 11 (1898): 15.

hours a day, while subjecting them to foul moods and violent tempers.[16] These abusive conditions came to the attention of private charities in the early years of the twentieth century, prompting a series of surveys and reform proposals to improve the lot of household servants. In 1903, the Warsaw-based Towarzystwo Higieniczne (Hygienic Society) conducted a study of the "sad situation" of serving girls. The report characterized the domestic as "a prisoner in the house of her employer, losing her personal freedom, and becoming a simple tool in foreign hands." Most mistresses, the study concluded, "were incapable of understanding the prospect of giving their maid so much as a moment in the day that is absolutely free of chores." Such thinking was "out of the question for most middle-class ladies of the house," the report determined. Instead, the poor girl was worked until utter exhaustion, taking "no account of the health of her body and soul."[17] The following year, the feminist weekly *Nowe Słowo* declared the situation of domestics in Poland to be "one hundred times worse" than that of household help in Berlin. "Everyone knows of the fatal conditions of life among servants," the paper opined, but "all agree there is no solution" to this crisis among lower-class serving girls.[18]

Work as domestic help was not highly sought among urban migrants, many of whom dreamed instead of salaried positions in factories or workshops. It was common knowledge among laboring women that conditions for maids were unhealthy and that servants were nearly starved in certain homes, despite official requirements that they be provided "modest" meals as part of their compensation.[19] Since most urban apartments were too small to provide separate sleeping quarters for their help, most domestics were fated to call the cramped and dank kitchen floor their home. In such settings, the servant was "accessible to everyone in the house at all hours of the day and night" and had "no corner to call her own" in order to sleep or relax from her endless workdays.[20] Among the most often cited reasons for quitting the service of a particular household, according to the Galician Association of Household Servants, were the living conditions. The cold, damp stone floor of kitchens purportedly caused rheumatism and other ailments.[21] Investigators noted that maids were given the worst food in the household, forced to

16. Sikorska-Kowalska, *Wizerunek kobiety Łódzkiej*, 57.

17. M., "W sprawie służących," 195–96.

18. "O położeniu służących w Berlinie," *Nowe Słowo* 3, no. 9 (May 1, 1904): 206.

19. "Inadequate supply of food" was one of the top reasons listed for servants to change positions. See "Dlaczego służące tak często zmieniają miejsca," 11–12.

20. I. Moszczeńska, "O służbie domowej," *Głos* 5, no. 25 (1900): 395–96.

21. "Dlaczego służące tak często zmieniają miejsca," 11–12.

live in a dirty corner of the kitchen, and permitted to leave the apartment only once or twice a week for a few hours. "A servant is essentially a slave," concluded one study. "They are traditionally treated no better than dogs."[22] Despite efforts to reform conditions for domestics throughout the Polish lands,[23] women working as household servants typically resigned themselves to "a lonely life and to committing all their time and effort to the home in which they served. They were entirely dependent on their employers and cut off from their families and friends. They had a guaranteed subsistence, but paid a high price for this: they lost their freedom and their personal liberty."[24] The housekeeper's lot was characterized as that of a complete "drudge" and a "pariah" from the rest of the household.[25]

Informal Prostitution in the Bourgeois Home

The working conditions and social isolation that shaped the lives of domestic servants in Polish cities drove many of them to search for other options. Some relied on household service as a stopgap while waiting for positions in nearby textile factories or needlework shops.[26] Others sought more informal methods for ameliorating their situation. Taking on lovers (often in exchange for small gifts), tolerating sexual advances from the master of the house, or socializing with criminal types in the neighborhood were all strategies serving girls adopted. Still others reportedly took their own lives when they could find no other options for advancement. One twenty-two-year-old maid threw herself under a train in Józefowa, near Warsaw, in 1913 after having "been a servant for the last three years in a situation where she was forced to work to exhaustion." Since she "could not think of a way out of the situation, she remained in the same position and waited patiently until she finally took the . . . step and committed suicide."[27]

---

22. Bujwidowa, "Idea demokratyczna w wychowaniu," 180.

23. Including the establishment of the Galician Society of Servants in 1898 with its press organ, *Przyjaciel Sług*, and the founding of the Society of Catholic Servants in Warsaw in 1907, whose deliberations were published in *Pracownica Polska*.

24. Sikorska-Kowalska, *Wizerunek kobiety Łódzkiej*, 58.

25. Najdus, *Rodzina i domownicy rzemieślnika*, 44.

26. Given the opportunity, Sikorska-Kowalska, writes, "most female servants fled for factory jobs and the freedoms they brought." *Wizerunek kobiety Łódzkiej*, 57. See also M., "W sprawie służących," 195–96.

27. Bolesława Białowąsówna reportedly threw herself under a train, an event that, according to the newspaper, so affected her former employer, Kazimierz Perdzyński, that he died of an aneurism of the heart a few hours later that same day. Given the number of household servants who became sexually involved with employers and who became pregnant through these relationships, it is also possible that household drudgery alone was not the sole cause of the servant's tragic decision. "Informacje i wiadomości: Samobójstwo służącej," *Pracownica Polska* 11 (June 1, 1913): 174.

Contemporary accounts often glossed over the abysmal conditions that prompted the turn from domestic service to prostitution, emphasizing instead the moral downfall caused by the absence of family and support networks. Yet characterizations of pure and protected country girls losing their way in the big city and "falling" into a life of prostitution failed to take full account of several factors guiding these young women's decisions. First, the informal sexual liaisons maidservants established might not have been experienced as acts of prostitution, although they were often recorded this way on police blotters. Like the "charity girls" in Victorian-era New York, many laboring women in Polish towns exchanged sexual favors for a meal, an article of clothing, or money. Those who maintained a full-time job while engaging in such practices on the side would not have self-identified as professional prostitutes.[28] Second, when serving girls exchanged sex for money, they arguably did so out of economic privation rather than because they were vulnerable innocents adrift in the city. Pundits and social workers characterized household maids as weak-willed and dim-witted, yet sometimes domestics simply calculated their options and turned to prostitution as the best of a limited range of alternatives. Certainly some were duped into turning to sex work, but the sleight of hand to which some witnesses testify was often the direct result of the specific conditions of life among household servants and their treatment by employers rather than a failure of will or a "fall from grace" from which they could not return.

Even journalists sympathetic to the plight of domestic servants emphasized the loneliness and social neglect they experienced, characterizing them as innocents corrupted by a hostile and unstable environment. Social reformers portrayed household employees as possessing little practical intelligence or ability to think independently. Because prospective servants typically had "only the lowest level of education," wrote one such reformer, "we must assume that they are unable to resist temptation and the advances of the stronger sex." The possibility of inculcating common sense or moral suasion into these rural girls was negligible, according to this view, because "they are recruited from the lowest spheres that have barely been touched by the smallest ray of civilization."[29] Whether the fall from virtue was prompted specifically by the social milieu from which they were recruited or from the conditions in which they found themselves after moving to the city, social reformers and charity workers generally agreed that most women employed as domestics lacked the will

---

28. On "charity girls," see Peiss, *Cheap Amusements*, 110–11.
29. Bilewski, "Służące a prostytucya," 33–39.

to resist inappropriate advances from coworkers or members of the household in which they worked. The servant's moral vulnerability, according to these arguments, arose partly from the utter loneliness of her work environment. Because housekeepers were "isolated in the home with no appropriate outlets to the outside world" and "lacked the camaraderie" of fellow workers, they often made poor choices. Moreover, serving in a stranger's home meant a lack of moral guidance and supervision. "There is no one to keep them on an honest path when they are desperate," the socialist activist Kazimierz Rząśnicki noted. Being fresh from the countryside, he observed, they "find themselves in conditions that are foreign to them and difficult to understand." This profound sense of disorientation, combined with lack of moral guidance and the misery of long hours of household drudgery, he implied, prompted many of them to view sex work as an enticing alternative.[30]

Such characterizations of the flow of servants into the ranks of prostitution ascribed little individual agency to young women who ended up on police registries. Instead, their social background, limited formal education, and lack of supervision prompted them to stray from the presumed virtue of their rural background. As the interwar prostitution expert Józef Macko noted in regard to this transition, "the village girl enters a foreign atmosphere in the city. Her 'career' as a servant begins very early in life when she has no worldly experience. She comes to an unknown world where she hears many strange new things." As if this sense of disorientation were not enough of a danger to a young woman's moral integrity, Macko suggested, once she took up a post with a bourgeois employer, a country girl was often bedazzled by the spectacle of city life with all of its inaccessible luxuries. "She grows accustomed to a certain level of comfort," he argued, developing new tastes and greater aspirations. Over time, young women became interested in "dressing in fine clothing" and "enjoying the comforts of a large city." The fresh migrant, according to Macko, quickly "comes to realize that there are people in the world who live in comfort and she wants to be among them." She grows "jealous of their comforts and dreams of a higher station in life." Finally, he concluded, "from these dreams comes the fall into the abyss of doom," the muck of lifelong prostitution.[31] Here again the descent into prostitution is mainly a psychological matter brought on by social isolation and class envy. Rarely did such scenarios make allowances for the dire economic straits or other circumstances driving women to these decisions.

---

30. Ibid.; and Rząśnicki, *Prostytucja a proletariat*, 8–9.
31. Macko, *Prostytucja*, quoted in Rosset, *Prostytucja i choroby weneryczne w Łódzi*, 17–18.

Social activists reinforced the notion that one sexual misstep could cast an otherwise innocent girl into a life of debauchery. The feminist Izabela Moszczeńska echoed the widely held belief that "every domestic was destined to fall and to become ruined." The widespread perception of country girls as ignoramuses unable to negotiate their surroundings in the big city fed the mythology of a seamless progression from domestic servant to streetwalker. "These crude, simple girls," Moszczeńska lamented, "quickly and thoroughly become acquainted with the great city and its scum of civilization," leading them down the road to sexual temptation and licentiousness. Recent migrants from the village, she believed, were "less confident and more fragile" than daughters of Warsaw's working classes. In fact, she complained that the step from village life to employment as a domestic in an urban home was among the most dangerous moves a young woman could make. Emphasizing the naïveté of rural parents, Moszczeńska complained that "only people living in the countryside see moving to the city to work as a domestic as useful to a girl's career . . . and it is precisely such girls that are thrown onto the pavement of the big city, deprived of moral support and left on their own, so that all of the morally harmful miasmas are absorbed into them."[32] Again, the very act of moving out of the supposedly protected bucolic environment to the morally compromised setting of urban decadence with its dangerous vapors established the preconditions for a young woman's "fall."

Out of the challenging conditions of household service, thousands of women made the transition to prostitution in Polish cities at the turn of the twentieth century. Police blotters throughout the region recorded their sexual activities, but their motives and their understanding of the meanings behind their actions are more difficult to render. What emerges from contemporary studies, observations of those who worked with "fallen women," and testimonies from prostitutes and former prostitutes themselves is a picture of a gradual transition to part-time or informal sex work, often beginning within the milieu of the bourgeois home itself. The investigative reporter Janusz Bilewski, for example, described the slow corruption of serving girls' morals after they took up work in private households. The urban courtyard in these depictions becomes the locus of a new ethic straddling village expectations and Victorian-era attitudes about sexuality. Young men and women on their own devised new social codes, incorporating a greater degree of sexual licentiousness than might have been tolerated on the family farm, while not necessarily countenancing multiple sex partners or the exchange of cash for

---

32. Moszczeńska, "O służbie domowej," 396.

sexual favors. Country girls freed from the authority of their rural communities established ties with other unattached young people. "They begin by
flirting with acquaintances of their own social station whom they see in the
courtyard of their building," Bilewski observed. Because they were "generally in the company of other serving girls who have already 'fallen,'" such
behavior was normalized.[33]

The flexible schedules and inconsistent supervision over household
maids sometimes permitted them the opportunity to pursue these flirtation
relationships. Even while masters and mistresses maintained strict rules of
domestic conduct, they could not monitor employees' behavior at all times.
Instead, the servant's initial sexual transgression was typically committed "on
the grounds" of the household she served, frequently in the very courtyard
where she socialized. This liaison was typically with "a countryman"—
someone from the woman's original village or a neighboring settlement in
her native region.[34] In this way, the moral code and attachments of the village
were transferred to the urban setting. Yet these practices were simultaneously molded to accommodate new social expectations in the freewheeling
atmosphere of young people adrift without the oversight of family or village
society. Statistics confirm that the initial sexual experience of lower-class girls
was typically with someone from their own social rank rather than with the
more powerful or wealthier individual often featured in melodramas of the
"fall" of country girls in the city.

An even more intimate route to sexual debauchery involved males—delivery
boys, drivers, stablemen, and other service employees—who drifted into the
kitchen of bourgeois establishments and befriended young women working
there. Sources complain of young ladies who "have access to a number of
bachelors through their positions and often entertain them or have 'trysts'
with them in their rooms." Journals offering advice to household servants
chastised domestics to beware of "entertaining their boyfriends without
shame in the kitchen."[35] Although the professional regulations of household
service forbade such visits, young men often presented themselves as the servant's brother or as a fiancé in order to gain access to the home. One article
joked that perhaps the official service regulations should explicitly forbid
"having three to five fiancés at the same time and returning from these visits
at dawn." Persuasive young men were rumored to have coaxed serving girls
out of their savings or part of their salaries, as well as "organizing customers

---

33. Bilewski, "Służące a prostytucya," 33–39.
34. Ibid.
35. "Dlaczego służące tak często zmieniają miejsca?"

for them, exploiting them, threatening them, and taking part of their wages."
One study of these "kitchen pimps" claimed in 1904 that "roughly twenty
thousand such 'kitchen' procurers" were taking advantage of vulnerable serving girls in Warsaw alone.[36]

Incidents of an employer or his son forcing himself on the maid were not
uncommon, though it is difficult to know whether the practice occurred as
often in reality as it did in the popular imagination. Regardless, the prospect
of sexual advances from the gentlemen of the household played into the
transition many young women experienced in their attitudes toward sexual
promiscuity. The Galician Association of Household Servants described as
the "saddest of all reasons for household servants to change positions" the frequent incidence of "immoral advances and attacks from the gentlemen and
their sons."[37] According to the Servants Association, the son of the household
often considered young domestics "free game" and pursued them, beginning with an innocent peck on the cheek and escalating to greater liberties.
Some girls who lost their "virtue" in this way were victims of violent rape
by young gentlemen who, using a notion left over from the days of serfdom,
believed they had the "legal right" to do so. The serving girl was typically
unclear of her rights, lacked friends to advise her, and was afraid to complain
about the abuse.[38] Although on the first occasion a servant might be forced to
have sexual relations, she sometimes continued voluntarily to maintain these
affiliations so as to win approval of the gentleman or in exchange for small
trinkets like blouses, shoes, or eventually money. She might even imagine
that the son of the family would eventually marry her. Despite dramatic dif-
ferences in social class, poor young women like the one in the introductory
segment to chapter 2 still dreamed of being swept off their feet by a gentleman of higher social rank, a hope that may have played into their willingness
to succumb to such advances.

Between courtyard liaisons and relations with members of the household,
a servant might take a succession of lovers, each of whom rewarded her with
small nonmonetary compensation. Sometimes such women ended up in
brothels; more often they found themselves on the list of "suspected" prostitutes maintained in municipal police stations. Meanwhile, they typically continued to function as household servants, moving from place to place when
the mistress of the house discovered their activities. In some cases, Bilewski

36. "Kuchenne sutenerstwo," *Przegląd Tygodniowy* 38, no. 15 (1904): 176–77; and Moszczeńska,
"O służbie domowej," 395–96.
37. "Dlaczego służące tak często zmieniają miejsca?"
38. Bilewski, "Służące a prostytucya," 33–39.

suggests, servants even found themselves "flirting" with the master or the young gentleman at their place of employment, a practice he terms "a sort of recreation," but one that might also help garner them limited employment security.[39] This was dangerous business since discovery by the household mistress or becoming pregnant could result in the servant's dismissal with a poor reference.[40] Nonetheless, as much as contemporaries believed that those who engaged in such forms of sexual misadventure "did not stay long in orderly homes" or "ended up as street prostitutes," the transition to a life of full-time prostitution was not always so clear or permanent.[41]

Admittedly, a subset of young women did turn to full-time prostitution, whether independently or in an established brothel, after a period employed as domestic servants. In some cases, they appear to have been duped into making this initial step, though explanations of trickery, force, and volunteerism are wound closely together, often in contradictory ways, in the testimonies of former prostitutes. In others, it was a self-conscious decision based on the hardships of a servant's life. We have very little evidence, however, that the sexual advances of gentlemen or the courtyard antics of fellow workers were directly responsible for the transition. Rather, household servants, overworked, often physically abused, and pitifully compensated, responded to a wide variety of indicators that appeared to offer them more comfortable circumstances. That their calculations were sometimes misguided does not make their decision making less self-conscious or their strategies for survival any less cogent.

One serving girl in Warsaw, for example, befriended a girl on the street near her employer's residence. The friend invited the maid to join her at a soup kitchen where she was "plied with liquor" by a man who turned out to be a pimp. The man then "did with me what he wanted" and told her "now you must be my lover," she later testified. Here the narrative becomes confused and the degree of agency on the part of the young woman unclear. Although the man "showed me a knife as long as his arm and threatened to stab me if I did not agree to live with him" and then "took me to the [Police-Medical] Committee and ordered me to register and tell them I wanted to be a prostitute," the former servant was not necessarily dissatisfied with her new life. The pimp forcibly enrolled her in a local brothel, yet she readily admitted that "at the beginning, I thought I might have benefited from this

---

39. Ibid.
40. Władysław Chodecki, "Co pchna służące w objęcia prostytucyi," *Zdrowie* 22, no. 8 (August 1906): 563–66, as cited in Sikorska-Kowalska, *Wizerunek kobiety Łódzkiej*, 58.
41. "Kuchenne sutenerstwo," *Przegląd Tygodniowy* 38, no. 15 (1904): 177.

arrangement—that I might be better off, that I might be able to dress better and not work as hard." In the end, however, the young witness lamented, this did not turn out to be the case. Instead, she ended up "ashamed, hungry, poorly treated, and now also sick."[42] Testimonies such as this suggest an intricate interplay of the passive, "fall from grace" narrative, with a degree of independent decision making on the part of women transitioning into the world of paid sex. Whether young women approached brothel life with a sense of calculation, hoping that such employment might make them "better off" and permit them to "not work as hard," or whether, instead, they were tricked or coerced into becoming professional sex workers is difficult to assess. Clearly, though, not all of those who ended up in brothels perceived their predicament to be wholly negative.

Domestic servants looked beyond the confines of their urban households when seeking a path out of drudgery. They searched the streets and neighborhoods near their workplaces for solutions to their misery. Young women such as J. turned to prostitution after being mistreated by their employers. J. took a position with Mrs. X, who brought her personally from the smaller town of Witebsk to Warsaw. Mrs. X. reportedly returned late one night from the theater and flew into a rage at the girl (for reasons not clarified in the girl's testimony), throwing her out of the house with her things. Despondent and frightened, the girl spent the night sitting with the night watchman and then, not knowing anyone else in town, allowed the watchman to conduct her to the nearest brothel.[43] Again, the line between a desperate lack of alternatives and a degree of individual initiative is very fine. Such tales cut against the grain of the prostitution melodrama many contemporaries told themselves about young women seduced and abandoned and reduced to selling sex as the only socially acceptable alternative.

Many household employees wavered between a willingness to suffer the harsh conditions of domestic service and an equally strong desire to escape, even if it involved association with frightening underworld characters. One enterprising serving girl searched for boyfriends among the neighborhood ruffians near her place of employment, only to find herself shut up in a brothel. As she later recounted,

> I was working as a servant for the X. X. family and got to know a certain girl, who stood on the corner in the evenings. She told me that she would find me a lover, and she sent him to me, but when I saw him he appeared so repulsive that I grew frightened, especially since

---

42. Moriconi, "Przyczynek do sprawy prostytucyi," 176.
43. Ibid., 173.

the watchman told me he was a thief. I told the couple [for whom I worked] that I did not want him to call on me, that he was likely to harm both them and me. Then I saw the same girl on the street and she told me that with a different lover I would have an easier time earning bread. I was on my way to go find her when five *alfonses* [pimps] trapped me and sold me to a place. The watchman told me this was a brothel and one of the women there warned me not to try to escape because they would knife me. The following day, they made me go to the [Police-Medical] Committee [and register as a prostitute].

It is difficult to imagine that this young woman was unaware that the girl who "stood on the street corner in the evenings" was a prostitute or that the "lovers" who might help her "earn bread" more easily were in fact pimps. Nonetheless, the witness maintained her victim status in her narrative by referencing moments of entrapment by five hideous pimps and by relaying her fear of being harmed by knife-wielding procurers. Still, even as she paints herself as having been coerced and manipulated into brothel work, the young servant's tale contains elements of independent action in her insistence that she "agreed to register" with the police as a public prostitute primarily because she was "hoping that after a while I would be sent to the hospital and in that way get out of this misery."[44] Pitiful though this reasoning might seem, it suggests an element of strategic thinking on the part of poor and homeless young women.

In still other cases, housekeepers appear to have succumbed almost unconsciously to sex work. They were not always pushed, coerced, or violently forced into the practice. Yet their lack of other resources meant that prostitution became one of their few options when their original plan to gain work as a domestic went sour. One young girl, for example, left her rural home at age eleven, driven by unspeakable hunger in her household, and searched for a position as a servant in Warsaw. Her age and upbringing meant that she lacked solid qualifications as a domestic, and her shoddy work led to frequent changes of position. In the end, according to her own testimony, "not knowing where to rest her head," she ended up in a house of prostitution. Another young woman, R., who moved to Warsaw from Radom to work for an affluent woman, lost her position after only two weeks. She went hungry for a week and slept at the night watchman's headquarters, then was approached by a prostitute as she sat crying in the courtyard of an apartment house one evening. The prostitute conducted the desperate woman to a brothel where she remained for some months.[45]

44. Ibid., 177.
45. Ibid., 171.

In these and other ways, the explanations many practitioners of prostitution supplied about their turn to the sex trade do not always correspond to the melodramatic explanations of their actions offered in the mainstream press. As much as bourgeois commentators sought to paint the worlds of proper urban families and degenerate sex workers as discrete universes, the pattern of interaction between these spheres was both more complicated and more constant than literary portrayals suggested. Police records, contemporary interviews, and legal testimony reveal a story that was dramatically different from the perception of prostitution as separated from bourgeois life. First, as these stories suggest, many women functioned simultaneously as prostitutes and as full-time household servants, nannies, or wet nurses.[46] Analysis of police records for prostitutes in 1900, for example, demonstrates that fully 22 percent of those on the registry were servants at the time they registered, and an additional 24 percent were laborers of some type who were former servants. Twenty-one percent were seamstresses and waitresses who had also formerly served as household helpers. In essence, then, fully three-quarters of those under police supervision had at some point served to maintain order and hygiene in middle-class households.[47] Women who served in these menial positions by necessity often supplemented their meager salaries with commercial sex, tacitly violating the purity of the bourgeois home through their immoral street activities.

Second, women who worked as registered prostitutes did not always experience a permanent fall from grace. Rather, the step into prostitution under some circumstances was reversible. Young women who found themselves without means appear to have been able to sell sex for a short time before marrying, starting a business venture, or gaining other forms of "legitimate" employment. The 1905 police registry in Lwów, for example, suggests a degree of permeability between the world of commercial sex and more mainstream pursuits for poor women. Six registered prostitutes were already married, four of whom "conducted this business with the agreement of their husbands," while eight left the police rolls during the year to get married, twelve when they took up "honest work," and three were signed off the registry by family members.[48]

And finally, the decision to sell sex, although an unfortunate reflection on the level of economic desperation in the lower social strata, appears frequently

---

46. Prostitution Registry for Cracow, APKr, DPKr 439–440.

47. K. Męczkowska, "Ze statystyki prostytucyi i nieprawych dzieci," *Świat Płciowy* 1, no. 1 (May 31, 1905): 37–41.

48. "Prostytucje we Lwowie," no. 7 (February 1906): 32.

to have been taken as a matter of conscious choice. Quite apart from the passive "fall" from innocence represented in much of the contemporary literature, the turn to sex work may have been a strategic move upwardly mobile girls and women made as a way of employing the limited resources at their disposal. As Christine Stansell and others have shown, many poor women viewed prostitution as "part of everyday life: a contingency remote to the blessed, the strong and the fortunate, right around the corner for the weak and the unlucky. Prostitution was neither a tragic fate, as moralists viewed it . . . nor an act of defiance, but a way of getting by, of making the best of bad luck."[49] Yet it is important also to recognize that economic necessity alone did not drive the move into sex work. Not all indigent women resorted to prostitution and many admitted to an element of choice in opting for the practice. Prostitutes themselves often rejected the victimization paradigm and stressed their own agency in choosing prostitution in the context of other available alternatives.[50]

Nonetheless, the tendency to equate poverty with prostitution and the working poor with sexual license prompted the imposition of new regulations throughout the Polish lands. Ironically, even as literary melodramas rendered prostitution a permanent, full-time profession, police investigators charged with supervising systems of tolerated prostitution increasingly assumed the practice to be instead a part-time, temporary means of dealing with contingency and the unpredictable exigencies of urban life. Not only did vice squads in the Polish Kingdom require all female factory workers and waitresses to register with the municipal police medical committees beginning in 1883, but female waitresses and shopkeepers in Lwów were also subject to registration as "discreet" prostitutes from 1905 on. By 1913, Galician household servants were also subject to police medical inspection.[51] Through these occasional prostitutes who existed at the margins of the bourgeois world, the moral contamination of licentious sex regularly permeated the protected realm of honest urban households. The domestic servant, a vital symbol of middle-class respectability, became emblematic of this contamination.

---

49. Stansell, *City of Women*, 175–76.

50. Stansell notes that William Sanger's 1855 survey of prostitution in New York revealed that one-quarter of his respondents turned to prostitution because of "inclination," including being "too idle to work," "wanting an easy life," or having been ill treated by parents or other relatives. "Structural factors alone," she argues, "cannot clarify why some women took up prostitution and others in similar straits did not." Stansell, *City of Women,* 178.

51. The chief medical inspector justified the practice by estimating that some 75 percent of serving girls suffered from venereal diseases. "Informacje wiadomości. Nadzór nad służbą," *Pracownica Polska* 7, no. 12 (June 15, 1913): 189.

Poor and Pregnant in the Polish City

The rigors and instabilities of domestic service represented one route by which young women made their way to the prostitution rolls in partitioned Poland. The predicament of poor, urban females was further complicated when they became pregnant as a result of one of their various sexual liaisons. A serving girl falling victim to the sexual advances of her employer could expect instant dismissal once her condition became known. Rarely would the master of the house admit responsibility for his actions. Neither did a young housekeeper's courtyard lovers typically have the means to support a child.[52] Pregnancy would mean an end to her salaried position since domestic servants were generally required to be both single and childless.[53] Although in some cases a pregnant servant might seek employment as a wet nurse after giving birth, this was risky and typically short-lived. Moreover, such a solution did not resolve the issue of where a woman might place her own child while caring for the offspring of her employers. Nonetheless, thousands of household servants turned up pregnant each year, accounting for by far the largest number of unwanted pregnancies in the Polish lands. Between 1898 and 1905, over half of all illegitimate infants in Cracow were born to domestics.[54]

Faced with loss of employment and the prospect of being ineligible for future positions, single, pregnant women faced a host of dismal alternatives. Abortions were dangerous and illegal. Giving up a child to a foundling home or "angel factory" meant the infant's likely death from malnutrition.[55] A small number of working girls brought their infants back to the countryside to be raised by relatives, though the shame and expense was hard for most rural families to bear. Others simply abandoned their babies in coal bins or railway stations, sometimes in the hope that the child might be found and raised by a more prosperous family. Each of these options presented risks to new mothers. The absence of clear solutions to the problem of unwanted

---

52. Bilewski, "Służące a prostytucya," 35.

53. Among domestic staff in Galician towns at the turn of the twentieth century, 92 percent were single and childless and 4.5 percent were widows. Kurkowska, "Birth Control in the Industrial Age," 161–65.

54. Poor women in Polish cities were by no means exceptional in their efforts to navigate the urban environment once they became pregnant. Rachel Fuchs examines the options impoverished expectant mothers in nineteenth-century Paris faced as they worked through medical and philanthropic institutions. *Poor and Pregnant in Paris: Strategies for Survival in the Nineteenth Century* (New Brunswick, NJ, 1992).

55. Foundling homes were commonly known as "angel factories" in this period because of the likelihood that an infant deposited in such a facility would die of hunger or malnutrition within weeks of its arrival and become a "little angel."

pregnancy accounts for part of the turn to full- or part-time paid sex. Ironically, prostitution was one of the few professions open to females in nineteenth-century Polish cities that permitted them to keep their children with them. The 1888 Regulations governing prostitution in Galicia, for example, authorized prostitutes to "keep their own children with them . . . so long as the house is run in such a way that the children would not be harmed."[56] We know that roughly 8 percent of the prostitutes registered in the Polish Kingdom in 1889 had children to support.[57] Moreover, experts on prostitution in the 1920s noted that "it was not unusual" to meet prostitutes who were burdened with children and that "the birth of a child is something prostitutes celebrate and all enjoy playing with the baby."[58] The 1930 prostitution registry for Łódź included ten newly registered prostitutes who were mothers of legitimate children and thirty-seven with illegitimate offspring, making a full 15 percent of all Łódź prostitutes mothers in that year.[59]

The dangers implicit in each of the alternatives poor pregnant women faced help suggest some of the paths that brought them to the threshold of prostitution. In many senses, the fate of single mothers magnifies the constrained circumstances all unskilled females in Polish towns endured. First, pregnant working women sought to abort their pregnancies, despite the risks the procedure posed to their own health. Laws governing Polish society in the late nineteenth century banned abortion at any stage of pregnancy, yet the popular belief that a fetus consisted of only dried blood during the first trimester meant that women had few scruples about abortion in the early period of gestation.[60] Those who sought to abort relied on a range of techniques from home remedies—such as heavy doses of onion, parsley, or ergot root—to potentially lethal mixtures of nitric acid, carbolic acid, or ammonia. Many also ingested large doses of mercury, lead, chrome, iron, or magnesium, or consumed more toxic substances such as phosphorus, arsenic, or antimony, with potentially damaging or lethal consequences. In some cases, women turned to professional abortionists, who also served as midwives, for help in obtaining these substances. Even more potentially harmful were procedures for "restoring menstruation" or "causing miscarriage" through uterine puncture using tools such as awls, spindles, quills, wires, hat pins scissors, or

56. "Regulamin zachowania się dla prostytutek," 1221–24.
57. Sikorska-Kulesza, "Prostitution in Congress Poland," 132.
58. Rosset, *Prostytucja i choroby weneryczne w Łodzi*, 14–15; Zaleski, *Prostytucja powojenna*, 113.
59. Rosset, *Prostytucja i choroby weneryczne w Łodzi*, 14.
60. According to the Austrian Penal Act of 1852 (sections 144–48), the German penal law of 1871 (sections 218–20), and the Russian code of 1885 (sections 933–35), abortion was forbidden at any stage of pregnancy. Kurkowska, "Birth Control in the Industrial Age," 165.

toothpicks. Women seeking help eliminating an unwanted pregnancy could easily locate a midwife, wet nurse, or girl friend with information about these methods, or they could read ads in city newspapers promising "help in discreet matters" or a willingness to take on "women suffering from weakness."[61] Such remedies were far more likely to cause injury to the mother than to abort the fetus, but for the most part women could rely on these procedures without fear of prosecution. Only a small handful of women were convicted in the Polish lands for the crime of abortion during the fin de siècle period and medical professionals performing abortions were not subject to prosecution.[62]

Those who brought their pregnancies to term had several options for giving up their babies, most of them unsavory. Only one overtaxed foundling home operated during the late nineteenth century in all of Polish territory. After the closure of two such institutions in Cracow and Lwów in 1873, Warsaw's Dom Podrzutków, located adjacent to the Infant Jesus Hospital (Szpital Dzieciątka Jezus), came under enormous pressure to accommodate abandoned infants from everywhere in the former Polish state and even from the western gubernia of Russia.[63] Christian and Jewish parents alike brought their children to the home in ever increasing numbers when poverty, the shame of an illegitimate child, a mother's illness or her need to find work as a wet nurse with a private family made it impossible to keep the child at home.[64] Business was brisk in the orphanage, which until 1878 accepted children without question, many anonymously through the "wheel" or revolving door where mothers could place newborns without being seen. In a two-year period during the late 1860s close to seven thousand children were

---

61. See for example, the classified ad published in *Kurier Warszawski*, January 17, 1883, noting, "I receive women suffering from weakness; discretion guaranteed."

62. During the period 1896–1899, only nine women were convicted of aborting their fetuses in Congress Poland; in Galicia, three women were sentenced for it in 1906; and in Poznania, seven people were convicted in 1906. France, Austria, and Germany had dramatically higher rates of trial and conviction for abortion (656 accused in Germany in 1906 and 186 in Austria outside of Galicia). Józef Kończycki, *Stan moralny społeczeństwa polskiego na podstawie danych statystyki kryminalnej* (Warsaw, 1911), 80–81.

63. The Cracow facility, known as the Hospital Magnum, was established in the sixteenth century and remained the only organization of its kind in Poland caring for foundlings in a systematic way until Father Pierre Baudouin, a follower of the Vincent de Paul Order, opened his orphanage in Warsaw in 1732. Marian Surdacki, "Dzieci porzucone w społeczeństwach dawnej Europy i Polski," in *Od narodzin do wieku dojrzałego: Dzieci i młodzież w Polsce,* Part 1, *Od średniowiecza do wieku XVIII,* ed. Maria Dąbrowska and Andrzej Klonder (Warsaw, 2002), 185.

64. Elżbieta Mazur, "Opieka nad sierotami w dziewiętnastowiecznej Warszawie," in *Od narodzin do wieku dojrzałego: Dzieci i młodzież w Polsce*, Part 2, *Stulecie XIX i X*, ed. Elżbieta Mazur (Warsaw, 2003), 40–41.

deposited in this way, with nearly 40 percent of them succumbing to malnutrition in their first year of life. A controversy surrounding high death rates in the foundling home prompted the institution to eliminate the "wheel" in 1870 and force women to hand over their children personally, but the perennial shortage of wet nurses kept mortality rates higher than in the general population. When the Warsaw Welfare Council (Rada Dobroczynności) decreed in 1878 that only children born within the city limits would be accepted into the orphanage, a firestorm erupted in the press. Warsaw residents complained both about the bureaucratic complications mothers faced in documenting their child's birth location as well as about the limited state funds the Russian imperial government made available to support the facility. Nonetheless, large numbers of local women continued to leave their children at the orphanage and the infant mortality rate continued to exceed the incidence of newborn deaths in the population at large.[65]

Alongside this state-supported facility, smaller private initiatives for tending the offspring of poor women arose in Poland's larger cities. The Warsaw Charitable Society, for example, ran nurseries for working women beginning in 1838 that were intended to look after the children of mothers employed in local factories and workshops. Modeled on West European preschools, these facilities took in children between the ages of three and seven who were orphans, half orphans, or whose parents were working full time. Children remained at the facility only during their parents' working hours, however, and returned home at night. They had to be delivered promptly each morning, clean, clothed, and fed.[66] Such requirements were impractical for many working women and for live-in servants who were not permitted to keep their children with them. Moreover, they did not provide a solution for the care of newborns. By the 1880s, a new philanthropic society in Warsaw, the Care for Poor Mothers (Opieki nad Ubogimi Matkami), focused on helping impoverished pregnant women during their confinement and tending to children in need until their seventh year of life. These private efforts remained small, decentralized, and poorly funded, however. Designed

---

65. Warsaw papers highlighted a controversy over mortality rates among infants under the care of the orphanage. Although 26 percent of those accepted into the foundling home and resident in Warsaw in 1899 died before their first year of life, the life expectancy of the babies sent to the countryside to be cared for by wet nurses was significantly higher. See Stanisław Kamieński, "Warszawski Dom Wychowawczy w świetle statystyki porównawczej (z powodu artykułu 'Niwy Polskiej')," *Gazeta Lekarska* 16, no. 7 (1901): 177–82; and Zofia Podgorska-Klawe, "Warszawski dom podrzutków (1732–1901)," *Rocznik Warszawski* 12 (1974): 139–40.

66. Hanna Markiewiczowa, *Działalność opiekuńczo-wychowawcza Warszawksiego Towarzystwa Dobroczynności 1814–1914* (Warsaw, 2002), 146–54.

explicitly to reduce the ever growing numbers of foundlings and infanticides in the Polish lands, they nonetheless failed to prevent steadily increasing rates of infant abandonment.[67] In 1886, for example, a year after the society opened its doors, some 1,843 infants were received in Warsaw's foundling home, bringing the total number of children under its care to 4,879.[68]

Public attention to the issue of foundlings peaked in the 1880s following a series of scandals involving women who accepted payment to care for the infants of poor mothers. Such women, many of them also serving as midwives, became known as "angel makers" after a well-publicized trial in 1883 of one Mrs. Skublińska for murdering nineteen infants she had agreed to look after.[69] Cases like that of Skublińska highlighted the limited options available to poor women for disposing of unwanted children. During the early 1870s, Skublińska operated a thriving business transporting newborn infants to the Warsaw foundling home. Records of the facility indicate she handed over a total of 1,258 babies, averaging between 200 and 250 infants each year. But Skublińska continued accepting infants after the home restricted its admissions criteria in 1878. The ban on undocumented children and, for a short time, on illegitimate children left the defendant with dozens of babies who lacked a home. She was convicted of slowly starving, and in some cases strangling, infants in her care, then scattering their corpses around Warsaw. She was sent to Siberia.

Other private nurseries charged lower fees than Pani Skublińska and continued to accept children, some deliberately or accidentally causing their death. Many of these advertised their services brazenly in local newspapers, addressing themselves, for example, to "those who would like their child to live on somebody else's keep" or of receiving "upon payment of 15 rubles, those who are expecting weakness, including intake of the child." In Cracow, after the Foundling Home at St. Lazarus Hospital was shuttered in 1873, a number of local women made a business out of helping to raise the children

---

67. Bolesław Prus commented in 1885 on the activity over the past several weeks of the society, noting that its efforts were focused particularly on reducing "the numbers of foundlings and cases of infanticide" in Warsaw and on keeping pregnant women out of the hands of the midwives "who take endless advantage of them these days." Many midwives also doubled as abortionists, which may well have been part of Prus's meaning here. Prus, "Kroiniki," *Kraj* 16 (1885), reprinted in Prus, *Kroniki* (1957), 8: 277.

68. Dr. Antoni Okolski, "O domach podrzutków," *Biblioteka Warszawska* 193 (January 1889): 21–26.

69. Skublińska became a cause célèbre in the Warsaw press during her 1883 trial and was dubbed a "maker of little angels" by the editors of *Kurier Warszawski,* seemingly the first time the term was used. See Kurkowska, "Birth Control in the Industrial Age," 172–74.

of wet nurses or domestic servants. One couple was convicted in February 1879 of starving the children they had been paid to raise. Forensic evidence presented at the trial revealed that the children died of emaciation, pneumonia, or bronchitis from being kept in the extreme cold, being poisoned, or finally from "death by means of a blunt tool." One settlement near Cracow was even described in a public-medicine periodical as "specializing in the production of little angels"; several women in the commune engaged in the practice of slowly murdering infants.[70]

Although poor women had long relied on infanticide to rid themselves of illegitimate children, rates of child murder skyrocketed once Warsaw's foundling home ceased accepting infants from outside the city.[71] Working mothers who failed to abort their unwanted child and did not have the documents necessary to turn it over to the foundling home often set out initially to keep their illegitimate children. Their efforts were stymied by the need to hide such offspring from their employers, however, as in the case of Stanisława Zadorożna, a housekeeper in Lwów who was accused of throwing her infant into the chimney in the home where she worked. Zadorożna testified that she had decided to keep the child with her rather than taking it to its usual caregiver because it was so weak it was not eating. In an attempt to keep the child's existence secret, she claimed, she left it in the chimney during the day and only brought it with her to the kitchen, where she slept, in the evenings. She discovered the baby was dead one morning when she checked on it to bring it milk. Not knowing what else to do and "having no money for a funeral," she left the remains in the chimney.[72]

The degree of intentionality in this case is difficult to pinpoint, yet surely many new mothers were torn by anxieties over their conflicting responsibilities as mothers and as wage earners. Servants' magazines were full of anecdotes depicting domestic helpers who were arrested for attempting to rid themselves of an infant they could not care for. One 1902 story, entitled "degenerate mother," described the tale of Anna Lużna, a serving girl who

---

70. Kurkowska, "Birth Control in the Industrial Age," 172–74.

71. The number of reported infanticides in the Galician province ranged from twenty-four to thirty-six annually in the 1870s when foundling homes were still available. In the Congress Kingdom, some eighty cases per year were reported for the period 1848–1860, a rate that increased by half again in the period 1860–1875. Contemporary experts believed infanticide was the recourse of single mothers in the countryside more than in the cities, but anecdotal evidence indicates the practice was common in both milieus. Okolski, "O domach podrzutków," 22; and Kończycki, *Stan moralny*, 80–81. "Sprawy bieżące," *Niwa*, no. 5 (1890): 79–80, discusses the problem of climbing rates of infanticide among those denied entrance to the foundling home in Warsaw.

72. "Z kroniki policyjnej," *Gazeta Narodowa*, March 8, 1905, 2.

was arrested for abandoning her two-week-old son at the train station.[73] Similarly, Marykówna, a thirty-one-year-old servant in Cracow, became a "fallen woman" despite her "mature years" and left the product of her illicit liaisons in a coal bin at the home of her employer.[74] The press often held up such examples as morality tales to discourage young women from taking their first steps toward "falling" into a life of debauchery.[75] At the same time, these stories reinforced middle-class assumptions about the impious behavior of working girls with their casual sexual practices and horrific solutions for dealing with the attendant pregnancies. Prostitution would become one alternative for young women whose "legitimate" employment options were closed because of rumors of scandalous behavior or the reality of bearing a child out of wedlock. As long as bourgeois households refused to permit unwed mothers to serve them, as long as charitable activity throughout the Polish lands remained limited, and as long as unskilled women could not rely on their impoverished families for support, prostitution would remain an option in times of economic stress.

Prostitution: A Family Affair

Desperation over the harsh conditions of domestic service or the responsibilities incumbent on a new mother were not the only routes to prostitution. Young women also ended up on the public registry because of pressure from their immediate families, from a stepparent, or after the death of one or both parents. Quite apart from serving as a moral check on young women's behavior, as many contemporary publicists believed, impoverished families sometimes encouraged or even coerced their daughters to take up paid sex as a supplement to the family income. Alcoholism, unemployment, and other misfortunes (such as discord within the family) pushed young women to register as prostitutes with the full consent and even support of their parents. Moreover, a small but consistent number of women on the registries were listed as married and performing prostitution with the knowledge and consent of their spouses.[76]

---

73. "Wyrodna matka," *Przyjaciel Sług* 1, no. 8 (August 3, 1902): 126.

74. "Niemówle w pace z węglem: Matka morduje nowonarodzone dziecko," *Nowiny dla Wszystkich,* May 24, 1907, 3.

75. On the role of the new boulevard press in shaping urban public opinion, see Wood, *Becoming Metropolitan.*

76. Three of the total 488 public prostitutes registered in Lwów in 1904 were married. Dr. Wł. S-I, "Prostytucya ze szczególnym uwzględniem," 11.

The possibility that prostitution formed part of the family economy in some communities challenges the dominant stereotype of young women falling from the moral high road into the gutter of debauchery after losing their virginity and being abandoned by their seducer. Instead, as we have seen, selling sex appears to be one of many mechanisms employed within poor families to survive in times of scarcity. The turn to prostitution for many women was by no means a permanent choice. Rather, they slipped on and off the prostitution registry for any number of reasons including the return to "honest" work, marriage, and reintegration with their birth families. As one specialist commented in 1905 about former prostitutes in Lwów, "some do over time choose to leave the registry and become married, often becoming good and honest women."[77] None of these realities fit well with the paradigm of a permanent fall from grace on which many publicists relied.

Families could be integrally involved in marketing their daughters to international sex traffickers and in overlooking the activities of suspected procurers, a topic to be discussed in chapter 4. Some poor parents appear also to have been complicit in encouraging their daughters to take to the streets within their local neighborhoods. Interviews conducted among registered prostitutes in the Lwów police station in 1905 indicate that family pressures were the most common reason women gave for joining the ranks of registered prostitutes. "In the majority of cases," the interviewer noted, "parents drove their daughter onto this road in order to benefit from her earnings." The stresses rising from a second marriage or a blended family led stepmothers and stepfathers to drive young women "into the arms of prostitution in order to force them out of the house." In at least two cases, "the woman's own mother forced her daughter into this condition because she was going to be remarried and did not want her grown daughter in the vicinity of her second husband lest they grow romantically involved." Admittedly, the interviewer notes, "these are the most abominable, most miserable motives for prostitution, but unfortunately they are the most frequently occurring."[78]

Even when parents were not directly complicit in driving their daughters to the street, family considerations still played a role. The death of one or both parents and the absence of other relatives could put a young woman in a vulnerable position, prompting her to turn to the streets. One Russian

77. Ibid., 11–12.
78. "Prostytucje we Lwowie," 27–28.

physician cited statistics demonstrating that 87 percent of registered prostitutes in the Russian Empire as a whole and 85 percent of those in the
Polish Kingdom had no parents. Moreover, 75 percent had no siblings, and
18 percent no relations at all, suggesting the turn to paid sex was driven at
least partially by lack of family support.[79] As Jolanta Sikorska-Kulesza has
argued, "information about [prostitutes'] family background, the structure
of their families, and their material status brings one to the conclusion that
they were brought up on the street, deprived of adults' care, left to themselves
since childhood, and living in utter penury" before turning to prostitution.[80]
It may be difficult to distinguish between families that pushed young females
directly into the practice of prostitution and women who turned to it out of
desperation when the family was unavailable. Nonetheless, the numbers of
underaged girls engaged in professional sex work suggest a subculture replete
with dysfunctional families. Warsaw records indicate, for example, that the
vast majority of registered prostitutes were minors, under the age of eighteen,
and independent researchers at the time found that a significant portion of
them were as young as eleven, twelve, or thirteen, ages at which families
might be expected to maintain some knowledge of their children's activities
if not influence over them.[81]

Elsewhere, anecdotal evidence suggests prostitution was at least occasionally used to support a family. Such was the case with Ludwika G. of Lwów,
who claimed she applied all her earnings to support her two younger sisters
in a convent. Still others joined the ranks of registered sex workers in order
to avoid the threat of incarceration in a convent. Finally, in at least one case,
prostitution became a temporary alternative to avoid an unhappy marriage.
This was the explanation Bogumila R. provided for fleeing to a brothel when

---

79. Petersen, *Enquêtes sur l'état de la prostitution* (Brussels, 1899), 281–82, quoted in Wysłouch,
Ohyda Wieku, 4–5; and *Prostitutsiya v rossiyskoy imperii po obsledovaniyu 1-go avgusta 1889 g.*, ed. A.
Dubravskiy (St. Petersburg, 1890), quoted in Sikorska-Kulesza, "Prostitution in Congress Poland,"
132.

80. One irony of the structure of most prostitutes' families is that legally only a parent, husband, or
evidence of an "honest" job sufficed to remove a woman from the prostitution registry. Without living parents, it was more difficult for registered sex workers to find a way off the police rolls. Rząśnicki,
Prostytycja a proletariat, 11–14; and Sikorska-Kulesza, "Prostitution in Congress Kingdom," 132.

81. The legal minimum age for serving as a prostitute was sixteen, but police typically did not
require proof of age. "Prostytucje we Lwowie," 31–33. Aleksander Świętochowski discovered that in
1889 there were at least three girls in Warsaw brothels eleven years old, three who were twelve, and
one that was only ten. Świętochowski, "Liberum veto," 130. According to the 1895 Warsaw police
registry, 69 percent had become public prostitutes as sixteen-year-olds. The following year 275 out of
the 418 "fresh" recruits to the list were minors. Most contemporary specialists believed girls inflated
their age to sixteen to be eligible for legal registration as prostitutes. Wysłouch, *Ohyda Wieku*, 5.

facing the unsavory prospect of marriage to a Galician official.[82] Examples of parental pressure or the absence of family support do not discount the financial motivation many prostitutes cited for their turn to paid sex. Instead, they complicate contemporary images of prostitution as driven primarily by moral failure. As we have seen, the reality of turn-of-the-century Polish city life was that employment for single women was inadequate and poorly paid, that few solutions existed for supporting unwed mothers, and that families were at best able to provide only limited support for their independent daughters and at worst guilty of pushing their offspring in the direction of paid sex in order to benefit from the proceeds themselves.

Definition: Life on the Prostitution Registry

Women who turned to commercial sex and others in their social circle had various incentives for their decisions. What, then, was the larger legal and professional structure that greeted those who turned to the sex trade? As we have seen, prostitution was intricately woven into the fabric of everyday life in fin de siècle Poland in a number of distinct spheres—the practice of poor females supplementing their wages through part-time sex work, women who flowed on and off police registries as temporary prostitutes in times of financial stress, and the coexistence in bourgeois households of "virtuous" middle-class women and domestic servants who were also part-time prostitutes. Because of the pattern of women combining paid sex work with other professional activities, the work of police officials in registering professional prostitutes was made all the more difficult and matters of definitions were a challenge for officials at every level of the regulatory system. Police investigators responsible for supervising prostitutes faced a wide spectrum of scenarios that could plausibly be labeled "prostitution." By the latter years of the nineteenth century, licensed prostitutes no longer were shut up in regulated brothels in a town's red-light district. Instead, increasing numbers of women operated out of private homes scattered around urban neighborhoods, making the job of police supervision more challenging. To make matters worse, police were expected to exercise control over an enormous contingent of women who sold sex part time, "camouflaged" by honest employment.

Police all over Polish territory dealt with this lack of definitional clarity by establishing the three separate registries for sex workers: the open or public (*jawny*) status for those self-identifying as professional prostitutes, the *tajny* or

---

82. "Prostytucja we Lwowie," 29–30.

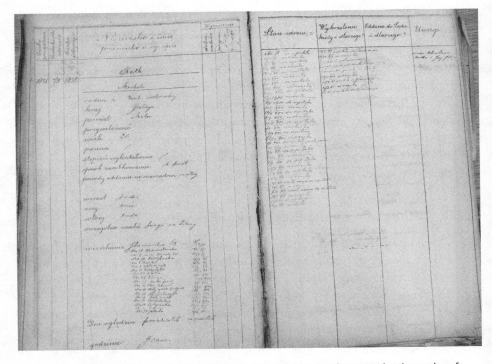

FIGURE. 3.2A Page from the sanitary registry for the city of Cracow, demonstrating the number of hospital stays and changes of residence for each registered prostitute. This record is for Rachela Roth, daughter of Abraham Roth, who was likely of Jewish background. Roth was first inscribed in 1898 at the age of twenty. She had no formal education and was a professional prostitute without other occupation. She was hospitalized sixteen times and changed apartments eighteen times during her years on the registry, finally "disappearing" from police supervision in 1905 at the age of twenty-seven.
Courtesy of the National Archive in Cracow (Archiwum Państwowe w Krakowie).

secret registry for women suspected of selling sex but not officially inscribed, and after 1905, the "discreet" registry for part-time prostitutes who also held jobs with legitimate employers. The complexity of this registration system reflected a deeper dissonance in official Polish society about how prostitution should be defined and where the legal limits of female sexuality lay. As one lengthy article explaining the practice of regulated prostitution noted, any female sex act was "treated as illegal if it is not sanctioned by marital bonds and the natural sexual drive." In other words, even women who "do not take money for sex but are described by the term profligacy [*rospusta*]" were viewed as prostitutes in the eyes of the (Austrian, in this case) law.[83]

---

83. Ibid., 18–19.

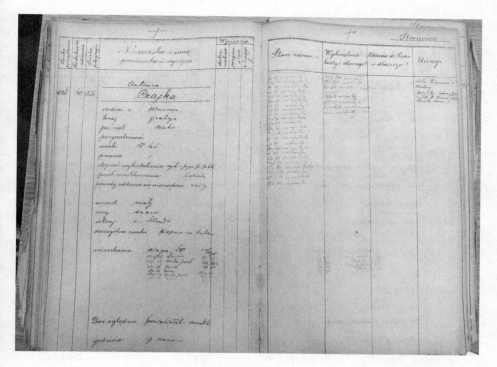

FIGURE 3.2B This record for Antonina Czajka indicates that she was a waitress by occupation but also practiced prostitution occasionally. She was placed under police-medical supervision at age eighteen. Czajka, who appears to have been Catholic, was hospitalized repeatedly and finally died of consumption in 1905 at the age of twenty-five. The cross at the top of the page shows the registrant is deceased.
Courtesy of the National Archive in Cracow (Archiwum Państwowe w Krakowie).

FIGURE 3.3 Warsaw's Szpital Dzieciątka Jezus (Baby Jesus Hospital) and its nearby Dom Podrzutków or Foundling Home, the only one of its kind in all the Polish territories. Photographed in 1916.
Courtesy of National Archive in Cracow (Archiwum Państwowe w Krakowie).

Of Brothels and Madams

Paid sex represented a more prominent challenge to bourgeois morality in the early years of the twentieth century as changing police regulations forced greater numbers of women onto the official registries. The simplest category of prostitution for police to identify remained those who committed themselves to full-time work in a brothel. Regulations inherited from Prussian rule initially permitted prostitution only in public houses. These official bordellos typically housed a few dozen prostitutes, a mixture of so-called first-class and second-class girls. They were managed by a madam and regulated by clear rules of behavior. Brothel employees were required to register with police before entering the establishment, a process that entailed entering their names onto the registry of "public" prostitutes, answering a series of questions about their personal background, and supplying the address of their intended residence. Thereafter, the women submitted to semiweekly medical examinations and were incarcerated in the venereal ward of the nearby hospital when they became ill. They had few rights within the brothel and were not permitted to leave its premises except with the permission of the madam. Each brothel employee was expected to accept the clients assigned to her without question, to maintain decorum, to bathe twice a week, and to report any sign of infection she noted. She was obliged to inform police authorities whenever she changed residences.[84]

The virtue of the brothel system for police and for medical personnel was that madams controlled the activities of their workers, limiting their exposure to the world beyond the bordello. A public-health doctor could easily complete his examinations on site and guarantee that ill patients were transferred to a venereal hospital. But the restricted existence of brothel workers, the limits on their personal freedom, and the myriad abuses madams imposed led to a strong preference on the part of practitioners for conducting prostitution out of private homes. Late nineteenth-century imperial laws permitted this transition in the venues of tolerated prostitution, driven partly by efforts to clean up the seedier parts of towns and disperse the obvious presence of venal sex from city centers. Many professional prostitutes in the Polish lands left formal brothels behind by the last decades of the nineteenth century,

---

84. The second-class girls were obliged to serve those in the first class, whose salaries were higher. This might include washing their laundry and providing refreshments for their clients. First-class workers were "absolutely never permitted to go outside into the world" except with the permission of the administration for very important matters. Franciszek Giedroyć, *"Domy wilczkowania"* *(Projekt organizacji wewnętrznej zamtuzów w Polsce)* reprinted from *Przegląd chorób skórnych i wenerycznych* (Warsaw, 1912). See also, Wysłouch, *Ohyda Wieku,* 10–11.

preferring instead to operate independently out of rented apartments in poorer neighborhoods. The reduced reliance on houses of assignation was partially the result of police pressure to conceal prostitutes from the public gaze by positioning bordellos away from schools, religious establishments, and shops.[85] As cities expanded and became more crowded, complaints about the "dangerous miasmas and sexual offenses spreading" from the bordellos "to the healthy portions of the population" increased and police were forced to close down the larger urban houses in close proximity to other public institutions. Still, as Lwów Police Chief Łepkowski noted with regret in 1912, having hundreds of prostitutes "living in private residences throughout the city is more harmful to public morality than a bordello because [they] come into contact with innocent women and through their demoralized behavior find new victims."[86] Since prostitutes living in private rooms were forced to locate their own clients, the very effort to protect bourgeois morality from the sight of inner-city brothels contributed to the dispersion of public women in the city streets.

Yet even inhabitants of licensed brothels were often ambivalent about their identification as professional prostitutes. Experienced brothel employees told stories of agents and procurers who tricked them into agreeing to enter a public house and registering with the police, suggesting that some degree of coercion did accompany entry into the business in certain cases. Though it is always difficult to assess the stories former prostitutes told about their earlier experiences, examples abound of those who claimed to have been entrapped and forced into a brothel against their will. Such testimonies remind us that the line between a desperate turn to sex work and forced entry into the business was fine but nonetheless significant. Young Z's story of a female agent who approached her while she was working in the construction business in Minsk is a case in point. The woman promised Z. a comfortable position in Warsaw, but then reportedly brought her directly to a brothel. "There she was shut in a room without windows that appeared to be intended as some sort of a prison," according to the manager of a shelter for fallen women, who later took in the traumatized girl. "For two days she refused to eat and on the third she started to eat and began to feel intoxicated as though she was going to lose consciousness. After five days, a man came to her and raped

---

85. Correspondence of Lwów Police Chief Łepkowski to the C. K. Ministerstwo Wewnętrzne, August 21 and September 19, 1912, AGAD, CKMSW, sygn. 213. Here, Łepkowski notes that "following the massive growth of the city with its new buildings, public institutions, educational facilities and schools, the Imperial Central Police Directory has repeatedly . . . sought to eradicate several brothels."

86. Łepkowski to C. K. Ministerstwo Wewnętrzne, August 21, 1912, AGAD, CKMSW, sygn. 213.

her. Then more men came to her. After this, she was taken to the [Police] Committee to register."[87]

The very act of registering with the police seems to have been fraught with confusion for some young women who were not familiar with the world of prostitution. Because household servants were required to register with local municipal authorities to obtain their employment booklets, procurers often convinced their prey that the medical examination at the police station was part of qualifying them to serve as domestics. One young woman left her village home after giving birth to an illegitimate child and placing it in an orphanage. She traveled to the nearby town of Mława (100 kilometers north of Warsaw) to find an employment agent who could help her obtain a position as a servant in Warsaw. The agent claimed she had a position and took the young lady to a "certain house," whereupon the mistress informed the young serving girl that she "liked [her] very much and was taking [her] to the servant's central office so [she] could be registered." As it turns out, the young woman recalled,

> She took me, as I later determined, to the Medical–Police Committee to be registered as a prostitute. At the Committee, the lady asked me whether I was happy at her place; I said that I was very happy and that I wanted to remain with her. Then they registered me and took me for a [medical] inspection. I resisted in the beginning, but it was explained to me that in Warsaw all servants must be inspected because it is the law, and I figured I was not guilty of anything so it didn't matter. The lady took me back home and then took me upstairs, assigned me a room, told me to dress in a red outfit and brought me to a large and elegant hall. At this point, I figured out that this was a house of prostitution. I started to cry and began to scream, but there was no way out.

Similarly, R., who had been living with her parents in the countryside, was approached by a female acquaintance who promised a wonderful position in Warsaw. The woman took her directly to the Police-Medical Committee, leading her to believe that she was participating in the domestic servant's inspection process.[88] Though it is difficult to determine if such testimonies reflected a tendency on the part of public women to channel the melodrama of deception enshrined in fictional accounts of the turn to prostitution, they certainly reflect an atmosphere of confusion surrounding the initial entry into the world of paid sex.

---

87. Although Moriconi recognized that many of the women under her care had led sexually indecorous lives, this case was one of two she proclaimed to have been "completely innocent when they were sold to brothels." Moriconi, "Przyczynek do sprawy prostytucyi," 175–76.

88. Ibid., 175.

Streetwalkers and Pimps

As we have seen, the system of enclosing women within a brothel where they were supervised by a madam and a police doctor was waning in the latter part of the nineteenth century. Increasingly prostitution in the Polish lands was conducted outside of established houses in the rented apartments of its practitioners, a situation that contributed to the urban panic among residents in surrounding neighborhoods. By the turn of the twentieth century, the independent sex worker operating out of a shared apartment was far more typical in most Polish towns. Laws governing prostitution all over Polish territory permitted women to sell sex from their own apartments as long as they did not attempt to entice customers in the surrounding neighborhood. Women working as prostitutes thus tended increasingly to rent flats in working-class districts, where they were more integrated into the life of the community than they might be while residing in a brothel.

These more permissive regulations made the work of police vice squads more challenging. Most street prostitutes avoided registration at all costs. Sanitary exams were painful and humiliating, and those diagnosed with venereal disease faced lengthy mandatory hospital stays with attendant loss of income. More important, registration transferred what might have been a part-time or temporary activity to the status of a permanent, full-time profession. Young women whose names appeared on the police record often experienced the process as one of public shaming or "branding" with a label they saw as inaccurate. Worse, registration required a woman to exchange her internal passport for a "black booklet" (or deep purple in some cases) on which her new status and health records appeared. Without official identification, she would be unable to garner "honest" employment, thereby formalizing her status as a public prostitute.[89] In this way, the registration system could turn casual sexual liaisons into a permanent casting out of polite society, forcing women to shift from occasional sex work to full-time prostitution. It is no wonder that most women resisted the process as long as they could.[90]

---

89. As Rząśnicki points out, "the passport booklets . . . were documents that proved they had completed their health examinations, but they were also their primary form of identification for other purposes. If a woman wanted to apply for an 'honest' job or return to the village of her birth to take up 'honest' work, or even move to a distant city to start over, she had to show the passport and then her secret would be out. Thanks to these booklets, occasional prostitutes (or those forcibly inscribed in the registry) became *professional* prostitutes because they could find no other means of living." *Prostytucja a proletariat,* 11–14.

90. Contemporary observers regularly assumed that only one-tenth of all women conducting prostitution were registered with the authorities. This figure is difficult to confirm and probably somewhat exaggerated.

Despite official regulations governing removal from the prostitution registry, the average length of time women spent on the police registry tended to be relatively brief. Although some women are listed as simply having "disappeared" from police supervision, others were expunged from the public record because of marriage, taking a legitimate job, or moving to another location. The successful removal of hundreds of women each year from official prostitution lists suggests a return to "normal" life was at least theoretically possible. For example, 488 women were inscribed on the public record in Lwów at the end of 1904, but of these, 225 were removed during the course of the following year and 129 new women were registered in their places.[91] Similarly, if the Cracow records are to be believed, prostitution was a relatively short-lived phenomenon for many practitioners there. Roughly one-third of all licensed prostitutes in Cracow worked for less than one year during the 1890s and the early years of the twentieth century, while an additional 30 percent stayed on the registry for two to three years total. Only 40 percent of those on the police rolls remained longer than three years. As Michał Baczkowski concludes in his study of Cracow prostitution records, "if the legal registry is to be believed, most girls did not practice prostitution for their entire professional lives."[92] Instead, they appear to have relied on sex work during particularly challenging transitions in their lives and then left the practice behind once their fortunes and employment situations stabilized.

With few women taking on the burden of registration voluntarily, it was left to police officials to round up those suspected of selling sex and record their names and vital information. To this end, vice squads engaged in regular surveillance of seedy neighborhoods in major city centers. They toured cafés, restaurants, and pubs where they believed prostitutes solicited customers. They searched army barracks, public baths, and city parks. Police conducted roundups in larger towns, detaining women suspected of selling sex and placing their names in the registry of "secret" prostitutes. The scene in the police station the evening after such a roundup could be hellish, with the "crying, sobbing, cursing, threats, and insults" of the accused reverberating throughout the jail cells.[93] Police had wide latitude in determining whom to detain in these roundups and could escort any woman suspected of conducting

---

91. "Prostytucje we Lwowie," 31–33.

92. Baczkowski, "Prostytucja w Krakowie."

93. Bolesław Limanowski reflected on the night he spent in jail at the police station in Lwów in the late 1870s. He was kept awake the entire night by the sound of women's voices coming from the women's cell bloc. The next day he was surrounded by scores of shabbily dressed women, heads in hands, awaiting medical examinations. Limanowski, "Regulamentacyja występku," 363–64.

prostitution to the police station for an examination. Liberal imperial guidelines for identifying suspected prostitutes put any single woman in a public area at potential risk and, as such, were the focus of frequent criticism. Police were authorized to pick up any female found alone in the company of an unrelated man in a hotel room, a café, or a bar. A woman walking late at night with several men or in a public place could also be accused, as could one spotted among men not related to her in the vicinity of military barracks or in the company of other prostitutes.[94] Suspected women could be forcibly inscribed onto the prostitution registry at the behest of the officer in charge and the medical inspector. No court of law, witness, or defense was required.[95] Only when a prospective registrant was discovered to be a virgin could she easily slip out of the requirement to registry. In other cases, those who resisted vigorously against inscription onto the "public" prostitution book were placed on the "secret" register rather than the "public" one.

The criteria police employed for spotting prostitutes was fraught with opportunities for misidentification, leading some contemporaries to wonder about the point at which a woman crossed the line from being protected by local police to being subject to police supervision and control.[96] Social reformers and liberal journalists worried about "honest" women being mistaken for prostitutes and devised numerous means for officials to identify the "real" streetwalkers. The Warsaw-based *Nowe Słowo* circulated a proposal in 1903 for solving the long-standing problem of police mistaking honest women for prostitutes. The article noted with concern that "police often pick up honest women thinking they are prostitutes and subject them to great unpleasantness," and suggested that authorities be provided guidelines to help identify prostitutes based on their clothing and outward appearance. Professional prostitutes should, according to the proposal, be assigned "special clothing and an external stamp" in order to "protect 'moral' women from being mistaken as prostitutes." Such notions served to underline the anxiety many single women faced when traveling or shopping on their own in city centers.[97]

Laboring women were frequently confused for prostitutes and subject to sexual attacks and police harassment. Examples abound of poor women

---

94. S-I, "Prostytucya ze szczególnym uwzględnieniem," 11–15; and Rząśnicki, *Prostytucja a proletariat,* 11–14.

95. Rząśnicki, *Prostytucja a proletariat,* 11–14.

96. See, for example, "Prostytucya we Lwowie," 18–19.

97. The original article was published in the Viennese journal *Die Wage*. The title was cited as "Prostytutki i ich strój" in a review by Stanisław Kelles-Krauz, "Kroniki," *Nowe Słowo* 2, no. 12 (June 15, 1903): 277.

alone on city streets who became the targets of upper-class sexual aggression. One particularly aggressive gentleman grabbed the arm of a seamstress in March 1888 and attempted to force her into his bachelor apartment. A blacksmith apprentice heard the victim's cry for help and came to her rescue. A few days later, a local businessman in his fifties brutally attacked a Miss M. at an intersection nearby. The shocked girl yelled for assistance and a passerby came to her aid.[98] Sometimes police misinterpreted the behavior of lower-class women and they were caught in the regular evening roundups. The sociologist Bolesław Limanowski noted that most of those arrested on suspicion of prostitution were "shabbily dressed girls, most likely domestic servants or seamstresses."[99] Young women traveling alone by rail were equally the targets of indiscreet advances, as in the 1896 case of a girl forced to jump off her train en route from Warsaw to Lublin when she was physically abused by some male passengers. Another "honest" girl was the victim of a sexual attack by two conductors; she responded to their entreaties simply by screaming. The columnist Bolesław Prus summed up the problem of "girls traveling alone by rail frequently (very frequently!) [being] solicited by men." As these examples suggest, some "defended themselves by screaming," whereas others reportedly had "the urge to commit suicide." Such "innocent" girls had the right to expect protection from society rather than harassment, Prus argued.[100] Again, the point at which public officials shifted from protecting young women to supervising and controlling them as presumed prostitutes was unclear and threatened the well-being of all single women in the Polish lands.

"Discreet" Prostitutes

In addition to prostitutes formally registered with a brothel and those operating independently out of their homes, police faced a new category of prostitution in the early twentieth century. During the aftermath of the 1905 Revolution in Russia, when numerous migrants were fleeing the Polish Kingdom for Galicia, police in Lwów established an additional

---

98. Bolesław Prus, "Doraźna kara," *Kurier Warszawski*, March 3, 1888, 3; and "Znowu donżuaneria," *Kurier Warszawski,* March 6, 1888, reprinted in Prus, *Kroniki*, 11: 311–12.

99. Limanowski had been incarcerated for public drunkenness and spent the evening sitting in his cell observing the behavior of women caught in police roundups for alleged prostitution. Limanowski, "Regulamentacyja występu," 364.

100. Prus, "Kroniki tygodniowe," *Kurier Codzienny,* January 24, 1897, reprinted in Prus, *Kroniki*, 15: 22–25.

means of supervising what they viewed as a "new and innovative form of prostitution." This new "type" of prostitution took account of a category of women "about whom it is generally known" that they engage in prostitution and yet "it is for some reason not possible to register with the police." The regulations passed in March 1906 thus defined "discreet prostitution" as all those sexual encounters attached to the professions that were "known to be inclined to selling sex." These new policies both acknowledged that many working-class women sold sex part time to make ends meet and, at the same time, painted all poor females with the brush of sexual indiscretion. The regulations tacitly assumed that every clerk or waitress an urban spectator met in a shop or café upheld standards of virtue far different from her bourgeois sisters and that her customers and clients could safely regard her as a de facto prostitute. The regulations applied, above all, to "waitresses and cashiers in coffee shops and low-class locales" whom "every guest and even more so the police know are available to anyone for money and that many of them are actually prostitutes."[101] Women in these categories of employment were officially placed in the category of "discreet prostitutes" as of March 1, 1906 and their names inscribed onto a third prostitution registry.

The new law was explicitly intended to bring those whose sexual practices might be masked by "legitimate" employment under the police supervisory gaze. It was rooted in police frustration at the inability to inscribe women in these employment categories onto the prostitution registries and mandate regular medical exams for them because "their employers would be within their rights to protest against placing them on the registry of public prostitutes." As will be discussed in chapter 7, public anxiety about the spread of venereal disease had reached near-panic levels during the 1905 Revolution and police were convinced that much of the contamination occurred because unlicensed prostitutes were not obliged to be screened for contagious illnesses. The commentary surrounding the announcement of mandatory examinations for all women in the service professions sought to soften this premise somewhat, noting that only "those girls on whom the police have concrete evidence will be declared discreet prostitutes." Nonetheless, authorities expected that those women who were currently "screened by their work" would "energetically and desperately protest against being declared discreet prostitutes."[102]

---

101. "Prostytucya we Lwowie," 24–26.
102. Ibid.

The Permeable Boundaries of Bourgeois Family Life

The advent of new regulations authorizing police investigators to require medical checkups for service personnel reflected a new way of thinking about the intersection of class, sexuality, and gender. On the one hand, poor women were increasingly assumed to function as part-time prostitutes in addition to performing their duties as household servants, bartenders, waitresses, or shopkeepers. According to this assumption, lower-class females did not earn enough in these positions to support themselves, they were greedy for lavish clothing and other luxuries, or they were sexually licentious as a group. Such expectations effectively categorized working women as existing in a world apart from their middle-class sisters, with morals and patterns of behavior alien from upstanding middle-class family life. The brusque and demeaning treatment suspected prostitutes received in police stations in many ways reflected these assumptions about the links between poverty and sexual permissiveness. By categorizing huge subsets of poor women as potential prostitutes, Polish society effectively distanced lower-class females from the elite universe of obligation, compartmentalizing them as less moral, less pious, and less virtuous than women of higher social rank. Just as bourgeois commentators sought to keep prostitution off the city streets and away from middle-class neighborhoods, so too did the implementation of legal regulations about the varieties of prostitution practices involve distancing poor young women from the moral site of upstanding urban residents.

These desperate attempts to isolate lower-class immorality from the world of the Polish urban elite also reveal a more complex side of the prostitution equation and more points of intersection between the world of prostitution and the surrounding social milieu. In fact, the very regulations mandating treatment of all working girls—be they factory workers, household servants, or service personnel—as de facto prostitutes also tacitly acknowledged the presence in upper-class homes of prostitute nannies, domestic servants, and wet nurses. They recognized that many, if not all, of the attractive young women who served bourgeois families in restaurants and coffee houses were also involved in some aspect of the sex trade. According to this view, female assistants in workshops and stores were also engaged in part-time sex work. In reality, then, the patterns of middle-class urban life in Polish cities involved constant interaction with part-time prostitutes, who were both socially alienated from the middle-class consumer and, at the same time, culturally linked to him. As awareness of the ravages of venereal disease circulated, panic over the proximity between bourgeois families and diseased women increasingly drove the prostitution discussion. Even more immediately threatening than disease to many families, however, was the prospect of having one of their innocent daughters whisked away by an international trafficker, a subject to which we now turn.

CHAPTER 4

Narratives of Entrapment

> "Is it true that they snatch girls off the streets and
> carry them away to Argentina?"
> "They go there by themselves."
>
> —Isaac Bashevis Singer, *Scum*

Poles soon became aware that their concern about paid sex on the domestic front also had international ramifications. Word of innocent women forcibly transported across national frontiers for illicit purposes captured the public imagination worldwide, filling the columns of daily newspapers and fueling coffeehouse gossip.[1] By the close of the nineteenth century, girls forced from their homes and transported to foreign brothels had become the subject of melodramatic exposés penned by purity activists, charity workers, legal experts, and police reporters from New York to Singapore. Polish observers were no exception to this flood of commentary. Capitalizing on readers' fascination with narratives of dark strangers lurking on shadowy street corners to whisk away vulnerable passersby, periodicals warned of girls disappearing from urban neighborhoods, train platforms, or off steamers bound for foreign ports. An army of social

---

1. On white-slavery scares throughout Europe and the Americas at the turn of the twentieth century, see Edward Bristow, *Vice and Vigilance: Purity Movements in Britain since 1700* (Dublin, 1977); Kathleen Barry, *Female Sexual Slavery* (New York, 1984); Kaplan, "Prostitution, Morality Crusades, and Feminism," 619–27; Connelly, *Response to Prostitution in the Progressive Era*; Egal Feldman, "Prostitution: The Alien Woman and the Progressive Imagination," *American Quarterly* 19 (1967): 192–206; and Donna Guy, "White Slavery, Public Health, and the Socialist Position on Legalized Prostitution in Argentina, 1913–193," *Latin American Research Review* 23, no. 3 (1988): 60–80.

reformers and government officials investigated the claims of these unfortunates. Journalists circulated powerful stories that shaped popular perceptions of prostitution. Imagery from these accounts colored an anxious public's views of sexual danger, gender expectations, and ethnic stereotypes. Antitrafficking activists worked to combat the incidence of coerced sex migration, warning against women traveling alone and wily businessmen who offered them luxurious positions. In the end, as we will see, those who took the lead in circulating cautionary tales about trafficking effectively controlled the narrative around it, influencing the way sex migration has been understood in the historical literature. Important for our study, the problem of "white slavery" was characterized in these narratives as a phenomenon that touched Polish society with particular force, contributing to an ongoing sense of national vulnerability and social insecurity.

Rarely were the women who were the subjects of trafficking tales analyzed from the perspective of their own goals and aspirations and the choices they made en route to their new homes. The purpose of this chapter and the two that follow is to provide some context for assessing the genesis of the white-slavery vocabulary, for understanding the actors who participated in transatlantic networks of sex migration (chapter 5), and for assessing the ethnic component of trafficking, particularly among local Jews (chapter 6). In contrast to the melodramatic rhetoric of the contemporary white-slavery narratives, recent historians argue that white slavery itself—the pattern of mass coerced migration specifically to fuel the international sex industry— was largely a construct "born out of a particular interpretation of sexual danger in a specific social and historical context."[2] This chapter unpackages the rhetoric surrounding the white-slavery scare and suggests ways in which trafficking imagery can be understood as a window into contemporary sexual anxiety in the Polish lands. Although most migration was voluntary and those who turned to sex work in foreign countries were typically experienced prostitutes, the "myth" of passivity and naïveté nonetheless caught hold of the public imagination.[3] It is our task to investigate what propelled the trafficking story forward in the Polish case and to assess the effects of its broad circulation during the early years of the twentieth century.

---

2. Petra de Vries, "'White Slaves' in a Colonial Nation: The Dutch Campaign against the Traffic in Women in the Early Twentieth Century," *Social and Legal Studies* 14, no. 1 (2005): 42.

3. As Frederick Grittner points out, such myths do not necessarily imply events that are false. Rather, a myth can be understood as "a collective belief that simplifies reality." In other words, "a myth can help explain the world and justify social institutions." Frederick Karl Grittner, "White Slavery: Myth, Ideology, and American Law" (PhD diss., University of Minnesota, 1986), 7.

Origins of a Metaphor

Use of the term "white slavery" as a general reference for prostitution was popularized during Josephine Butler's antiregulation campaign of the 1870s. The designation was originally used in the 1830s among members of the British and American labor movements to describe the low wages and intolerable working conditions that characterized early Anglo-American industrial settings. Its first usage in a sexual context was in an 1870 letter Victor Hugo wrote to Butler decrying the fact that "the slavery of black women is abolished in America," whereas the "slavery of white women continues in Europe and laws are still made by men in order to tyrannize over women."[4] Butler quickly adopted the allusion, employing it in her 1875 description of the inherently oppressive relations she saw at the core of all prostitution. She argued that the system of regulated prostitution prevailing across the whole of Europe was one of "slavery, of buying and selling of human beings, of oppression, of imprisonment, and of slow murder," which was not for the "rich man's cotton fields" but for "the secure gratification of man's lust."[5] Taking their cues from Butler, abolitionists frequently relied on the white slavery image to stand in for *all* prostitution, domestic and international, forced and voluntary, and thereby focus attention on the evils of state regulation.

By the 1890s the term "white slavery" took on a more specific meaning connected with the forced kidnapping and transfer of girls to brothels outside of Europe.[6] The reputed practice of placing European women in sexual bondage came to represent a moral inversion of earlier slave relationships and typically involved "alien" or non-Christian traffickers such as Jews overpowering innocent white girls, a relationship that made the phenomenon all the more frightening for its racial component. "Buyers," in turn, were characterized as swarthy Hispanics, Muslim Turks, Indians, Chinese, Jews, or any of a number of nonwhite population groups. "White slavery" would become the centerpiece of the 1902 Paris Antitrafficking Conference, a meeting that drew Bertha Pappenheim's attention to the issue and resulted in the

---

4. Cited in Mara L. Keire, "The Vice Trust: A Reinterpretation of the White Slavery Scare in the United States, 1907–1917," *Journal of Social History* 35, no. 1 (2001): 2. Alfred S. Dwyer, another of Butler's allies, used the term more specifically to refer to involuntary brothel prostitution. Alfred S. Dwyer, *The European Slave Trade in English Girls* (London, 1880). On the semantic shifts in the meanings of white slavery, see Corbin, *Women for Hire,* 275–80.

5. Josephine Butler, *A Letter to the Members of the Ladies National Association* (London, 1875), 19.

6. De Vries, "'White Slaves' in a Colonial Nation," 43–44; and Jo Doezema, "Loose Women or Lost Women?: The Re-Emergence of the Myth of 'White Slavery' in Contemporary Discourses of 'Trafficking in Women,'" *Gender Issues* 18, no. 1 (2000): 4.

passage of the first International Agreement for the Suppression of the White Slave Traffic. Ratified by a dozen governments, the agreement committed the international community to take action against "procuring women and girls for immoral purposes abroad," an injunction that would lead the United States to the passage of the Mann Act in 1910.[7]

In Europe as in the United States, an anxious public was deluged with articles, brochures, plays, novels, and educational materials painting the tragic lives of kidnapped women in almost pornographic detail and warning otherwise innocent girls of impending doom if they strayed out alone. The story had all the appeal of a lurid melodrama, complete with underground intrigue, conspiracy, and seduction. For a late-Victorian audience the drama provided almost voyeuristic access to the world of paid sex.[8] Fears about trafficking reached "epidemic proportions" in the early years of the twentieth century, prompting the rise of rescue societies, international conferences, and multilateral agreements devoted to curtailing the traffic in innocent women and children.[9] By 1914, experts estimated that some one billion pages had been written on white slavery in North America alone.[10] Yet the overblown media coverage did not necessarily reflect a corresponding spike in prostitution or in international sex migration. As with other waves of moral panic, the increase in public *concern* about trafficking had its roots in a much broader set of fears related to gender roles, female sexuality, and the behavior of single women.[11] Although female migration out of Europe experienced a sharp rise in the late nineteenth century, the number of documented cases of forced migration to brothels is extremely small.[12]

Contemporary experts on domestic and international vice challenged the validity of the white slavery narrative where they could. A series of 1912

---

7. On the international research that agents of the US Immigration Commission conducted, see the letter from the Immigration Commission, Washington, DC, October 30, 1908, to Chief of Police in Vienna, BPdWA, "Prostitution und Mädchenhandel," 1907/I. The Mann Act forbade the transfer of women across state lines for the purposes of prostitution. Barry, *Female Sexual Slavery,* 32.

8. Ruth Rosen stresses that just because white-slavery narratives tended to be melodramatic does not discount the existence of an element of coercion in prostitution at some level. In her view, "a careful review of the evidence shows us that a real traffic in women existed," though reformers may have exaggerated its conditions and extent. *The Lost Sisterhood: Prostitution in America, 1900–1918* (Baltimore, 1982), 112–16, 129.

9. Stephanie A. Limoncelli, *The Politics of Trafficking: The First International Movement to Combat the Sexual Exploitation of Women* (Stanford, CA, 2010); and Bristow, *Vice and Vigilance,* 190.

10. Bristow, *Vice and Vigilance,* 188–89.

11. Daniel Bell, "The Myth of Crime Waves," in *The End of Ideology: On the Exhaustion of Political Ideas in the Fifties* (Cambridge, 1962), 151–74.

12. De Vries, "'White Slaves' in a Colonial Nation," 39–60; and Mary Ann Irwin, "'White Slavery' as Metaphor: Anatomy of a Moral Panic," *Ex Post Facto: The History Journal* 5 (1996): 1–22.

interviews with British vigilance society representatives, police officers, and court commissioners, for example, failed to uncover any identifiable cases of entrapment in Britain. Assistant Commissioner F. S. Bullock, head of the Society for the Repression of the White Slave Traffic in London, confessed that despite widely circulated stories of women forced into prostitution, "I cannot call to mind a single case of forcible trapping of a girl or a woman by drugs, false messages, or physical force during the last ten years that has been authenticated or proved. I should say such cases were very rare indeed."[13] A longtime probation officer at the Thames Police Courts in London confirmed that "in every case known to me of a girl being dragged down to life in a brothel, she has been a willing though blind and misguided victim. . . . I have never found reason to believe that any girl is ever forcibly carried off."[14] Police records for the Habsburg Monarchy corroborate these observations. With rare exceptions, women reported missing and believed to have become victims of sex traffickers were either discovered pursuing "legitimate" professions or had willingly migrated to take up work in foreign brothels.

One way to reconcile the contemporary panic over trafficking with the limited number of documented cases is to treat white slavery as a metaphor, a "way of explaining a complicated and threatening reality" rather than as a direct reflection of actual events. Since white-slavery narratives invariably portrayed victims as passive and innocent, such stories provided an excuse for rescue agencies to treat the female migrant as someone in need of assistance and intervention rather than condemnation.[15] White slavery essentially gave the state and private charities permission to intervene in the lives of migrating women and impose "corrective" measures on them.[16] It is possible to look beyond the sensationalized accounts of trafficking tales and uncover the power relations behind these narratives. By reading the depictions of imperial agencies tracking women who migrated illegally against testimonies from the girls themselves, we see that the panic about "white slavery" disguises as much as it reveals. Young, single, female migrants were often, though not

---

13. Interview with F. S. Bullock, Central Authority in England for the Repression of the White Slave Traffic, cited in Teresa Billington-Greig, "The Truth about White Slavery," *English Review* 14 (June 1913): 439.

14. Eleanor Carey, sixteen-year veteran of the Police Court Missionary and Probation Officer at Thames Police Court, cited in Teresa Billington-Greig, "The Truth about White Slavery," 441–43.

15. Jo Doezema, *Sex Slaves and Discourse Masters: The Construction of Trafficking* (London, 2010), 11–13.

16. Stephanie A. Limoncelli suggests that efforts to combat prostitution at home led to increased control over women rather than increased liberties. *Politics of Trafficking.*

always, resourceful travelers who sometimes relied on selling sex to fashion a more promising future. Yet the public panic surrounding their exodus was nevertheless carefully crafted into a middle-class reform agenda that encompassed issues much broader than prostitution.

International Prostitution in Eastern Europe

In the Polish lands, women working as prostitutes had long crossed international frontiers to practice their trade. This kind of commerce was not labeled "trafficking" in contemporary reports until the late nineteenth century. During the 1850s, for example, professional prostitutes traveled regularly from towns across the Polish Kingdom to the annual fair in Nizhny Novgorod, famous for its lively brothel trade. They disguised themselves as female harpists or as members of a "singing choir" when crossing the frontier. Newspaper and police reports referred to such activity as mainly voluntary on the part of the migrating women. Only very rarely were organizers of this cross-border trade accused of coercion. Instead, the diplomatic corps and police officials alike overlooked the migration of women to work in brothels and failed to punish its ringleaders.[17] Beginning in the 1860s, traffic in young women moving across Eastern Europe to ports in Western Europe and then on to Latin America and Asia came to the attention of the Austrian government. In 1864, a Hungarian decree called attention to the shipment of girls bound for American brothels, and in 1867 Hungarians living in Egypt petitioned their consulate to take steps against human trafficking.[18] According to Dr. Josef Schrank, a contemporary Austrian specialist in trafficking issues, Hungarian girls were brought regularly to Vienna for the purpose of sexual exploitation throughout the 1850s and 1860s, but the police closed their eyes to this trade "as long as the human goods were not Austrian."[19] Indeed, throughout the period 1865–1885, Budapest's mayor ostensibly permitted the bribing of local authorities in order to facilitate the peaceful transfer of women and children across international lines. By 1880, the migration of women from the Polish lands bound for brothels in the Americas had risen dramatically, with elaborate schemes for bribing border guards in place. And yet few Polish newspapers or charity groups capitalized on the images of oppressed and abused young women marketed abroad.[20]

---

17. Milewski, *Ciemne sprawy dawnych warszawiaków*, 118.
18. Corbin, *Women for Hire*, 277–78.
19. "Handel kobietami na Węgrzech," *Czystość* 5, no. 26 (June 26, 1909): 406–9.
20. Macko, *Prostytucja*, 349–50.

Not until 1874, when the Austrian Chamber of Deputies called for an international conference to deal with the problem, did imperial attention focus on the movement of girls and young women across borders to work in the sex trade, and only in the last decade of the century was transnational prostitution the subject of imperial regulation. Despite pressure by the Chamber to insert language into the Austrian penal code prohibiting forced migration for prostitution, only in 1892 did Reichsrat deputies take up reforms to improve methods for the international tracking of missing girls.[21] In 1897, the German Reich added a clause to the Reich Criminal Code, punishing with two to five years imprisonment anyone who "by concealing his intentions, persuaded a women to emigrate with the purpose of delivering her into prostitution." At the same time Germany also signed extradition treaties with neighboring countries.[22]

At a popular level, narratives of sexual abduction began circulating in European media in the last decades of the nineteenth century. The hysteria surrounding the 1885 "Maiden Tribute of Modern Babylon" series published in the English newspaper *Pall Mall Gazette* sparked British public interest. The case introduced the paradigm of vulnerable "virgins ravished" rather than highlighting the sale of experienced, willing prostitutes to foreign brothels, as was more typical of international sex migration.[23] Later reports demonstrated that tales of British gentlemen capturing young women and transporting them overseas were greatly exaggerated. Nonetheless, the story took on a life of its own and helped sell papers by the thousands, giving opponents of regulated domestic prostitution fuel to stoke their campaigns. Such scandals proved useful for social reformers intent on conflating notions of slavery and coercion with the domestic brothel industry. By claiming that all prostitution involved coercion, opponents of the domestic trade leveraged images of racialized slavery to gain traction against the sex industry at home. Reformers employed tropes and vocabulary similar to those used in discussing the abolition of black slavery to describe the slavery of prostitution, adding moral power to their movement.[24] After the retraction of the British Contagious Diseases Acts in 1886, the antiprostitution activist Josephine Butler brought her campaign to abolish police-regulated prostitution

---

21. "Von Nah und Fern," *Arbeiter-Zeitung: Organ der Österreichischen Sozialdemokratie*, November 18, 1892, 1.

22. Corbin, *Women for Hire*, 277–78.

23. On the revelations of markets in young girls dealing out of London, see Walkowitz, *City of Dreadful Delight*; and Corbin, *Women for Hire*, 275–77.

24. De Vries, "'White Slaves' in a Colonial Nation," 44.

to continental Europe, traveling to Warsaw and Lwów, among other places, with her message about the abuses of tolerated sex work.

White Slavery in the Public Eye: The 1892 Lwów Trafficking Trial

The wider Polish public first gained access to detailed depictions of trafficking schemes through the well-publicized October1892 trial of twenty-seven accused traffickers in the Galician administrative capital of Lwów.[25] By highlighting the vagaries of commercial sex, the case turned the attention of Poland's social elite to the moral corruption of young girls.[26] Witnesses and readers of the daily press were treated to vivid accounts of the coercion, deceit, and physical abuse trafficked women suffered over a decade-long period. Stressing the presumed purity of the "victims," Polish- and German-language periodicals depicted victims as "white lilies" who had been "tricked" into going off to foreign lands and forced into "public debauchery."[27] Ten days of testimony allowed witnesses to recount their tales of abduction and the promises made to them for money, jobs, and husbands. They told of the humiliation of being auctioned off in the Ottoman capital and of their inability to escape their employers before paying the cost of their passage. The crowd of onlookers in the courtroom swelled each day as the city's bourgeois residents gazed on the poor unfortunates returned from their odyssey in the sexual jungles of the Middle East. Local newspapers published retrospectives of the "disappeared" while taking administrative authorities to task for their failure to launch rescue efforts sooner.

The Lwów trial captivated a public already preoccupied with the dangers of young women traveling unaccompanied on city streets. Proceedings unfolded in the broader atmosphere of a wave of concern about rising rates of female migration, increasing rates of domestic prostitution, and the enhanced

---

25. Educated Polish readers had access beginning in 1890 to Dr. V. M. Tarnovskii's studies depicting the techniques, prices, and trade routes traffickers employed to round up girls as young as nine and sell them to houses of prostitution. Venjamin Tarnovskii was Russia's premier authority on venereal disease and prostitution, whose work was translated into several European languages in the 1890s. See, for example, Tarnowsky [Tarnovskii] *Prostitution und Abolitionismus* (Hamburg, 1890), 33–51; and "Z badań nad prostytucyą," *Nowe Słowo* 3, no. 23 (December 1, 1904): 536. On Dr. Tarnovskii's career as a proponent of regulated prostitution and a follower of the Italian forensics specialist Cesare Lombroso, see Engelstein, *Keys to Happiness*, esp. 134–44.

26. On the details of the trial, see Bristow, *Prostitution and Prejudice*, 80–81; and Stauter-Halsted, "'A Generation of Monsters,'" 25–35.

27. "Z tajemnic społeczeństwa: Handlarz dziewcząt," *Gazeta Narodowa*, July 9, 1892, 2; and "Handlarze dziewcząt," *Gazeta Narodowa*, October 19,1892, 2.

visibility of a very mobile population of Jewish merchants. Just as the urban panic of the late 1890s helped distill the image of streetwalkers into distinct types in the public imagination, so too did the Lwów case introduce wide audiences to the terms by which sex trafficking would be understood in the period leading up to the First World War. In the two decades following the trial's conclusion, accusations of trafficking and stories of abducted women filled the pages of the mainstream press throughout the Polish lands.[28] White slavery became the subject of colorful exposés, editorials, and cautionary tales warning young women to beware of strange young men offering lucrative employment opportunities or marriage proposals.[29] Immediately following the trial, reports of missing and abducted women skyrocketed in Polish-language periodicals. Newspaper editors warned young women to beware of "unknown agents who offer them golden positions abroad as schoolteachers or household companions" lest they "turn into unhappy victims taken to America . . . to rot away in houses of debauchery." As one Poznań paper lamented, "many a gullible girl falls for these golden words and accompanies such unknown agents, [ending up in] houses of prostitution where they lose their health and become lifelong invalids."[30]

Aid agencies highlighted the horrific experiences of young women trapped in foreign brothels and the heroic efforts to which victims resorted in order to escape captivity. Victims were passed from station to station, ending up on steamers crossing the ocean to South American, North African, or Asian ports of call, and then delivered into the hands of Jewish traffickers. Taken at face value, these reports emphasized the naïveté of the victims and the diabolical schemes of the traffickers in their endless quest for "fresh flesh" to sell to foreign brothels. Women were coerced or duped into believing they would be placed in honest positions as waitresses, seamstresses, or governesses. Meanwhile, gullible parents of migrating women were unaware of the potential dangers of their trip and willingly trusted migration agencies to fulfill the promises made before departure. Announcements of girls rescued from the brink of sexual slavery circulated widely in the boulevard press and young women who went missing on their way to church were feared to have "become victims" of renowned traffickers whose nefarious networks

28. See, for example, the cycle of articles under the heading "Naganiacze," published in Warsaw's *Niwa* in 1896; "Handel żywym towarem," *Kurier Poranny* (June 1897); and "Handel dziewczętami," *Słowo*, August 12, 1899, 3.

29. The most widely circulated discussions included Posner, *Nad otchłania*; Wróblewski, *O prostytucji i handlu kobietami*; and Schrank, *Mädchenhandel und seine Bekampfung*.

30. *Dziennik Poznański*, January 14, 1897, 1, 4.

FIGURE 4.1　Wojciech Weiss, "Demon (w kawarnii)" (Devil in a Café).
Courtesy of the National Museum in Cracow (Muzeum Narodowe w Krakowie) and the Wojciech Weiss Museum Foundation (Fundacja Muzeum Wojciecha Weissa).

ensnared unsuspecting maidens across the Congress Kingdom and Galicia.[31] Habsburg authorities tracked "known traffickers" across Europe, inserting frequent announcements of sightings and arrests in major newspapers.[32]

For the Polish public, the drama of young women whisked away from city streets tapped into deeper anxieties about national weakness and the debilitating poverty of the lower classes. Reports stressed the ways in which white slavery was a problem uniquely pressing in the Polish territories. "Experts" estimated, for example, that some ten thousand "white slaves" were transported each year out of the Polish Kingdom alone to sexual prisons "through trickery, treachery, and sometimes brute force."[33] Agents

31. See, for example, the tale of two serving girls detained at the Lwów train station en route from Sniatyń in eastern Galicia using tickets to Buenos Aires purchased for them by a "swarthy Jew" whom authorities suspected of trafficking. "Co tam słychać w świecie," *Przyjaciel Sług*, February 4, 1900, 30–32; "Zniknięcie," *Przyjaciel Sług* 1 (June 1, 1902), 92; and "Handlarze dziewcząt," *Przyjaciel Sług*, July 6, 1902, 111–12.

32. In July 1907, police in Poznań announced the arrest of traffickers from Warsaw whom Austrian officials had been trailing. Because the men were traveling with a seventeen-year-old girl, they were remanded to the court in Berlin for kidnapping. "Akt betreffend des Mädchenhandel nach dem Auslande, 1896–1911." *Posenauer Zeitung*, July 30, 1907, APP, PPwP, 1815–1918, sygn. 6297.

33. St. Annański, "Krytyka i sprawozdania: Dr. Aug. Wróblewski, 'O prostytucji i handlu kobietami,' Warsaw 1909," *Społeczeństwo* 35 (1909): 418–19. Reformers latched onto Dr. Wróblewski's wildly inflated estimate of forced emigration and cited it repeatedly thereafter.

from throughout Western Europe and Latin America reportedly took advantage of the region's inherited poverty and the growing demand for prostitutes in the New World to initiate a lively trade in women beginning in the 1860s.[34] Newspapers stressed that brothels in the Near East and Latin America were staffed primarily with girls smuggled out of the Polish lands. Exaggerated accounts of Polish women serving as prostitutes abroad did nothing to calm this anxiety. "The fact is," wrote one Polish journalist, that "in brothels in Buenos Aires and South Africa 90 percent of prostitutes are Polish girls of Christian and Jewish background."[35] The trafficking expert Major Wagener famously proclaimed Lwów as one of the "greatest centers of debauchery on earth" because of its centrality to the international sex trade.[36]

Coverage of the Lwów trial brought the anxieties of sex trafficking home to the Polish reading public. No longer could white slavery be portrayed as a distant problem plaguing only the countries of Western Europe. Indeed, by the aftermath of the first international trafficking conference held in London in June 1899, specialists on the sex trade estimated that the export of women and children was "most intense" in the Polish districts of Austria, Russia, and Germany. Polish writers warned "young people who want to go abroad" to be aware of this danger.[37] Reporters soon discovered a "formal system" of trade in girls based out of the Austrian crown land of Galicia. Austrian officials complained that the trade in women had "grown more lively" by the 1890s and Galician pundits repeatedly proclaimed that the vast majority of trafficked women originated in the Polish and Jewish communities of Galicia, which reportedly comprised "the most significant terrain" for trafficking outside of Romania. Galician Governor General Count Feliks Badeni lamented that hundreds of local girls were being "sold into slavery and delivered to foreign brothels by special commissioners traveling around the province. It may be difficult to fathom," Count Badeni admitted, but "this monstrosity has become a business, organized on a wide scale, operating arrogantly under the eye of the Austrian police."[38] Warning of culprits

---

34. Macko, *Prostytucja*, 347–49. Macko argues that the migration of young women to service the brothels of Latin America and elsewhere began in the mid-nineteenth century owing to the extreme poverty and relatively porous borders in some regions of partitioned Poland, and the improved rail and ship communications linking the Polish lands to other countries.

35. "Kronika," *Nowe Słowo* 2, no. 10 (May 15, 1903): 226.

36. "Przeciw handlowi dziewczętami," *Nowiny dla Wszystkich,* October 18, 1905, 4.

37. "Handel dziewczętami," *Słowo,* August 12, 1899, 3.

38. "Handlarze kobiet," *Słowo,* July 31, 1891, 4.

who sought to hire "single girls for immoral tasks," newspapers appealed to their middle-class readership to protect the virtue of their teenage daughters. Traffickers intending to "trade in human goods for the most hideous purposes" were on the prowl everywhere, they cautioned, and every young woman traveling unaccompanied was potentially vulnerable.[39] The ubiquitous reporting on the unhappy fate of women traveling alone encouraged readers to suspect the worst when a daughter failed to write home or a domestic servant quit without notice.

A World Turned Upside Down

All of these presentations contributed to a debate about the position of Poland within the continuum of civilized societies. Polish-language reporting on the sex trade stressed the inverted morality of light-skinned girls from the "civilized" world being whisked away by "darker" primitives. Images of Polish women turned Middle Eastern sex slaves "grated on the [public's] nerves," making readers wish they could wake up from the nightmarish scenarios, according to one editor. Realization that the captives were doubly demeaned, having been sold into sexual slavery and entrapped in a non-Christian or non-European environment, increased the anxiety of an already uneasy readership. Newspaper articles emphasized that "some horrible trafficker had sold them for pleasure to Turks and Brazilians," calling attention to the enslavement of Polish women by captors from "lesser civilizations."[40] Polish journalists uncovered other tales of trickery and sexual abuse in foreign brothels and used them to increase the level of public panic to a feverish pitch. They reported on the case of Katarzyna Adamowska, the daughter of a carpenter from Przemyśl, Galicia, who was sold along with an acquaintance to an agent in Pest. She was then transported to a bordello in Constantinople, where she remained imprisoned in a heavily guarded cell and was beaten regularly along with a dozen other Galician girls. Heroically, young Katarzyna escaped through a second-story window in the bordello and found her way to the Austrian Consulate. Agents there assisted her in getting back home to Galicia. A less savory fate awaited her young contemporary, Marya, whose story appeared in the Galician press during the summer prior to the Lwów court case. Marya had been transferred to the Ottoman capital, where her captors reportedly beat her to death for refusing to ply her trade.[41]

---

39. "Kronika: Towarzystwo młodzieży 'Ethos' w Krakowie," *Nowe Słowo* 6, no. 9 (1907): 218–19.
40. "Handlarze dziewcząt," October 19, 1892, 2.
41. "Handlarze kobiet," 4.

The Polish-speaking public read ever more frightening accounts of the cruel tactics traffickers employed and of the fate of their victims. Cracow's police director emphasized the parallels between the treatment of alleged victims of sexual exploitation and the experience of African slaves. "Once they fall into the net," he emphasized, "they become human goods, and traders treat them many times worse and more shamefully than black slaves," he reported to Warsaw's *Słowo*.[42] The trajectory of young women caught up in sex trafficking rings was distilled in many of these accounts into an expectation of certain death once they left their homeland. Drawing on existing paradigms of innocence corrupted that played out in discussions of domestic prostitution, reports claimed that "these pure girls, once they are shipped abroad, will never return again. The villains who capture them sell them to the harems of the pashas and the *begs* in the east, from which none of them will ever see the light of day again. Their life, their shame, their suffering and their tears, remain a secret hidden from us. . . . Their mothers can cry over them as if they were dead."[43] Sexual exploitation by Muslim pashas and *begs* made the possibility of a young woman returning to her previous existence all the more unlikely. Instead, they would be ravished both sexually and racially, making their reentry into mainstream European society a virtual impossibility. The Lwów case highlighted nonwhite Jewish traffickers in Muslim Constantinople as the primary setting for these crimes, offering all the unsettling elements of a world turned upside down. Innocent white Christian girls from "civilized" countries were enslaved at the hands of "dark Jews" in the barbaric Middle East. "Degenerate" people, according to reports of the crime, left girls in "shame and slavery, worse than death," more horrific even than "Jack the Ripper," who took "only the lives of his victims."[44] Poland here was the innocent and her rulers were standing by while rapacious "foreigners" kidnapped her pure young women.

Innocent Bourgeois Daughters?

Early reports from sex-trafficking trials portrayed forced migrants as reflecting the paradigmatic qualities of bourgeois femininity, a stereotype that fit some of the witnesses more aptly than others. Survivors of sex-migration schemes such as those caught in the net of the Lwów defendants were characterized as "overwhelmingly frail" and able to speak "only hesitantly," traits that contrasted

42. Ibid.
43. "Z tajemnic społeczeństwa," 2.
44. "Handlarze dziewcząt," October 19, 1892, 2.

sharply with the depictions of the brazen hussies lining Warsaw's commercial streets. In contrast to the hardened, streetwise prostitutes featured in the boulevard press, readers of trafficking reports discovered witnesses with faces "of purity . . . pale like sorrow," features characteristics of Victorian female virtue. Depictions of "sky-blue eyes, like veiled fog—and hair the color of straw" implied Polish Christian heritage rather than a Jewish background, though the particular witness's name—Róża Rosenreich—suggests otherwise. Young Róża, we learn, displayed an "enigmatic silence about her, as if having returned from the abyss of purgatory she is frightened to remember it and is worried she will be sent there again . . . her pale lips are stubbornly pressed together from nervousness." The presentation is in no way altered by the news, later in her testimony, that "it is true that before [her] seduction to Constantinople [she] sold love" for two years in her hometown in Poland.[45]

Such reports helped boost attendance at trafficking trials, the courtrooms of which appear ironically to have been the province of bourgeois females. Only a "scant dozen or so" observers made their way to the courtroom in the first days of the Lwów proceedings. But after sensational reportage equated international sex migration with kidnapping, slavery, a permanent fall from grace, and assigned primary responsibility to Jewish perpetrators, residents flocked to the trial in huge numbers. By the second day, interest in the proceedings was "feverish" and the gallery "overflowed with curious listeners." On day three, the crush of observers was so great the government required special identification cards for admittance, and the corridors and vestibules of the courthouse were choked with those denied entrance. Finally, the judge resorted to forbidding women from entering the courtroom, which resulted in a significantly smaller crowd at later sessions, suggesting much of the earlier attention came from the large population of bourgeois housewives in the municipal area.[46] In keeping with more widespread concern about protecting innocent women from contamination through exposure to sordid tales of debauchery, the judge may well have sought to insulate the city's middle-class female residents from particularly spicy testimony.

Yet press accounts also tacitly recognized a degree of conscious decision making on the part of the trafficking victims, suggesting that the young women on the witness stand may have been aware of what awaited them abroad and that they might not have been as cloistered before leaving home as they were initially depicted. Reports note, for example, that witnesses

---

45. "Z tajemnic społeczeństwa," 2.
46. "Handlarze dziewcząt," October 19–25, 1892, 2.

were often very much "reconciled to their fate."[47] In some cases, parents acknowledged accepting payment to release their daughters to the accused traffickers. Evidence from the 1892 trial indicates that at least one mother demanded 500 złoty in "compensation" when her daughter was taken away to Constantinople, a process of "selling" one's offspring that could only have implied illicit purposes. By 1911, Cracow newspapers reported that trafficking in women was frequently "conducted completely openly . . . under the protection of [the girls'] mothers."[48] Nonetheless, reporters stubbornly maintained the tropes of innocence and vulnerability even while recognizing that "many of [the victims] belonged to that class of women about whom one does not speak in society."[49] Some witnesses even openly confessed that they had *knowingly* accompanied their "captors" to distant ports; others depicted the harsh conditions in Turkish brothels as better than what they left behind back home in Galicia. "After all," testified one, "I would go there again."[50]

Despite the suggestion that women participated actively in the early stages of sex smuggling operations, images of innocent maidens disappearing off city streets helped foster a stereotypical understanding of sex migration in the popular press. Accounts of white slaves "allured through trickery and deceit and often with brute force" persisted despite evidence of much more complicated scenarios.[51] Over and over, tales of trafficking emphasized violence and deceit in smuggling women out of Polish territory to their sexual captivity overseas. "Again, girls are disappearing," wrote the editors of *Przyjaciel Sług*, the household servant magazine, in February 1900. The Friday before New Year's Day, Emilia Maryniak "disappeared without a trace" from Rakowicka Street and Marya Czerwinka vanished on December 21 from the Praga area of Warsaw.[52] "Two thugs" tried to drag away a young woman in broad daylight off Królewska Street in Warsaw in September 1909.[53] Such "disappeared" women were reportedly "hidden away in bordellos, and when they refuse to give themselves up voluntarily they [were] urged with the help of starvation, beatings, and torments of various kinds until they give in."[54]

The imperial police often unwittingly contributed to the trafficking scare, treating reports of kidnapped women in an unreflective way and passing on

---

47. "Handlarze dziewcząt," October 19, 1892, 2.
48. "Bagno wielkomiejskie," *Ilustrowany Kurier Codzienny,* May 5, 1911, 1–2.
49. "Handlarze dziewcząt," October 19, 1892, 2.
50. Testimony of Elka Jenner and Chana Herman, "Handlarze dziewcząt," October 20, 1892, 2.
51. Wróblewski, *O prostytucyi,* 7.
52. "Co tam słychać w świecie," February 4, 1900, 30–32.
53. "Raz na miesiąc: Gawęda," *Pracownica Polska* 2, no. 9 (September 1909): 15–16.
54. Wróblewski, *O prostytucyi,* 7.

fears of parents and local employers. The late 1880s and early 1890s saw a spike in media coverage of disappeared women throughout Galicia, putting the problem on the public's radar as never before.[55] In response to the Austrian Interior Ministry's charge for urban police departments to provide lists of suspected traffickers, authorities in Lwów drew up biographic details on some fifty-nine male and female suspects, along with information about dozens of young "victims" who had vanished from Galician cities like Tarnopol, Lwów, and Cracow or who were suspected of having been "abducted and ravished" or "taken to America."[56] In 1904, the Austro-Hungarian consul to Alexandria, Egypt, visited some of the young women who had been rescued from their ordeal and confirmed their pitiable status. The vice consul reported to Cracow's police commissioner that some "70 to 80 percent of the prostitutes in public houses in Alexandria were from Galicia and Bukowina" and that those he observed displayed obvious signs of having been abused. "It was clear to me from the first moment I saw them," he concluded, "that they were victims of trafficking." The girls, whom he referred to as "white slaves," were, he said, "often in a state of unbelief and often have been physically mishandled in the most extreme way."[57] Even without complete information about the conditions of their travel and the degree of voluntarism involved in their behavior, police were quick to associate missing women with sexual captivity and prostitution with physical abuse.

Depictions of female vulnerability in the face of crafty trafficking agents soon sprang up in mainstream Polish media. Like accounts circulating in Western Europe and North America, stories featuring debauched women on the borders leveraged testimony of victimized women to stress the sexual danger they risked when leaving the middle-class home. Popular papers ran urgent announcements of "girls disappearing," describing young women abducted by "some gentleman" and "headed off in an unknown direction."[58] Eighteen-year-old Marya Czajkowska, a Lwów serving girl, reportedly "disappeared without a trace" in 1902, having left for church one Sunday and never returned. "There is great fear that the young thing has become a

---

55. Polish newspapers had quietly covered trafficking rings during the preceding decade, but these cases never went to trial. See, for example, *Czas* 6 (1885); "Handel kobietami," *Kurier Warszawski* (1891); and *Tygodnik Ilustrowany's* 1891 rebuttal. Such stories were no doubt prompted by the sex trafficking case publicized in London's *Pall Mall Gazette* in 1885.

56. List of Lwów suspected traffickers, APKr, DPKr 110, 1203–1210.

57. Letter from Vice Counsel Szarvasy, Austro-Hungarian consul in Alexandria, Egypt, to the police commissioner in Krakow, dated Lwów, September 8, 1904 (Alexandria date March 24, 1904), APKr, DPKr 110, 1245–58.

58. "Co tam słychać w świecie?" *Przyjaciel Sług*, February 3, 1901, 24.

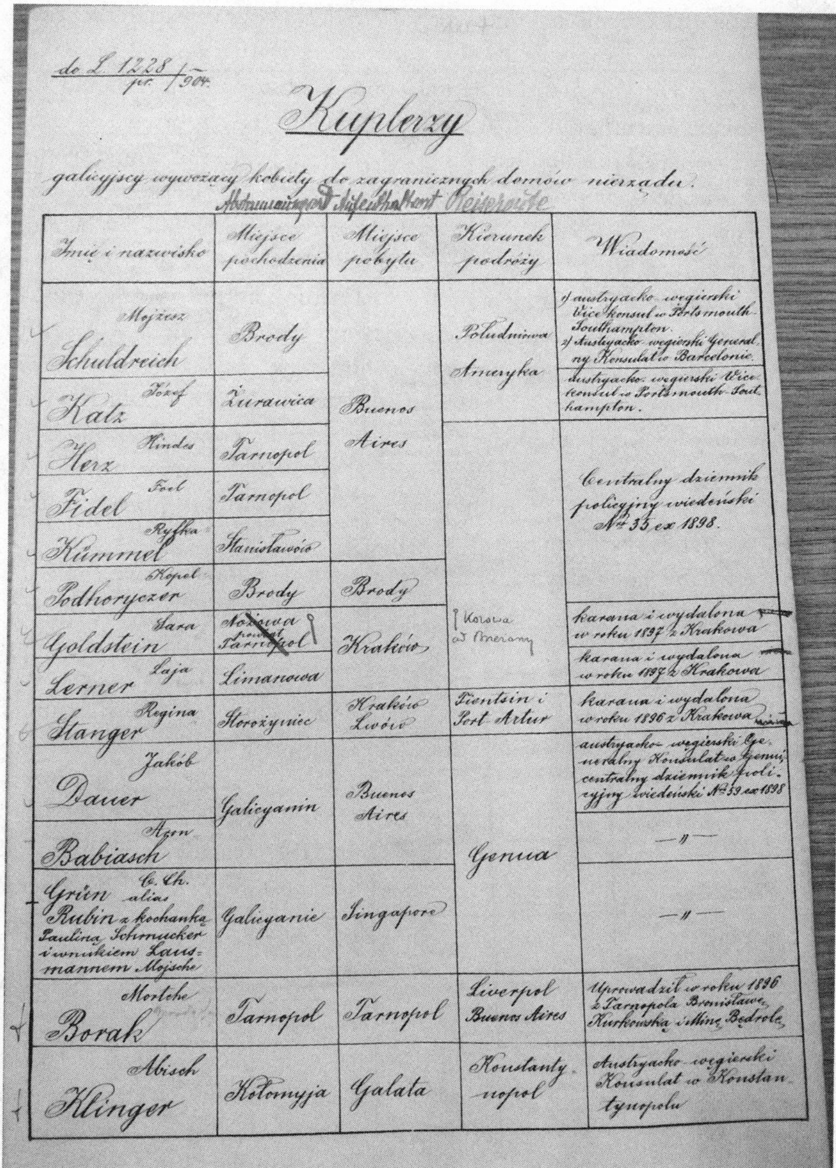

FIGURE 4.2 "Traffickers transporting Galician women to houses of prostitution abroad." In response to a 1904 directive from the Austrian Interior Ministry, the Lwów Police Department drew up this list of several dozen suspected traffickers and the locations of their bordellos. Note that the majority of the names on the list are typical Jewish names.

Courtesy of the Cracow National Archive (Archiwum Państwowe w Krakowie).

victim," the paper recounted ominously.[59] Anxiety about threats to the sexual order drove fears about the dangers threatening young women once they moved beyond the limits of parental control. Historians have noted that melodramatic warnings about the threat of white slavery often fell into a paradigmatic script that emphasized the perceived dangers of young women stepping outside their parental home. As the Dutch scholar Petra de Vries points out, "an innocent or rather stupid girl was apt to 'fall' by hanging around the street, going to the big city, travelling abroad or having 'bad' friends. In other words, dangers of a sexual nature did not seem to exist in the 'here and now,' but were projected beyond the cherished safe haven of marriage and family. Strange gentlemen should always be treated with suspicion."[60] Ironically, as de Vries stresses, the sexual danger to which young women were exposed within the private setting of bourgeois households where they functioned as service personnel was often greater than that to which they were subject in public spaces. Nonetheless, this private vulnerability was rarely discussed.

But even the parental home and the pure Polish countryside were not safe havens for innocent girls, since representatives of foreign brothels purportedly "sneaked their agents" into the most remote "peasant huts, and into the attics and cellars of great cities." Gangs of professional traffickers were reported to have roamed the villages searching intently for "poor, ignorant girls, blooming with the fat of youth," and captured their victims through "deceit and persuasion."[61] Anxiety about abductions soon reached a feverish pitch, prompting middle-class women's magazines to circulate repeated warnings for young women to "watch out!" for rapacious procurers and be suspicious even of close acquaintances making offers of well-paid work abroad.

Uses of an Image

The white-slavery narrative provided a common vocabulary that informed a number of themes connected with the nineteenth-century sex trade. From attitudes toward Jews, to concerns about social dislocation and the transatlantic movement of peoples, to anxiety tied to the industrializing economy, white slavery offered a framework for understanding a whole host of new

59. "Zniknięcie," 92.
60. De Vries, "'White Slaves' in a Colonial Nation," 47.
61. Marya Rygier, "Walka z prostytucyą," *Nowe Słowo* 2, no. 17 (August 1, 1903): 394.

challenges facing the population of late partitioned Poland. The sex-trafficking paradigm presented one way to analyze and control such disorienting phenomena. By the early years of the twentieth century, a broadening array of social reformers, political activists, and charitable societies began employing the rhetoric of sex slavery to mobilize public support for their particular causes. Descriptions of accused traffickers circulated in imperial police bulletins and in diplomatic exchanges between the Habsburg Monarchy and embassies in the Ottoman Empire, Egypt, India, China, and Argentina. The story took hold of the public imagination, prompting the birth of international organizations devoted to fighting the scourge of sex trafficking and defending the presumed virtue of its victims.

Closer to home, Polish antiprostitution reformers relied on sensationalist reports of trafficking victims to encourage the correlation of domestic regulated prostitution with international sexual "slavery" and to encourage the assumption that all prostitution was accompanied by violence, fraud, or abuse of trust.[62] Feminist organizations tied to Cracow's *Nowe Słowo* and Warsaw's *Ster* took advantage of missing-person reports to promote their campaign for the abolition of tolerated domestic prostitution. Activists neatly conjoined descriptions of the common process of trading young women among brothel keepers in a given location, on the one hand, with the coercion implied in women crossing state boundaries to practice prostitution, on the other. Leaders of antiregulation abolitionist societies began relying on the upswing in female migration to draw public attention to their cause. At the same time, anxiety about vulnerable female travelers helped propel the inauguration of rescue agencies.[63] Organizations such as the Society to Prevent Trafficking in Women (examined in chapter 7) portrayed the naïve and childlike prostitute as the appropriate beneficiary of their rescue and repatriation efforts. Purity campaigns, like Doctor Augustine Wróblewski's Ethos Society (discussed in chapter 7) played up the numbers of "white slaves" captured through "trickery, treachery and . . . brute force."[64]

The panic surrounding white slavery also tapped into a very real sense of anxiety about single, unaccompanied young women leaving European shores

---

62. Corbin, *Women for Hire*, 275–77.

63. Stephanie A. Limoncelli stresses the link between international trafficking fears and domestic social movements in *Politics of Trafficking*.

64. Stephanie Wahab points out that social-work responses to prostitution in the nineteenth century were heavily influenced by the notion that women needed to be protected, that prostitutes were weak and incapable of taking care of themselves, and therefore that increased social control was the best way to eliminate prostitution. "'For Their Own Good?': Sex Work, Social Control, and Social Workers, a Historical Perspective," *Journal of Sociology and Social Welfare* 29, no. 4 (2002): 1–2.

in droves each year during the decades around the turn of the century. Those who stayed behind, and especially the nationally conscious social elite, found this migration pattern unsettling. They worried about the breakdown of the family implied by increased female independence through transatlantic migration. Fears about the migrating woman, who was perceived as "passive, foolish, and naïve" (in contrast to her male counterpart, who tended to be viewed instead as "active, adventurous, brave, and deserving of admiration"), sparked concerns about the disintegration of the family, juvenile delinquency, and divorce.[65] Single women traveling alone risked tarnishing their reputation of sexual purity and challenging Poland's national honor. Women who left home, who abandoned native soil, and who at the same time exposed themselves to sexual danger also placed Poland's reputation as a culture at risk since that reputation was to some extent dependent on women's ability to uphold high moral standards.[66] Such women have often been vulnerable to a "boundary crisis" in which a community "draws a symbolic set of parentheses" around certain human behavior during periods of cultural stress, limiting the range of acceptable action.[67] White slavery may have contributed to such a boundary crisis, which in the Polish lands was made more prescient by ongoing concerns over the loss of national sovereignty.[68] These are the concerns to which we turn in chapter 5. Finally, the majority of those accused of international trafficking were Jewish, a fact that complicated contemporary discussions of the subject and that continues to underlie analyses of nineteenth-century trafficking. Any assessment of "white slavery" must take into consideration the anxiety caused by the visible Jewish presence in the sex trade, especially out of the Polish lands, both among non-Jews and within the Jewish community itself.[69] The position of Jews in the imagination of Polish commentators and in the lived experience of Polish migrants is the subject of chapter 6.

---

65. Doezema, "Loose Women or Lost Women?" 19–24. See also, William Thomas and Florian Znaniecki's classic work of sociology, *The Polish Peasant in Europe and America*, 3 vols. (Chicago, 1919), in which the peasant community's system of social morality is dissolved through industrialization and emigration.

66. Donna J. Guy, *Sex and Danger in Buenos Aires: Prostitution, Family, and Nation in Argentina* (Lincoln, NE, 1991), 7.

67. Kai Erikson, *Wayward Puritans: A Study in the Sociology of Deviance* (New York, 1966), 10, cited in Frederick K. Grittner, *Myth, Ideology, and American Law* (New York, 1990), 8.

68. On the importance of female public behavior in the cultural construction of national boundaries, see also Nira Yuval-Davis, *Gender and Nation* (London, 1997), 45–56.

69. The Austrian social reformer Bertha Pappenheim wrote extensively about Jewish involvement in trafficking out of Galicia. See Elizabeth Loentz, *Let Me Continue to Speak the Truth: Bertha Pappenheim as Author and Activist* (Cincinnati, OH, 2007), 123–56; and Kaplan, "Prostitution, Morality Crusades, and Feminism," 621.

Chapter 5

Sex Trafficking and Human Migration

Women who leave their countries and later are found
selling sex in someone else's . . . disappear from
migration studies . . . and reappear in criminological
[studies] . . . where they are called victims.

—Laura Agustin, "The Disappearing of a Migration
Category: Migrants Who Sell Sex"

Sex trafficking at its core is a migration prob-
lem. The pattern of young women traveling abroad on their own, often
with the help of intermediaries, was increasingly prevalent in the early years
of the twentieth century, part of a much larger movement of people out of
eastern Europe.[1] Economic deprivation in the underdeveloped, underindus-
trialized Polish territories created a pool of needy females, many of them
recent arrivals from the impoverished countryside to the swelling cities.[2] The
ubiquity of open borders and the crush of migrants traveling abroad in search
of "legitimate" positions provided camouflage for would-be traffickers and
their customers. Meanwhile, the boomtowns of Chicago, New York, Rio,
Buenos Aires, and the cities of North Africa and the Middle East supplied
the clientele to augment demand for prostitution outside of Europe.[3] This

---

1. On the relative percentage of female migrants out of Europe in the nineteenth century, see Donna
Gabaccia, "Women of the Mass Migrations: From Minority to Majority, 1820–1930," in *European
Migrants: Global and Local Perspectives,* ed. Dirk Hoerder and Leslie Page Moch (Boston, 1996), 90–111.
2. Ewa Morawska, "Labor Migrations of Poles in the Atlantic World Economy, 1880–1914," in
Comparative Studies in Society and History 31, no. 2 (1989): 237–72; and Annemarie Steidl, Engelbert
Stockhammer, and Hermann Zeitlhofer, "Relations among Internal, Continental, and Transatlantic
Migration in Late Imperial Austria," *Social Science History* 31, no. 1 (2007): 61–92.
3. On the growing demand for European prostitutes in Argentina, see Guy, "White Slavery,
Public Health," 60–80.

massive migration shaped the context in which the exodus of single females would be understood. Not only were the Polish territories a key source of voluntary labor migration, but pogroms and discriminatory legislation in the Russian Empire also left millions of Jews homeless and hungry, forcing them to search for livelihoods outside their customary communities.[4] Jewish refugees made their way by the thousands to the Habsburg Monarchy, Western Europe, and the Americas in search of religious tolerance and economic opportunity.[5] The prevalence of migrants and migration agents from the Jewish community across the region gave the trafficking tale a particular cast, complicating our understanding of interethnic dynamics at border crossings.[6] In short, labor migration and sex migration out of eastern Europe occurred at roughly the same moment, both engendered risks and abuses, and both were subject to nationalist pressures and imperial restrictions. In the Polish case, incorporating accusations of trafficking into the broader migration story allows us to read portrayals of coerced and duped women against the backdrop of more generalizable anxieties about national decline and population depletion.

To put the sex trade in this context, it is crucial to understand how disorienting and disruptive the larger movement of people in the nineteenth century was for both governments and the broader public. In the face of near-constant migration out of eastern Europe, government officials struggled to track the whereabouts of their subjects with any degree of accuracy, leading to wildly exaggerated claims about lost and kidnapped souls. The chaos surrounding the exodus of millions of illiterate and easily duped migrants prompted a series of elaborate migration scams and abuses, many of them publicized by imperial powers in an effort to slow the pace of emigration. Historians have long bracketed these migration streams, placing single female

---

4. Brigette Hamann looks at the mass migration of Jews out of the Pale of Settlement and their connection to the prostitution trade; see *Hitler's Vienna*, 330–35.

5. Jewish migration out of the Russian Pale of Settlement to the United States alone reached a pace of over eighty thousand per year by the end of the nineteenth century, with a total of 2.8 million Jews leaving Russia between 1880 and 1930. Antony Polonsky, *The Jews in Poland and Russia*, vol. 2, *1881–1914* (Oxford, 2010), 18–21. See also Jonathan Frankel, "The Crisis of 1881–82 as 'Turning-Point in Modern Jewish History,'" in *The Legacy of Jewish Migration: 1881 and Its Impact*, ed. David Berger (New York, 1983), 9–22; Zosa Szajkowski, "How the Mass Migration to America Began," *Jewish Social Studies* 4, no. 4 (1942): 291–310; and Hans Rogger, "Government Policy on Jewish Emigration," in *Jewish Policies and Right-Wing Politics in Imperial Russia* (Berkeley, 1996), 176–87.

6. According to a report from the Swiss Consul at Buenos Aires in 1897, for example, the international agents transporting prostitutes from Europe were mainly Polish Jews. The same report indicates that 40 percent of prostitutes in Buenos Aires originated in "Poland" and an additional 15 percent from Russia itself; 10 percent came from Austria. Those traveling from the Polish territories were characterized as heavily Jewish as well. *Le relevement social: Supplement*, June 1, 1897, quoted in Corbin, *Women for Hire*, 297.

migrants in a separate category from those traveling as part of families, and disaggregating Jewish refugees from Christian labor migrants. As a consequence, women who traveled independently and who sometimes turned to prostitution in their adopted homes have rarely been assessed in the context of the larger trends of migration history.[7] Instead, scholarly research has underrepresented the autonomy of these migrants, referring to them as "victims of trafficking," "forced migrants," or "prostituted women," labels that simplify their experience and turn them into passive participants in their own fate.[8] In this way, the scholarly framework repeats and reinforces the contemporary melodramatic narrative pattern of seduction and abandonment, a narrative that deprives female actors of agency and reduces the chaotic condition of migration and sex trade to familiar comprehensible tropes.

To address this lacuna, this chapter looks beyond the melodrama of kidnapping and coercion to examine young female migrants in the context of their lives at home before departing, their personal ambitions, and the difficult decisions they were asked to make.[9] Archival evidence suggests that many alleged trafficking victims in this period voluntarily accompanied their migration agents, at least on the initial leg of the journey, and that some even understood the activities they would be performing abroad. As we have seen, a close look at the details behind the "captivity narratives" circulating everywhere at the turn of the twentieth century suggests more human agency, more ambition, and more ingenuity on the part of female travelers than the standard story of passive victimhood implies. To evaluate the plight of young women caught up in what historians have recorded as sex migration, we need to follow Sara Rabinowitsch's advice above and assess more fully

---

7. On the limitations of research on the gendered components of migration history, see Stephanie Nawyn, A. Reosti, and L. Gjokaj, "Gender in Motion: How Gender Precipitates International Migration," in *Advances in Gender Research* 13 (2009): 175–202; Elinor Kofman, "Female 'Bird of Passage' a Decade Later: Gender and Immigration in the European Union," *International Migration Review* 33 (1999): 269–99; Sarah Mahler and Patricia Pessar, "Gender Matters: Ethnographers Bring Gender from the Periphery toward the Core of Migration Studies," *International Migration Review* 40, no. 1 (2006): 27–63; Donna Gabaccia, *From the Other Side: Women, Gender, and Immigrant Life in the U.S., 1820–1990* (Bloomington, IN, 1994); Gabaccia and Franca Iacovetta, eds., *Women, Gender, and Transnational Lives: Italian Workers of the World* (Toronto, 2003); and Pierrette Hondagneu-Sotelo, *Gendered Transitions* (Berkeley, 1994).

8. Laura Maria Agustin, *Sex at the Margins: Migration, Labour Markets, and the Rescue Industry* (London, 2007), 2–7.

9. On new approaches to understanding sex trafficking, see Laura Agustin, "The Disappearing of a Migration Category: Migrants Who Sell Sex," *Journal of Ethnic and Migration Studies* 32, no. 1 (2006): 29–47; and Maybritt Jill Alpes, "The Traffic in Voices: Reconciling Experiences of Migrant Women in Prostitution with Paradigms of 'Human Trafficking,'" *Human Security Journal* 6 (Spring 2008): 34–45.

the conditions prompting thousands of young women to seek a way out of economic misery by turning to migration.

Migration Fever, Migration Abuses

A huge portion of the population in the Polish lands was on the move during the decades leading up to World War I. Improved railway connections, low transatlantic fares, and effective telegraph communications helped drive the mass transfer of people out of the region. This heightened mobility brought with it chaos, corruption, and anxiety about the fate of loved ones across the sea.[10] Mediators who assisted prospective migrants with the purchase of rail and steamer tickets played a vital role in recruiting individuals of all kinds for emigration, but were also infamous for their fraudulent schemes. Steamship companies hired hundreds of such agents to scour the countryside in search of prospective passengers, while mining and industrial enterprises sent recruiters to locate sturdy laborers.[11] Local entrepreneurs often worked independently, skimming profits by charging inflated ticket prices. The ubiquitous presence of migration agents across the east European landscape confused the context in which travelers made decisions. Single young women, like their male counterparts, fell victim to fantastical tales and abusive tactics, sometimes agreeing to questionable commitments for positions abroad. The nature of the work and recruitment techniques varied, yet migrants of both genders were vulnerable to trickery, false promises, and even physical danger during their journey. The line between voluntary migration and trafficking was thinner than we might suppose.

In the Polish territories, much of the population dreamed day and night of relocating to a wealthier corner of the world. "Argentine fever," in the 1890s, like its earlier cousin "Brazilian fever," gripped whole communities, leaving village populations ravaged.[12] Residents were so confident they would be leaving for the New World soon that many sold all of their belongings in the expectation of imminent departure. The dire

---

10. John D. Klier, "Emigration Mania in Late-Imperial Russia: Legend and Reality," in *Patterns of Emigration, 1850–1914*, ed. Aubrey Newman and Stephen W. Massil (London, 1996), 21–30; and Gregorz Maria Kowalski, *Przestępstwa emigracyjne w Galicji, 1897–1918* (Cracow, 2003).

11. Tara Zahra, "Travel Agents on Trial: Policing Mobility in East-Central Europe, 1889–1989," *Past and Present* 223, no. 1 (2014): 161–93.

12. On Polish attitudes toward migration to Brazil in the 1890s and Argentina in the early years of the twentieth century, see Benjamin P. Murdzek, *Emigration in Polish Social-Political Thought, 1870–1914* (Boulder, CO, 1977), 61–69, 103–7; and Leopold Caro, *Emigracya i polityka emigracyjna ze szczególnym uwzględnieniem stosunków polskich*, trans. Karol Englisch (Poznań, 1914), 217–18.

poverty in many communities and encouragement from family members abroad combined to prompt rash decisions. Letters from earlier migrants convinced poor residents that "every colonist in Argentina [was] given his own plot of land" that was so rich that it easily produced "enough to support a family and then some." As one newspaper concluded, "it is not surprising that someone who has known only poverty since childhood would believe such things."[13] One consequence of this optimistic attitude toward migration was a tendency for young migrants to act "quite gullible and irresponsible" when presented with advertisements that promised them lucrative positions and tantalizing professional opportunities abroad.[14] Partially because of such enticements, more than three-quarters of a million Poles, Ruthenians, and Jews left Austrian Galicia alone during the thirty years preceding World War I.[15] Still others migrated internally, flooding in from the countryside to the sweatshops of Warsaw, Łódź, and Białystok or crossing from Russian Poland and Galicia into Prussia in search of seasonal agricultural jobs and positions in factories.[16] "Throughout the length and breadth of the country," a contemporary commentator summarized, "in the Polish and Ruthenian villages the population is moving."[17]

The sustained exodus prompted imperial concern about the loss of labor power and military conscripts. Austrian officials complained that the shortage of workers damaged livestock, reduced consumption in the cities, and caused meat to be sold at unprecedentedly high prices since the vast majority of migrants were peasants who were fleeing land shortages, high taxes, and crippling indemnity payments. Newspapers ran stories describing whole villages turned into ghost towns, emptied of all productive laborers. Government officials circulated elaborate warnings designed to discourage the flow of young workers from European shores. The harsh treatment of migrants en route from eastern Europe became legion, prompting state bureaucracies to

---

13. "Out of every ten craftsmen, barely five are needed, and out of five porters only one is needed," observed one commentator. "Argentyna," *Izraelita*, April 6, 1901, 173–74.

14. "Przeciw handlowi dziewczętami," 4. This report on the 1905 Bremen Congress on Combating Trafficking in Women quotes Major Wegener's [sic] reference to Dr. Chatelet's finding that some 59 percent of the girls who resorted to paid sex did so out of hunger.

15. Caro, *Emigracya i polityka emigracyjna*, 34–35.

16. Between 1885 and 1888, the Prussian government expelled at least thirty thousand Poles and Jews from its territory, arguing that they were unfit for permanent settlement. Tobias Brinkmann, "Why Paul Nathan Attacked Albert Ballin: The Transatlantic Mass Migration and the Privatization of Prussia's Eastern Border Inspection, 1886–1914," *Central European History* 43 (2010): 54; and Macko, *Prostytucja*, 347–49.

17. "Ludzie czy szakale: Emigranci a Towarzystwa przewozowe i ich agenci," *Gazeta Ludowa*, August 4, 1912, 4.

take on increased responsibility for protecting their subjects abroad.[18] Trafficking accusations were but one reflection of imperial anxiety over the loss of personnel and the potential threat to the liberty of their subjects.[19]

Meanwhile, Polish nationalists worried about the impact of mass migration on the demographics of a reborn Polish state. Opponents of emigration warned, for example, that the "nation . . . should not squander its strength and its blood in the service of foreigners . . . or in the improvement of conditions [abroad] that are of no concern to us."[20] Leopold Caro, a Polish lawyer and opponent of emigration, helped popularize the view that migration contributed to a decline in overall morality as families resettled in communities lacking adequate leadership from organized religion.[21] For Caro, migrants were exposed to a whole host of threats when they left home, including "brutal foreign employers, the neglect of religious practice, the ease of contracting infectious diseases, along with physical exhaustion." Those who left had no way of foreseeing the impact emigration would have on their health and psychological well-being, Caro argued. More concretely, local economies were adversely affected by the depletion of manpower from native soil. Across the Galician countryside, "crops are often left in the field, potatoes rot because of a lack of working hands; a shortage of farmworkers and girls to pasture cattle leads to general misery, which cannot be alleviated by the state."[22] No matter how high the wages émigrés garnered abroad, Caro concluded, they could not possibly make up for "the loss that the national economy must bear through the absence of its most vigorous workers."[23]

---

18. The Habsburg Monarchy passed legislation in 1905 shifting its responsibility from merely protecting emigrants before they left Habsburg territory to protecting them after their arrival overseas. Related to this, a Ministry of the Interior decree dated June 26, 1905 called for the Viennese police directorate to mediate with foreign officials in the battle against trafficking in women. Caro, *Emigracya i polityka emigracyjna*, 324; and Nancy M. Wingfield, "Destination: Alexandria, Buenos Aires, Constantinople; 'White Slavers' in Late Imperial Austria," *Journal of the History of Sexuality* 20, no. 2 (2011): 303.

19. On Austrian efforts to protect the personal liberty of imperial subjects and others on Habsburg territory, see Alison Frank, "The Children of the Desert and the Laws of the Sea: Austria, Great Britain, the Ottoman Empire, and the Mediterranean Slave Trade in the Nineteenth Century," *The American Historical Review* 117, no. 2 (2012): 410–44.

20. Caro, *Emigracya i polityka emigracyjna*, 9. See also Murdzek, *Emigration in Polish Social-Political Thought*.

21. The notion that the disruption of local communities during the migration process resulted in degeneracy and an overall collapse of moral standards was later popularized by William Thomas and Florian Znaniecki in their classic work of sociology, *The Polish Peasant in Europe and America*.

22. Caro, *Emigracya i polityka emigracyna*, 7.

23. Ibid., 67.

Fears about the loss of labor power and rumors of abuse contributed to an increased reliance on the language of captivity to discourage mass migration. Horrifying tales of unscrupulous migration agents appeared in the columns of daily newspapers. Many reports characterized mediators as hyenas who prowled around the countryside "seizing poor people and sending them into their misery in exile." Travel agents were described with wolflike characteristics or with stereotypically Jewish features. Migration facilitators were accused of relying on the worst kinds of tricks to exploit the defenseless poor and to "capture the maximum number of emigrants in their nets."[24] As with vulnerable young women swooped up by would-be traffickers, observers stressed that "dark" [ignorant] peasants were willing to accept the "greatest fairy tales about overseas countries" from ingratiating migration agents. Employees of transatlantic shipping companies made themselves indispensable to their clients, arguing that neither the Polish nor Ruthenian languages were adequate for the emigrant to negotiate with German officials on the border. The harsh methods many migration agents employed in transporting their clients prompted accusations that they were managing a modern slaving operation. Officials such as the Polish Reichsrat deputy Zygmunt Łasocki accused officials in the Galician travel agency Ojczyzna, for example, of "capturing our emigrants, sending them to Canada, and forcing them into slavelike conditions."[25]

A series of high-profile legal cases brought against migration agents exacerbated popular unease over the fate of labor migrants. Agents stood accused of charging dramatically inflated prices for steamer tickets, convincing travelers that they needed a special (and expensive) "certificate" to exit, and claiming their services were required for those evading military service to cross the border safely.[26] Since the passport required of émigrés exiting Russian territory was difficult to obtain, agents promoted their own services as vital to facilitating the border crossing.[27] Among the most widely publicized migration scandals was the Wadowice trial of 1889–1890, which exposed an elaborate system of exploitation established by agents of the Hamburg Amerika steamship line (HAPAG) operating on the frontier between the Austrian, German, and Russian empires.[28] Details of the trial echoed across

---

24. "News of the World," *Gazeta Powszechna*, March 24, 1910.

25. PAN KR, Oddział Specjalnych Zbiór, "Polskie Towarzystwe Emigracyne, 'Canadian Pacific,' 1908–28," sygn. 452.

26. Kowalski, *Przestępstwa emigracyjne w Galicji*.

27. Brinkmann, "Why Paul Nathan Attacked Albert Ballin," 55–56.

28. On the Wadowice trial as part of a larger campaign to discourage emigration out of east-central Europe, see Zahra, "Travel Agents on Trial."

FIGURE 5.1   Sketch demonstrating the trickery used on naïve would-be emigrants by corrupt migration agents. Here the travelers are fooled into believing their minders are in contact with America by the regular ringing of an alarm-clock bell. "Proces Wadowicki w portretach i scenach" (The Wadowice Trial in Portraits and Scenes), 1890.
Courtesy of Jagiellonian University Library (Biblioteka Uniwersytetu Jagiellońskiego).

eastern Europe, helping to link labor migration to images of coercion and abuse.[29] Anti-Semitism also played a role in the proceedings, as the accused in the case were sixty-five Jewish travel agents operating in the border town of Oświęcim, at the junction of the Austrian, German, and Russian railway lines.

Prosecutors set out to depict the agents as ruthless human traffickers who had transported thousands of Polish and Ruthenian peasants to hard labor in American factories and mines. They called on images of slavelike conditions similar to those later used in sex-trafficking cases. Prosecuting attorneys accused defendants of "introducing a slave trade into the free land of Austria."[30] Newspaper accounts depicted burly "drivers" who surrounded emigrants on the train platform, "beating them with fists and sticks" and forcing them "like cattle" to the agency's offices.[31] Anti-emigration activists

---

29. Kowalski, *Przestępstwa emigracyjne w Galicji*, 158.
30. *Der Galizische Menschenhandel vor Gericht* (Vienna, 1890), 205, cited in Zahra, "Travel Agents on Trial," 1.
31. *Galizische Menschenhandel*, 35, cited in Zahra, "Travel Agents on Trial," 175.

soon began using metaphors of slavery to depict the harsh conditions and low wages greeting labor emigrants in the United States and Canada.[32] The Wadowice trial highlighted frightening examples of emigrants who were incarcerated for days, forced to purchase clothing from the company store at exorbitant prices or to pay bribes to physicians conducting medical examinations.[33] Migrants were allegedly imprisoned in locked "pig stalls" and dark basements.

Later trials revealed that subagents routinely detained travelers at the train station in Cracow long enough to cause them to miss their connection to Hamburg and hence their steamer to America (and forcing a fine for a new ticket). In the border city of Mysłowice, in German Silesia, travelers were forced to sit for days in the waiting area after being examined by a doctor and were then transferred to a fourth-class train car with no bathrooms or food for the trip to Hamburg or Bremen.[34] Agents of the Canadian Pacific steamer company were no better. Called "hyenas" and emigration "parasites" by contemporary lawmakers, they operated in cahoots with railway officials and gendarmes, collectively tricking migrants out of hundreds of crowns and often sending them back home as medically unqualified once their money had been absorbed.[35] At least one Polish Reichsrat deputy was even accused of taking substantial bribes in exchange for channeling migrants to a particular steamer company.[36] The persistence of such stories helped convince many representatives of Polish society that all forms of migration were potentially harmful and risked jeopardizing the liberty of the traveler. And yet the poor continued to emigrate.

The Trauma of Female Migration

Public censure about leaving the homeland fell especially hard on female migrants. Like their male counterparts, women left home as a result of a wide range of factors and faced a host of potential risks along the way. Despite

---

32. Friedrich Hey, *Unser Auswanderungswesen und seine Schaden* (Vienna, 1912), 5, cited in Zahra, "Travel Agents on Trial," 177.

33. Caro, *Emigracja i polityka emigracyjna*, 82–86.

34. Ibid., 89–99.

35. PAN KR, Oddział Specjalnych Zbiór, " Polskie Towarzystwe Emigracyjny, 'Canadian Pacific,'" 1908–28," sygn. 452.

36. The Reichsrat deputy Jan Stapiński from the Galician Peasant Party (*Stronnictwo Ludowe*) was accused in 1912 of having siphoned off huge profits from the sale of steamer tickets on the Canadian Pacific line, an accusation he consistently denied. PAN KR, Rps. 4094, "Materiały Zygmunta Łasockiego dot. Emigracji Polaków do Kanady."

many shared experiences between emigrants of both genders, however, contemporary observers often singled out independent women travelers for particular criticism. Country girls were chastised for reaching beyond their station and taking unnecessary risks in their quest for fortunes overseas. Dreams of secure jobs and comfortable lives led them to fall carelessly into the traffickers' traps, nationalist journals warned.[37] Newspaper editors warned that the migration of young women deprived the nation of childbearing females. All of these concerns fed a growing anxiety about single female travelers and encouraged a receptive audience for tales of "white slavery."[38] Testimonies of women labeled as "trafficked" out of the Polish lands suggest that for the most part the initial impetus to leave was voluntary, though sometimes based on false or exaggerated information. Migrants chose to venture beyond their native shores for money, professional advancement, to see the world, to escape the routine of their hometown, or for love. Though at some stage migration agents might have employed force or continued deception to maintain control over their charges, women who turn up on the rolls of "white slaves" typically took the opening plunge into migration on their own without physical coercion. They may well have been coaxed into accompanying a migration agent by promises of employment or the prospect of meeting a wealthy husband, but such commitments are not dissimilar to those made to migrants everywhere.

Migration even in the best of times entailed risks on the part of the traveler, as our examples from the Wadowice case suggest. Agents frequently misled their clients into believing secure jobs awaited them. Labor contracts were cleverly arranged to disguise long-term commitments. Migrants were forced to repay the cost of their journey over many months or years, remaining in semibondage until the debt was paid. Job descriptions were vague and migrants had to be happy with whatever employment they could find after arriving in a new setting. Such abuses were certainly unfortunate, but they do not in themselves constitute coerced migration. Instead, evidence from diplomatic correspondence, local police files, and the testimonies of returning women suggests several ways in which the fate of presumed trafficking victims was misrepresented in the territories comprising partitioned Poland.

This chapter proposes a fresh set of perspectives for understanding the contemporary trafficking scare in the Polish lands, focusing on four ways in which traveling women or their family exercised a degree of power over

37. "Handlarze dziewcząt," *Niwa*, October 26, 1896, 729–30.
38. "Przeciw handlowi dziewczętami," 4.

migrants' fates. First, women who migrated and did not maintain steady correspondence with their families back home were often presumed to have come to a bad end. Their parents complained to their local police officials accordingly. Yet such women were often typical labor migrants wrongly categorized as victims of trafficking or sexual abuse. In the Austrian lands, local police were required to file missing persons reports with the Central Police Directorate in Vienna when a parent complained about a daughter they suspected had been taken abroad by force. Such cases were treated as trafficking episodes, although not all of their subjects ended in foreign brothels. Sometimes more banal outcomes explained the break in correspondence. As Mark Connelly argues in his study of the trafficking panic in early twentieth-century America, white-slavery imagery provided a plausible, "though admittedly macabre" explanation for wayward daughters who lost contact with their families.[39]

A second and somewhat more sinister explanation for missing teenaged girls involves parental complicity. Taking advantage of the rising demand for young women in boomtowns around the world, impoverished east European families sometimes accepted offers of compensation from migration agents to release their underaged daughters for transport overseas. Though certainly unsavory, such practices should not be confused with the forced kidnapping of young women off city streets. Rather, a degree of volunteerism was involved, at least in the initial parental agreement. Third, many female migrants arrived in their new homes intending to work in shops or factories, but opted instead to turn to prostitution as the best of a range of bad options. Women who traveled abroad and turned to paid sex in their new homes often made the initial decision to leave for reasons similar to other travelers. Though coercion may have been involved in their turn to sex work, they were not initially "trafficked" from their hometown or village.

Fourth and most important, professional prostitutes operating in eastern Europe migrated to burgeoning cities around the globe with the specific intent of pursuing work in the sex industry. If their testimonies can be believed, these women traveled abroad in order to improve their fortunes through work in foreign brothels, not because they were forced to do so. As Alain Corbin reminds us, the so-called white-slave trade was a "mere corollary of the trafficking officially tolerated by [domestic] regulationism" across Europe. The only difference is that there was "no longer unity of place." The international trade in women in many ways represented an extension

---

39. Connelly, *Response to Prostitution*, 124–26.

of local brothel systems in that many of the women and girls involved were well aware of what was expected of them and were willing to travel abroad initially.[40] Let us consider briefly the geographic spread of the trafficking phenomenon before turning to the various scenarios by which the transatlantic sex trade played out.

Routes and Markets

As with any other product or service, the international trade in women followed its own routes and had its own markets. This commercial geography shifted with new government-imposed obstacles and fresh forms of surveillance. The migration of sex workers out of the Polish lands followed three main paths, each subject to varying degrees of imperial and civilian control. Groups of women from the southwestern Russian Empire made their way by train, typically accompanied by a migration agent or a married couple facilitating the transaction, to passenger steamers shipping out of the Black Sea port of Odessa. Destinations varied, but most migrants followed the growing demand for prostitutes in Buenos Aires or the key cities of the Ottoman Empire.[41] In the eastern Mediterranean, Istanbul and Alexandria served as central marketplaces for agents traveling from Cairo, Bombay, and Shanghai to locate women in a legal atmosphere with few restrictions on sex trafficking. Odessa was the port of choice for thousands of impoverished Jewish and Christian girls from Ukraine and the southern Pale of Settlement, many of them fleeing discriminatory government policies and the abuses of their neighbors.[42] The distant tsarist bureaucracy imposed little

---

40. Alain Corbin argues that public concern over the white slave trade erupted in advance of the international conference to combat trafficking in women held in Paris during July 1902. The campaign to inform public opinion about white slavery was initiated by several large circulation Parisian newspapers, which had recently proved their power in the Dreyfus Affair. Ironically, the 1902 conference, by ratifying legislation to crush trafficking and punish its perpetrators, narrowed the definition of "coerced trade in women" so greatly that procurers were able to wriggle out of convictions regularly. Though the conference, according to Corbin, was certainly "the first demonstration of any concern on the part of diplomats with the problems of prostitution and the trade in women, it nevertheless ended up by recognizing the legality of most of that trafficking." Rather than suppressing the international trade in women, it "laid down the conditions that the traders must fulfill if they are to continue their activities without fear of interference." Corbin, *Women for Hire*, 285–98.

41. Wingfield, "Destination"; and Corbin, *Women for Hire*, 287.

42. Roshanna Sylvester looks at danger and sexual immorality among Jews in Odessa's port district, though her sources are inconclusive about Jewish involvement in international trafficking. *Tales of Old Odessa: Crime and Civility in a City of Thieves* (DeKalb, IL, 2005), 92–94. On the economic destitution of Odessan Jews after 1871, see Steven J. Zipperstein, *The Jews of Odessa: A Cultural History, 1794–1881* (Stanford, CA, 1986), 129–50. Brinkmann argues that legal restrictions were so strict at Russian ports that many imperial subjects opted instead to bribe border guards along the lengthy

regulation on this wild port town, which had regular passenger service to Constantinople, Genoa, Marseilles, and London, and then on to North Africa or Latin America. Odessa's port district was infamous for its "dangerous and disorderly population" of drunken dockworkers and homeless beggars who slept on streets lined with squalid taverns and unsavory flophouses. Migrants had to survive several days or weeks in this atmosphere, surrounded by "dirty," "half-naked," and "falling down" men and shameless, "barely covered," "public" women, before embarking on their long passage to their new homes.[43] International police reported that by 1905 whole companies of ten or more traffickers worked in tandem at the port, scouring the countryside for those who had "already fallen" and allegedly organizing three hundred women at a time on transports.

Émigrés from the Polish Kingdom often preferred the more carefully regulated ports in Germany and Austria, where police and customs surveillance contributed to a more orderly processing of travelers.[44] Agents who recruited girls from brothels in the Polish Kingdom, Galicia, and German Silesia collected them first in a network of restaurants and bars along the three-empire border, often compensating subagents 5 to 10 marks for each prospective migrant. Police believed forty such establishments with one hundred or more "serving girls" operated in Poznań alone, a town of some seventy-five thousand inhabitants in 1899.[45] Recruiters systematically bribed border guards at the Katowice crossing to transfer undocumented women from the Russian Empire into German territory. Trains were efficient and frequent to Hamburg, while facilities for waiting migrants, though often overcrowded, operated smoothly. Booking passage on steamers out of Hamburg was particularly challenging for migration agents, as customs officials and border police often challenged their claim to be taking women to legitimate work overseas, even interviewing young women traveling in the company of older men and closely examining their destination addresses for indications of known brothels. National Vigilance Society representatives patrolled the docks, pulling aside single women for special attention.[46] Finally, migration agents believed Austrian Trieste to be subject to less police supervision than Hamburg and hence ideal for trafficking in undocumented or suspicious cargo. The port

western border with Germany and Austria rather than risk being turned back by Russian officials. Brinkmann, "Why Paul Nathan Attacked Albert Ballin," 55–56.

43. Sylvester, *Tales of Old Odessa*, 30–34.

44. Brinkmann, "Why Paul Nathan Attacked Albert Ballin," 56.

45. "Handel dziewczętami," *Słowo*, August 12, 1899, 3.

46. "Co tam słychać w świecie?" *Przjaciel Sług*, March 6, 1898, 9–10.

was well served by the Austrian Lloyd shipping company, which ran some seventy separate steamers and over a quarter million passengers out of the port each year already in 1870.[47] Brothel owners in Trieste were closely tied to the overseas sex trade, providing a steady supply of willing prostitutes for agents shipping women off to Ottoman trading centers.[48] These port cities provided the last view of European shores for thousands of migrants and the first of many challenges as they started their new lives overseas.

Wayward Daughters

The exodus of young people seeking opportunities across the ocean placed significant strains on parent-child relationships. Migrants became preoccupied with their new lives and neglected to write home, leading to suspicions about their fate. Not every anxious parent complaining to local police about a "disappeared" daughter located her offspring in an overseas brothel. Karoline Eckert confided to Viennese police in 1906, for example, that her sixteen-year-old daughter had left home a year and a half earlier to take up work as a household servant in Helle, but that she had not heard from the girl in almost a year. Frau Eckert was afraid that her daughter, who was "a rather lovely tall girl with dark hair and blue eyes, [had] fallen into the hands of a trafficker," but no evidence of foul play was uncovered.[49] Another parent, Beruch Weinsicher, told police in Warsaw that his twenty-two-year-old daughter, Cyvia, had left town a month earlier and he had received no word from her since.[50] Again, police failed to locate any indication that she had been forcibly trafficked. Such complaints may well have been encouraged by the birth of the League to Combat Trafficking in Women, whose Austrian chapters were established formally in 1906. Members of the League regularly collected information about suspicious behavior or vulnerable young women

---

47. Frank, "Children of the Desert and the Laws of the Sea," 410–44.

48. The vast majority of prostitutes working in Buenos Aires migrated from the Russian Kingdom or Galicia through the port at Trieste, according to information provided by the Swiss Consul in Buenos Aires in 1897. See Corbin, *Women for Hire*, 286–88, for a relatively comprehensive account of the primary shipping lanes, destinations, and origins of the girls transported as prospective prostitutes. One of the most widely publicized trafficking trials, sensationalized in Stanisław Posner's 1903 publication, *Nad otchłania*, featured graphic depictions of smuggler activity in the small towns on either side of the Katowice crossing. See also Wróblewski, *O prostytucji i handlu kobietami*, 13–14.

49. Letter from Vienna Central Police Direction to Berlin Police Direction, Central Office of the Battle against International Trafficking, December 5, 1906, BPdWA, "Prostitution und Mädchenhandel," 1907/I.

50. Testimony of Beruch Mendelsohn Weinsicher, January 3, 1896, Warsaw police headquarters. BPdWA, "Prostitution und Mädchenhandel," 1891–1895.

about to make a misstep, though their reports often proved misleading or incomplete. One member of the Lwów chapter reported to police that she had word from Paris that a young woman in Lwów was on the verge of embarking on a trip to Argentina with the "notorious trafficker, Touran from Marseille." According to the League member, the girl awaited instructions from the alleged trafficker about her port of departure. Police dutifully tracked both the young woman and her alleged handler, but discovered no one by her name registered in Genoa and that the accused white slaver had died two months before the letter was written.[51] While the lack of evidence to support coerced migration does not in itself preclude foul play, the inability of imperial agents to confirm parental suspicions suggests that such accusations sometimes ended up being spurious.

Young women chose to leave home and migrate abroad or to the city for any number of reasons. In one case, Maria Klimek left her tiny native village of Golanka in the Galician district of Tarnów during the summer of 1913, bound for Buenos Aires. A twenty-one-year-old serving girl, Klimek had taken up with the thirty-year-old Stanisław Laszuk from the town of Ratibor in Prussian Silesia. According to her mother, their five-month relationship had "ruined her and caused a scandal" such that Klimek's mother happily contributed to the cost of her daughter's transatlantic passage and gave her full blessing to Maria's exodus. Laszuk's promise to marry the girl upon their arrival in Argentina no doubt strengthened the mother's support for the trip. Nonetheless, when Maria presented officials in the emigration hall at Hamburg the address of a known brothel as her destination, local police and Austrian consular officials initiated an investigation into possible trafficking charges against Laszuk and warned Maria's mother that her daughter might be in danger.

A few months later the mother was relieved to receive a letter from her daughter announcing she had secured employment as a tutor for the daughters of a wealthy local family. In reality, as local police discovered when they investigated the case, Maria was working as a domestic in the family's household. She had exaggerated her professional success in the correspondence with her mother, but had nonetheless avoided ending up in a brothel. Klimek had used her relationship with Laszuk to travel abroad, but told police that "once she learned of Laszuk's former life, she no longer wanted to have anything to do with him" and so landed a more pedestrian position.[52]

---

51. Report from Emma Lilien, member of Women's Protection Society, to police headquarters, Lwów, June 12, 1914, BPdWA, "Prostitution und Mädchenhandel," 1914/I.

52. "Maria Klimek, Victim of Trafficking," BPdWA, "Prostitution und Mädchenhandel," 1913.

Embarking on a transatlantic steamer with a known trafficker did not necessarily suggest a young woman was being duped or abused; sometimes the trickery could go the other direction and migration agents could be wrong footed by clever migrants. In Klimek's case, the "suspected victim" left the country voluntarily with the permission of her parent and found "honest" if unglamorous work abroad. Had Argentine police not investigated her whereabouts she might have been presumed to be a victim of trafficking. In fact, she was merely guilty of "creating a scandal" at home and fibbing to her mother about the nature of her work in Buenos Aires.

Parental Complicity

The promise of well-paid work abroad and desperate poverty at home helped convince some parents to give up their daughters to suspicious agents, often in exchange for immediate compensation. Already in the early days of "Brazilian fever" investigators preparing criminal cases against alleged traffickers discovered that "special agents travel throughout Galicia . . . buying up girls from their relatives." More and more, they found, "daughters are sold into slavery and debauchery by their own parents," a process that was partly responsible for the spike in sex trafficking, according to investigators.[53] Austrian police documented the case of Mili Bochsler, aged fourteen, in 1913. Mili's father had sent her to a dance engagement at the well-known nightclub Casino de Paris, in Lwów, where she was expected to serve as a prostitute. Quickly realizing the place was a "house of debauchery," the girl demanded the proprietor pay her way back home. But the case did not stop there. Imperial police prosecuted the father for, among other things, "shirking his parental duty." They were able to confirm his suspicious behavior partially because he was already under surveillance for sexual crimes. In the end, the father stood accused of "handing over his daughter to a strange, morally depraved person and in this way abandoning her to a life of misery." Mili, for her part, was able to wriggle out of the arrangement partly with the support of the police and representatives of the League to Combat Trafficking in Women.[54]

But parents were not always aware of the situation into which they sent their offspring. Hundreds of girls from eastern Europe responded to advertisements to travel to America during Chicago's 1893 Columbian Exposition,

---

53. "Handlarze kobiet," 4.

54. "Correspondence from Switzerland regarding daughter in Lwów brothel," September 27–October 14, 1913, AGAD, CKMSW, sygn. 213.

many of them falling into the hands of agents who encouraged them to engage in prostitution or shipped them on to Asia.[55] One father in Silesia paid the cost of this daughter's travel to Vienna in 1898, where she was intending to work as a servant. He was heartened to receive a letter soon after the girl's arrival announcing she had found work. When he subsequently failed to hear from her, he traveled to Vienna and tracked her down in a brothel. The Austrian trafficking expert Josef Schrank theorized that "many . . . parents in Galicia have a suspicion about the fate of their daughters, but out of poverty they decide to divest themselves of the burden in their households."[56] Like their daughters, parents of poor women found themselves attracted to the rosy scenarios migration agents painted.

Often opportunities appeared so enticing that even the most vigilant parents were tempted. After all, patterns of migration from the Polish lands had been established for centuries.[57] Long before concerns about sex trafficking surfaced, Poles left home to work in Germany, the United States, South America, and Australia either temporarily or permanently. The ubiquitous and long-standing presence of migration facilitators may have encouraged parents to accept the assistance of agents who promised lucrative employment and safe passage for their daughters.[58] Talent agents roamed across eastern Europe, searching for young women interested in opportunities abroad. Some served as legitimate representatives of band, choir, or dance troupes. Others were procurement agents for foreign brothels and sex rings. Police, parents, and consular officials struggled to distinguish between legitimate migration agents and dangerous criminals who abused the trust of young women. Musical and artistic productions were often used as cover for procuring operations. Evidence of their activities is inconclusive, but suggests an intricate overlap between the entertainment world and that of clandestine prostitution. The "supposed" theater director Mieczysław Jagodziński was probably insincere, for example, when he engaged several "very young and pretty girls as dancers and singers under "the most brilliant conditions" for his "of course not really existing Berlin Theater," according to a German news

---

55. Wróblewski, *O prostytucji i handlu kobietami*, 11–12.

56. Augustyn Wróblewski, "Handel kobietami," *Czystość* 5, no. 23 (May 14, 1909): 354–56.

57. For a general overview of Polish migration patterns, see Adam Walaszek, "Wychodźcy, Emigrants, or Poles: Fears and Hopes about Emigration in Poland, 1870–1939," *Association of European Migration Institutions Journal* 1 (2002): 78–84; and Edward Kołodziej, "Emigracja z ziem polskich od końca XIX wieku do czasów współczesnych i tworzenie się skupisk polonijnych," in *Emigracja z ziem polskich w XX wieku*, ed. A. Koseski (Pułtusk, Poland, 1998), 11–24.

58. On the culpability of migration agents and their influence on waves of emigration from the Polish lands, see Murdzek, *Emigration in Polish Social-Political Thought*, 134–37.

report. Herr Jagodziński was reported to have offered prospective employees "jewels and other items of gold that he had acquired on credit and immediately pawned." Berlin police intercepted Jagodziński's correspondence with "infamous houses abroad," revealing his intent to transport girls to brothels rather than to the theater.[59]

The choirmaster Leon Hackmayer of Bukovina was similarly suspected of trafficking, but Austrian officials were unable to prove conclusively that his itinerant search for talented young women to join his troupe was inauthentic. Hackmayer reportedly "engaged exclusively Jewish women from Galicia and Bukovina," scouring Europe and sailing out of Trieste to Singapore, where his Musikkapelle performed regularly. The choir director corresponded with his wife and business partner, Bertha, "in veiled language suggesting that they are dealing with some kind of illicit trade," according to police investigators. Austrian authorities, along with consular officers in Cairo, Singapore, and Bombay, suspected the Hackmayers of engaging in sex trafficking but could prove nothing. Interviews with one of the ostensible singers, Klara Zitterer of Bukovina, revealed simply that some six months previously Frau Hackmayer had "reached an understanding" with Miss Zitterer's father in Radautz, Bukowina, to engage her for four years in a choir in Singapore. Klara traveled along with several other girls from Trieste to Singapore and later testified that "Herr Hackmayer [had treated her] well, like a student, and conducted her in a strict way of life."[60] The opportunity to travel abroad under the supervision of an artistic director was compelling enough both for Klara and her impoverished Bukovinan parents to take risks that left them feeling uncertain and vulnerable.

Not surprisingly, parents whose daughters embarked on such artistic or musical tours worried about the welfare of their children. Concerned mothers and fathers often sought to track young women who took employment with enterprising migration agents to confirm that their children were safe. Consulates everywhere fielded requests to investigate the whereabouts of girls who had arrived from abroad without their families. Austrian officials in Warsaw, for example, caught up with Emilie Schrammell and Antonie Keitl to investigate their treatment in the Oettlessy Troupe, which had ostensibly been performing in Warsaw under the direction of one Martin Faust throughout the spring and summer of 1914. One of the girls had written

---

59. *Breslauer Zeitung,* May 2, 1899, dateline Krakau, B PdWA, "Prostitution und Mädchenhandel," 1897–99.

60. "Testimony of Klara Zitterer," K.u.K. Konsul in Singapore, July 8, 1914, B PdWA, "Prostitution und Mädchenhandel," 1912/I, 1913.

home from Kharkov complaining about her situation, but by the time the troupe reached Łódź later that year the problems had dissipated and the girls were no longer unsatisfied with their positions.[61]

Government officials often suspected the worst but found it difficult to prove claims of sexual abuse. Nonetheless, suspicion about ulterior motives was embedded in the life of the migration agent. The Galician governor general's office in Lwów, for example, circulated stern warnings to young women approached with offers of engagements with the director Fryderyk Frankenstein and his Murthaler from Graz singing troupe, even though Herr Frankenstein had never been arrested on charges of trafficking. Austrian police cautioned that they had information suggesting Frankenstein traveled "the whole world with his troupe of singers, who serve as the playthings for men . . . they are often left in foreign countries without the means to support themselves." Officials at the Austro-Hungarian Consulate in Shanghai sought, in particular, to discourage Katarzyna Hohmann, who had recently been engaged to sing in Shanghai, from traveling there, warning that it was difficult for women to find honest work in China and that they should safeguard their passports at all costs.[62] Parents were cautioned to exercise "care and prudence" when sending their daughters abroad.[63]

Casual observers had their own agenda for complaining about suspected traffickers. Austrian police received a lengthy complaint in 1912 about one Harry Simpson, an alleged artistic agent for a dance troupe based in Vienna. The letter writer accused Mr. Simpson, who was legally married, of keeping a concubine whom he "sent out onto the street to support him." Simpson frequented the local movie theater "almost daily" in order to "make the acquaintance of young girls," leading the interlocutor to "imagine he was perhaps a trafficker in women."[64] The report acknowledged that Simpson recruited female dancers from Lwów to his school in Vienna to study, employed them in his theater, and secured promising engagements in "first-class houses" for them. So what was it that raised the ire of this observer? The letter of complaint includes an allusion to two aspiring young dancers who had reportedly been sent to Lwów to perform in the hinterland rather than at

---

61. Austro-Hungarian Consulate in Warsaw to k.k. Polizei Direction in Vienna, June 15, 1914; report of Österreichische-Hungarische Hilfsverein in Lodz, n.d., BPdWA, "Prostitution und Mädchenhandel," 1914/2.

62. Prezydyum c.k. Namiestnictwa, "Okólnik do wszystkich Panów c.k. Starostów do Panów c.k. Dyrektorów Policyi we Lwowie i Krakowie," Lwów, October 29, 1911, APKr, DPKr 110, 1109.

63. "Handlarze dziewcząt," Niwa 45 (October 26, 1896), 729–30.

64. Letter from Emanuel Hollstein [pen name of Karl Romer] to Viennese central police headquarters, June 7, 1912, BPdA, "Prostitution und Mädchenhandel," 1911.

a venue in Vienna, as they had originally been promised. Sometimes tensions among talent agents affected trafficking allegations, in this case prompting police surveillance of Simpson for at least two years.

False Promises

The third type of scenario contributing to women ending up in foreign brothels was connected to commitments made prior to their departure. The lack of opportunity for professional advancement prompted many unskilled women to risk migration from eastern Europe, often acting on utopian descriptions communicated to them in the initial phases of their journey. Accused traffickers testified convincingly that they never transported women against their will, but rather relied on verbal and sometimes material enticements to convince their clients to travel abroad. Promises were often mundane, involving meager but important increments of social mobility, such as the possibility that a peasant girl might find work indoors as a lofty domestic servant, or a maid might be promoted to a cashier or a shopkeeper. Such elevations of employment status were surprisingly difficult in the east European social economy but could be more easily facilitated in a foreign milieu where one's background and personal circumstances did not serve as markers of success.

Migration agents frequently emphasized opportunities for social mobility among women they accompanied abroad. Marya Sabat and M. Kawecka, for example, were approached while working in the fields near the provincial town of Czernowitz and promised positions as household servants if they traveled abroad. Before they knew it, the two were on a steamer bound for Constantinople, where they landed in a brothel. Elka Jenner was already employed as a servant in a small town in the Polish Kingdom when an acquaintance offered her "good money" if she accompanied him to Istanbul. She agreed to pay an intermediary a 500 złoty fee to make the arrangements and was shipped out of Trieste.[65] Golda Reinerman, in turn, became involved with a group of migration facilitators when one approached her at the Sosnowiec railway station in upper Silesia, offering her a position as a barkeep in nearby Będzin, along the Russian-German border. "In Będzin," Reinerman related, "they brought me to the home of the Hendlers [a known trafficking ring] and Mrs. Hendler persuaded me to go abroad" with them. Reinerman's testimony is tinged with initial gratitude for the opportunity to travel.

---

65. "Handlarze dziewcząt," October 20, 1892, 2.

As she tells it, Mrs. Hendler explained to Golda that "thanks to her help many girls have been able to go . . . and that she herself had received many presents for her interventions," including a large stash of diamonds, which seems to have impressed the prospective migrant.[66] In all of these cases, the women were placed in Turkish brothels after arriving in Istanbul. They appear not to have suffered physical coercion at the hands of agents while departing Europe, yet their facilitators clearly were less than forthcoming about the activities the girls would perform after arriving at their destination. Moreover, sticking to a narrative about false promises allowed girls and young women caught up in trafficking activities to insist on their status as unwilling victims even in cases where prospective migrants might have been reasonably confident of the outcome in store for them at the end of their journey.

Even relatively pedestrian commitments agents made to their clients typically featured depictions of a luxurious and carefree existence. As Captain Bielski, head of the Będzin district police in Silesia explained during his 1901 testimony, traffickers preyed on the suffering and poverty of their young clients, painting idealized pictures of high wages and plentiful jobs in America—not unlike agents seeking workers for companies abroad. Even the promise of a position as a lowly barkeep or a waitress could be compelling when migrants traveled first class, received housing in luxury accommodations, or were escorted to theater performances on their route out of the country.[67] Emilja Rosentretter, for example, met her contact in Katowice, where he promised her and her friend waitress jobs in Buenos Aires. Along the route out of the country, the agent purchased tickets in the sleeping car of the train and brought them to the theater, activities seen as so luxurious they were highlighted in Emilja's court testimony against her accused trafficker.[68] Similarly, Blima Znaderówna was working long hours as a domestic for a butcher's family when she met a migration agent who offered her a position as a cashier if she traveled with him to "Stambul." She fell for his promises and departed for Constantinople, where she was reportedly sold to a house of prostitution. Even more pitiful, young Feiga Kupferman was a fourteen-year-old orphan when the wife of a trafficker approached her promising good and honest work if she went to America. Her sojourn there would allow her to accumulate enough wealth to return to her native land before long, she was told. But instead of being

---

66. Posner, *Nad otchłania*, 19–20.

67. Józef Macko notes that a particular type of trafficker operated between Berlin, Vienna, Moscow, Warsaw, Odessa, and the Baltic ports and always traveled with his clients first class and in a "high style." Many of these were sons of the owners of long-standing trafficking businesses who had learned the trade since childhood. Macko, *Prostytucja,* 351–52.

68. Posner, *Nad otchłania*, 16–20.

transported to America, Kupferman was swept up in the Mediterranean traffic to Constantinople, where she too soon found herself in a Turkish brothel.[69] Personal ambition and a desperate desire to better their material circumstances led each of them to trust unsavory migration agents.

As simple country girls lacking professional skills aspired to jobs in stately homes, fine restaurants, or elegant shops, critics chastised them for taking inappropriate risks. Dreams of secure jobs and comfortable lives led female migrants to fall carelessly into the traffickers' traps, argued one editorialist, stressing that "the fault here lies in part in the recklessness of girls. Today unfortunately hundreds of uneducated or poorly educated maidens, school-teachers, governesses, wet nurses, and actors abandon themselves to some fantastical or unrealistic dream. Their father's background and humility does not suit them, but instead it seems to them that they were born for something better, something higher. They have the desire to cross over into the sphere of the gentry, travel abroad, pursue their dreams to dress well and to glitter. They want to earn the most possible money. Often they imagine that under foreign skies, in the home of some famous or wealthy family, they will have a wonderful party."[70] The crime here appears to have been striving for upward economic mobility, something denied to many young women on Polish territory. On other occasions, police and antitrafficking activists tracked girls suspected of having fallen into hostile hands only to find an element of volunteerism that handicapped their ability to prosecute the agents or return girls to their families. The "admirer" of one young woman from Czernowitz complained to local police that Erna Denk had been "taken away alone" in February 1907 from the coffeehouse where she worked. A few days later the young man received a letter from her indicating she had taken a position at the "Krauk" coffeehouse in the nearby district of Starożyniec and "apparently (to all appearances) had become a prostitute." Despite the obvious consternation of her gentleman friend, the police's hands were tied since Denk's correspondence indicated "she was ready to limit her personal freedom."[71]

Trafficking and Domestic Prostitutes

Just as lowly cleaning women and seamstresses sought social mobility through migration, so too did women already working as prostitutes at home approach emigration as a route to professional advancement. This is the fourth and

---

69. "Handlarze dziewcząt," October 22, 1892, 2.
70. "Handlarze dziewcząt," 729–30.
71. Case of Erna Denk, no. 3900, BPdWA, "Prostitution und Mädchenhandel," 1906.

by far the most common scenario for young women who entered the sex trade in emigration. It is also the least recognized route to sex migration, one that is rarely acknowledged explicitly among contemporary social activists who preferred to characterize female migrants as innocent and easily duped maidens. Some of these migrants believed relocating to a new environment would offer the chance to start a new life in a more "legitimate" profession. Others wanted to improve their working conditions or increase their profit margins. Contemporary rescue workers had to face the reality that luxurious settings and exotic conditions abroad made the life of a transplanted prostitute attractive and thwarted efforts to repatriate them. One British pamphleteer complained that trafficked women often refused the efforts of charity workers simply because the excitement of their new homes made a return to "respectable life" unattractive. "A young woman living an immoral life is under the constant spell of excitement. She receives attention from men; she is the recipient of gifts. . . . Night after night she is given dinners, suppers, and theatre. . . . Modern rescue workers recognize that you cannot expect a girl or a woman to come straight from the glamour of the unfortunate's life and plunge immediately into a routine of study work and implicit obedience."[72] Instead, rescue workers were encouraged to convince the immoral woman that she should work to "regain her self-respect and realize the responsibilities life entails"—not a terribly attractive substitute for the luxury and excitement of these migrants' new lives.

Specialists on sex migration in the late twentieth century have argued that most women who sold sex before leaving home were aware that they would be expected to perform work with a sexual aspect once they relocated.[73] Similarly, a significant portion of those who left eastern Europe at the turn of the twentieth century and made their way to brothels overseas were recruited directly from houses of prostitution in their home countries. Testimonials from trafficking trials suggest that brothels along the borders of the Polish territories were the primary source of supply for those trading in women and that the women involved generally understood their future prospects. Subagents collected women working as prostitutes from a wide swath of territory and assembled them in public houses near train stations at border crossings.[74] As Stanisław Posner

---

72. [n.a.], *In the Grip of the White Slave Trader* (London, 1911), 100–101.

73. Agustin, "Disappearing of a Migration Category," 36–39.

74. The 1901 case against John Meyerowicz for international trafficking held in Bytom, Prussian Silesia, reflects this pattern. Meyerowicz allegedly worked with a phalanx of subagents recruiting prostitutes from across the border in Russian Poland. The bulk of Meyerowicz's "cargo" were recruited from brothels in the border towns of Będzin and Sosnowiec and transported over the border at Katowice, then on to Wrocław, Berlin, and London.

emphasized in his study of trafficking along the Prussian-Russian border, the greatest problem was the "link between the domestic brothel trade and the international traffic in women," an issue that was virtually ignored by imperial governments and private charities alike.[75] Edward Bristow points out that of the large numbers of migrants out of eastern Europe in the nineteenth century, "prostitutes were among those who were increasingly mobile."[76] Their previous activities aside, such women opted to migrate abroad partially because, like all migrants, "they dreamed and longed for another life."[77] Knowledge that their new conditions might entail some sexual activity did not necessarily preclude a whole range of abuses at later stages of migration. Itinerants are always vulnerable to unexpected shifts in their professional situation, and those who labor in the sex industry are not alone in experiencing abuse. Many made informed decisions only to discover that promises of luxury, wealth, or a stable existence in a "legitimate" profession were unrealistic.

Despite the pattern of seasoned prostitutes relocating to foreign brothels, contemporary journalists and prosecutors alike struggled to portray them as sympathetic figures, carefully avoiding any allusions that might suggest they were self-aware individuals who willingly accompanied their captors. Public depictions during trafficking trials stressed the poverty and personal tragedy that compelled women into prostitution in the first place, describing them as "prompted by the misery of their life to market their own bodies."[78] "Victims" were painted as having been pushed into the world of commercial sex through the inexorable logic of economic necessity and the struggle for human survival. Many had been driven to the streets "in order not to die of hunger," because of "the cruel treatment of an aunt," or after being left indigent following the death of a parent.[79] The realities of financial hardship prompted women to take desperate measures and turn to prostitution, but these activities were painted as more of a reflex than a conscious decision. In contrast to many depictions of women who sold sex on native soil, those featured in trafficking stories were characterized as more economically desperate than morally challenged. Such images of passive and vulnerable women fit neatly into the white-slavery narrative,

---

75. "Kroniki: St. Posner, 'Nad ochłania,'" *Nowe Słowo* 5 (March 1, 1903): 114–15; and Posner, *Nad ochłania*, 6–9.

76. Bristow, *Vice and Vigilance*, 177.

77. "Z tajemnic społeczeństwa," 2.

78. Ibid.

79. "Handlarze dziewcząt," October 22, 1892, 2.

allowing trafficking imagery to serve a dual purpose as a cautionary tale for young women in public spaces.

Yet testimonies of returning migrants did not always correspond to these stereotypes. Some admitted they had emigrated willingly and other witnesses often corroborated their testimonies. The accused trafficker Schaefferstein, for example, testified that he never transported girls against their wishes and that when his clients expressed misgivings in transit, he simply left them behind. In keeping with this policy, Schaefferstein deposited Mindla Bas in Stryj en route to Constantinople, a fact that was later corroborated by a waiter in the hotel there.[80] Others agreed to travel the entire route and were returned home later when they informed their agents they were "home-sick" for eastern Europe. Even the convicted trafficker John Meyerowicz explained that he returned to Prussian territory from Buenos Aires in 1897 primarily because his ritual wife of many years, Liza Berger, "was homesick for her native land."[81]

Several young women explicitly sought out agents who offered to sponsor their travel abroad and told authorities they were well aware of the trafficker's intentions. Fana Aufseher was tempted after the death of her father to accompany a migration agent to America when he promised her "treasure and wealth." Along the way, the man revealed he was really transporting her to Istanbul to work in a brothel, so she escaped. Several years later, however, after Aufseher's mother died, the young woman relocated the same trafficker at a brothel in Stryj and this time agreed to make the trip, knowing full well what was involved.[82] Likewise, Chana Herman took up work in a brothel in Nadwórna after her mother died and she could not find a permanent position anywhere else. Seeking still greater fortunes, she later relocated to Lwów, where she found work in Mr. Schaefferstein's brothel. Schaefferstein then convinced Herman to travel with him to Constantinople. Herman complained of the hard life in Turkey, but compared with the conditions she left in her eastern Galician shtetl home, she testified that she welcomed it.[83] Seventeen-year-old Golda Praeger from Zborów, Galicia, told Austrian consular officials in Constantinople that she had traveled there on her own without the assistance of mediators and with "no one accompanying" her

---

80. Testimony of Maks Schwaechter, waiter in "Three Crowns" Hotel in Stryj. "Handlarze dziewcząt," October 20, 1892, 2.

81. Meyerowicz appears to have married Liza Berger in a ritual marriage in Wrocław in 1888, suggesting the two had been together for nearly a decade when he traveled back to Prussian Poland with her. Posner, Nad ochłania, 6–7.

82. Testimony of Fana Aufseher, "Handlarze dziewcząt," October 22, 1892, 2.

83. Testimony of Chana Herman, "Handlarze dziewcząt," October 22, 1892, 2.

after practicing prostitution in Lwów for a time. Her testimony may have been intended to protect a trafficker, but young Golda was clearly not eager to be transported back home to Zborów.[84]

The business of prostitution was a mobile profession under ordinary circumstances. Police registries throughout central Europe reflect high levels of travel between imperial towns and across international frontiers. A single page in Cracow's police registry might reveal entries for women born in Brno, Budapest, Lwów, Silesia, and small-town Russian Poland. An August 1910 medical report for a Viennese brothel included residents from Limanowa (Galicia), Cracow, lower Austria, and Silesia; by January 1911 the inhabitants of the same house included a woman from Hungary, one from Russia, and another from Moravia. The Wallenstein bordello, also located in Vienna, was inhabited in 1906 by a total of thirteen prostitutes, four of whom were born in Hungary, one in Dresden, and one who had traveled from England.[85] Prostitutes relocated for any number of reasons: to avoid police harassment, to present themselves as exotic and new, or to avoid being recognized by family members or former acquaintances. They were often eager to improve their financial situation by seeking out wealthier clients. Those working in brothels fled the captivity and control of restrictive madams for the freedom of private rooms; freelance hookers working out of private apartments were ambitious to resettle in upscale neighborhoods with well-heeled customers. All of these motivations prompted hundreds of prostitutes to change locations and register in new municipalities each year. The informal network among registered prostitutes assembling at twice-weekly medical exams, reconnecting during extended hospital stays, or chatting together in brothels or local pubs helped circulate the latest information about opportunities available in the trade. In many respects, the decision to relocate overseas can be understood as an extension of an already itinerant occupation.

Migration agents sought out ambitious prostitutes, tempting them with untold fortunes in the New World, Asia, or the Near East. Women recruited from the bordellos of Będzin and Sosnowiec, in Russian Poland on the border with German Silesia, for example, were promised money, expensive dresses, and jewelry if they traveled to Buenos Aires. They were told "there were very few women in America" so their services would be highly valued.[86] In Bukowina, police admitted they had detailed information about a society

---

84. Case of Lea/Lotti Holz, BPdWA, "Prostitution und Mädchenhandel," 1906/II.

85. Registries for Viennese Brothels, BPdWA, "Prostitution und Mädchenhandel," 1906/I.

86. Posner summarizes the May 1899 trial in Piotrków district, where a gang of traffickers were tried for shipping women to Buenos Aires. Posner, *Nad otchłania,* 15.

of traffickers who regularly shipped women out of Trieste to brothels run by associates in India, Transvaal, and America. Despite the evidence in their possession, however, local officials were unable to prosecute the gang because members carefully "traffic only in girls who are conscious of their fate and thus manage to defend their trade to the courts."[87]

Individual prostitutes interviewed in police headquarters often told the same story: they traveled abroad voluntarily in search of opportunities and not as a result of coercion or abuse by international traffickers. Peppi Beiner of Rozdol, eastern Galicia, insisted she alone was responsible for the decision to relocate internationally. Peppi's mother had died when she was nine, and at age fifteen she left Galicia for Budapest, where she took up work as a professional prostitute. However, "in terms of material conditions," she was not prospering and so after five years she decided "completely on my own" to travel to Constantinople and then on to a brothel in Salonika. According to Peppi's deposition, her migration to the Ottoman Empire had been entirely voluntary, prompted only by the suggestion of an acquaintance at the bordello in Budapest, and she did not use the services of a professional trafficker. To be sure, consular authorities in Constantinople doubted Peppi's story, not least because she was carrying false identity papers. Yet even in the safety of her own consulate (which might well have been persuaded to transport her back home), Peppi stuck to her tale of human agency and individual initiative rather than presenting herself as a victim of international trafficking.[88] Another prostitute who had worked at a brothel in Buenos Aires testified that she had been "sold" by the owner of her original bordello in Pińczów (Kielce province) to a Warsaw trafficker who took her to Berlin and then on to South America. She stressed, though, that after working in Buenos Aires for seven months, she grew intensely homesick and the owner eventually sent her back to Europe at his own cost.[89]

As these stories suggest, even experienced prostitutes could be duped. Female travelers frequently took the decision to migrate abroad willingly. They were nonetheless subject to hyperbole, false promises, and entrapment after arriving in their new homes. Two residents of an Odessa brothel realized firsthand the dangers of traveling on their own when they agreed in 1901 to leave for London with the help of a married couple who had befriended

---

87. "O handlu żywym towarem," *Czystość* 8, no. 22 (1909): 344–46.

88. The report from the Austro-Hungarian Consulate in Istanbul notes that Peppi "made this testimony full of lies in order to protect the trafficker from punishment." BPdWA, "Prostitution und Mädchenhandel," 1906/I, Karoline Merczel file, 1.

89. Posner, *Nad otchłania*, 20.

them. Vjera Karamuszka and Anisja Pisko were promised cushy jobs in London and given 25 rubles apiece before boarding a steamer in Odessa. After arriving in England, however, the money was taken from them and they were informed that the London position did not exist. The group would be continuing on to South Africa, where there were some "great opportunities" for which the girls would be recommended. Their "protectors" promised to cover the cost of the trip, an astronomical 700 rubles, but they would be expected to repay the loan after a few months' work in their new home.

The girls caught the attention of National Vigilance Association representatives, who were struck by the unusual site of a young Jewish couple chaperoning two attractive Christian girls. Nonetheless, despite the assumptions of Vigilance workers, the women insisted they had voluntarily arranged with the owner of their Odessa establishment to transfer to a brothel in London. Once there, even after stern warnings from the Vigilance Association and local town police, the young women opted to continue on their journey to Buenos Aires, probably to try their hand in the brothel trade there.[90] Authorities in Odessa expressed similar frustration that "those who are arrested simply explained that they are only intermediaries, that the girls after all wish to further their own interests by being conducted abroad on their own free will, and [the arrested] speak to them openly" about their prospects overseas.[91] Again, poor young women who had already resorted to sex work at home and saw "only shame and humiliation" before them (according to local police) sought to improve their prospects by emigrating—not unlike thousands of other migrants leaving Russian territory during the early years of the twentieth century.

Traffickers were not saints and frequently employed false promises and exaggerated descriptions of wealth to capture the imaginations, if not the bodies, of their prospective clients. Fourteen-year-old Feiga Kupferman, who was already working as a prostitute in Galicia, was promised she would be able to find honest work in America, quickly accumulate a dowry, and return home as an eligible marriage prospect. Migration agents instead shipped her to Constantinople and deposited her in a brothel, where she was poorly paid.[92]

90. The experiences of the young women, aged nineteen and twenty-one, reflects the pattern of migration from smaller towns to larger cities and then abroad, as well as the tendency of migrant women to train in a specific trade and then turn to prostitution to supplement or replace scarce income from "legitimate" work. The girls were originally from Elisavetgrad and Kishinev, where one of them had been employed as a seamstress and the other as a milliner. The story also provides insight into the activities of the Vigilance Association, which famously failed in its repeated attempts to "rescue" vulnerable young women. Posner, *Nad otchłania*, 23–26.

91. "Handel dziewczętami," *Świat Płciowy* 1 (May 31, 1905): 48.

92. "Handlarze dziewcząt," October 22–23, 1890, 2.

Others were given the same story, replete with promises of easy treasure, a short sojourn, and returning as wealthy women. Most were not told specifically where they were headed until after they had boarded the ship and could not turn back.[93] One gang of traffickers in Kiev posed as legitimate employment agents, offering to send girls on work assignments in other towns, then forwarding them to brothels after their arrival in their destination.[94]

Prostitution was a rough business at every level and efforts to convince unwilling young women to travel abroad sometimes involved violence. Whereas some traffickers willingly released those who backed out of transatlantic commitments, others employed physical techniques to persuade them. The manager of a hotel in Będzin (Russian Poland), for example, testified that he approached one of the prostitutes who rented a room from him after hearing commotion coming from her apartment. Maria Konopka related to him that her pimp had beaten her because she refused to go abroad with him.[95] The culprit was Mr. Hendler, longtime manager of several dozen prostitutes working out of inns in Silesian border towns, who invited traffickers from Russian Poland to select among them for those they wished to transport to brothels in Buenos Aires. Ordinarily, verbal persuasion and false promises sufficed to convince them, but clearly Hendler was not above getting rough with his prospective clients.[96]

Regardless of whether women who made their way to foreign brothels were experienced prostitutes, many were nonetheless capable of manipulating their own surroundings in order to benefit from the migration experience. The story of Tauba Schliwek is a case in point.[97] Schliwek reported to the Austrian Antitrafficking League that a migration agent named Israel Londner approached her in Będzin about working in his "business" in America, offering to help pay for her passage. Londner agreed to sponsor her on the condition that she would repay him later. Schliwek cleverly disembarked in Paris, where she had a sister, yet after only a few days, "things did not go well" for her and she determined to take Londner up on his original offer

93. "Z tajemnic społeczeństwa," 2.

94. "Handel 'żywym towarem,'" *Przyjaciel Sług* 1 (1902): 13. This magazine, intended for domestic servants, featured sensationalist reporting on the subject of white slavery.

95. Posner, *Nad otchłania*, 18–19.

96. Ibid., 16.

97. Tauba's story comes to us from an interview she conducted with Celestine Truxe, general secretary of the Austrian League to Combat Trafficking in Women. There are significant gaps and inconsistencies in the tale that suggest she may have been practicing prostitution before leaving Poland. It is difficult to explain the persistent appearance of the accused trafficker Israel Londner in several establishments where Tauba worked if she was not somehow associated with the brothel business in the Polish Kingdom and in Galicia.

to travel to America. After arriving at the hotel to meet Londner, however, Schliwek reported that her clothes were taken from her and she was raped by one of the accused traffickers. She still refused to report the incident to the authorities, yet when police later raided the hotel, Schliwek testified that if the accused traffickers "had said as much as one word about taking me to a bordello, [she] would not for any amount of money have gone." Yet her original incentive—to seek new opportunities in another town where she already had relatives—was a classic migration scenario. The initial step into sex trafficking was taken willingly and only later was any form of coercion used.[98] In this and other cases, it is unclear when persuasion becomes intimidation and when knowledge crosses over into deceit.

Migration literature is careful to stress that serving as a prostitute in one location does not preclude the use of force to transport women to foreign brothels. Still, we have ample evidence to suggest that experienced prostitutes often volunteered to relocate in order to practice their profession. When such cases ended up in the police files, they reveal a remarkable degree of self-awareness on the part of prostitutes, who often manage to manipulate the situation to their own benefit. The odyssey of Fani Wajner and Liza Kowal demonstrates this pattern. A female procurer approached the young women on the streets of Lwów and invited them to a bordello. From there they were transported to Hamburg, where they boarded a ship bound for Rio de Janeiro. After a year and half working in a Brazilian brothel, the girls were shipped to yet another bordello in Bombay, India. At each stop, migration agents took the girls to private rooms, brought them food and drink, and promised them large quantities of cash. On occasion, according to a letter the young women penned at the end of their journey, they would cry because "it was very tiring for us." But then they "began to grow accustomed to it and it was a little better . . . and they were promised money and presents."

The complaint mailed to the Lwów police commissioner references a luxurious existence in a string of international brothels. The women met "elegantly dressed fellow[s]," attended late-night parties, and were rewarded with steady infusions of fancy food and alcohol. The letter does not mention escape attempts or allude to any type of coercion. Instead, the rambling note claims the girls never sought to leave the bordellos because they "tried to be patient until the Lord God might help" them. In the end, their report concludes, "we

---

98. After police raided the Viennese hotel where the group was staying, Schliwek was delivered into the hands of the Austrian League to Combat Trafficking in Women (Liga Bekämpfung des Mädchenhandels), where General Secretary Celestine Truxe debriefed her. "Interview conducted by general secretary of the Austrian league to Combat Trafficking in Women, Celestine Truxe, July 31, 1907," BPdWA, "Prostitution und Mädchenhandel," 1907/I.

managed to be saved because the tolerated house [in Bombay] burned down and everyone escaped." Because the girls did not have money to pay for their return trip home, however, they asked the police commissioner to "send for us and end our eternal suffering . . . and let us travel back to our people gratis." Sadly for the young travelers, however, their story could not be corroborated and the police refused them any money. Austrian consular authorities in Bombay noted that they could not "confirm the girls' story since in the last ten years none of the public houses located here in the vice district have burned." And even the Austrian representatives in Rio were unable to follow their trail because of the "large number of prostitutes from the provinces of the fatherland [Austria-Hungary] here."[99] It is not out of the question that some degree of psychological pressure was employed on these young women, who no doubt had few other options once they were housed in foreign brothels. Nonetheless, the story reads a bit like a picaresque novel, with wily young women dreaming up a means of returning home once the adventure wears thin and they run out of resources. Even in their extended rambling missive, few complaints emerge beyond their situation being occasionally "tiring" and the unwillingness of their managers to return them home.

Young women who went missing from jobs and homes throughout Polish territory migrated abroad for any number of reasons. Some sought to escape the shame of a personal scandal. Others wanted a route out of inherited poverty and limited professional options. Still others were attracted to the opportunity to travel and see the world, perhaps in the company of a dance or music troupe. Many had worked as prostitutes in their homeland and hoped for better conditions, more money, or a fresh start. Nearly all of them were assisted in some way by a migration agent, who helped them supply the necessary papers to cross the border, purchased the rail and steamer tickets for them, and provided an address for them in their arrival port, without which they would often not be permitted onto a transatlantic ship.[100] Not all of them ended up in brothels in their new homes, though we know that many foreign bordellos were staffed with women from the Polish lands. A significant portion of the women that police and consular authorities labeled "white slaves" at the turn of the century either chose to travel abroad aware of the activities expected of them, left their native country in the company of a known trafficker but then turned to another livelihood after arriving, or

---

99. "Case of Fani Wajner and Liza Kowal," BPdWA, "Prostitution und Mädchenhandel," 1907/I.

100. On restrictions placed on migrants at European ports by shipping companies seeking to avoid the cost of returning passengers rejected at foreign ports, see Brinkmann, "Why Paul Nathan Attacked Albert Ballin," 56–58.

agreed to travel with a migration facilitator believing the agent's promises of well-paid "honest" work.

As with labor migrants, the initial decision to emigrate must be disaggregated from any subsequent coercion women may have experienced after leaving native soil.[101] The evidence available for women involved in trafficking cases suggests that both at the moment of departure and later when the situation soured for them, traveling women were capable of manipulating their fates. Rarely did traffickers kidnap or drug women in order to take them across international borders, though we do have some examples of physical coercion.[102] Most young women were attracted to and excited about their prospects in Buenos Aires or Chicago, Shanghai or Istanbul, and willingly accompanied their benefactors on the initial journey. Only later, after their arrival in the strange land, did many learn what work was expected of them and decide to resist their situation. And resist they did. Their resourcefulness in extricating themselves from unpleasant situations also suggests more control over their fate than images of powerless victims would suggest. At the same time, some of them may have preferred sex work in a foreign brothel over what they viewed as the hopelessness of small-town eastern Europe.

In many respects, women who sold sex after transplanting to foreign shores followed similar migration trajectories and were driven by similar motives as other labor migrants of their time. Their use of commercial sex as an instrument to facilitate their relocation should not blind us to other classic aspects of their migration stories: their ambitious entrepreneurship, their financial desperation, or their interest in starting new lives. Some of these largely unskilled, uneducated migrants were guilty of naïveté, ignorance, and a misguided sense of trust, yet the historical record suggests that they could also be clever, manipulative, resourceful, and pragmatic. During extended moments of intense overseas migration such as the decades preceding the First World War, many travelers joined the exodus abroad without a clear plan or with an incomplete picture of the future. This is the fate of most migrants, and the women under examination here need not fall out of that category merely because of the work they may have performed after arriving in their new homes. Once we look beyond the white-slavery mythology promoted by contemporary actors and reconnect these women with their homes, families, and working conditions at home, we can begin to understand them as an integral part of the history of Polish migration rather than as an exception to that narrative.

---

101. Alpes, "Traffic in Voices," 34–36.

102. Even Ruth Rosen's sympathetic account of the sex trade in progressive-era America concludes that white slavery "was probably experienced by less than ten percent of the prostitution population." *Lost Sisterhood*, 133.

CHAPTER 6

The Devil's Chain

> From beginning to end, the guilty ones, the agents,
> their associates, and all the links in this devil's chain
> are of Jewish faith.
>
> —Stanisław Posner, *Nad otchłania*

> How long will the jackals continue to feed on our
> live flesh?
>
> —"Handlarze kobiet," *Słowo*, July 31, 1891

One of the most overwrought themes in Polish prostitution narratives is the image of the powerful and omnipresent Jew dominating overseas trade in women. Unlike domestic prostitution, which was perceived as an ethnically heterogeneous enterprise, the business of transporting women abroad to work in foreign brothels was marked as a Jewish practice.[1] If consular documents, police transcripts, and court testimonies are any indication, the vast majority of suspected traffickers and most of those convicted and imprisoned for coerced migration were Jews. Leading Polish antiprostitution activists made no secret of their assumptions that Jews were central to sex trafficking operations. The legal scholar Professor Stanisław Posner, himself of Jewish origin, famously proclaimed in 1901 that "from beginning to end, the guilty ones, the agents, their associates, and all the links in this devil's chain are of Jewish faith."[2] Josef Schrank, a Viennese physician and a member of the Austrian Vigilance Society, pointedly labeled

---

1. Police records reflect the ethnic diversity of registered prostitutes, yet brothel owners and managers tended to be Jewish, a situation that helped drive the vice district riots in Warsaw during May 1905. Popular opinion occasionally characterized prostitution itself as a Jewish practice, but registries in key cities—Cracow, Lwów, Warsaw, Łódź—indicate Jewish prostitutes represented a proportion roughly corresponding to their residence in each of these cities.

2. Posner's comments appeared in serial form in 1901and were later reprinted in his longer study *Nad otchłania*.

trafficking in human goods "a special occupation of the Jews."[3] Abolitionists like Augustyn Wróblewski agreed, noting, "procurers in Poland are mostly Jews."[4]

At the popular level, Polish readers were exposed to a nearly constant barrage of reports on young women disappearing at the hands of Jewish kidnappers. Lurid details of Jewish merchants enticing girls into overseas travel bombarded audiences of every social station. Working women, among them the legion of household servants toiling in urban apartments, were warned against "villainous Jewish procurers" bustling about city streets in search of prey. "Most often Jewish," these "factors" purportedly loitered near exchange houses looking for desperate women. Agents ostensibly approached "passing servants, seamstresses, and shop girls" in neighborhood parks, ensnaring them in a web of intrigue.[5] A steady stream of Jews arrested on trafficking charges reminded readers that Yiddish-speaking agents scoured the countryside "luring young girls" to sell in far-off lands.[6] "Caftans" were said to marry and later abandon their "wives" in South American brothels.[7] Meanwhile, the right-wing press explicitly characterized trafficking as "a historical calling of the Jewish nation."[8] Everywhere, "Jewish men and women" appeared as the main perpetrators of the "abominable traffic" in "Polish blood" to "houses of shame" abroad.[9] In all of these respects, the dark, kaftan-wearing Hebrew was central to the drama of international sex migration, serving as the villain to the naïve (Christian) female heroine.

Historians of trafficking have largely accepted this presentation of Jews as central to the coerced trade in women, echoing the impressions of contemporary observers. Wacław Zaleski's 1923 portrayal of Warsaw-based trafficking rings assigns primary responsibility for the trade to enterprising "Litvaks" (Jews from the Lithuanian region).[10] Stanisława Paleolog, head of Warsaw's interwar Women's Police Battalion, graphically depicts "souteneur-husbands" in the Polish Jewish community and their links to the Latin

---

3. Quoted in Augustyn Wróblewski, "Handel kobietami," *Czystość* 5, no. 23 (May 14, 1909): 354–55.

4. Wróblewski, "Handel kobietami," 354–55; Wróblewski, *O prostytucji i handlu kobietami*, 18.

5. "Raz na miesiąc: Gawęda," *Pracownica Polska* 3 (October 1909): 3–4.

6. "Co tam słychać w świecie," *Przyjaciel Sług* 2 (March 5, 1899): 54–55.

7. The journal for domestic servants, *Przyjaciel Sług*, printed regular sensationalist reports of Jewish traffickers, as in the reference to "a whole gang of so-called *caftens,* that is, traffickers in human goods, who have been conducting a systematic procedure over a long period of time." "Handel dziewczętami galicyjskimi," *Przyjaciel Sług* 1, no. 4 (1902): 59–61.

8. Wróblewski, "Handel kobietami," 354–56.

9. "Raz na miesiąc: Gawęda," *Pracownica Polska* 3 (September 1909): 15–16.

10. Zaleski, *Z dziejów prostytucji*, 87–91.

American criminal world.[11] Even contemporary Yiddish writers and dramatists embraced the figure of the wealthy but corrupt Jewish trafficker, turning him at times into a charismatic protagonist, at times a tragic figure.[12] Jewish philanthropists were equally struck by the prevalence of Jews in the trafficking business, emphasizing the financial desperation that drove the business. Bertha Pappenheim returned from her 1903 travels through Galicia concluding that "Galician trafficking in women should not be treated as an isolated phenomenon. Its cause is rooted much more in general economic and spiritual poverty, on the one hand, and in the insecurity of existence brought about by the continual fluctuation of the Jewish population from place to place and from state to state, on the other."[13] Drawing on such testimony, more recent scholars such as Marion Kaplan, Edward Bristow, and Ruth Rosen have offered sympathetic accounts of the Jewish role in international trafficking, citing the extreme poverty, legal restrictions, and cultural limitations of east European Jewish communities that conditioned the turn to the overseas trade in women.[14] Despite these added perspectives, however, accounts of Jewish "migration agents" rarely address the complex relationship between Jewish mediators and their female "customers," nor do they adequately problematize the uses of trafficking imagery in Polish nationalist discourse.

This chapter considers contemporary discussions of Jewish "traffickers," placing them in the broader context of Jewish cultural realities and of Jewish interactions with migrating clients. Without accepting at face value the dominance of Jews in long-distance procurement and sex migration, the analysis here considers how the figure of the Jewish entrepreneur came to figure so predominantly in stories of sexual captivity. The chapter takes into account the unique hardships under which Jewish merchants across the Polish territories operated and explores the dynamic that evolved between traveling women and their (often) Jewish handlers. It also challenges the victim/perpetrator, angel/demon, Jewish/Christian dichotomies that are so paradigmatic

11. Stanisława Paleolog, *The Women Police of Poland* (London, 1957), 5–7.

12. See, for example, Sholem Aleichem, "The Man from Buenos Aires," in Tevye the Dairyman and the Railroad Stories (New York, 1987); and Sholem Asch, God of Vengeance, trans. Joseph C. Landis, The Dybbuk and other Great Yiddish Plays. New York, 1966. For more on this representation, see Mir Yarfitz, "Caftens, Kurvehs, and Stille Chuppahs: Jewish Sex Workers and Their Opponents in Buenos Aires, 1890–1930," (paper presented at UCLA Center for Argentina, Chile, and the Southern Cone Interdisciplinary Workshop, April 7, 2009).

13. Bertha Pappenheim and Sara Rabinowitsch, *Zur Lage der Jüdischen Bevölkerung in Galizien* (Frankfurt, 1904), 67.

14. Kaplan, "Prostitution, Morality Crusades, and Feminism, 619–27; Bristow, *Prostitution and Prejudice*; and Rosen, *Lost Sisterhood*.

in contemporary understandings of transatlantic prostitution. In so doing, the argument complicates the larger narrative of Polish national history, which has occasionally allowed the malevolent Jew to stand in for a whole host of shortcomings plaguing the captive nation. It reassesses the Polish media's portrayal of Jewish agents as "dark" or "alien" and their behavior as "unnatural" or "inhuman"—depictions that helped Polish society distance itself from the problem of forced migration. In the end, the portrait of the Jewish sex broker was multivalent, communicating at times sexual danger, exploitation, abuse, or an alien threat to Polish integrity, and at other times social and economic opportunity. The anti-Jewish trafficking narratives under our consideration helped position Jews at the margins of the Polish national narrative and at the same time they embraced the vulnerable young women ostensibly caught in the traffickers' clutches as central figures in that story.

The presence of Jewish "agents" thus complicated the meanings of prostitution in the Polish imagination. The figure of the sinister Yiddish speaker appears both as a threat to female Christian purity and as an unnatural figure who traded on the virtue of his wife and daughters. As dichotomous images of the sexually rapacious Jew and his vulnerable young target crept into the Polish vernacular, they fed a growing hysteria about unattached women wandering freely in urban centers and the open sexuality they represented. The mythology around white slaves—as passive victims, permanently fallen, socially isolated, and entrapped by Jewish agents—masked an etiology that might otherwise trace these notions back to the Polish household and the Polish community as a whole. The white slavery narrative, though grounded in some truth (since Jewish migration agents did at times assist prostitutes and other young women traveling abroad), thus made it possible to externalize paid sex and its economy and to attribute primary causality to Jewish ringleaders. Polish society, in effect, relied on images of malevolent Jewish actors to offload a whole range of social ills that it often did not wish to confront directly.

The Culpability of Partitioning Powers

Highlighting the dangerous Jewish middleman also allowed contemporary observers to stress Polish exceptionalism. Nowhere outside the Polish territories, experts claimed, did Jews play such a central role in the forced migration of women.[15] According to this argument, the partitioning powers

---

15. Trafficking experts and specialists on the domestic sex trade both characterized the Polish territories as uniquely plagued by high rates of prostitution. Posner, *Nad otchłania*; Wróblewski, *O prostytucji i handlu kobietami*; Schrank, *Mädchenhandel und seine Bekämpfung*; and Macko, *Prostytucja*.

refused vigorous remedies to combat the sex trade and tolerated the sexual enslavement of Polish women. As one exposé put it, "this monstrosity has become a business, organized on a wide scale, operating arrogantly under the eye of the Austrian police and even . . . with the cooperation of some of its members. . . . The [Austrian] Consulate [recommended] that it was better for the entire Austrian province [of Galicia] to keep the matter quiet and not to discuss it." Blaming the occupying empires for the prostitution explosion allowed Polish critics to attack both the external imperial foreigner and the alien within. By deflecting responsibility for the sex trade, Polish chauvinists sought to exculpate their own national community of blame for the moral downfall of a whole generation of compromised young women. Discussions of why the sex trade was so lively in Polish-speaking areas invariably stressed the legal disadvantages the Polish territories suffered that allowed easy procurement of women. One Warsaw columnist noted cynically that "the answer" to the question of why the center of the sex trade is based in Warsaw "is not difficult." The eighteenth-century partition rendered Poland unable to protect itself from criminal elements. "Nowhere else in all of Europe is a society as deprived of the means necessary to defend itself" as was Poland. The trade in women was an open secret on Warsaw's city streets and yet civil authorities took no measures to temper this public menace. Imperial neglect was partnered, according to this view, with the peculiar influx of Jewish brokers into Polish territory. The large numbers of destitute Jewish refugees from Russia "with their colorful clothing and wonderful jewelry" lent an exotic atmosphere to the Warsaw market in women, as did the rich varieties of Yiddish they spoke.[16]

After the 1905 Revolution the trade in "human merchandise" was conducted somewhat more furtively, but nonetheless continued to flourish, according to this view. Local observers claimed the very presence of Jewish merchants (who traded in a variety of wares, both legal and illicit) guaranteed the continuity of the business. As one commentator described it, "there is no city [like Warsaw] within whose walls reside so many thousands of dark individuals driven from the East." This desperate population, the author explained, "which was completely deprived of moral scruples and searching for easy profit," accounted for the volume of trade in prostitutes and the range of techniques used to attract women to it.[17] The Warsaw-based sex trade was enormous and was said to be growing between 1905 and the outbreak of the Great War. Especially "with respect to the prostitution of

16. "Handlarze kobiet," *Słowo* 4 (1891): 4.

17. Orion, "Echa prawdy: Z tajemnic Warszawy," *Prawda* 35 (1913): 2.

children, Warsaw is the *most degenerate city in the world*," pundits proclaimed (emphasis in the original).[18] The problem had international ramifications as well. As far away as Brazil, local brothel keepers and procurers were popularly assumed to be "traffickers who had originated in Galicia, the Kingdom of Poland, or in southern Russia"; local prostitutes were known as *polacas*.[19]

Trafficking Trials and the Polish Imagination

Anxiety about Jews in the prostitution underworld grew increasingly acute in the late nineteenth century as the public's attention was drawn to a series of court cases against alleged traffickers. These prosecutions played out in an atmosphere of heightened ethnic and confessional tension. Dozens of ritual-murder accusations across the Habsburg Monarchy and the Russian Empire gave currency to the notion that Jews sought the blood of Christian innocents, including traveling maidens.[20] Reports of anti-Jewish attacks inundated Polish readers, from discussions in the Viennese City Council to the streets of Paris, Hungary, and Bohemia.[21] Ritual-murder accusations in Austrian Galicia increased dramatically with the much-publicized Ritter case in 1881 to a pitch of some six officially investigated accusations in 1899 alone.[22] The Dreyfus Affair made headlines across the region beginning in 1894. Such cases provided the backdrop to references subtly linking the trade in human "flesh" with rumors of Jewish blood-libel atrocities. The headline introducing the 1892 trafficking trial in Lwów queried, for example, "how long will the jackals continue to feed on our live bodies?" helping to conjure up memories of recent ritual-murder prosecutions. Reports from the prosecution

---

18. "O handlu żywym towarem," 344–46. The author cites Dr. Schrank's study on white slavery in reference to the number of traffickers operating in Austria in 1905.

19. *Wagener Report* (1906), 402. See also, Yarfitz, "Caftens, Kurvehs, and Stille Chuppahs."

20. On turn-of-the-century blood trials across the region, see Hillel J. Kieval, "The Rules of the Game: Forensic Medicine and the Language of Science in the Structuring of Modern Ritual Murder Trials," *Jewish History* 26, nos. 3–4 (December 2012): 287–307; Kieval, "Neighbors, Strangers, Readers: The Village and the City in Jewish-Gentile Conflicts at the Turn of the Nineteenth Century," *Jewish Studies Quarterly* 12, no. 1 (2005): 61–79; and Helmut Smith, *The Butcher's Tale: Murder and Anti-Semitism in a German Town* (New York, 2002).

21. On the Vienna City Council, see "Burz a antysemicka," *Związek Chłopski,* November 1, 1897, 242.

22. For a summary of officially investigated ritual murder accusations in Galicia, see Andrzej Żblikowski, *Żydzi krakowscy i ich gmina w latach 1869–1919* (Warsaw, 1994), 292–93. On the four-year trial of the Ritter family for the ritual murder of a Christian girl in a west Galician village, see Simon Dubnow, *History of the Jews*, vol. 5 (South Brunswick, NJ, 1973), 490–94. Finally, in October 1897, Jakub Jarmark, a Jew from the village of Łodzina, was sentenced to death for the murder of a local Christian farmer. See "Na karą śmierci," *Związek Chłopski*, October 11, 1897, 223.

offered graphic depictions of Christian girls entrapped, seduced, beaten, and left to die. One young maiden demanded a return to Galicia after learning she was bound for a Turkish brothel, prompting her captors to pummel her to death. In the ultimate humiliation, the young [Christian] woman's remains were buried in the local Jewish cemetery.[23] Playing on the imagery of the blood libel, these representations helped solidify the dichotomous paradigm of perpetrator and victim, Jew and Christian, wealthy entrepreneurs and impoverished naïve girls, not to mention cannibal and cannibalized.[24]

Publicity surrounding trafficking cases placed the villainous Jewish trafficker at center stage, helping to shape the ways the sex trade was understood. Media coverage in these trials emphasized the Jewishness and outsider status of the defendants, who were often made to bear the responsibility for an entire system of paid sex. The Lwów trial attracted attention as far away as Cracow, Warsaw, and Vienna, where the *Reichstag* devoted a fiery discussion of the "shameful outrages of the Jewish people" in the affair.[25] In this and other trafficking scenarios, Polish observers—although not always explicitly anti-Semitic—helped draw a link between Jews and the sex trade in the popular imagination. Reports emphasized the Yiddish and Hebrew terms at play among members of organized sex gangs, characterizing the "main organizers [as] Jews." Those they procured were identified as "a poor Christian girl," "a Polish girl," or the "daughter of a farmer," even as significant numbers of the prostitutes themselves were Jewish.[26] By attributing primary responsibility to Jewish procurers and discounting the agency of the women involved, such reports provided the raw material for analyses that would make Jews the chief culprits in the ongoing sexual degeneracy of Polish society. Rather than focusing on the socioeconomic ills that helped drive the apparent increase in sex migration, the Galician elite instead turned to a pattern of scapegoating that emphasized racial purity and the salvation of the nation. Not only did alien men entrap Christian maidens but the young women also fell into a distinctly *Jewish* net. Many were treated by Jewish doctors or mistakenly

23. "Handlarze kobiet," July 31, 1891, 4.

24. On the role of the press in fanning the flames of ritual murder accusations, see Daniel M. Vyleta, *Crime, Jews, and News: Vienna, 1890–1914* (New York, 2007).

25. Quote from the motion introduced to the Austrian parliament by Professor Schlesinger on November 11, 1892 after the conclusion of the trial. The motion, signed by fourteen other deputies, asked the prime minister "what . . . precautions [he] was taking to build an effective claim against the shameful outrages of the Jewish people in Austria?" *Stenographisches Protokol über die Sitzungen des Hauses der Abgeordneten des Österreichischen Reichsrats in den Jahren 1892 und 1893,* session 9, vol. 7 (Vienna, 1893), November 11, 1892, 7638–39ff. See also, "Von Nah und Fern," *Arbeiter-Zeitung,* November 18, 1892, 1, for a report of the same debate.

26. "Handlarze dziewcząt," October 19, 1892, 2; and "Handlarze kobiet," July 31, 1891, 4.

buried in Jewish cemeteries. They engaged in sexual relations with their Jewish perpetrators.[27] As with references to trafficking in the popular press, the depictions here are of a world turned upside down. Rather than Christian Europeans with a civilizing mission enslaving pagans, as European colonizers were doing in Africa or the Near East, power relations (and sexual interactions) were reversed in this scenario. "Monstrous," "satanic" Jews had established networks of predatory agents to dupe Christian girls into sacrificing their virtue and their freedom. In this reverse enslavement process, Christian Poles were removed from European soil and transported to the Near East and North Africa, ending up in the Muslim-dominated sites of Constantinople, Alexandria, and Cairo.

Well-publicized trials of confessed Jewish traffickers in the Russian-Polish border towns of Bytom and Sosnowiec in July 1901 fed an anxious public's thirst for a more colorful and intimate account of trafficking operations.[28] The proceedings stressed the shocking details of migration agents slipping into Galicia and the Congress Kingdom to "collect" women and transport them abroad. Crossing the border at Katowice, the women were reportedly sent on to Wrocław, Berlin, London, and Buenos Aires.[29] Later prosecutions, such as the June 1912 arraignment of three Jewish merchants in Lwów, included accusations that traders forcibly escorted a "lengthy list of girls" to brothels in America or engaged in regular business trips to Galicia to collect "fresh merchandise" for Latin American bordellos.[30]

Othering the Trafficker: Sex Migration as a (Jewish) Family Affair

Although the merchants featured in trafficking trials were residents of Polish territory, Christian observers could still sidestep responsibility for high rates of prostitution by identifying them as members of an alien ethnic community. This proved to be a delicate rhetorical dance: the women themselves could be presented as weak or "corrupted" but not as immoral or dangerous. By contrast, those who facilitated their emigration were assigned blame for their "fall" into prostitution and their abandonment of native soil. The victims were portrayed as "honest, innocent, and poor girls allured through trickery, deceit, and often brute

---

27. "Handlarze dziweczat," October 20, 1892, 2.
28. Posner, *Nad ochłania,* 3–9.
29. Ibid., 12–17.
30. "Handel żywym towarem," *Wiek Nowy,* June 1912, 3.

force," as one reviewer of a study on trafficking summarized.[31] Characterizations of the trade played up its foreignness, exoticism, and even social deviance every step of the way. Key to portraying the sex trade as a problem rooted outside of Polish society was a persistent focus on the "unnatural" character traits and strategies of migration agents, while emphasizing the "normality" of those they preyed on. If the individuals who compelled others to migrate were themselves "abnormal" in some way, then the problem of sexual immorality could be laid at the feet of the trafficker and his or her social "deviance." By focusing on the peculiar proclivities of those who squired young girls to foreign brothels, public scrutiny was trained on the facilitators of these immoral actions and not the actors themselves. Accordingly, contemporary reports addressed the gender imbalance in traffickers' networks, the violations of bourgeois marriage standards and family practices, and the duplicitous Jewish "factors." In all of these ways, the debate over sex trafficking was skewed to focus more on the flawed character of the intermediaries than on the problems that drove women to paid sex. The purity of Polish womanhood could remain unchallenged, or at least unexamined, as attention concentrated on other aspects of the sex-trafficking triangle.

Polish media portrayed purported traffickers as "alien" and unnatural. Wives, children, and other "innocents" frequently played key roles in their operations, for example, suggesting unsavory business practices and lack of family values. Of particular concern was the notion that Jewish traders sold members of their own families into sexual slavery. Spectators at the 1892 Lwów trial heard testimony confirming this practice. "Can we believe that Jankiel Berger sold his own niece?" asked the prosecuting attorney. Katowice police chief Maedler affirmed that in fact Berger sold his seventeen-year-old niece to a brothel in Argentina, as was the case "frequently in the Congress Kingdom, where Jews sell their own daughters to brothels." A second defendant, Moszek Zalc, was accused by a fellow trafficker of selling his fiancée to a third trafficker for 47 rubles. In a complex plot twist that played out during the trial proceedings, this third agent decided to inform local police about the entire operation only after he discovered the traffickers also intended to sell his fiancée.[32] Such examples of horse trading with the bodies of daughters, sisters, wives, or fiancées helped underline the public's assumptions about Jews' inherent immorality and their consistent violation of normative standards of morality. Worse yet, even Jewish parents who were not themselves

31. St. Annański (S. Auerbach), "Zagadnienie prostytucji w świetle higieny społecznej," *Wiedza* 1, no. 3 (1910): 80–83. Annański was reviewing Wróblewski's book *O prostytucji i handlu kobietami*, which prompted a heated debate in the Polish press about trafficking in women.

32. Posner, *Nad otchłania*, 12–17.

involved in the international trade allegedly sold their children into sexual slavery. As one newspaper report claimed, in Warsaw dozens of girls are "brought to this state [of prostitution] at the hands of their own parents."[33]

Accused international traffickers also upset gender norms by assigning women—often wives of merchants managing "export" businesses—to accompany female migrants as they exited Polish territory. Police everywhere in the three empires documented the activities of such female agents, charting their routes out of the country and taking note of the dozens of young women they squired about. Viennese police were especially vigilant about the female role in facilitating migration after the 1906 founding of the Association to Combat White Slavery, based in the imperial capital. The Association traced the activities of Golde Stern, for example, a tailor's wife from Vienna who reportedly traveled across Galicia searching for likely prospects to transport to foreign bordellos. In Czernowitz, eastern Galicia, police reported that Lotti Schachter Riemer was assisting her husband, Aron Riemer, in gathering young women for brothels in Shanghai, information they passed on to the Vienna police and Association leaders.[34] Everywhere police looked, they found Jewish women deeply embedded in trafficking operations. Regional police in Szczakowa, upper (Austrian) Silesia, solicited help from the Cracow authorities to track the activities of the suspected trafficker Chaja Ewelsmann. The Cracow police station confirmed that the Russian subject had crossed into Austrian territory in order to locate and transport Polish girls to South Africa.[35] Authorities in the east Galician towns of Czernowitz, Czortków, and Kołomea similarly reported that Adele Eder, a resident of Constantinople, was "buying women" in each of these places with the intent of sending them to "the Orient."[36] And police in Lwów received an anonymous tip that Rosa Eingross Blocksberg was forwarding local women to Brazil, Bombay, and Egypt.[37]

Those who sought to expose the inverted moral universe of Jewish traffickers often stressed the intimate level on which extended family members took part in the "business" of trafficking young women to distant bordellos. One particularly disenchanted citizen from Buenos Aires complained to police about a Jewish family from Czernowitz operating a trafficking ring based in Argentina with connections to Warsaw, Lwów, Vienna, Trieste, and

---

33. "Z motworności wielkiego miasta," *Ilustrowany Kuryer Codzienny,* July 27, 1913, 2–3.

34. BPdWA, "Prostitution und Mädchenhandel," 1906/I, case no. 4032/06.

35. Police office in Izczakowa to police director in Cracow, January 5, 1905, APKr, DPKr, 1233–37.

36. BPdWA, "Prostitution und Mädchenhandel," 1906/II, case no. 4942.

37. BPdWA, "Prostitution und Mädchenhandel," 1906/II, Blochsberg file.

various spa towns in central Europe. The complainant, Señor Hellich Sterling, emphasized in his letter to Argentine police that "the criminal" Isak Kohn worked closely with his wife, Itzi, scouring Bohemian spa towns for young women to become "live goods" for their business. Even more shocking, the husband and wife team was particularly successful because their South American business had the support of Kohn's mother, who procured women from Austrian spas, his sister Rosa, who assisted the mother, and another sister Esther, who operated several bordellos together with her husband and son. Esther's two brothers-in-law also ran brothels in Buenos Aires. Sterling's letter appended a long list of traffickers ostensibly transporting women between Galicia, the German Empire, Russian Poland, and Argentina, most of them husband-and-wife teams.[38] In the view of many Christian observers, the social order was already threatened by the practice of false marriage proposals, exaggerated promises of employment, and other techniques to attract single female migrants. The advent of women serving as the heads of alleged criminal operations exoticized the Jewish business world still further.

Jewish Poverty, Jewish Business

Many such claims of overall Jewish culpability were exaggerated or incomplete. They were born of deepening public insecurity about emigration, national purity, and the protection of vulnerable members of society. Jews were constructed as scapegoats, standing in as the cause of ills plaguing the Polish lands. At the same time, these tales of Jewish intrigue also reflected tensions around a very real shift in the status and conditions of east European Jewish life in the waning years of the nineteenth century. The restrictions facing Jews after the pogroms of 1881–1884 in southwestern Russia and the imposition of the restrictive May Laws placed them in a uniquely dismal position.[39] Prevented from settling in small towns and villages and separated from the peasant population with which they had traditionally traded, the new regulations forced the Jews of the Pale into already overcrowded cities with little hope of earning a decent livelihood.[40] Since a substantial fraction

---

38. Letter from Senor Hellich Sterling, Buenos Aires, June 25, 1912, to Central Police Direction, Vienna, BPdWA, "Prostitution und Mädchenhandel," 1912.

39. Kaplan, "Prostitution, Morality Crusades, and Feminism," 620–23; and John Klier, *Russians, Jews, and the Pogroms of 1881–82* (Cambridge, 2011).

40. The 1882 May Laws imposed new regulations on Jewish employment and new residency restrictions on Jewish settlement. They were inconsistently enforced, leading to still greater insecurity among the Jewish population of Russian Poland. Polonsky, *Jews in Poland and Russia,* vol. 2, *1881–1914,* 5–17; David Vital, *A People Apart: The Jews of Europe, 1789–1939* (Oxford, 1999), 883–84.

of the Jewish population in Russia already lacked permanent, stable employment, the new decrees increased their pauperization. "In some communities," David Vital has observed, "the pauperized—meaning those devoid of skills, resources, and specific occupations and largely or even wholly dependent on charity—might form as much as 40–50 percent of the population." One contemporary described Russian Jewish poverty as "utterly without a cure" and complained that the Jew had "no available means for improving his condition" in the post–May Laws Russian context.[41]

Even harsher than the regulations themselves was the tacit permission they seemed to give local authorities to harass and exploit the Jewish population by demanding bribes, closing schools, and openly encouraging them to emigrate.[42] Within a few years, when it became apparent that the "temporary" decrees of 1882 were to remain in force and with them the grinding poverty and persecution by Christian neighbors, Jews flocked to the ports and land borders of imperial Russia and headed for North and South America, South Africa, Palestine, and Australia. Together with migrants who traveled only as far as Western Europe, the exodus out of Russia became a mass flight. The steady trickle of about 40,000 Jews who made their way to the United States between 1871 and 1880 turned into a stream of 135,000 in the decade following the pogroms. The real flood took place between 1891 and 1910 when almost a million Jews emigrated to the United States and an additional one and a half million left Russia for other destinations.[43] In addition, a substantial portion of the 800,000 impoverished Jews of Galicia fled to other shores. Despite this substantial exodus, however, natural increase more than kept pace with emigration and the overpopulated Jewish communities of Russia and Galicia continued to swell.[44]

It is no coincidence that the years of overpopulation, oppression, pauperization, and migration among east European Jews corresponded with the popular panic about the Jewish role in trafficking. Jews were indeed intricately involved in migration processes—as facilitators, as agents, and as émigrés themselves. In many respects, human trafficking became a Jewish problem because migration was a Jewish issue at the turn of the century. As the chief rabbi of Britain related to an audience at the 1910 Jewish International Conference on the suppression of trafficking, "we can trace

---

41. Vital, *A People Apart,* 302–3.

42. H. H. Ben-Sasson, ed., *A History of the Jewish People* (Cambridge, MA, 1994), 883–84.

43. Zvi Gitelman, *A Century of Ambivalence: The Jews of Russia and the Soviet Union, 1881 to the Present* (Bloomington, IN, 2001), 1–13. Polonsky, *Jews in Poland and Russia,* vol. 2, *1881–1914,* 18–21.

44. Vital, *A People Apart,* 299–302.

this deplorable change [in Jewish participation in trafficking] directly to the recrudescence of active Russian persecutions in 1881."[45] Edward Bristow poignantly characterizes government-sponsored repression as central to the story of the more than four million Jews in the Pale of Settlement. "Official anti-Semitism meant economic deprivation, a condition of life shared too by the bulk of the Jews in the neighboring Hapsburg provinces of Galicia and Bukovina, and in Rumania," he notes.[46] Without the particular Jewish experience of pogroms, crippling anti-Semitic legislation, and grinding poverty, Bristow argues, "there would have been very little participation in the overseas [sex] traffic."[47]

In many respects, Jews were attracted to the overseas trade in brothel employees for similar reasons other migrants might have been. They had ever diminishing opportunities to earn a livelihood in the Russian Empire as a result of tightening occupational and residency restrictions. They often possessed personal and family connections that helped smooth the transition into dealing in "live goods" on an international scale. And they—like all migrants—had a desire to get ahead and the business of transporting young women abroad represented a potential way out of poverty. The problem, though, is that the more Jews were seen as integrally involved with the business of trafficking, the more contemporaries began to draw conceptual links between poverty and immorality in the Jewish community, reinforcing the notion that east European Jews (in contrast to their West European coreligionists) were uniquely involved in sexually degenerate practices.

Major W. E. Evans-Gordon, a British MP and member of the Royal Commission on Alien Immigration, drew some of these connections in his 1903 report covering his two-month tour through Jewish settlements in Russia and Poland. The genesis of Jewish trafficking, Evans-Gordon claimed, lay in the filthy, morally challenged communities he surveyed.[48] Even in Vilna, relatively well-off by east European standards, Evans-Gordon was struck by the desperation reflected in the "miserable dens and cellars in which the people live." He found the "walls of the houses . . . blistered and rotting, as if poisoned by the pestilent atmosphere within. Two or three families would be found in one miserable room or cellar."[49] This impoverished environment

---

45. *Report of the Jewish International Conference on the Suppression of the Traffic in Girls and Women* (London, 1910), 94.

46. Bristow, *Vice and Vigilance*, 179.

47. Bristow, *Prostitution and Prejudice*, 48–50. For a slightly exaggerated account of Jewish vulnerability to trafficking, see also Hamann, *Hitler's Vienna*.

48. Major W. Evans-Gordon, *The Alien Immigrant* (London, 1903), 48–49.

49. Royal Commission on Alien Immigration, *Minutes of Evidence* (London, 1903), 451–66.

conditioned the prostitutes who migrated to London from the Pale, Evans-Gordon argued. After visiting the garrison town of Dvinsk, not far from Riga on the Baltic coast, he reflected that "people . . . no doubt, are often driven by circumstances into undesirable courses and occupations. The immorality that prevails in towns like Dvinsk may, I think, in large part be accounted for in this way. People are born and have to live. As the struggle for life becomes keener scruples disappear ... it is unquestionable that sexual immorality is prevalent in these overcrowded towns in the Pale, and that the procuring of very young girls is quite a common incident. It is from the lower strata that a considerable proportion of the emigrants come, and of course such tendencies reappear among them in London."[50] For Evans-Gordon, prostitution and international trafficking among Jews were extensions of similar practices established in eastern Europe. Other contemporary observers agreed, viewing Jewish involvement in the overseas sex trade as tied to specific elements of Jewish life. In particular, the traditional institution of ritual marriage, the long-standing Jewish role as employment agents or "jobbers," and the growing influence of Jews in facilitating migration of all kinds helped to situate them at the core of the trafficking world.

Ritual Marriage as Recruitment

The first of these peculiarities was the pattern among east European Jews of establishing marital unions based on a religious ceremony alone, bypassing all civil procedures.[51] These so-called ritual marriages were adapted further among poor families who lacked dowries and often did not have access to a rabbi. All that was required was the permission of the bride's father and two adult witnesses; no state license or fee need be filed. Sometimes the ceremony was even simplified to exclude the rabbi if one was not available and to omit the second witness. Contemporary white-slavery accounts stress the prevalence of such marriages as a method of seducing innocent girls from Orthodox Jewish homes. Handsome and elegantly dressed bachelors would court the daughter of a destitute family and ask the father for her hand in

50. Evans-Gordon, *Alien Immigrant*, 89–90. See also his index, p. 296, for examples of girls emigrating and becoming prostitutes in London.

51. The institution of ritual marriage in Austria dates to a 1773 imperial order that forbade Jews "under penalty of expropriation of property and . . . corporal punishment to enter into the covenant of marriage . . . without a license from the government and without paying the set tax in advance." These new regulations, designed to slow the growth of Jewish families, prompted a pattern of performing religious ceremonies without the accompanying civil document in order to avoid paying the marriage tax. Israel Bartal, *The Jews of Eastern Europe, 1772–1881*, trans. Chaya Naor (Philadelphia, 2005), 72.

marriage, insisting there was no time to wait for the rabbi because the groom had urgent business abroad. The marriages remained unregistered with civil authorities and were not valid once the couple relocated to a foreign country. Trafficking depictions stress resort to ritual marriage as a frequent method for entrapping young women. As one vivid testimony recounted, "in order to capture girls more easily . . . the kaftans . . . trick them into marrying millionaire Americans, or the kaftans themselves marry their victims in Europe, acting as though they are American millionaires. After the wedding they travel to America, where they sell their wives." One such culprit was said to be "sitting in prison in Buenos Aires," having married in this fashion an astounding thirty-five times.[52]

The frequency of false marriages—also called "wild" marriages in legal parlance—in the pre–World War I Galician Jewish community is legion.[53] A significant minority of male migration agents took advantage of this administrative loophole to locate fresh young "brides" to transport abroad for nefarious purposes. Bertha Pappenheim became aware of this problem in her 1903 travels through Galicia, writing about it in some detail.[54] The institution offered several advantages to the family, among them saving money, eliminating bureaucratic delays, and bypassing unnecessary exposure to the imperial authorities. At the same time, the practice increased the likelihood of convincing unsuspecting parents to release their daughters to relative strangers for the purpose of accompanying them abroad. Although clearly only a subset of the women transported abroad on suspicions of sex slavery belonged to this category, the façade of a ritual marriage did allow parents of migrating Jewish girls to maintain the fiction that their daughters were complete innocents.

Isabel Vincent describes one such ritual union in *The Jewish Prostitutes of South America*. Thirteen-year-old Sophia Chamys was courted by a wealthy businessman who visited her shtetl and asked her father for her hand in marriage. The couple claimed they had no time to wait for a rabbi to officiate at the ceremony, so instead two witnesses were rounded up and the girl left the next day with her new "husband." As Vincent explains, "even though the wedding was organized in such haste, and would not be officiated by a religious leader, the Chamys family probably would not have thought anything amiss" because these kinds of weddings were common in the smaller,

---

52. "Handel dziewczętami galicyjskimi." *Przyjaciel Sług* 1, no. 4 (1902): 59–61.

53. John Meyerowicz was described as living in a "wild marriage" with Liza Berger during his 1901 court case for trafficking. Posner, *Nad otchłania*, 6.

54. Bertha Pappenheim, *Sisyphus: Gegen den Mädchenhandel-Galizien* (Freiburg, 1992); and *Zur Jüdenfrage in Galizien* (Frankfurt, 1900).

poorer shtetls where rabbis were rarely present. Commonly referred to in Yiddish as a *stille chuppah* or "silent wedding," Vincent explains, "the ritual marriages had absolutely no validity under civil law, so women entering into these compromising situations had no legal protection." Channeling the contemporary sense that ritual marriage was primarily a plot used by malevolent traffickers, Vincent claims: "Of course, this was very convenient for pimps like Isaac Borowsky, for whom the *stille chuppah* became a very important tool, allowing them to entrap ignorant women and rob them of their civil rights. It is not known how many impoverished young women Isaac married in these 'silent weddings.' It is clear that pimps working in America would typically return to Eastern Europe and travel from *shtetl* to *shtetl* acquiring multiple wives in *stille chuppah* ceremonies."[55] "Brides" such as these would often accompany their husbands abroad or promise parents a wedding after arriving in South America only to find that their marriage was not legally binding. Migration agents who snared women in this way reportedly deposited their wives in foreign brothels or abandoned them, forcing them to fend for themselves in an unfamiliar land where they lacked language skills. Jewish women who had married "ritually" suffered equally if they refused to accompany their new "husbands" abroad, since Jewish law required the girl to obtain a "get" or religious divorce from her husband before she could remarry. Such women were trapped in marital purgatory, lacking the support of a male wage earner but unable to court anew. They were left to support themselves by any means possible, often, according to some accounts, by prostitution.[56]

Ritual marriage as a weapon of international trafficking gangs is one of the most overmythologized and underresearched aspects of east European prostitution. Isabel Vincent devoted five years to uncovering the story of women abandoned in Argentina, but was refused access to relevant documents. Bristow and others discuss the practice uncritically. Marion Kaplan acknowledges that a minority of girls may have actually been kidnapped. Yet "most," she argues, "were semi-willing victims whose desperate desire to emigrate caused them to accept dubious job or marriage offers hastily."[57] More likely, young prospective migrants were promised work in a factory, a

55. Isabel Vincent, *Bodies and Souls: The Tragic Plight of Three Jewish Women Forced into Prostitution in the Americas, 1860 to 1939* (New York, 2005)

56. Kaplan, "Prostitution, Morality Crusades, and Feminism," 620–23. Research on the problem of ritual marriage of Jewish traffickers and brothel keepers is incomplete. Vincent faced difficulties accessing documents on the subject in Argentina, and other accounts are inconsistent about the degree to which women were aware of their destination when they entered these marriages.   ·

57. Kaplan, "Prostitution, Morality Crusades, and Feminism," 620.

place to live, and free passage if, as one 1902 newspaper reported, they agreed to travel with a certain agent.[58] Ritual marriage to a migration facilitator no doubt helped gain permission from a "bride's" family for her to leave home and minimized awkwardness at border crossings, where young women traveling with unrelated older males were often singled out for special questioning. Ruth Rosen points out that in order to "secure entry into foreign countries, women were often declared to be wives or relatives of the procurer who accompanied them."[59] To prove to customs officials that the women were actually related, migrant agents took great pains to teach them how to answer questions likely to be asked on the border. Regardless of whether the marriage was "ritual" or completely fabricated, false marriages were used as a tool of migration agents to ease the transfer of women across international boundaries.

Reliance on such tactics does not in itself demonstrate force or deceit, since the women may well have been complicit in the charade, nor does it preclude deception as part of the migration experience. Evidence from European archives documents the repeated travels of Jewish import–export merchants between Polish territory and the port cities of Latin America, Africa, and the Middle East, often in the company of young women to whom they claimed to be married. Yet some of these materials complicate the story of marriage and abandonment. Harry Halberg, a tailor from Janów (today's Dolina, south of Lwów), for example, married Chaja Rochmes, the daughter of a synagogue beadle, in July 1900. The couple immediately departed for Buenos Aires, where Chaja took up residence in a brothel. Harry was back on the radar of Austrian police six years later when he took a steamer to Marseille under a false name, intending to travel on to Lwów to obtain a divorce from his wife. Habsburg authorities believed him to be a professional procurer looking for "fresh goods" to transport back to Argentina. Interestingly, however, consular documents make reference to the couple's daughter, whose birth date suggests she was born very soon after the couple's marital union was finalized. Either Chaja had engaged in a more extended relationship with her fiancé than the standard ritual marriage trope implies or he had married her in spite of her preexisting pregnancy. Regardless, when Chaja's parents granted their daughter's marriage and agreed to her emigration, their

---

58. In this newspaper story, a father recounts his search for his two daughters who had migrated with the help of an employment agent to Buenos Aires; however, when they arrived at the port, the girls were met by "two ladies claiming they were relatives" of the factory manager, who escorted them to a brothel. "Handel dziewczętami galicyjskimi," 59–61.

59. Rosen, *Lost Sisterhood*, 119.

consent may have been more related to the shame of an illegitimate pregnancy than it was to being duped by a clever trafficker.[60]

Similarly, Kohos Baruch, a butcher's helper from Czernowitz, married Jetti Flegl in a ritual marriage in 1908. Soon after this, they left for Buenos Aires. International police were alerted to Kohos because of his frequent, lengthy tours of Europe, his absence of any visible profession, and because he gave as his permanent address the Philosophy Faculty at the University of Buenos Aires. He claimed he had "no idea what his wife lived off of in Buenos Aires" while he was traveling, thus arousing suspicion that she worked as a prostitute. But Argentine authorities reported Jetti was not registered as a prostitute and that neither she nor her husband had a police record of any kind in South America. Jetti Flegl had been registered in Czernowitz as a prostitute prior to her marriage to Baruch. Surely he knew she had worked in the sex trade before marrying her. Perhaps they left Czernowitz in order to start over in a new community and not merely as part of a trafficking scheme. Again the marriage did not follow the pattern of a union between a sheltered Orthodox girl and a dashing bachelor on a brief visit to town. Both bride and groom were longtime residents of Czernowitz and could have been expected to know each other's background prior to their engagement. Moreover, they remained married for at least six years, according to the police deposition taken in February 1914.[61] Both of these couples were clearly hiding something from police. Baruch gave a false address and no indication of his livelihood, whereas Halberg (in the previous story) was traveling under an assumed name. But the couple's relationships to each other, to international trafficking, and to the larger practice of prostitution are much more complicated than the trope of "abandoned wife" suggests. In both cases, it is conceivable that the bride, the groom, and the bride's family were all involved in hatching plans to emigrate. Sneaking past police and customs officials does not point undisputedly to kidnapping and forced migration, as much of the white-slavery literature suggests. In fact, as one contemporary noted, parents themselves were sometimes in on the plot. "Many Jewish parents in Galicia," Wróblewski claims, "have a sense for the fate that awaits their daughters but out of poverty they decide to rid their households of their burdens."[62]

The large number of Jewish girls squired abroad after fictitious marriages raises doubts about how much families knew of the fate of their offspring.

---

60. Letter from Hungarian Consulate to Vienna Central Police Headquarters, June 11, 1906, BPdWA, "Prostitution and Mädchenhandel," 1906/I, case no. 3529/06, 1–3.

61. "Baruch Kohos, Mädchenhandelsverdacht," BPdWA, "Prostitution und Mädchenhandel," 1914/2.

62. Wróblewski, *O prostytucji i handlu kobietami*.

Take, for example, the case of Rifka Fingerhut, an unemployed serving girl living with her family in Kałusz, a small town in eastern Galicia. Fingerhut met Josef Libo (born Blumenzweig) in the nearby town of Stryj. Libo promised he would marry her, take her back to Turkey with him, and find her well-paid work at a beer hall. The two traveled to Lwów and shared a room in a hotel, whereupon Libo convinced Fingerhut to return to her family in Kałusz while he collected travel money to bring her back to Turkey. The young couple's plans were interrupted, however, when Galician police arrested Libo on an anonymous tip from Constantinople accusing him of procuring women for a bordello in Lwów.[63] Rifka Fingerhut's story is not unlike many thousands of others. She was already somewhat worldly, having worked on her own as a serving girl, and was willing to take the social risk of traveling alone with a man to the regional capital and even sharing a room with him. Moreover, according to her own testimony, Fingerhut fully intended to travel abroad with her "fiancé" on the promise of well-paid work. She probably did not foresee being placed in a brothel upon arriving in Turkey, yet this does not discount the level of independent decision making she exercised up to that point.

Part of the difficulty in assessing the degree of coercion to which female migrants were subjected lies in the prism through which we learn of their stories. Police and social-welfare agencies often assumed the worst intentions of those with previous criminal records. What, for example, did the future wife of Harry K. believe about his plans when they met in Lwów while he was home visiting his family? Claiming he was the representative of a gold mine, the elegant bachelor made the acquaintance of the (Jewish) daughter of a prominent citizen. He soon expressed his desire to marry her and the parents agreed. After the civil wedding, the newlyweds left on a trip to Vienna. However, from there Harry K. appears to have sent his new wife alone to Buenos Aires, where she was immediately placed in a brothel. Having gone along with the migration from her hometown to Vienna and on to South America, the young woman now realized the fate her new husband intended for her and resisted. Her efforts to extricate herself from this situation came to the attention of an official at the Austrian Consulate, who helped "rescue" her. Nonetheless, Harry K. proved in a trial at the consulate in Buenos Aires that he was married to the woman and appealed successfully to the courts to return his legitimate wife to him.[64] Apart from demonstrating a stunning

---

63. BPWA, "Prostitution und Mädchenhandel," 1906/I, Jozef Libo file, 1, 9, 11.

64. *La Plata* (November 7, 1901), cited in Posner, *Nad otchłania*, 90–91. A similar story is repeated in a doctoral thesis by Dr. S. Maxin, "Der Mädchenhandel, Social-und-criminal-politische Studie,"

degree of power that a husband was legally permitted to exercise over his wife—including the right to prostitute her—such cases also suggest a pattern of limited agency on the part of poor females. Women such as Harry's wife may have willingly assented to the initial migration and yet also resisted when things did not go as expected.

Even when young women were warned against traveling abroad with new husbands, many insisted on going anyway. The Polish press recounted, for example, the tale of Ludwik Berger, originally from Hungary, who became engaged to the daughter of a "decent Berlin family." Since the Berlin police were already aware of Berger's record as a trafficker, they summoned the young woman and her parents to inform them of the future son-in-law's involvement in the trafficking business. The daughter, however, refused to believe the accusations about her intended and escaped from her parents' home to travel with him. The couple was last reported in Vienna still "planning" a wedding. From there, the young bride appears to have traveled on to Cairo, whence her parents received a postcard signed "from your deeply unhappy daughter."[65] Clearly, something had gone badly wrong with the girl's original plan to flee with her fiancé and start a better life. Yet we cannot assume that there was no affection involved in the attachment. As the migration authority Maybritt Jill Alpes proposes, relationships between trafficker and migrant tend to be dynamic and multileveled. "Patterns of coercion and exploitation do not work as one expects," she explains. "They change over time and hence there can be elements of help and gratefulness even in the relationship between a trafficker and a trafficked woman."[66] It is important to note that "the 'trafficker' at first is somebody who brings help" to an individual searching for a way out of her current circumstances. Sources suggest that even without the veiled "legitimacy" of a marriage offer, prospective migrants found ways of reconciling the risk of traveling alone with their desire to improve their economic status. They replied to advertisements for positions abroad that promised work as "a housekeeper for a lonely widower" or in the home of a "young man of means [who was] seeking acquaintance with a young person with serious intentions," situations that suggested some degree of compromised behavior.[67]

completed at the University of Freiburg in 1904. Here the trafficker's name is Harry N. and he finds his wife in Cracow rather than Lwów, however, the rest of the details remain the same. Cited in H. Polańska, "Handel dziewczętami," *Świat Płciowy* 1, no. 3 (October 1905): 21–23.

65. Maxin, "Mädchenhandel," cited in Polańska, "Handel dziewczętami," 21–23.

66. Alpes, "Traffic in Voices."

67. Polańska, "Handel dziewczętami," 21–23.

Of Jobbers and Malevolent Migration Agents

The second important tendency that helped channel Jews into the trafficking business was the long-standing phenomenon of Jewish "jobbers" or "factors," who functioned as intermediaries in linking poor clients up with employment opportunities. The precarious financial and legal position of east European Jews encouraged them to pursue a wide range of dangerous, unethical, or even illegal employment options. Because a large number of livelihoods were legally restricted or discouraged by custom to Jews, many resorted to international trade to eke out an existence. Smuggling of all kinds, including transporting undocumented women, was but one of these shadowy livelihoods. Jews relied on their historic status as a middleman minority during these years, a function that grew out of their long-standing occupation as shopkeepers or managers of taverns.[68] As more and more Jews were displaced from their secure livelihoods, they increasingly came to serve as mediators of all kinds—communicating news, trading information, and eventually locating jobs for needy applicants. Trading in goods on an international scale was but an extension of these earlier professions. Sometimes the "products" in which Jews traded were women who wanted to emigrate; at other times they were luxury goods in high demand among local populations. The transportation of women across international boundaries may well have formed one component of a larger trade in perfume, women's clothing, lingerie, cigars, or jewelry.[69] As one accused trafficker explained about his choice of livelihood, "generally I did whatever I needed to earn money."[70]

Police records suggest Jewish peddlers frequently smuggled goods across the borders of east European states under the noses of customs agents to avoid penalties or to dodge customs duties. Border guards at crossings along the Russian, Austrian, and German frontiers often detained Jewish merchants on suspicion of trafficking in women, only to discover large quantities of luxury

---

68. On the middleman minority status of Polish Jews, see Keely Stauter-Halsted, "Jews as Middleman Minorities in Rural Poland: Understanding the Galician Pogroms of 1898," in *Antisemitism and Its Opponents in Modern Poland*, ed. Robert Blobaum (Ithaca, NY, 2005), 39–59; and Hillel Kieval, "Middleman Minorities and Blood," in *Essential Outsiders: Chinese and Jews in the Modern Transformation of Southeast Asia and Central Europe*, ed. Daniel Chirot and Anthony Reid (Seattle, 1997), 213.

69. John Meyerowicz claimed at his 1901 trafficking trial in Bytom that he traded in "cigars, lingerie, and women's clothing," in addition to "showing foreigners around Buenos Aires." Nussem Lechner testified in a 1913 deposition that he had been trained as a pretzel baker in his hometown of Grzeminów, but left at age twenty-two to help his uncle peddle perfume in Cairo. Posner, *Nad otchłania*, 8; Letter from Austro-Hungarian Consulate in Shanghai to Vienna Central Police Headquarters regarding case of Nussem Lechner, September 16, 1913, BPdWA, "Prostitution und Mädchenhandel," 1913.

70. Meyerowicz, quoted in Posner, *Nad otchłania*, 8.

items or foreign currency in their possession.[71] One suspected trafficker from Czernowitz was arrested in 1890, for example, with a billfold full of French francs, Austrian gulden, and Chilean pesos totaling about $25,000 in 2010 value, along with an expensive watch, a gold chain, and a diamond ring.[72] Dealing in contraband accounts for the wealthy men who "lacked a visible profession" and their unexplained periods of travel across multiple international boundaries.[73] Such suspicions prompted police to track the activities of businessmen like Wolf Goldenberg. The Jewish tailor from Warsaw received a telegram while taking a cure in the Austrian spa town of Bad Hall: "Be so good and take the clocks from the clockmaker there and send them on to me here."[74] The trouble lay in determining which contraband items Goldenberg and his associates were preparing to ship.

East European Jews functioned not only as a middleman minority in the Polish lands, delivering smuggled goods across international frontiers, but also as migration and employment brokers. As we have seen, the omnipresent Jewish "factor" who hung around employment agencies was an icon in nineteenth-century Polish culture. But the stereotype was based on real conditions, and many supplicants counted on contacts with local Jews to locate positions. The Jewish employment agent was easily confused with the Jewish procurer of brothel women, however, and no doubt he was sometimes the same person. These overlapping functions—jobber and pimp—helped facilitate trust among migrants seeking a livelihood in a new city. The long and infamous role Jews played as international migration agents also gave them easy access to young women to be transported—willingly or unwillingly—to foreign brothels. Their service as migration facilitators helped taint Jews with the sin of encouraging the various waves of emigration out of Polish territory during the decades prior to World War I. As successive waves of migration emptied border areas of the Polish territories in the late

---

71. Rubin Eliasz Grunberg, Mendel Wieser, and Josel Simpel were arrested on suspicion of trafficking in women and arraigned in Lwów in June 1912. The evidence against the three men consisted of the observation that they "spent long periods of time in America," "made excursions from time to time around Galicia," and were in possession of "a mass of costly goods" when they were arrested. "Handel żywym towarem," *Wiek Nowy*, June 5, 1912.

72. Josef Münzer admitted to operating a bordello in Buenos Aires. He was arrested at the port in Bremen on suspicion of trafficking girls, with over 3,000 francs (equivalent to about $600 in 1890), 1,000 gulden (about $500 in 1890 terms), and a handful of pesos in his pocket. BPdWA, "Prostitution und Mädchenhandel," 1887–1890, Josef Münzer file.

73. Vienna police report, BPdWA, "Prostitution und Mädchenhandel," 1914/2, Baruch Kohos file.

74. Case of Wolf Goldenberg and Consorts, Trafficker. Letter from Bad Hall, August 2, 1907, k.k. Landes-Gendarmerie-Kommando Nr. 8 to k.k. Polizei-Direktion, BPdWA, "Prostitution und Mädchenhandel," 1907/I.

nineteenth century, the Polish elite came to perceive the departure of their countrymen as "actuated from without," especially by Jewish facilitators. Rather than blaming the economic situation at home or the attraction of jobs abroad, Polish intellectuals, clergy, and gentry regarded migration as a "fever," something that they could not control and that Jews appeared to be stimulating in every way. As Benjamin Murdzek argues, nineteenth-century commentators perceived emigration as "a sort of mass hysteria, a mob action, in which the individual participants were incapable of rational consideration or appraisal of the realities of their existence."[75] The prime cause of this "mass suggestibility" was the migration "agent," often seen as "the malignant instigator," the "Pied Piper leading the ignorant masses to their inevitable doom." The malevolent figure of the "agent-demon" played a central role in most nineteenth-century discussions of the causes of emigration, especially during the "Brazilian fever" of the 1890s. In particular, the Galician lawyer Leopold Caro made the exposure of the underhanded schemes of these agents one of his central campaigns.[76] Generalized anxiety about migration was thus compounded by images of the nefarious agent, effectively intensifying negative public opinion around Jewish international merchants.

Despite the negative press to which Jewish employment agents and migration facilitators were subjected, young women continued to seek their help in locating positions both within the Polish lands and abroad. Yet the multiple functions Jewish businessmen performed made it difficult for prospective clients to predict the outcome of their negotiations. When Scheindla Szymanowa Żyto met Jozel Goldmann and his wife on the train from Kiev to Lwów, for example, she could not have known he was an experienced procurer of women for Argentine brothels. Goldmann convinced her that for 30 rubles he would provide her passage on a steamer to Buenos Aires, where Żyto looked forward to joining her parents. At the time of his arrest, Goldmann had a "large bundle of documents, including photographs of women and letters written in Yiddish, Polish, and German," suggesting he was transporting "live merchandise" abroad on a large scale. Authorities concluded Żyto was being taken directly to a bordello in Buenos Aires and arrested Goldman for trafficking.[77] Similarly, Viennese police tracked the

75. Murdzek, *Emigration in Polish Social-Political Thought*, 133.

76. Leopold Caro, "Das Problem der Auswanderungsfrage," *Volkswirtschaftliche Wochenschrift*, nos. 1215, 1217, 1218 (1907), as cited in Murdzek, *Emigration in Polish Social-Political* Thought, 135–37. See also, "Unserer überseeischen Auswanderer und die Enquete vom Jahre 1905," *Zeitschrift für Volkswirtschaft, Sozialpolitik und Verwaltung* (November 1907); "Wychodźtwo Polskie," *Ekonomista* 2, no. 7 (1907): 1–14; and "Unsere Auswanderer in Brasilien," *Österreichische Rundschau*, February 1, 1908.

77. "Aresztowanie handlarza żywem towarem," *Wiek Nowy*, June 21, 1912, 10.

author of a 1904 advertisement seeking a pretty girl "to correspond with" and "eventually to marry," partially because the ad stressed the gentleman's wealth and his Argentine connections. Authorities claimed the newspaper appeal was part of a larger trafficking racket, but the women who responded to it may not have been aware of this context.[78] And Mendel Piernick was picked up by police at his London bootery and accused of conspiring to procure a recent immigrant for "improper purposes." Piernick was certainly guilty of inviting Marjem Lie Giek, a young Polish Jewish woman with whom he had become acquainted before leaving Łódź in 1902, to follow him to London. She did so and shrugged off the efforts of the Society for the Protection of Jewish Women, only to find herself in a brothel disguised as a bootery.[79] The Jewish mediators in all these cases plied so many indeterminate occupations—functioning variously as petty merchants, import-export dealers, jobs brokers, and migration agents—that smuggling young women across international boundaries was merely an extension of other more-or-less legitimate livelihoods.

At other times, however, trafficking was a full-time occupation, something defendants occasionally acknowledged under interrogation. Wolf Berkowicz and his wife, Sara, from Kielce, testified that they left the Polish Kingdom in 1911 and went to Buenos Aires, where Berkowicz owned a public house. Having made his fortune, he returned home in 1913, acquired property in Kielce, and established a bordello there. All the while, he maintained connections to Brazil and over the years "sought out girls interested in turning to prostitution and . . . sent them on to his wife, who would take them to a certain Joskowicz, a former acquaintance from Kielce who kept a brothel in Buenos Aires."[80] In a more transparent case, Mendel Proffer was arrested in Cracow while traveling with a group of "consorts" in March 1912 and served fourteen days for procuring. Proffer was already under suspicion, having been arrested for depositing his ritual wife in a New York brothel in 1903 and for domestic procuring in 1899.[81] Finally, the case of Nussem Lechner, the Galician-born pimp sought by authorities on three continents for trafficking, left little doubt about the suspect's line of work. Lechner's case reveals the chaos of overlapping schemes, while highlighting the level of petty crime and abuse common to the underworld of international prostitution. In 1905 at the

---

78. "Heiratsantrage," *Neue Freie Press,* August 31, 1904, BPdWA, "Prostitution und Mädchenhandel," 1906/II, case no. 8272.

79. Evans-Gordon, *Alien Immigrant,* 296.

80. Berkowicz was eventually arrested in 1926 and served out a three-year prison sentence for trafficking. BPdWA, "Prostitution und Mädchenhandel," 1914/2.

81. BPdWA, "Prostitution und Mädchenhandel," 1911.

age of twenty-four, Lechner (born Nute Spieler) reportedly began making his living off prostituting a certain Rina in Cairo. The following year found him living in the vice district of Shanghai with a registered prostitute who claimed to be his ritual wife. Lechner traveled regularly between Cairo and Port Said, where he sent girls to yet another mistress who was running a tolerated house in India. In 1912, he deposited Regina Spaeklin in a bordello in Shanghai, then departed for Singapore, where he lived for a time "off the immoral proceeds of prostitution," according to Singapore police reports. Meanwhile, authorities in Rio de Janeiro reported they had evidence he was procuring women for brothels there, and Sarajevo police detained him in the company of his supposed new fiancée, Schiffre Ikifmann. Through it all, Lechner managed to avoid detention on the grounds that he had become a Turkish subject and traveled under the protection of the French Consulate.[82]

Lechner's activities fit neatly into the employment profile of many east European Jews: He worked variously as a pretzel baker, a perfume peddler, a jewelry merchant, and in a string of hotels. He had business relations across the globe and traveled widely, often abusing the tradition of ritual marriage to transport young women across international boundaries. Nevertheless, with the exception of one Russian prostitute who unsuccessfully brought a case against him in 1909, Lechner was never explicitly accused of forced procurement. Indeed, when Czernowitz police tracked down one of the women he had transported to Buenos Aires almost twenty years before (at the instigation of the woman's brother), she wrote to say she did not wish to return home, preferring to remain in Buenos Aires managing what appears to have been a brothel. In Lechner's case, serving as a migration facilitator, like engaging in multiple ritual marriages, was not coercive on the face of it. Lechner was a petty criminal, a pimp, and probably also a smuggler. He was reported to have a "harsh nature" and an unsavory personality, but we have little evidence that he forced young women into prostitution against their will. Instead, the transport of prostitutes between countries may well have been a mere extension of larger international smuggling rings with which Lechner and others were heavily involved.

Clearly a large part of the motivation for enticing young women to leave the country was the healthy compensation everyone in the chain received for their services. Even "subcontractors" who procured women locally and turned them over to migration agents could make well over 500 rubles per girl, sometimes as much as 1,000 rubles for "the prettiest specimens."[83] In

---

82. File of Nute Spieler/Nussem Lechner, B PdWA, "Prostitution und Mädchenhandel," 1913.

83. Some of the smaller players in the drama testified to these amounts at the trial. One by the name of Hendler reported he received 1,100 rubles for delivering two girls to a trafficker in

contrast to the compensation even the best-educated Jew could garner in "legitimate" professions in Congress Poland, these were impressive rates of pay. And the risk of apprehension and conviction was minimal, especially until the Paris Congress of 1902 brought the problem of international trafficking to public attention. Until then, border guards were easily bribed, local police overlooked charges of procurement, and courts had difficulty convicting defendants in the absence of compelling evidence. Although twenty-two of the twenty-seven defendants in the 1892 Lwów trial were convicted, they were found guilty of the lesser charge of (local) procurement rather than international trafficking, and were sentenced for only six months to one year of prison time. The wide range of witnesses at the 1901 Bytom trial, by contrast, allowed the judge to find the three defendants guilty of the more serious offense of trafficking and sentence them to three to five years hard labor (perhaps because in this case, the prisoners confessed they were transporting women to brothels). Yet trials of this nature were relatively rare. More often, police assembled circumstantial evidence on possible sex trafficking rings, collected complaints from family members, and tracked the activities of individual migration agents. Even those who were occasionally sentenced for their activities appear to have returned to their previous endeavors almost immediately after serving their time.

Contemporary activists who sought to dissuade young women from falling into the hands of traffickers tacitly acknowledged the appeal of material gain and recognized that coercion was rarely used in convincing migrants to go abroad. Experts such as Dr. Maxin acknowledged that "trickery" was not the key to success in appealing to potential sex migrants. In fact, "hunger and poverty are the greatest allies of these men." Moreover, "sometimes the girls give them their hands of their own free will." In particular, he noted, "the most unhappy of the unhappy come from the very environment in which thousands of victims are dying of typhus."[84] Migration agents were tricky, insincere, and often desperate businesspeople, but their activities were sometimes assisted by willing—or at least reckless—young women desperate for the opportunity to improve their circumstances and willing to accept risks to do so.

There is ample evidence that Jews were well represented in the sex trade in the Polish lands—as they were in most urban professions and international

---

Katowice. A prostitute not directly involved in international trafficking testified that she had learned from Hendler's wife that he traveled abroad three times a year with "goods," which he sold to agents who took them to Buenos Aires. He received 400–500 rubles per girl for as many as eight at a time. Posner, *Nad otchłania*, 16–17.

84. Polańska, "Handel dziewczętami," 21–22.

trading networks. Yet it is equally clear that by turning the trafficking problem into a primarily Jewish issue, the Polish public effectively dodged responsibility for a whole host of causal factors that were responsible for maintaining a thriving prostitution industry in Poland and beyond. A deep underlying malaise about the dislocation of rural–urban migration, the shortage of jobs for single women, the dangers of emigration, and the abuses of the household servant system was sidestepped by making wily Jewish procurers the chief cause of the widening system of paid sex. The melodramatic projection of Polish anxieties about these social ills onto sinister Jewish protagonists had the added effect of replicating a familiar pattern in Polish national discourse. Constantly defeated by selfish aristocrats or aggressive foreign powers, the Polish elite could too easily blame others for the ills of modernity rather than engage in vigorous debate about real solutions to domestic problems. Granted, the powers governing Polish territory imposed certain restrictions on the range of solutions available to them. Yet by the early years of the twentieth century, the increasingly liberalizing regimes of Austria and Russia made possible a real discussion about the sources of and solutions to some of the issues that underlay the thriving trade in women's bodies.

As most of the cases discussed here suggest, those involved in the overseas transport of women did not act out of pure malevolence. Rather, they were desperate people reacting to challenging situations. Sometimes they cleverly manipulated legal loopholes or used their status as middlemen to arrange unsavory employment for migrating women. They frequently relied on a network of their own family members to assist in smuggling schemes. More often than not, the women they accompanied to foreign brothels were part of a much broader wave of young Jewish migrants fleeing a whole range of injustices and hardships in their east European homes. The melodramatic stereotype of the vicious agent coercing his entirely ignorant client into compliance was a severe misrepresentation of events and is sorely in need of revision. Once we complicate the picture of forced migration, a whole host of deeper problems reflecting the darker side of east European modernity reveal themselves. It is to these that we turn in the next chapters.

CHAPTER 7

Female Activism and the Shadow State

> The events of the last several days have awakened our social consciousness in the greatest possible way. We have had to divest ourselves of our indifference and instead take the most vigorous action. . . . Never before have we had before our eyes such gloomy images, never before have such falseness and hypocrisy appeared in social relations to such a degree. Everything that was hidden now stands before us in all its nakedness and is appalling in its immensity, an abomination, overflowing our hearts with boundless and gloomy sadness.
>
> —"Kilka słów w kwestyi prostytucyi z powodu ostatnich pogromów," *Nowe Słowo*, October 15, 1905

Anxiety surrounding the disappearance of young women and their ostensible Jewish captors soon exploded on Warsaw's city streets. In May 1905 a crowd of angry workers stormed the city's red-light district, attacking Jewish-run bordellos, smashing furniture, tearing hinges off doors, and shattering windows. Pianos, paintings, crystal, porcelain, and bedding flew out of second-story rooms as a cloud of feathers descended on nearby neighborhoods. Knife fights bloodied the streets and an upturned meat wagon left carnage in its wake. The violence and destruction continued for two days. By the time police restored order forty people, including many owners of public houses, lay wounded or dying. The bedlam all but eliminated the brothel trade in the center of the former Polish capital. Pimps fled the city, setting up business out of private residences on the edge of town. None of the public houses destroyed in the rioting reopened in central Warsaw until after the revolutionary events of the 1905–1907 period, leaving just two Christian-owned facilities in the Old Town out of the dozens operating prior to the riots.[1] The unrest followed a winter of strikes and demonstrations across the Polish Kingdom and the Russian Empire as a whole. The focus

---

1. "Krwawy dramat," *Słowo*, May 25, 1905, 3; "Precz z prostytucyą i nierządem." *Czystość* 1, no. 1 (June 20, 1905): 5–6. ; and Zaleski, *Z dziejów prostytucji w Warszawie*, 76–78. Zaleski's assessment is based on Warsaw police reports.

of the spring mayhem, however, was unique: the violence was directed only at known sites of tolerated prostitution and it concentrated exclusively on Jewish-owned brothels.[2]

The "Alfonse Pogrom," as the Warsaw press quickly labeled the May events, marked a turning point in popular attitudes toward commercial sex, sparking increased public awareness of prostitution across the Polish territories. Along with the other events of 1905–1907, the riots also ushered in a more permissive political atmosphere in the Russian Empire, allowing a boom in organizational initiatives to combat commercial sex. As pimps and procurers became the chief objects of public opprobrium, prostitutes were increasingly painted as deserving objects of humanitarian intervention.[3] Following the 1905 Revolution, residents of the Polish Kingdom were able to attack prostitution head-on, founding a broad range of philanthropic, charitable, and educational initiatives. Female activists led the charge in this effort, followed by doctors and eventually eugenicists and legal experts. This initial feminine activism was based on a new sense of resolve that the behavior of the prostitute was linked to the health of the nation as a whole and that bringing reform to the world of prostitution would by extension improve Poland's national fortunes.

This chapter outlines the genesis of women's public activism and traces the shift in public perceptions on which it was premised, including an increased willingness to discuss openly the prospect of a return to national sovereignty. Female aid workers stepped in to take advantage of new opportunities for reform. In the process they carved out a public role for themselves in Poland's newly open civic space. The chapter suggests that the cohort of feminine activists that emerged after the 1905 Revolution, most of them members of professional or intellectual families, helped constitute a "shadow state" that worked to shape and transform Polish society in preparation for independence. Concentrating specifically on the women caught up in the world of paid sex, they set out to improve conditions among Poland's lower orders in order to strengthen the health and welfare of the nation itself.

---

2. Historians disagree about the genesis of the riots. Norman Davies calls them a working-class attack on urban vice, arguing they emerged as a "spontaneous demonstration against Warsaw criminal elements." A closer examination of police reports, however, reveals that the events were an outgrowth of a turf battle between two rival groups of pimps in downtown Warsaw and that, in fact, both the rioters and the victims were Jews. Despite this, the public continued to refer to the May Days as the "pimp pogroms." Norman Davies, *God's Playground: A History of Poland,* vol. 2, *1795 to the Present* (New York, 1982), 273; "A Jewish Fracas in Warsaw," *Gazeta Narodowa,* May 26, 1905; "Krwawe sądy w Warszawie," *Nowiny dla Wszystkich,* May 26, 1905, 3–4; and Zaleski, *Z dziejów prostytucji,* 75–84.

3. L. Straszewicz, *Kurier Warszawski,* May 26, 1905, quoted in "Prasa o pogromach," *Słowo,* May 27, 1905, 3.

Penitent or Partner?: Victorian-Era Prostitution Reform

Part of the cognitive process involved in extending aid to women in the sex industry involved a conceptual transformation of the prostitute from sexual predator to innocent victim, a status that more clearly justified the offer of charity. To facilitate this shift, aid organizations focused on the social context that produced the need for prostitution. Rather than ascribing the "fall" into commercial sex to inborn degeneracy or an aberrant sex drive, as was the case in earlier periods, twentieth-century activists implicated the society itself that allowed them to sink into sexual slavery.[4] The protofeminist paper *Słowo*, for example, reminded its readership that "the implications of prostitution are more deeply and generally damaging than many people imagine" and that "society" had a responsibility to take up arms and battle the problem. The paper called on its readers to help return former prostitutes to normal life, but to do so without condescension or scorn.[5] "Let us go to them and raise them from their fallen status, give them our hands, envelope them with our warm hearts," editors—most of them women—bid in the weeks after the brothel riots. For the volunteers of the early twentieth century, prostitutes were "our sisters, bones of our bones, blood of our blood," potential members of the same national community.[6]

Yet the notion of streetwalkers as innocent victims of a neglectful society rather than morally corrupt seducers was relatively new in the Polish case. Earlier philanthropic efforts focused on the moral failings of former prostitutes and the need to retrain brothel workers' moral compass to allow their return to polite society. The few institutions on Polish soil that addressed the growing prostitution problem in the nineteenth century typically fell under the supervision of religious orders or aristocratic philanthropists and tended to offer self-restraint, humility, or religious piety as remedies to extricate their subjects from the sex trade. The tendency here was to remove prostitutes completely from their native environment, isolating and insulating debauched women in a convent-like setting focused on penitence and prayer. The network of shelters that opened across the Polish territories in the 1880s, for example, went so far as to create new names and personalities

---

4. Jolanta Sikorska characterizes the tendency of the women's movement and members of socialist parties to turn prostitutes into objects of social remorse as a phenomenon of the last quarter of the nineteenth century. The public portrayal of the iconic prostitute might better be characterized as a duel between angels and harlots, victims and corrupt aggressors. Only later did images of sex workers settle into a consistently passive and naïve portrayal, and this only for a few years at the start of the twentieth century. See Sikorska-Kulesza, "Prostitution in Congress Poland," 123–33.

5. "Przystań dla kobiet," *Słowo*, May 31, 1905, 2.

6. "Mój pochód krzyżowy," *Czystość* 1, no. 2 (July 1, 1905): 9.

for their clients. Pity, condescension, and social distance characterized these early institutions, many of them also managed by female proprietors or religious orders. A few examples from this era will highlight the change of tone affected by activists in the post-1905 period.

The Magdalene Asylums

Early forms of humanitarian assistance in the Polish lands reflected a sense of social condescension on the part of reformers. The most common form of refuge for prostitutes through the late nineteenth century was the so-called Magdalene system, a string of small shelters focused on productive work and religious training. The institution sought to teach village and urban working-class girls how to accept their station in life rather than aspiring to easy money or social mobility.[7] The aristocratic women who founded the chain of "Magdalenki," or Zakład Opieki Najświętszej Panny Marii, across the former Polish territories based them on the model of Magdalene asylums in Ireland, England, and Scotland, which operated on the assumption that male seducers, "bad company," or a negligent upbringing were to blame for a woman's decline into vice.[8] Magdalene homes sought clients who were relatively young, had only recently "fallen," and were still capable of feeling guilt and shame.[9] Such penitents were more easily rehabilitated, according to early reformers.

This process of rescuing women from the wages of sin was premised on the strict separation of prostitutes from every aspect of their former lives.[10] The facilities were heavily guarded and their inhabitants cordoned off from intruders. Residents, or "penitents," as they were called, were forbidden to speak of their past or to utter the word "prostitute" while residing in the shelter. The "cleansing" of one's past included a new name, a new profession, and a new morality. Women were only accepted into the facility if they came of their own free will and were fully committed to establishing a new way of life. Recidivism was punished by eviction from the facility.[11] The

---

7. See Mahood, *Magdalenes*, 75–94.

8. Magdalene homes were established in Warsaw, Dyrdy (upper Silesia), and Łagiewniki near Cracow. Elsewhere, in Lublin and in Poznań, the Good Shepherd Order of nuns (Dobry Pasterz Sisters) managed similar facilities. On the Polish Magdalene Foundation's goals and strategies, see "Nowoczesnie niewolnice," *Słowo*, June 21, 1899, 2.

9. Linda Mahood's discussion of the ways Scottish philanthropists portrayed prospective clients of Magdalene asylums mirrors the views of Polish organizers a century later. Mahood, *Magdalenes*, 56–59.

10. Maria Luddy, *Prostitution and Irish Society, 1800–1940* (Cambridge, UK, 2007), 76–123.

11. Bolesław Prus, "Kroniki tygodniowe," *Kurier Codzienny*, December 5, 1897. Reprinted in Prus, *Kroniki*, 15: 227–28.

institutional philosophy of the Magdalenki held that rehabilitation could be achieved only by means of a complete substitution of a young woman's idle and debauched ways with a new set of habits. Residents were occupied in a daily regime devoted almost exclusively to work, prayer, and silence.[12] The transformation of residents' morals would come about through the adoption of an orderly lifestyle, subservience to authority, religious piety, and expertise in household chores necessary to take up service in bourgeois homes. The lengthy period of "training," between four and six years, limited the number of clients the homes could accept, while also assuring that graduates might be "cured" of their immoral habits by the time they left to take up employment with a local family.[13]

Unsurprisingly, the strict regime in Magdalenki discouraged many girls from taking refuge there. The shelter on Żytnia Street in Warsaw, for example, established through the largess of Countess Ożarowska in 1882, reflected the intense work regime of the West European institutions on which it was modeled.[14] The roughly two hundred clients who entered the facility each year were assigned vocational tasks from embroidery and weaving to washing and ironing. This work was undertaken with the nearly constant recitation of prayers. "During work hours, which is nearly the whole day," noted one visitor to the home, the girls "pray loudly or sing."[15] At the sound of a bell, residents moved robotically to a new type of prayer. The girls were forbidden to speak about their past, yet were constantly reminded of it by means of colored necklaces that represented their relative level of virtue. Inmates greeted visiting benefactors in their factory-like uniforms by kissing their shoes and addressed their superiors as "mother." Everywhere in the homes, the "cult of Catholicism" dominated and physical comfort was deemphasized.[16] Visitors to the home noted a shortage of washbasins and an overall low level of hygiene in the facility, an impression reinforced by the prevalence of girls who were physically scarred by the effects of syphilis.[17]

---

12. Most of the girls were occupied from before dawn until 10:00 p.m. with sewing, embroidery, crocheting, washing, ironing, and linen making. The rest devoted their time to house cleaning or cooking. Laundry was a particularly prevalent way of earning incoming for the institutions, though it is unclear how central this was to Polish Magdalene asylums. Wróblewski, *O prostytucji*, 85–88.

13. Prus, "Kroniki tygodniowe," December 5, 1897, in Prus, *Kroniki*, 15: 227–28.

14. The Dom Opieki in Warsaw was housed on Żytnia Street, with an auxiliary facility on the Derda estate. It served 210 women in 1899, one of whom died and twenty-one of whom left the establishment prepared to accept handicraft work of some kind. The remaining 188 women remained in the facility for "further improvement and education." A. Gagatnicki, "Skrzynka do listów: Opieka nad kobietami," *Kurier Warszawski,* April 8, 1900, 6.

15. Prus, "Kroniki tygodniowe," 3.

16. Wróblewski, *O prostytucji*, 86–87.

17. Wróblewski, "Przytułki dla upadłych kobiet," *Czystość* 5, no. 2 (June 26, 1909): 414.

The emphasis on moral purification continued to dominate even as other charities focused increasingly on vocational skills for needy women. The growth of visible poverty in urban centers attracted the attention of several orders of Catholic nuns in the 1890s, many of whom focused on rescuing women from city streets. In Poznań, Sister Maria Karłowska established a chain of Good Shepard (Dobry Pasterz) convents including the Zgromadzenie Sióstr Pasterek od Opatrzności Bożej (Congregation of the Good Shepard of Divine Providence). Similar facilities in Lublin, Toruń, Łódź, and elsewhere helped train girls from the margins of society to become proficient servants and to take up employment in wealthy homes. Sick prostitutes were directed to the facilities from the library at hospitals where they underwent treatment for the effects of venereal diseases. The Good Shepherd homes were at first quite small, housing no more than a dozen or so girls, and were slow to find patronage. By 1905, however, the sister had established a ten-room shelter in Lublin housing some fifty girls.[18]

Karłowska institutions differed from the Magdalenki in that they were managed entirely by nuns whose "sense of charity [was] more pronounced than that of the Magdalenkis." The sisters accepted anyone who came to them, and the social "chasm" between care providers and charges that existed in Magdalene asylums was ostensibly absent here. Visitors reported that the nuns "actually [became] fond of the unfortunates." Rather than sending seriously ill patients back to the hospital, the Good Shepherd nuns nursed them personally. The mother superior even counted herself fortunate to "have the horrible venom" of venereal infection under her roof, believing that dying of the disease was a "sign of holiness" and the first step in achieving sainthood.[19] The primary purpose of the shelters was to train girls in a usable skill so they could find work after leaving the facility. Like the Magdalenes, the girls took in laundry. But the homes also trained their residents in textile making, hosiery manufacture, sewing, gardening, and general housekeeping in preparation for work in domestic service.[20] The Good Shepherd facilities hardly challenged the social order in their emphasis on appropriate class-based vocational skills, but they did provide a model of practical training for unskilled women to help prevent their slide back into sex work.

Neither the Magdalenki nor the smaller Church-sponsored facilities in Russian Poland made significant inroads in addressing the high rates of

18. "Przytułek św. Antoniego w Lublinie dla upadłych dziewcząt," *Czystość* 1, no. 7 (September 1905): 61–62.

19. Wróblewski, "Przytułki dla upadłych kobiet," 414–15.

20. "Przytułek św. Antoniego w Lublinie," 62.

prostitution. Their capacities were limited relative to the need, and most young women were unwilling to take up residence in such a restricted environment after making their way to large cities. The Magdalenki in particular only managed to place 10 percent of their registrants in full-time service positions. So inconsequential were their efforts that the politician and economist Władysław Grabski was unaware they were still functioning in 1900, speaking of them only in the past tense. "It's true we had Magdalenki," Grabski observed, "but this single institution was barely a tiny light in the gloom." He contrasted local efforts with those organized in Chicago, London, or Paris, compared to which Polish institutions lagged severely behind. Although aristocratic Poles had the resources to help their less fortunate sisters, most of them avoided offering assistance, he complained, refusing to reach into the "muddy depths" for fear of "touching filth" in the process. "Under the cover of the nightly gloom hundreds of fallen women search for bread daily in sin and debauchery," Grabski mourned, and yet even when they "wanted to shake themselves free of the muck, no one shows them the road, no one gives them a bowl of water, or helps to return them to among the pure."[21] Overall, efforts to uplift morally compromised lower-class women and integrate them into "legitimate" society faced constant challenges. Initiatives to turn former prostitutes into demure domestic servants were often impractical, of limited scope, and deeply unpopular with their intended audiences.

Piaseczna

Charitable institutions often struggled to improve the lives of their charges even when they were governed in an atmosphere of generosity and acceptance. Nonetheless, a handful of facilities began by the turn of the century to operate with the hope of accomplishing a complete rehabilitation of former sex workers and even the expectation that their charges might marry and bear healthy children of their own.[22] One of the most popular shelters for former prostitutes was established in the Warsaw suburb of Piaseczna in the 1890s. Founded and managed by Countess Ludwika Moriconi, the home operated on the founding principle that despite a lifetime of hardship some prostitutes could leave their old practices behind. This view reflected a shift in contemporary thinking about the causes of prostitution. Rejecting

---

21. Władysław Grabski, "Listy z Krakowskiego Przedmieścia," *Kurier Warszawski*, April 1, 1900, 2–4.

22. At least one early twentieth-century Warsaw shelter reported upward of fifty successful marriages among former residents. St. Poraj, "Dusza prostytutki i śródki słuszące do jej odrodzenia," *Ster* 1, no. 9 (1907): 375–78.

theories of the "born prostitute" (see chapter 9), Moriconi saw prostitution as not innate but correctable.[23] She insisted it was not the sex worker herself who was inherently flawed, but rather the "atmosphere in which the soul of the prostitute is created that is almost always degenerate."[24] If the domestic background and family setting in which young girls were raised could be improved, she suggested, rates of prostitution would drop.

Hundreds of professional prostitutes made their way to Moriconi's shelter, having learned of it from other streetwalkers or from fellow patients in the St. Lazarus Hospital venereal ward.[25] The countess managed to retrain over three hundred girls in fifteen years of operation and placed many of them in "honest" jobs, but she faced enormous challenges in recovering women who had faced lifetimes of abuse and her rates of recidivism remained high. The vast majority of the residents in her shelter came from damaged family backgrounds. Some did not know who their parents were or were foundlings with no connection to parents at all; many were orphans or half orphans. The combination of poverty and the absence of family support meant that many of Moriconi's charges took the plunge into sex work out of financial desperation at a painfully early age.[26] They were predominantly illiterate, had no vocational training, and lacked even the most rudimentary skills for survival. Most also lacked experience in practical matters such as sewing and cooking, and "in general have no sense for order and work," according to the shelter's outspoken director.[27] The typical family environment of the women who appeared at her shelter, Moriconi explained, was enveloped in "laziness, the greatest cynicism, incessant lying, and alcoholism."[28] Nevertheless, Moriconi expressed great empathy for the residents who passed through her shelter, believing that they could be made whole again and return to productive life. "It is not true that a prostitute's soul is always degenerate," she insisted, "and that she is made of some special material, as if from clay." Rather, her true character could shine through once she was removed from the negative environment that caused her suffering.

---

23. On the tension between the views of criminal anthropologists such as Cesare Lombroso and abolitionists throughout continental Europe, see Corbin, *Women for Hire*, 227–29.

24. Moriconi, "Przyczynek do sprawy prostytucyi u nas," 168–73.

25. Wróblewski, *O prostytucji*, 87.

26. The vast majority of the former prostitutes in Moriconi's care entered the trade before they were eighteen, nearly half of them before they were sixteen, and thirty-six of the three hundred began selling sex as young as eleven or twelve.

27. Moriconi, "Przyczynek do sprawy prostytucyi," 168–73.

28. Lecture by Ludwika Moriconi, December 16, 1907. Summarized in Poraj, "Dusza prostytutki," 395–97.

Galician Rescue and Redemption

Philanthropic and charitable assistance to prostitutes during the last years of the nineteenth century reflected contemporary social and gender norms. Prostitutes "saved" from the trade were expected to embrace vocational training in preparation for a life serving in bourgeois households. Little effort was put into challenging the system of gender expectations or the overall economic conditions driving women to the streets in the first place. Few institutions stepped forward to assist migrating women or to help locate jobs and housing for those who did not wish to take on positions as domestics. Conditions for charitable assistance in Austrian Galicia were somewhat more favorable than in Russian Poland, thanks partly to the jurisdiction of the provincial Sejm Krajowy (National Diet), yet here too the structure of aid agencies reflected contemporary patterns of social organization. Support provided through the Sejm helped maintain a network of training schools designed to prevent recent migrants to the city from resorting to prostitution, but rested on the assumption that work as domestics was the best future their students could hope for. A new Cracovian order of nuns, Sisters of the Sacred Heart (Zgromadzenie Służebnic Najświętszego Serca Jezusowego, or Sercanki), for example, launched one of the most successful efforts to prepare rural girls for positions as housekeepers.[29] The program of vocational training was efficient, short term, and effective. Residents received free housing, but were required to labor in the laundry facility or in the kitchen in exchange for their board.[30] Women typically spent two or three months at the convent, where they learned cooking, laundering, and sewing, while also being steeped in spiritual reading and prayer. Most left to take up positions as domestic servants, though some were sent to hospitals after their short stay. Only a handful remained on the premises after the three-month training sequence, among them the women who had determined to take vows in the order.[31]

The school benefitted from a close connection to a network of education establishments scattered throughout the Galician countryside and coordinated by the Society of People's Education (Towarzystwo Oświaty Ludowej), an affiliation that helped provide legitimacy in the eyes of female rural migrants. In its first year the Cracow facility served 180 pupils,

---

29. The Sercanki shelters were the brainchild of Jagiellonion University Professor Father Józef Sebastian Pelczar, who worried about recent migrants to the city "falling into the hands of evil people" such as pimps or socialists. "Statut Bractwa Najświętszej Panny Marii Królowej Korony Polskiej," *Posłaniec Bractwa Najświętszej Marii Panny Królowej Korony Polskiej* 1, no. 1 (1893): 37.

30. "Przytulisko i szkoła praktyczna dla służących" *Posłaniec* 1, no. 1 (1893): 49.

31. In 1894, nine girls were sent to hospital out of a total of 260 who took advantage of the shelter. *Posłaniec* 3, no. 4 (1895): 32.

growing to 317 in 1895.[32] By 1896, a second home opened on Garncar-ska Street and the clientele grew still more rapidly, peaking at some 547 students at both Cracow institutions in 1910. Meanwhile, the Sercanki opened a facility in Lwów that quickly surpassed the Cracow branch, as well as a smaller school in Zakopane. Unlike the Magdalenki homes, the Galician shelters enjoyed contributions from public funds. The Cracow town council donated a portion of the convent's operating budget each year from funds allotted to it by the Galician Sejm Krajowy.[33] The remainder of the facility's support was made up of subscriptions sold to town residents and profits from its highly successful laundry business. In stark contrast to shelters in Warsaw and elsewhere, Sercanki were intended as preventative measures to keep girls off the street, not as rescue missions.[34] The Sercanki represent an important exception to earlier forms of charity in their commitment to educate and employ women rather than simply sequestering them from their former lives.[35]

Societies for the Protection of Women

The pattern of social care stemming from conservative gender expectations began to shift in the new century with the rise of the equal-rights agenda. The movement for women's rights comprised a significant undercurrent in Polish public life during the last decades of the nineteenth century, fitting

32. Jadwiga Kupczewska, *Praca o szkołach rolniczych*, MA thesis, Jagiellonian University, 45–48; and "Przytulisko i szkoła praktyczna," 49.

33. The Cracow town council contributed 200 zloty to the school's annual budget of 600–700 zloty in 1893–1898. The rest of the operating expenses were covered by private donations from over three hundred Galician notables and residents, as well as small contributions from the church treasury. "Sprawozdanie Ksawerego Konopki, skarbnika Bractwa Najswieszej Panny Marii Królowej Korony Polskiej, z wpływów i rozchodów kasy tegoż Bractwa za rok 1894," *Posłaniec* 1, no. 2 (1893): 32; *Posłaniec* 5, no. 6 (1897): 40; *Posłaniec* 7, no. 7 (1898): 43.

34. Warsaw boasted several shelters specifically intended for unemployed female professionals, including one for schoolteachers, two for seamstresses, and another for out of work domestic servants. These facilities were small and inadequate, however. The combined beds in the two homes for needleworkers totaled seventy-eight, hardly sufficient for the thirty thousand or more seamstresses in Warsaw alone. The Shelter for Female Teachers opened in 1882 on the initiative of Mrs. A. Helwich and Father Chełmicki; M. Wostkowska founded the the first shelter for seamstresses in 1894. Soon thereafter, the St. Jadwiga House and the St. Józef Shelter for Servants opened to serve unemployed domestics. "Opieka nad kobietami, poszukującymi pracy," *Nowe Słowo* 3 (December 1, 1904): 544.

35. Other Galician shelters, such as the one at the convent of the Sisters of Divine Love (Siostri Boskiej Milosci), imposed excessively restrictive rules, requiring women to document that they were unemployed domestics who were "in good health and of good moral standing" before granting them admission. Such requirements made the shelter impractical for assisting former prostitutes. "Dom opieki dla Sług u Siostr Boskiej Miłości w Krakowie," *Przyjaciel Sług*, February 1, 1898, 7–9.

in well with the focus on economic and cultural improvements among the lower classes after the failed 1863 Uprising.[36] The gradual relaxation of imperial restrictions on civic organizations in the Polish Kingdom and in Galicia also helped create opportunities for the growth of cross-border associations to advance equal rights for Polish women. By the last years of the nineteenth century, women's organizations began to focus explicit attention on the problem of international traffic in women. Sex-trafficking trials were receiving top billing everywhere and women's rights organizations quickly discovered they could leverage popular anxiety about white slavery to call attention to the vagaries of commercial sex at home.

The campaign to address the implications of tolerated vice received a boost with the series of international conferences to combat white slavery around the turn of the new century. Beginning in June 1899, the London-based National Vigilance Association brought together delegates from across Europe and the Americas to discuss the trafficking epidemic. Polish representatives from all three empires took part in the proceedings and in the conferences that followed over the next several years. Each new gathering generated a wave of activity among local reformers intent on combating the sources of prostitution at home.[37] Representatives returned to their countries and threw themselves into organizational activity, establishing national Committees for the Protection of Women in sixteen countries by 1902. Branches of the Vigilance Society opened offices in key cities and set about compiling statistics on female migration. Members worked to track suspected traffickers, patrol ports and train stations, and monitor employment agencies suspected of shipping women abroad for illicit purposes. Those returning from brothel work abroad or who had been threatened with a trafficking scam were subjected to extensive interviews at police stations across the Continent.

Polish-speaking activists participated in these early congresses, but were deeply embarrassed to report no organizational initiatives of their own. Nor did the governments to which they belonged ratify the treaty that resulted from the 1902 Paris proceedings. Returning from the 1899 London conference, Polish delegates reported that national committees were urged to

---

36. On the movement for Organic Work or Positivism in Polish culture, see Blejwas, *Realism in Polish Politics*; and Piotr Wandycz, *The Lands of Partitioned Poland, 1795–1918* (Seattle, 1974).

37. The June 1899 London conference established national committees in each of sixteen countries that sent delegates to successive international meetings held in Amsterdam (1901), Paris (1902), Frankfurt (1903), Geneva (1904), Dresden (September 1904), Zurich (September 1905), and Geneva (1908). See coverage of congresses in Kaplan, "Prostitution, Morality Crusades, and Feminism," 620–25; Ruth Rosen, *Lost Sisterhood*, 116–17; Bristow, *Vice and Vigilance*, 182–83; Macko, *Prostytucja*, 353–62; and Posner, *Nad otchłania*, 51–79.

establish societies at home "dedicating to fighting evil." "Perhaps," representatives conjectured, "even among us a group of people will be found who will devote themselves specifically to this matter and will want to establish a new organization."[38] Polish representatives soon set to work devising remedies to aid those who had long been the focus of public opprobrium. Situating prostitution and international trafficking as the centerpiece of their reform agenda provided Polish female activists the chance to advance the broader goals of the nascent women's movement while also benefitting the collective needs of the Polish people.[39] Work to aid trafficked women provided a well-defined and socially acceptable space for philanthropy that benefited the national cause without challenging the political dominance of the governing powers.

Jewish-Christian Cooperation

A full generation after the abolition of tolerated prostitution in Britain, Polish representatives had been embarrassed to report to the London meeting that "nothing was happening" to combat human trafficking in their homelands.[40] The resulting sense of national urgency prompted the birth of four separate institutions designed to combat human trafficking out of the Polish lands: three in Warsaw and one in Cracow. These organizations combined the efforts of Christian and Jewish philanthropists, who worked alongside one another or in closely collaborating affiliations. In Warsaw, Dr. Józef Zawadzki, editor of the influential Warsaw medical journal Kronika Lekarska, took the initiative in establishing the Warsaw Christian Society for the Protection of Women (Chreścijanskie Towarzystwo Ochrony Kobiet) in 1900.[41] Two years later, Jewish philanthropists opened a parallel branch, the Jewish Society for the Protection of Women (Żydowskie Towarzystwo Ochrony Kobiet), as a direct response to the overly religious character of the original protection society.[42] The Christian and Jewish branches of the protection

---

38. "Nowoczesnie niewolnice," 2.

39. Posner, Nad otchłania, 51; Macko, Prostytucja, 353–58; and "Handel dziewczętami," Słowo, August 12, 1899, 3.

40. Z. Grotowski, Rozwój zakładów dobrocznnych w Warszawie (Warsaw, 1910), 204–9.

41. The organization operated informally for a time until the Russian Interior Ministry formally approved its application for official status in December 1901, and began its official existence as of January 1902. Posner, Nad otchłania, 4–7.

42. The publicity surrounding the birth of the Christian Society—and the "delicate warnings" influential Warsaw Jews received reminding them that the society's services were intended primarily for Christian girls—prompted Jewish leaders to open a parallel institution. "Odgłosy," Izraelita, April 13, 1901, 19. On the evolution of Jewish women's organization from charity to social work,

societies worked closely together, often jointly patrolling train stations or staging combined meetings of activists. Each group employed dozens of female volunteers, though neither appears to have gained significant influence over its intended charges. Both institutions "sought to have political, cultural, and educational influence over women," according to Elżbieta Mazur, but "little of this actually came to fruition."[43] The two protection societies were soon joined by a third Warsaw agency, this one much more radical in its aims. The Polish Society of Abolitionists (Polskie Towarzystwo Abolicjonistów), also established in the immediate aftermath of the London Congress, aggressively opposed the institution of regulated prostitution in the Russian Empire. Because of its direct challenge to imperial policies, the association was forced to remain hidden from Russian authorities, meeting clandestinely in taverns during its early years so as not to antagonize the imperial government. Only during the heady days of the 1905 Revolution were the abolitionists able to function in the open without fear of imperial reprisal. Just as with the Christian Protection Society, physicians took the lead in organizing the Abolition Society's activities and agenda.[44]

Meanwhile, in 1903 residents of Galicia founded a chapter of the Austrian League to Combat Traffic in Women (Österreichischen Liga zur Bekämpfung des Mädchenhandels), a Vienna-based organization that worked with police to track and rescue lost women. Similar to the Warsaw societies, League members monitored the Monarchy's train stations, erected warning signs for traveling women, and offered legal advice for victims of trafficking. The organization ran a shelter in Vienna and also aspired to serve as an employment agency, although this function was little discussed in its annual reports.[45] In the spring of 1903, Galician philanthropists established local chapters of the League in Cracow, Czernowitz, and Lwów, where Count

---

see Marion A. Kaplan, *The Making of the Jewish Middle Class: Women, Family, and Identity in Imperial Germany* (New York, 1991), 192–219.

43. Mazur, *Dobroczynność w Warszawie*, 77.

44. Dr. Leon Wernic, later head of the Polish Eugenics Association, and Dr. Teodora Męczkowska, one of the first female doctors in the Polish lands, were among its founders. They were joined by Dr. Stanisław Posner, a legal and trafficking expert and a Sephardic Jew. Dr. Witold Chodźko, *Prostitucja i choroby weneryczne jako zjawiska społeczne* (Warsaw, 1939), reprint from "Prostytucja i choroby weneryczne jako zjawiska społeczne," *Opiekun społeczny* 30, no. 3 (1939).

45. The main chapter of the Austrian League was approved by the Ministry of Interior Affairs on November 12, 1902. The president of the League quickly submitted a letter to Cracow's *Nowe Słowo* on November 26, 1902 announcing its birth and stating that "it is our hope that by publishing this in Galicia, whence hundreds of white slaves are carried away ... we can focus attention on this problem and attract assistance. The letter was published in "Kronika," *Nowe Słowo* 2 (May 15, 1903): 226–27. Information about the newly formed association also appears in "Handel dziewczętami," *Przyjaciel Sług* 4 (December 7, 1902): 190.

Andrzej Potocki served as the official protector. In Cracow the feminist newspaper editor Maria Turzyma organized patrols of the train station and worked closely with police to help rescue young women headed out of the country under false pretenses.[46] Agents of the Warsaw and Cracow protection societies worked closely with the Austrian League for the Suppression of the Traffic in Young Women headquartered in Vienna, maintaining correspondence about missing women and forwarding depositions from trafficking victims.[47] Austrian League Chairwoman Truxe appears to have been a force of great energy, traveling the region and interviewing women exposed to international prostitution networks.

In contrast to the separation of aid societies in the Polish Kingdom into distinct religious communities, Jewish activists in Galicia worked alongside their Christian colleagues in charitable organizations designed to assist women of all confessions. Perhaps encouraged by the visit to Cracow of the Viennese Jewish philanthropists Sarah Rabinowicz and Bertha Pappenheim, Jewish leaders joined their Christian colleagues in generating support for the Galician chapter of the Austrian League.[48] Rabinowicz and Pappenheim were sent to Galicia as the official delegates of the International Committee for Trafficking in Women to explore the causes behind the long-standing assumption that some 90 percent of women shipped out of Europe to service brothels in other parts of the world were Galician born.[49] Pappenheim spoke at a meeting of female intellectuals of both Catholic and Jewish background at the offices of *Nowe Słowo* in Cracow in April 1903, complaining that the annual exodus of some eight to ten thousand Jewish girls from Galicia to Muslim and South American countries was "a source of danger and pestilence for the entire world, the cause of immorality and vice among men." Pappenheim encouraged local philanthropists in their work, but insisted on cultivating a class-based approach to charity and addressed the problem with a tone of condescension about the Galician lower classes. Prostitution, she averred, was the direct result of the morally challenged social substratum in the crown land. Young women in Galicia received a "poor upbringing both

---

46. "Kroniki," *Nowe Słowo* 2 (April 1, 1903): 156–57.

47. On Austrian efforts to combat the traffic in women, see Jürgen Nautz, "The Effort to Combat the Traffic in Women in Austria before the First World War," *Journal for Police Science and Practice* 2 (2012): 87–91.

48. "Kroniki," 1903, 156–57; "Kroniki," *Nowe Słowo*, May 15, 1903, 224–25.

49. On the condescending attitude toward east European Jewish women expressed by Pappenheim and other female German welfare workers, see Elizabeth Loentz, *Let Me Continue to Speak the Truth: Bertha Pappenheim as Author and Activist* (Cincinnati, OH, 2007), 123–56; and Kaplan, *Making of the Jewish Middle Class,* 209–19.

FIGURE 7.1   Bertha Pappenheim and other members of the Weiblich Fürsorge (Women's Relief Organization) that worked with Jewish women in Galicia in danger of falling into prostitution. Frankfurt am Main, 1904. Pappenheim is in the front row, second from the left.
Courtesy of the Leo Baeck Institute.

at home and in school." As a result, lower-class women had internalized a certain laziness and a severely "underdeveloped desire to work."[50]

The tenor of Pappenheim's comments appears to have resonated with her audience. The self-proclaimed feminists who flocked to her speech were pleased to see themselves included in the proclamation that "progressively thinking people" were "actively engaged in the question of vice and its link with the so-called traffic in women." Pappenheim's appearance galvanized Galician feminist society. Her listeners quickly committed themselves to supporting the needs of the poor women in their midst.[51] She explicitly criticized the shortage of charitable institutions available to young women in Galicia and appealed to middle-class women to volunteer their services. They needed to create the infrastructure necessary to prevent the resort to

50. "Kroniki," *Nowe Słowo* 2 (May 15, 1903): 224–25.

51. Pappenheim only briefly touched on the "poor working conditions or the complete absence of available work" in the crown land as a causal agent for the massive turn to prostitution in Galicia. Ibid.

paid sex, Pappenheim stressed. "Educated women from the intelligentsia," she emphasized, should become the "communicators of culture and enthusiasm for work" by establishing shelters for midwives and newborns, schools to care for the sick and for children, kindergartens, and professional schools to educate women in a trade.

Partially in response to Pappenheim's appeal, activists in Cracow created an ambitious new chapter of the Austrian League to Fight Trafficking in Women, headed by Dr. Waldman. Again, Jewish and Christian organizations worked together to more effectively combat the dire conditions in Galicia. This small band of aristocratic and bourgeois women labored, along with their male titular heads, to affect increased opportunities for needy women. But progress was slow and the imperial government put up roadblocks to impede their work. Organizers successfully inserted warnings to traveling women and to servants seeking positions to beware of unscrupulous migration facilitators and would-be employment agents. Both *Nowe Słowo* and *Przyjaciel Sług* published alerts in their columns, cautioning their readers "not to believe promises that they will receive paid work" abroad or propitious marriages, because only "certain doom" awaited them in America. Reformers circulated descriptions of "known traffickers" who had been spotted on ships bound for Poland from Buenos Aires to recruit young women to work in brothels there.[52] We have little evidence that these wider functions were fulfilled to any significant degree. The two organizations remained "quite small" and focused mainly on intercepting new arrivals to the city who might be vulnerable to false offers of employment, and on debriefing victims of trafficking ruses. The societies worked carefully to remain within the bounds of their official charge, avoiding direct opposition to state-regulated prostitution.[53]

Charitable Activism and the Shadow State

This feminine "shadow state" of aid workers, newspaper editors, educators, and social activists flourished under the three empires partly because charitable societies were permitted to operate legally with the emperor or tsar's consent. Membership in political associations was strictly forbidden across the Russian Empire until after 1905 and remained the exclusive terrain of males even thereafter. For this reason, private charities expanded their purview to include a broad spectrum of activities that went beyond simple material

---

52. "Kroniki," *Nowe Słowo* 2 (October 15, 1903): 471–72.
53. Posner, *Nad otchłania*, 1–4.

assistance and were able to operate freely as instruments for the preservation of national identity.[54] Their day-to-day activities interacting with less fortunate individuals allowed them to embody the general interests of the broader society. It is important to note that much of the language around the establishment of institutions to combat prostitution took aim at the occupying imperial powers for their complicity in upholding the system of registered prostitution. Even as Warsaw reformers began addressing the inadequacies of the regulation system, they grew weary of Russian bureaucratic delays and the seemingly intentional obfuscation of reform efforts, insisting that private individuals, not government institutions, were key to social reform.[55] In the Polish context, men and women of means formed an alternative source of assistance, helping to supply the services not offered by the governments of the partitioning powers. In so doing, they stood in for the absent Polish state and helped to train a generation of public actors ready to "act national" in the event a sovereign Polish state materialized.

The eruption of humanitarian institutions in the late nineteenth-century Polish lands was part of a wider bourgeois effort across Europe to civilize the laboring classes by imparting middle-class values to them.[56] In the Polish context, the approach was tied to the shortage of state-sponsored aid agencies in the empires governing national territory.[57] Prostitution became one important point of contact between Polish intellectuals and the poor women newly arrived in the cities. As the equal-rights activist Stefanja

---

54. Mazur, *Dobroczynność w Warszawie*, 155; and Czesław Kępski, *Towarzystwa dobroczynności w Królestwie Polskim 1815–1914* (Lublin, 1993), 3–4, 93.

55. In the aftermath of the May riots, for example, Governor General Czertkow established a government commission to study the regulation of prostitution in the Polish Kingdom. The commission, which included local physicians and members of the government, proved so bungling and incompetent—even permanently misplacing the minutes from its early meetings—that social reformers soon redoubled their efforts to take control over prostitution reform and remove it from the hands of imperial officials. "Nierząd w Warszawie," *Świat Płciowy* 1 (October 1905): 48.

56. In France, for example, associations devoted to fighting registered prostitution proliferated from the 1870s on; by the end of the century, over 1,300 associations specifically devoted to "saving" fallen women had been registered there. Agustin, *Sex at the Margins,* 121.

57. Charitable initiatives in eastern Europe helped fill a gap left by a shortage of state-run facilities to cater to vulnerable populations. Whereas the governments of the French Third Republic and the German Empire introduced centralized welfare institutions in the late nineteenth century, the Habsburg and Russian empires depended instead on private initiative for social assistance. See David Ransel, *Mothers of Misery: Child Abandonment in Russia* (Princeton, 1988); David I. Kertzer, *Sacrificed for Honor: Italian Infant Abandonment and the Politics of Reproductive Control* (Boston, 1993); and Mazur, *Dobroczynność w Warszawie*, 137–62. For the dramatic growth in private charitable activity in Łódź at the end of the nineteenth century, see Czesław Kępski, "Łódzkie Żydowskie Towarzystwo Dobroczynności w latach 1899–1918," *Biuletyn Żydowskiego Instytutu Historycznego w Polsce*, nos. 3–4 (1990): 93–94. On the growth in the authority of medicine and public health, see Sikorska, *Zło tolerowane*, 50.

Rygier Cekalska later observed, given the almost complete absence of state-sponsored welfare support, "the battle with prostitution" before World War I had to be "conducted by society itself." Humanitarian organizations offered a limited substitute for the material support that might have been expected had Poles enjoyed a national government—and that many West European states had begun to offer their populations. "The needs in this field," Cekalska noted, "demanded a well-planned, organized campaign, supported with a strong material base, such as that which the state organs or local government could provide" if they had been inclined.[58]

A generation of mostly female activists thus leveraged the public panic over prostitution and international trafficking to establish a role for themselves in civic affairs. Their efforts focused explicitly on strategies for assisting vulnerable women, yet their networks of shelters, vocational schools, and reform associations did little to affect the plight of poor women. Still, by colonizing the antiprostitution campaign and dominating subsidiary reform projects, philanthropic females earned the credibility they needed to insert themselves into day-to-day public affairs throughout Polish territory. By the end of the first decade of the twentieth century, female reformers had earned positions on local boards, editorial commissions, and charitable societies. They contributed to and edited prominent newspapers, held public meetings, and conducted interviews with former harlots. The ultimate failure of these philanthropic efforts to "solve" the prostitution problem and the intransigence of many of its practitioners would eventually help fuel renewed cynicism about the permanence of the sex trade and prompt activists to turn to other, more militant strategies for solving sexual immorality and disease.

Acting National in the Public Sphere

The period of civic openness ushered in by the 1905 pogroms allowed activist women the opportunity to challenge imperial agendas more directly and in so doing to create for themselves a presence in the national public space. Their initiatives did not achieve great success in rehabilitating prostitutes, nor were they well subscribed by their intended audience. Moreover, female activists quickly splintered into several factions, reflecting radical and conservative feminist directions. Yet the passion and combined purpose of their activism, much of it directed at lambasting the occupying empires for their policies on prostitution, shaped a field of open debate on national issues and

---

58. Stefanja Rygier Cykalska, "Samoobrona społeczeństwa w walce z nierządem," *Zagadnienie Rasy* 2, no. 8 (July 1920): 7.

legitimized their participation in this broader conversation. In the end, the problem of commercial sex offered an opportunity for feminist activists to join in nationwide discussions about health, morality, legal affairs, economics, and other issues of wider social concern. The implicit critique of the occupying powers reflected in these debates further accentuated the degree to which female activists were "acting national" in the course of their work among the prostitutes.

The Warsaw riots thus represented an epiphany in prostitution reform in several important respects. The 1905 events would come to symbolize the moment when the fight against commercial sex in the Polish lands shifted and activists began to launch increasingly open attacks on the institutions of regulated prostitution. This fresh onslaught came about as a result of at least four changes in the sociopolitical environment of the Polish territories. First, the climate for political activism temporarily relaxed across the partitions in the immediate aftermath of the Warsaw violence, permitting the birth of dozens of civic organizations devoted to the rescue and rehabilitation of prostitutes. Second, the Polish public embraced the need for change and initiated a lively debate about the options for reform. Third, public animosity increasingly concentrated on male perpetrators as the focus of their ire and elevated prostitutes as victims, prompting a new focus on charitable assistance. These changing conditions provided the context for the fourth shift, the entrance of female activists into the public sphere and their adoption of poor women likely to slip into the sexual underworld as a key focus of their work.

To begin with, the extended revolutionary moment in Congress Poland, starting with demonstrations in Łódź in January and continuing with anti-Russian school strikes throughout the Polish Kingdom, helped inaugurate a new era of popular participation in civic life in all three sections of divided Poland.[59] The new Russian constitution reinstated Polish-language rights in private schools and allowed representation in the Russian Duma, where a Polish Circle was inaugurated in 1906. Censorship across the Russian Empire was relaxed, allowing a flood of new journals reflecting a broad range of political sensibilities. More permissive regulations governing public associations were introduced, paving the way for the burgeoning of a robust civil society.[60] Meanwhile, the Habsburg state, already comparatively liberal in its

---

59. Robert Blobaum, "The Revolution of 1905–07 and the Crisis of Polish Catholicism," *Slavic Review* 47, no. 4 (1988): 667. See also Blobaum, *Rewolucja: Russian Poland, 1904–1907* (Ithaca, NY, 1995).

60. On the liberalization of censorship in the Congress Kingdom after October 1905 and the effect of the March 4, 1906 law regulating the activities of social organizations, see Jerzy Franke, *Polska prasa kobieca w latach 1820–1918: W kręgu ofiary i poświęcenia* (Warsaw, 1999), 197.

press laws, introduced universal male suffrage, permitting men over the age of twenty-five to vote for delegates to the *Reichsrat*. Finally, Polish subjects of the German Empire launched school strikes in 1906–1907, inspired partly by the earlier precedent in Russian Poland.[61]

Second, the pimp riots brought Warsaw's sex trade to the attention of the Polish public in an increasingly visible way. As the town's central neighborhood erupted in violence and destruction, bordellos were emptied of their occupants and exposed to the curious stares of passing onlookers. City residents could for the first time witness the concrete reality of an entrenched vice-based economy. Varsovians were shocked and embarrassed by what they saw, complaining that the events reflected the "primitive, barbarian, and uncultured instincts" of Warsaw inhabitants.[62] More than anything, they were concerned about the impact news of the rioting might have on their international reputation. "Critically thinking people who are highly educated," the editors of *Kurier Warszawski* feared, would view the street fighting as a reflection of the "lowered level of ethics and morality of the population as a whole."[63] Such worries were confirmed with the circulation of the German activist Major Hermann Wagener's comment about Lwów as the greatest center of debauchery in all of Europe" made during an antitrafficking conference in Bremen the following September. The quip quickly rippled through the Polish activist community, helping prompt a call to arms in the fight against prostitution.[64] Across the Polish lands, commercial sex was becoming a recognized eyesore that reflected poorly on the Poles' national honor.

Third, unlike the moral panic of the 1880s, the 1905 mob violence targeted pimps and procurers as the source of debauchery rather than the women who worked in the sex trade. A decade of sensationalized reporting about white slavery had effectively turned public opinion against Jewish brothel managers and in support of their female employees. Warsaw residents widely perceived the events as a legitimate response to years of public powerlessness, a moment of "reckoning" for those who ran the sex trade.[65] Social activists

---

61. Davies, *God's Playground*, 373–77.

62. "Prasa o pogromach," 3.

63. L. Straszewicz, *Kurier Warszawski*, May 26, 1905, quoted in "Prasa o pogromach," 3.

64. See, for example, "Prostytucja we Lwowie," *Świat Płciowy* 7 (February 1906): 20–21. Wagener repeated this claim in his 1911 pamphlet, *Mädchenhandel*, noting that "typically the work [of trafficking] occurs in areas where there is material; for this reason most of the trafficked girls come from Poland, Hungary, Galicia, Romania, and Southern Russia." Major D. H. Wagener, *Mädchenhandel* (Berlin, 1911), 33.

65. "Odezwa," *Czystość* 1, no. 2 (July 1, 1905): 11–12; and Marya Wojnarowa, "Zbudźcie się kobiety," *Czystość* 1, no. 4 (August 1, 1905): 41–42. The daily press throughout Polish territory reported on the riots. See, for example, "Krwawy dramat," 3; "Warszawa," *Nowiny dla Wszystkich*,

recast the problem of commercial sex, identifying male agents as the aggressors and preparing to take action against them. This shift in public attitudes helped prompt the birth of shelters and other aid agencies designed to rehabilitate the victims of the commercial sex industry.

Finally, the perceived need for charitable assistance provided an opening for female activism and established a newly gendered dimension to prostitution reform. The vast majority of the initiatives to aid "fallen women" introduced during the aftermath of 1905 grew out of women's organizational efforts.[66] By embedding themselves in the lives of streetwalkers, these aid workers became implicated in the economy of prostitution. They adopted the plight of sex workers as their cause, defending the needs of fallen women and devising social programs to accommodate them.[67] Some of their proposals represented a continuation of philanthropic efforts begun in earlier decades. Others arose out of the newly formed equal-rights movement, which sought to revolutionize gender roles and transform the institution of marriage. In both cases, voluntary efforts to assist prostitutes provided the opportunity for middle- and upper-class women to "act national."[68]

Female activists were able to "perform" national care by opening shelters, patrolling train platforms, and stocking hospital libraries. Humanitarian activities like these helped establish the framework of a state without a state, a civil society of social care aimed at rescuing vulnerable women. The daily routines of these charitable activities—tracking trafficking victims, staffing municipal hospitals, managing homes for wayward women—and the

May 26, 1905, 1; "Prasa o pogromach," 3; and "Ksiądz Józef Żyskar," Czystość 1, no. 4 (August 1, 1905): 25–31. For an overview on press reactions to the events, see Jolanta Sikorska-Kulesza, "Sądy doraźne nad prostytucją w Warszawie w maju 1905 roku w świetle prasy," Rocznik Warszawski, 45 (2007): 111–27.

66. In Warsaw alone, over thirty organizations devoted to women's issues were established in the period between 1905 and the outbreak of the First World War. During the period 1906–1914, Russian authorities approved the founding of 1,202 organizations in the Polish Kingdom. K. Konarski, "Ruch stowarzyszeniowy w Warszawie w latach 1905–1915 (w świetle akt kancelarii gubernatora warszawskiego)," in Z dziejów książki i bibliotek w Warszawie, ed. S. Tazbir (Warsaw, 1961), 495.

67. Women's groups in Galicia remained small and slow to take on prostitution as a primary focus during the early years of their activity. Marja Biniękówna, a peasant daughter who became an activist within the women's movement, commented on this history in "Wolny głos włościanki: Kilka słów o mieszkańcach wsi polskiej," Ster 1, no. 2 (1908): 68–72. See also "Statut Stowarzyszenia 'Związek kobiet,'" Nowe Słowo, April 1, 1904, 145–48. The total membership of the Galician Związek kobiet was only 170 in 1904, of which over half were behind in their membership dues. "Ze stowarzyszeń," Robotnica, June 15, 1904, 7–8. In the Poznań district women's organizations like the Polish Union of Professional Women (Polski Związek Zawodowy Żenski) began rendering assistance to combat "the constantly growing ranks of prostitutes" only in 1902. D. L. to Nowe Słowo, "Korespondencye," Nowe Słowo 2 (January 15, 1903): 36–38.

68. On the nation as an event rather than a static entity, see Rogers Brubaker, Ethnicity without Groups (Cambridge, MA, 2004), esp. 12–14.

rituals that surrounded them helped give the future Polish state meaning both for those who provided the care and those who were the recipients of it.[69] By stepping in for the absent nation-state, charitable organizations effectively functioned as a medium for national activity. As Elżbieta Mazur has argued about Warsaw voluntary associations, "charitable activity went far beyond the mere scope of material help, fulfilling during the period of political subjugation the role of an agent for preserving national identity."[70] Yet the network of shelters and aid societies at first found little traction among desperate young women. It was only with the advent of programs for vocational training and a women's rights vocabulary that the prostitution problem would be tackled from a more holistic standpoint, addressing the double sexual standard of Victorian society and the inequities in wages that drove women to the streets. Nevertheless, the gesture of reaching out to a previously scorned social group can be read as a genuine act of inclusion even when the schemes were relatively inconsequential or were rejected by their intended recipients.

Only in the aftermath of the 1905 Revolution, when imperial governments provided a brief window of loosened control over censorship and diminished restrictions on public assembly, were antiprostitution activists able to make significant inroads with the population of prospective sex workers. In the meantime, a whole generation of bourgeois women made their entrée into the world of public activism on the wings of Polish harlots. Their advocacy of prostitutes helped cement for the reformers a permanent sphere of social activism. Just as desperate lower-class women left their families and small communities and entered public life through the economic realm of sexual exchange, so too did their middle-class sisters create a platform for public action outside their bourgeois apartments by taking on the plight of fallen woman. Females of all social strata began in this way to reconfigure and extend the prescribed boundaries of their private worlds. They managed to combine efforts to better the conditions of the struggling classes while leveraging prostitution reform to gain access to and influence over much broader social issues.

---

69. Jean H. Quataert has argued in the German case that female philanthropists helped demonstrate the concrete ways in which the German state "cared" and in so doing made the dynamics of gender an integral part of state building. *Staging Philanthropy: Patriotic Women and the National Imagination in Dynastic Germany, 1813–1916* (Ann Arbor, MI, 2001), 6–8. In the Russian Empire, women's private charity substituted to a great degree for the assistance of the state. Here too a civic role for female philanthropists grew out of their charitable duties. Adele Lindenmeyr, *Poverty Is Not a Vice: Charity, Society, and the State in Imperial Russia* (Princeton, NJ, 1996).

70. Elżbieta Mazur, *Dobroczynność w Warszawie XIX wieku* (Warsaw, 1999), 161.

A central component of feminist activism in this period was the belief in a "self-organized society" that could reform and modernize the Polish community in preparation for eventual independence. The conviction that intervention in the lives of the lower classes was both necessary and possible drove these mostly middle-class activists to pursue a broad-ranging social-work agenda. Women's aid organizations introduced their charges to Polish culture and scientific progress as a means of expanding and reconstituting the Polish nation. If lower-class women could be taught vocational skills and moral standards, activists theorized, they could become a useful force for resurrecting Polish sovereignty.[71] The broader equal-rights message was intended as a response to the sexual double standard that permitted male sexual promiscuity before and during marriage but required female chastity before and monogamy within marriage. The image of the prostitute with her downtrodden, morally ruined demeanor became the iconic emblem of women's status overall. Until the prostitute could be rescued, reformed, and reintegrated into mainstream society, women everywhere would suffer from sexual inequality, activists argued. Prostitutes, in this conception, represented the potential fate of all women so long as procurers, traffickers, and pimps roamed city streets, and as long as society's double standard created a market for sexual labor.[72]

Women's groups adopted the image of the trafficked woman to promote a host of related causes. Foremost among these was the effort to draw public attention to the domestic prostitution industry, long smiled on by police and state authorities, by presenting the export of sex workers as part of a connected system of vice and abuse. The irony of the state-sponsored effort to combat international sex trafficking was not lost on Polish activists. The very governments that sent delegates to high-profile European congresses, established national committees to prevent trafficking, and made grandiose claims about the dangers of white slavery were the same administrations that tolerated prostitution within their own borders. "The very existence of brothels creates the traffic in human goods," the feminist press proclaimed, since bordellos throughout the Polish lands provided an ongoing supply of women for export. The Russian, Austrian, and German

---

71. On the goals of nineteenth-century women's philanthropy in the Polish lands and its links to wider European trends, see Dietlind Hüchtker, "Enlightenment—Education—Social Reform: Concepts of Sociopolitical Activities in the Habsburg Province of Galicia," in *History of Social Work in Europe (1990–1960): Female Pioneers and Their Influence on the Development of International Social Organizations*, ed. Berteke Waaldijk and Sabine Hering (Wiesbaden, Germany, 2003), 161–69.

72. On shifts in the attitudes of European feminists toward prostitution reform, see Richard J. Evans, *The Feminist Movement in Germany, 1894–1933* (London, 1976), esp. 145–70.

governments all tolerated public houses within their borders yet opposed the international trade in women.

Equal-rights proponents set out to highlight the horrors of sex migration and in so doing to draw critical attention to the tolerated domestic trade. They complained that advertisements about local brothels circulated freely on the streets of major cities and appeared in every "bawdy rag found in candy stores . . . and displayed in shop windows." Nonetheless, publications highlighting the horrors of young women sold as live goods were confiscated by the Austrian authorities, creating "yet another double standard of morality."[73] Women's rights activists objected that they were forbidden from discussing "immoral acts that violate the standards of public shame and morality [and] . . . the pain and misery experienced by women shut up in public houses regulated by the police and hence tolerated by the state." They complained of the "inconsistency" of their governments tolerating public houses at home and legislating against trafficking abroad. Editors of women's rights journals set out to "build the consciousness" of these tragic circumstances among their reading public in order to move forward the "battle with lies and hypocrisy."[74]

Even conservative organizations like the Friends of Household Servants complained about the negligence European governments showed in the face of legally sanctioned immorality. Sporadic government involvement was simply not enough to staunch the bleeding of young girls from Polish soil, the housekeeper society complained. More sustained state-sponsored programs were necessary to address the growing crisis. Yet they saw little sign that the partitioning powers were addressing the problem in any concerted way.[75] In Warsaw, Countess Moriconi complained that the task of rehabilitating the prostitutes who came through her shelter was made all the more challenging because of inadequate public support for abandoned and neglected children, who were the main practitioners of venal sex. Under conditions of imperial rule, the absence of state-sponsored welfare agencies made the rehabilitation of prostitutes painfully inadequate. The Congress Kingdom administration offered virtually no social care for orphans, foundlings, or illegitimate children, and Warsaw's municipal government was ill equipped to staff such agencies.[76]

---

73. Wróblewski, O prostytucyi, 2–7; and "Kronika," Nowe Słowo 2 (August 15, 1903): 370–71.

74. Nowe Słowo editors complained bitterly, for example, that their August 1, 1903 issue was confiscated because of a novella about a girl traded as a "live good." Nowe Słowo 2 (August 15, 1903): 370–71.

75. "Handlarze dziewcząt," Przyjaciel Sług, July 6, 1902, 111–12.

76. Ransel, Mothers of Misery, 43.

Taking on the Empires

In a dramatic shift from earlier associational activity in partitioned Poland, many of these new affiliations took direct aim at the partitioning powers for permitting the escalation of tolerated prostitution while refusing to lift a finger to combat pimps, procurers, and traffickers in Poland's city centers. Reformist journalists criticized the Russian government's refusal to intervene against Warsaw vice, a situation they blamed for the 1905 rioting. "The authorities provided no help," editors lamented. "Instead, they tolerated official debauchery, and the godless youth did not offer help themselves, sunk in debauchery as they were." Again, Polish "society" turned to its own resources in addressing the problem of public debauchery. *Czystość* editors even presented the outbreak of street violence as an acceptable response to Russian policies. The imperial government, they argued, "showed the most horrendous criminals excessive lenience" by officially tolerating the domestic sex trade.[77] *Nowe Słowo*, in turn, attacked governments that "sanctioned and regulated" prostitution even though "society knows" that "tolerated prostitution is the source for trafficking in women" and no amount of state control will reduce the spread of disease. "The state system of toleration" had clearly "not achieved its goals," the paper concluded summarily. Registering their disappointment with the Russian government's support of the prostitution industry in the aftermath of the pimp riot, *Nowe Słowo* editors concluded that "never before have such falseness and hypocrisy appeared in social relations. . . . Everything that was hidden now stands before us."[78] "Where is the government that allows such injustice?" wondered *Czystość*. "After all," the paper concluded piously, "the government should protect the weak."[79]

Everywhere the more open political environment following the 1905 Revolution created space for open criticism of imperial inadequacies. Cracow's young boulevard paper *Nowiny dla Wszystkich* boldly blamed the May unrest in Warsaw on Russian authorities' tolerance of the criminal subculture surrounding regulated vice. "Warsaw police," the paper complained, permitted "the greatest abuse" from knifemen and other pimps.[80] At the October 1905 Congress of Polish Women held in Cracow, Pani Teodorczuk argued that the growth of prostitution in Galicia was largely a result of the 1852

---

77. "Ksiądz Józef Żyskar," 35–41.

78. "Kilka słów w kwestii prostytucji z powodu ostatnich pogromów," *Nowe Słowo* 4 (October 15, 1905): 391–95.

79. Wojnarowa, "Zbudźcie się kobiety," 41–42.

80. "Krwawe sądy w Warszawie," 3–4.

Austrian regulations governing the registration of prostitutes in towns and cities. Since the registration system's introduction, little opposition to tolerated prostitution had materialized in Galicia. Now was the time, she insisted, for feminists to fight the prostitution plague on *both* moral and on political grounds. "A dual battle!" Teodorczuk proclaimed. The meeting encouraged the formation of a Society to Combat Regulated Prostitution and Human Trafficking in Galicia that emulated the Warsaw Society and focused on establishing shelters for former prostitutes on the model of the Warsaw shelter system. Whereas "up to this point, it was not possible to work" in the Polish territories on anything but half measures to combat prostitution," according to Professor Augustyn Wróblewski, head of the abolitionists, the new climate for civic activism after 1905 meant that it was possible to address the historic intransigence of imperial governments and tackle moral reform.[81]

To take account of the neglect of state and local authorities in controlling moral contaminants, Polish reformers mapped out new tactics that did not require direct government involvement. They introduced measures—many of them building on earlier charitable initiatives throughout Polish territories—to discourage women from taking up commercial sex in the first place. They worked through international organizations to apply moral pressure on state agencies and allow them a wider sphere of civic activism. Increasingly, in the period after 1905, these efforts were pursued in an explicitly nationalizing register. Indeed, just as the prevalence of open prostitution was perceived as a threat to national health, so were efforts to reform sexual morality approached as a central element in the campaign to restore national sovereignty. Dr. Antoni Wysłouch made this connection explicit, observing that all social improvements oriented to reducing prostitution also effectively "improved the welfare and health of the nation."[82]

By 1908, Polish antiprostitution activists began openly discussing links between regulated domestic prostitution and the overseas transport of women to work in foreign brothels, demanding an end to government hypocrisy. The Socialist Adolf Rząśnicki, for example, encouraged delegates to international antitrafficking meetings to consider the connection between trafficking and public houses in Europe. "It is necessary," he stressed, "to battle the brothels as well as the existence in most of the great states of Europe of regulated prostitution. These brothels are often the sites where traffickers organize the women to be traded," a link delegates to the 1908 Geneva Conference

---

81. "Protokol I. Zjazdu kobiet polskich w Krakowie który odbył się w dn. 20, 21, 22, 23 października, 1905 r.," *Nowe Słowo* 4 (November 15, 1905): 410, 424–30.

82. Antoni Wysłouch, *Prostytucja i jej skutki* (Poznań, 1905), 37–38.

willingly pursued.[83] The Geneva Conference explicitly debated the question of whether "lawmakers who oppose trafficking in women can support tolerated procurement in other forms." Delegates agreed that "tolerating one contributes to the other problem." Nonetheless European states continued to support "legislators [who] oppose trafficking but tolerate domestic procurement," while human trafficking itself was widely believed to "take place under the noses of the authorities, completely openly."[84] At the same time, the empires were not averse to fighting back in an effort to discourage oppositional activity in the guise of charitable aid. Several aspects of charity work faced impediments from imperial authorities. Already in early 1902, an activist in the Society for the Protection of Girls (Stowarzysenie opieki nad dziewczętami) who described herself as "occupying an important position" in the organization complained anonymously that she faced roadblocks in her work from Austrian government agencies, including the Northern State Railway Headquarters (Dyrekcji kolei Północnej i Państwowej), which had forbidden her to post warnings for traveling women on train-station walls and to install members on train platforms to warn arriving women of the danger of trafficking agents.[85] Female activists soon sought other means to put pressure on state governments

The 1905 Call to Action

The bloody events of May 1905 breathed new life into these disparate women's groups, enlivening their campaigns against the prostitution industry and prompting a rethinking of antiprostitution reform. Cracow's *Nowe Słowo* editors commented that seemingly overnight, "even those who before this did not participate in any social action" were now "committed to do battle with this plague." Varsovians who had long managed to ignore the prostitution problem now recognized the "social wounds" it caused and openly called for an investigation into its causes.[86] The revolutionary atmosphere of the 1905–1907 period brought to light two sharply divergent directions

---

83. A. Rząśnicki, "W sprawie walki z handlem żywym towarem," *Społeczeństwo* 3, no. 44 (1909): 530–31.

84. "Kongres Międzynarodowy Federacyi Abolicyonistycznej we Genewie," *Ster* 2, no. 10 (November 16, 1908): 152–53; and Wróblewski, *O prostytucji*, 49–51. See the depiction of open efforts by traffickers to enlist young women from a Lwów café in sex work, dialogues that took place completely in the open. "Handlarze żywy towarem: Stręczenie posad kowiarnianych," *Gazeta Codzienna,* March 1, 1911, 1–2.

85. "Listy do '*Przyjaciela Sług*,'" *Przyjaciel Sług*, January 5, 1902, 9–10.

86. "Kilka słów w kwestyi prostytucyi," 391–92.

in prostitution reform, reflecting contrasts between the social conservatism of Cracow and the more progressive atmosphere of Warsaw and Lwów. In the weeks following the unrest, two new journals devoted to reforming prostitution made their appearance, representing these dueling reform agendas, *Czystość* (Purity) in Cracow and *Świat Płciowy* (Sexual World) in Lwów. The following year, a new and more progressive feminist journal,

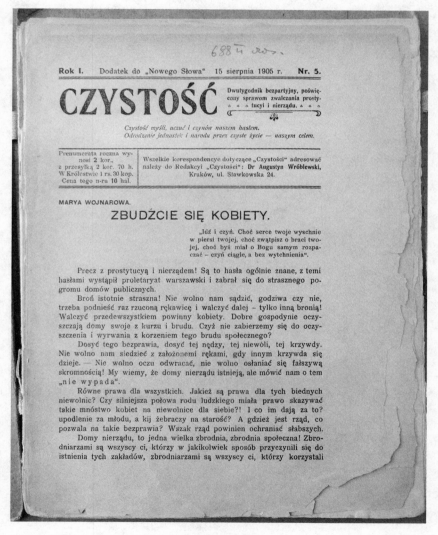

FIGURE 7.2 Front page of *Czystość* (Purity), the Cracovian journal founded in 1905 to combat sexual immorality and disease.

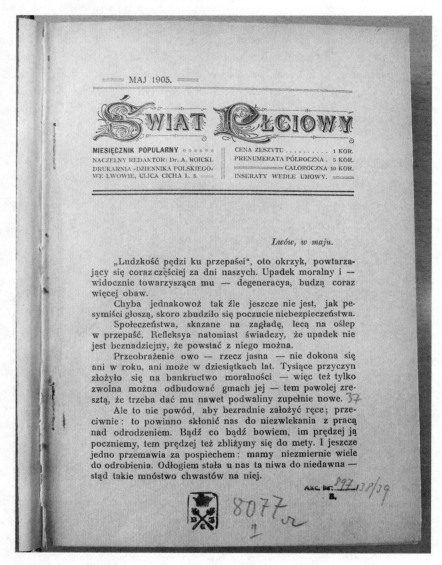

FIGURE 7.3 Front page of *Świat Płciowy* (Sexual World), established in Lwów in 1905 with a focus on the sexual double standard implied by Victorian gender relations.

Ster (The Helm), set up shop in Warsaw, joining its sister paper, *Nowe Słowo,* in Cracow as an alternative voice of the nascent Polish equal rights movement. The two sets of journals—*Czystość* and *Świat Płciowy, Nowe Słowo* and *Ster*—reflected alternative responses to concerns about prostitution and moral degradation in general. The feminist group around *Nowe Słowo* in

Cracow, for example, was less politically combative than its counterpart in Warsaw and expressed greater concern for the reform of morals than for concrete economic improvements to help vulnerable women.

Social activists responded to the local violence stemming from the sex trade with a host of new institutions, pouring new energy into several moribund organizations. Associations such as the Warsaw Society for the Protection of Women, founded in 1901, turned from an almost exclusive focus on human trafficking to a heightened concentration on domestic prostitution.[87] Immediately after the conclusion of the riots in late May 1905, the society acquired a facility in central Warsaw and set about establishing a women's shelter to "save fallen creatures whose souls have been left in the gutter."[88] With the help of a coterie of female reformers, they set to work rescuing and retraining former prostitutes.[89] Within two weeks of its founding, the new shelter arranged for the purchase of sewing machines to help train residents in a trade and already had partial orders to produce underwear from a local vender.[90] It is important that the facility sought to train former prostitutes not in the lower-ranked vocation of housekeeper but in the more "modern" professions of seamstress or factory worker in one of the kingdom's booming textile plants, relatively prestigious positions for lower-class women.

At the same time, the Warsaw-based Polish Society of Abolitionists received confirmation of its legal status in 1906. Its work paralleled that of Cracow's newly formed Society of Abolitionists.[91] Physicians and progressive intellectuals headed up both associations, which drew heavily on women as founding members. The *Nowe Słowo* editor Marya Turzyma and her sister Bronisława were instrumental in initiating the new organization, as was Marya Wojnarowa and other members of Cracow's female elite.[92] The societies took a public-health approach to prostitution reform, arguing that regulation was ineffective and even damaging to the battle against contagious diseases since it legitimized extramarital sexual relations. Leaders also

---

87. Wojnarowa, "Zbudźcie się kobiety," 41–42.

88. "Przystań dla kobiet," 2.

89. Like other shelters of the time, the titular head of the facility was a member of the clergy, Father Gaweski. Nonetheless daily affairs were in the hands of bourgeoisie women. The economic section of the new enterprise was headed by Pani Przewóska, Pani Wielowiejska ran the educational unit, Pani Buchwald coordinated efforts to locate families to take in rehabilitated women, and Pani Dzierzkówna was governor of the shelter itself.

90. "Ochrona kobiet," *Słowo*, June 15, 1905, 2.

91. The Cracow-area Abolition Society was granted authorization from the Austrian Ministry of the Interior in November 1906. AGAD, CKMSWwW (C. K. Ministersto Spraw Wewnętrznych w Wiedniu), sygn. 169, Mikrofilm no. A-23380, 807–11.

92. The founding document of the Cracow Abolitionists includes the signatures of eighteen women and only one man. AGAD, CKMSWwW, sygn. 169, 811.

broadened the usual medical proscriptions to encompass ethical guidelines. The solution to the dangers of venereal disease, the society proposed, lay in a dramatic campaign to reform sexual mores. Not only should prostitution be outlawed and the entire class of "enslaved women" thereby liberated but young people of both genders (beginning with society members) must also commit themselves to a life of abstinence before marriage. To do so required maintaining a "completely hygienic life, devoid of temptation and sensual flirting." This sexual "purity" was to be encouraged through advertisements, education, and scientific research to help enlighten the public about sexual diseases. In contrast to the Societies for the Protection of Women in Warsaw, the Cracow abolitionists invited membership from all religious and political backgrounds and either gender to join their ranks.[93]

These efforts drew explicitly on Josephine Butler's antiregulation campaign in England of two decades earlier.[94] Having sustained their program for a generation on unobtrusive social activism and educational initiatives, leaders of the Polish women's rights movement were ready to make a bolder move. The sensationalism surrounding the white-slavery scare combined with the publicity generated from the 1905 pimp riots gave female activists the perfect opportunity to move their cause into a more public arena. They resolved to join the collective outrage about commercial sex and, at the same time, use the spotlight to publicize their message of equal rights, sex education, and marital reform. In short, crafting reform programs to aid fallen women also assisted the equal-rights activists in their efforts to push forward their feminist agenda. Even as they critiqued the behavior of public women as being "against the nature" of femininity and emphasized the rejuvenating effects of marriage and motherhood, early Polish feminists themselves devoted long hours away from their homes to the cause of moral reform, some of them avoiding marriage or motherhood altogether.[95]

Equal Rights and the Prostitute: Whither Gender Reform?

In the years leading up to the Great War, opposing camps of Polish feminists would find themselves sharply divided on the issue of prostitution reform.

93. Cracow's abolitionists adopted the feminist protoeugenics newspaper *Czystość* as their press organ, reflecting a distinct emphasis on ethical reform rather than medical solutions to prostitution and the threat of venereal diseases. AGAD, CKMSWwW, sygn. 169, 811.

94. Macko, *Prostytucja*, 269–72.

95. Marya Turzyma, the editor of Cracow's *Nowe Słowo*, had a short and childless marriage to a syphilitic who passed the disease on to her, causing her to go blind eventually. Ludwika Moriconi,

Two factions of female reformers competed for public support of new directions in police regulation. The sexual liberation and gender equality emphasized among feminist groups in Warsaw and Lwów was reflected in the pages of journals such as *Ster* and *Świat Płciowy*, press organs that would be loosely linked to the neoregulation campaign of prostitution reform. The Lwów muckraking journal *Świat Płciowy* focused on exposing sexual scandals, highlighting police corruption, and revealing details from the spicy lives of local waitresses and barkeeps. The paper featured the miserable lives of lower-class women, highlighting their limited economic horizons. Cracow's *Nowe Słowo* and its supplement *Czystość*, by contrast, became the mouthpieces for the abolition camp, which set about eliminating all forms of paid sex and dismantling the police regulation system. *Czystość* addressed prostitution from the perspective of abstinence before and monogamy within marriage for both partners, stressing reforms in the upbringing of male children, in sexual expectations for young men, and the need to clean up society's standards of morality. Both publications placed paid sex at the center of their agenda, taking advantage of the heightened interest in prostitution after the May riots to further their competing agendas of eliminating or "rationalizing" regulated prostitution.[96]

The relaxation of imperial restrictions on civic organization in the Polish Kingdom and in Galicia also opened up the field for the growth of a cross-border equal-rights agenda. Marya Turzyma's feminist journal *Nowe Słowo* helped establish Cracow as a base for feminist activity from 1902 until Paulina Kulczycka-Reinschmitt's founding in Warsaw of the more explicitly political *Ster* in 1906. The political stances of the two journals continued to reflect the differing relationships Polish subjects maintained with their constituent empires. In keeping with the politically conciliatory environment in Galicia, for example, Turzyma's journal advocated social and economic advancements for Polish women without explicitly criticizing the Habsburg authorities.[97] By contrast, the revolutionary atmosphere of Warsaw after 1905 created an opening for a women's movement that espoused much more explicitly political aims. The Warsaw feminist journal

---

the manager of one of Warsaw's largest and most long-lived rescue shelters for fallen women, emphasized the curative powers of motherhood on her charges but remained single and childless herself. See Marya Turzyma, "Ekonomiczne przyczyny prostytucyi," *Nowe Słowo* 4 (December 15, 1905): 458–60.

96. "Nierząd w Warszawie," 48.

97. On the distinctions between *Nowe Słowo* and, especially as regards ethical matters, see Anna Pawłowska, "Kwestie etyczno-obyczajowe w prasie kobiecej przełomu XIX i XX wieku (na łamach 'Steru' i 'Nowego Słowa')," *Studia historyczne* 30, no. 4 (1987): 571–88.

Ster, declared the official "organ of the Polish equal-rights movement" in 1907, united the Polish Kingdom's two overlapping feminist entities, the Polish Society of Equal Rights for Women (Polskie Towarzyszenie Równouprawnienia Kobiet), and the Union of Equal Rights for Polish Women (Związek Równouprawnienia Kobiet Polskich).[98] The *Ster* program was closely modeled on West European feminist agendas, calling for women's right to participate in legislative bodies, testify as legal witnesses, and share property equally with males. This radical agenda demanded the elimination of separate law codes pertaining to men and women and their replacement with one type of citizen. Self-consciously representing the women's movement across Polish territory, the paper provided a sharp critique of gender relations in Galicia as well as in the Congress Kingdom. Especially after the passage of universal male suffrage for elections to the Austrian Reichsrat in 1907, editorials highlighted the additional legal inequities remaining in the Habsburg Monarchy, including a wife's legally subservient status within a marriage, her legal powerlessness over her own children, and the prohibition on female participation in political societies.[99] *Ster* was remarkable both in its radical vision of a society without legal gender distinctions and in its seamless interweaving of social activism in all three partitions of the Polish lands. Work to improve the position of women within Polish culture effectively strengthened the national community by expanding its active citizenry. The society *Ster* envisioned was one in which all Polish women obtained "an equal role in the battle for the rights of [the Polish] nation, in the work for its future." Women, in sum, were "demanding to take part in the building of the national edifice [gmach]" and in so doing improve the moral standing of the nation's active citizens.[100]

This vision of Polish equal rights also applied to the realm of sexual politics. Feminists throughout Polish territory sought to remedy the moral dysfunction they perceived, at the heart of which was the sexual double

---

98. The existence of two separate women's rights organizations stemmed from the movement's separate constituencies. The Towarzystwo was intended to serve a mass audience that included peasants in Poland's far-flung provinces, whereas the Union appealed to a more professional audience of teachers, doctors, attorneys, etc. See "1907," *Ster* 2, no. 1 (1908): 1–4.

99. As of 1907, all males over the age of twenty-four had suffrage rights in the Habsburg Monarchy as well as the right to join political parties, privileges denied to women. Moreover, an 1811 Austrian law required women to "obey [her husband's] commands and seek to accomplish his bidding." Women were also forbidden, along with the mentally handicapped and criminals, from serving as witnesses to wills or members of juries. "Zasada równouprawnienia kobiet," *Ster* 1, no. 2 (1907): 87–88; and "Mężczyźni i kobiety Austrji wobec ustaw," *Ster* 1, no. 3 (1907): 149.

100. Speech by Dulębianka presented at the Third Congress of Polish Women in Warsaw, June 1907. Reprinted in Marja Dulębianka, "Polityczne stanowisko kobiety." *Ster* 1, no. 7 (1907): 257–62.

standard reflected in the system of police-regulated prostitution. The notion that women should "remain pure before marriage and faithful afterward" while men were permitted to take lovers both before and during marriage "so long as [they] provide[d] for [their family] materially" was, according to the feminist activist Iza Moszczeńska, a root cause of the prostitution industry. Societal expectations preventing "good" women from engaging in sex outside of marriage meant "the formation of a whole separate class of fallen and contemptible women" to provide sexual services for single males. The depreciation of wages in the late nineteenth century meant that upper-class males were forced to marry late, compelling them to employ the services of prostitutes during their years of sexual maturity prior to marriage.[101] The result, according to the feminist author Teresa Lubińska, was that the moral purity of middle- and upper-class women was dependent on working-class girls selling their sexual services. In the end, the Victorian sexual economy was premised on class inequality: bourgeois women maintained their virtue at the cost of their lower-class sisters. Regulated commercial sex implicated all women, and society as a whole bore responsibility for upholding the regulation system. "Every woman who lives in purity at the cost of the shame of her sister prostitutes is guilty," Lubińska stressed. "All of humanity is guilty."[102]

Polish feminists were united in their fundamental opposition to regulated prostitution. But beyond putting pressure on intransigent imperial governments, they diverged on the strategies appropriate for curing society of the prostitution disease. Two sets of overlapping agendas evolved in the Polish public space, each concerned with addressing the fundamental causality behind the turn to paid sex. The equal rights movement as it developed in the Polish Kingdom stressed civil and economic rights for women, along with education about sexuality. For Warsaw activists associated with the journal *Ster,* prostitution reform was a women's rights issue best addressed by granting political rights to women. "Women must govern themselves with new laws in the area of ethics," noted Weychertowna. Only then can they "do battle with the abomination that is prostitution."[103] To this end, men and women needed a more equitable distribution of wage-earning capacity. Work for women was both "poorly paid and highly unpleasant," activists acknowledged. However, even more important than increasing wages

---

101. Iza Moszczeńska, "Podwójna moralność," *Nowe Słowo* 2 (March 1, 1903): 97–101.

102. Teresa Lubińska, "Handel żywym towarem i prostytucja," *Ster* 2, no. 6 (1908): 220–24.

103. Weychertowna, "Źródła społeczne i etyczne handlu żywym towarem," *Ster* 2, no. 6 (1908): 212–16.

and improving professional training for female workers was challenging the assumption that only males worked outside the home. By encouraging "both men and women to be wage earners" the inequalities within marriage could be addressed and the sexual double standard eased.[104] At the same time, Warsaw activists envisioned a changed approach to the way children were educated about sexuality. They believed it was vital to "recognize the sexual urge as a natural biological phenomenon." Children should be taught personal responsibility and both sexes should receive information about sexuality, sexual diseases, and reproductive processes. Even charity activists like Ludwika Moriconi, founder of the Warsaw shelter, recognized that "the sexual instinct is one of the strongest instincts in an individual." The key, according to Moriconi, was to reorient that sensibility toward "normal" functions of life (i.e., marriage) rather than allow it to be pursued through extramarital commercial relationships.[105] Warsaw equal-rights activists advocated sex education in schools, the teaching of sexual responsibility to adolescent boys, and family planning.

All of this depended on the creation of an atmosphere of intellectual openness, one that women should be instrumental in shaping. As Dr. Julja Blay argued at a 1913 meeting of the Union of Equal Rights for Polish Women, the disappearance of prostitution from Polish society could only be accomplished by creating a completely "new culture" and allowing the discussion of sexuality to "come out from the shadow of prejudice."[106] Sexuality, gender roles, and reproductive issues must be openly discussed among adolescents if a reeducation of the younger generation was ever going to come about, an educational revolution vital to redirecting Poland's social morality. With this in mind, the Union would appeal in 1913 to Polish deputies in the Russian Duma to support a proposal to "close public houses in all forms" and "destroy regulated prostitution." This, argued equal-rights activists, was both a feminist and a nationalist issue. Legislation to abolish tolerated prostitution was vital to the national cause, they insisted. "Let the whole world hear that the Polish nation wishes Warsaw to stop being the so-called factory of white slaves," alluding to the prevalence of Polish women in foreign brothels. Poland, they claimed, wished to eliminate the brand "'Polish goods' on the international market." Closing the public houses and crushing regulated prostitution would raise Poland's ethics to the level demanded by her national needs.[107]

---

104. Report on series of three lectures by the Union of Equal Rights for Polish Women activist Dr. Julja Blay, "O czym kobiety nie mówią," *Ster* 7, no. 1 (January 10, 1913): 4.

105. Poraj, "Dusza prostytutki," 375–78.

106. Blay, "O czym kobiety nie mowią," 4.

107. The Russian League of Equal Rights for Women proposed a motion to "close the public houses in all forms" throughout the Russia Empire and to "conduct a fight against venereal disease on

Warsaw's equal-rights activists shared an optimistic perception of human nature, viewing prostitutes as victims of poverty and immoral circumstances who could be guided back to a more wholesome path. The reformability of hardened prostitutes was vividly demonstrated in discussions of the clients in Moriconi's rescue shelter. After spending only a short time in her care, Moriconi claimed young women became "repulsed by lying." They were "drawn to the truth" and to the "nobility" of motherhood. The combination of equal rights, social sympathy, and mutual trust along with good hard work led former brothel residents to "return to an honest road." Overall, most Warsaw activists believed that former prostitutes could be redeemed and could serve a useful purpose in society, if only to raise strong and healthy children.[108]

Yet former prostitutes, equal-rights activists complained, were treated with contempt by those around them, making their return from this life all the more difficult. Women's rights activists depicted sex workers with increasing empathy for their plight, characterizing their lives as "dark and impoverished" and being "spat upon" by "honest" members of society with whom they came into contact. When charity workers got to know these "outcasts" better, as when they conducted educational programs in the prisons, they often discovered a passionate desire to learn and to better their position in life. One such activist was struck by a professional prostitute who burst into tears of joy at the opportunity to study, never having had the chance before in life. "This one had a soul," acknowledged the charity worker. "If it was possible to rescue her from the jaws of fate, it might be possible to rescue a second, even a tenth," she proclaimed hopefully.[109] Increasingly, women's groups in Poland and elsewhere came to view prostitutes as no different from any other women. Sex workers were neither fatally flawed nor marked at birth for a life of crime and degeneracy. Instead, it was the prostitute's surroundings that were unhealthy and prompted her to turn to the sex trade. Economic and environmental conditions, and especially their status as orphans or illegitimate children, encouraged the turn to prostitution.[110] Once such women were lifted out of their damaging home environments, provided with jobs training and life skills, and given the prospect of honest work, they could rise above the "muck" of their origins. This was a project that reflected a changed attitude toward the sources and solutions of sexually promiscuous behavior. It was also an increasingly political stance that

---

the general principle of the battle with infectious diseases." The motion was supported by forty-four deputies in the Duma. "Do społeczeństwa," Ster 7, nos. 19–20 (December 1913): 113–14.

108. Poraj, "Dusza prostytutki," 375–78.

109. Weychertówna, "Zródła społeczne," 212–16.

110. Lubińska, "Handel żywym towarem," 220–24.

envisioned dramatically reforming the laws of all three partitioning powers in order to abolish regulated prostitution and eliminate the sexual double standard that supported it.

Cracow's Moral Reformers

Moriconi's comments on the reformability of former streetwalkers spoke directly to a core issue in the debate about prostitution. Could women who sold sex be resurrected from the moral muck and reintegrated back into society? Warsaw feminists believed this to be possible and based their rescue initiatives on the hope of redemption. Activists associated with the Cracow movement approached the prostitution problem from a more skeptical standpoint. The distinctions between the two movements on the subject of prostitution reform remind us that despite regular exchanges between the two groups, conditions in the three empires helped shape distinct political and cultural sensibilities that would color Polish public life for a long time to come. Cracovian activists expressed serious doubts about the return to a "normal" life for those who had once worked the streets.

Writers associated with Marya Turzyma's Cracow journal understood prostitution to stem from the overall degeneracy of the lower classes. Turzyma, who had herself been contaminated with syphilis by her philandering husband, traced a link between poverty, crime, and prostitution. A high percentage of "morally degenerate" children were born to the lower classes, she argued, causing 95 percent of the registered prostitutes to trace their origins to "degenerate criminals of the poorest classes." Following Cesare Lombroso, the Italian criminal anthropologist, Turzyma attributed the rise in prostitution to the inborn traits common to Poland's poorer strata and the damaging effect of their impoverished environment. "Take a good female worker, often under the influence of alcohol, who has a child at her bosom." If the woman continues working, she can't spend time with the child. She lives with the child in a "crowded and sultry hut" together with many immoral characters. As the child matures, it is exposed to "fights and cursing, noisy drunken orgies, and the secret sessions of well-mannered criminals." By the time such children are teenagers, Turzyma proposed, the girls were naturally attracted to the "easy wages" of the female lodger who "sleeps all day, dresses nicely, goes out on walks at night, and comes back full and drunk."[111] Given the tension implied here between nature and nurture in shaping a prostitute's impulses, Cracow feminists increasingly emphasized inborn qualities over

---

111. Turzyma, "Ekonomiczne przyczyny prostytucyi," 458–61.

the possibilities of nurturing a sex worker back into the social mainstream. This pessimistic view would find a voice in the social control impulses of the eugenics movement in later years.

Cracovian feminists also deemphasized the economic argument behind the turn to prostitution. They resisted the call for women wage earners to stand alongside their husbands in public life, arguing instead that the presence of women laborers effectively decreased wages for males, causing men to marry later. In the meantime, bourgeois males tended to rely on the services of prostitutes during the long hiatus between sexual maturity and marriage. This trend toward late marriage, in the view of *Nowe Słowo* writers, led to an overall reduction in the number of children born to Polish families. If fewer women were wage earners, they argued, wages for men would be higher and would allow them to marry earlier, decreasing reliance on prostitutes and encouraging larger families. Perhaps most tellingly, the Cracovian circle viewed high rates of prostitution as indicative of a deeper social malaise. The unbridled male libido was responsible for the spread of incurable venereal diseases and the overall "degeneration of the race" as a whole, which was permanently damaged by congenital syphilis. The pattern of late marriage made possible by the availability of inexpensive sexual liaisons meant that fertility rates had decreased. "Fewer children" were born in the early years of the twentieth century, according to the *Nowe Słowo* correspondent Iza Moszczeńska, in comparison to times when prostitution was less rampant. A significant number of these offspring were "deficient" or fell to infanticide, starvation, or diseases.[112] As other writers argued, the recent "trend toward free love" and the "complete freedom of desire" for males resulted in disastrous harm for honest women. The solution lay in encouraging sexual restraint outside of marriage. "Men must be taught in their youth to fight their instinct and have relations with just one person," activists stressed.[113] These concerns would be further reflected in the work of medical associations to be discussed in chapter 8.

Women's Rights and the Prostitute: A Route to National Activism

The permissive atmosphere for publishing and civic association after 1905 helped widen the rift between the wings of the Polish women's movement. The two camps of women's rights activists advocated sharply divergent

---

112. Iza Moszczeńska, "Prostytucya i praca kobiet," *Nowe Słowo* 1 (December 15, 1902): 370–75.
113. Edward Carpenter, "Małżeństwo: Rzut oka na przyszłość," *Nowe Słowo* 2 (July 15, 1903): 315–19.

solutions to the problem of prostitution. The more politically aggressive Warsaw camp quickly incorporated assistance to profligate women into its overall equal-rights agenda. Warsaw feminists switched course sharply after 1905 and worked to include women of loose morals in their plan of action. They presented this agenda as part of a delicate symbiosis involving improved conditions for women while strengthening the Polish national movement. The founder and longtime leader of the Polish women's rights movement, Paulina Kulczalska-Reinschmitt, claimed in a slightly exaggerated fashion that "the women who belonged to the Polish equal rights movement . . . have supported as a point in their program from the very beginning the abolition of regulation [police-regulated prostitution] and have always treated it as a central component of their twofold concern about moral purity and the physical health of the nation." Kulczalska-Reinschmitt presented the women's movement as the *only* organized association in the Kingdom of Poland that viewed the fight against regulated prostitution as a core programmatic goal.[114]

The long-standing reticence among women's rights activists to engage seriously with the plight of less advantaged women changed dramatically when the events of 1905 riveted society's attention on the deep inroads prostitution had made in lower-class female culture. The Warsaw press brought the issue of prostitution to the attention of charity groups as never before. The pediatrician and child pedagogue Janusz Korczak demanded in the pages of Warsaw's *Głos* that reporters move beyond metaphorical depictions of the prostitution problem and investigate specifically "where the unhappy girls spend their time, who feeds them, [and] who provides them with housing."[115] Rather than claiming that prostitution was of no concern to broader society or that it was a problem that was "difficult to remedy," Korczak insisted that "much, much more could be learned" about the world of prostitution. Until the better-off portions of society took it upon themselves to work among the masses, he cautioned, "the wounded will continue to bleed."[116] Even as the debris from the May events was being cleared away, antiprostitution activists marshaled their forces for a new attack on the hated system of registering young women as professional prostitutes. Taking a page from Josephine

---

114. Paulina Kulczalska-Reinschmitt, "Reglamentacja prostytucji jako środek zapobiegawczy zarazie chorowenerycznych," in *Pamiętnik Wystawy Walka z Chorobami Zakaznemi, Maj 1915 roku* (Warsaw, 1915), 68–73.

115. Cracow's Ethos chapter found reflection in Warsaw, where a similar ethic society was established in the wake of the 1905 riots. "Odezwa," 11–12.

116. Janusz Korczak, *Głos*, 20, no. 22, May 21, 1905, 322–23. Korczak was particularly concerned with the prostitution of girls as young as ten and twelve through various cover schemes. This article highlights a prostitution ring operating out of a warehouse for women's hats.

Butler's earlier crusade, reformers announced that "a new generation" had arrived, one that could take inspiration from Mrs. Butler's "fervor." Polish activists resolved to join with the broader international effort to combat prostitution. Alongside the Italian, French, German, Russian, American, and Spanish agencies involved in the effort to combat prostitution, "should there not also be a place for us in this battle?"[117] Statelessness would no longer be seen as prohibitive to the foundation of effective self-help associations to serve the interests of vulnerable women.

During the frenzy of social activity after 1905, the philanthropic energies of women's groups found an open civic space. Compelled by the harm they witnessed in the world of pimps, procurers, and prostitutes revealed to them by the 1905 riots, bourgeois women entered the public sphere in unprecedented numbers. They set out to remedy the ills they saw and to highlight the clear responsibility borne by the empires in propping up the outmoded system of regulated prostitution. Their activism brought them in conflict with one another and with the imperial powers. Nevertheless, civic engagement and public debate about solutions to key social issues allowed women to "act national" in new and important ways. Still, the optimistic notion that social assistance could remedy the vagaries of commercial sex was comparatively short lived. A more masculine, scientific medical discourse soon overcame this social-reform agenda as physicians' societies and eugenics organizations took over the debate about prostitution in the Polish lands. Frustration with the results of these labors would prompt tensions and divisions in the antiprostitution forces. Sympathy toward the prostitute waned as medical science portrayed her as more a danger to Polish society than an object of pity. The failure of the humanitarian efforts to "solve" the prostitution problem and the intransigence of many of its practitioners helped fuel a renewed cynicism about the permanence of the sex trade and prompted activists to turn to other, more militant solutions for sexual immorality and disease. It is to the genesis of this solution that we turn in the next chapter.

---

117. "Mój pochód krzyżowy," 9.

CHAPTER 8

The Physician and the Fallen Woman

> Police doctors must expand their sphere of activity
> and their powers such that all means are used to
> guarantee the examination of *every* prostitute—
> especially those who avoid regulation and those who
> have been recently removed from control.
>
> —"Ankieta w sprawie zwalczanie—Chorób u
> młodzieży szkoł"

Physicians stood at the center of the universe
of regulated prostitution. Their reach extended into every aspect of the practice. Police doctors determined who would be inscribed onto the public
registry and who would be sent to hospital for treatment. They inspected
the bodies of professional prostitutes, conducted examinations at tolerated
houses, and managed venereal wards in city hospitals. Army medics monitored the health of troops returning from garrison brothels. Municipal physicians kept detailed records and maintained transcripts of disease, hospital
stays, and changes of residence among public women. As actors central to
the drama of supervised prostitution, Polish doctors saw an enormous rise
in their authority during the extended turn-of-the-century era of anxiety
about public sex. In the early days of regulation, they approached their task of
supervising public women with relative optimism, striving to achieve greater
efficiency and to employ modern medical techniques in their work. In the
Polish lands, as across the Continent, faith in science encouraged the belief
that the venereal threat could be brought under control through efficient
application of medical knowledge. Syphilis and related maladies might be
prevented if not cured by keeping infected women off the streets and out
of the brothels. But over time, the seemingly limitless supply of women
suspected of selling sex combined with new and frightening information
about the horrors of venereal diseases prompted a rising tide of cynicism

among many medical practitioners. This chapter demonstrates how physicians effectively leveraged the panic over prostitution to expand their powers in unprecedented ways, carving out a new status for themselves as the moral conscience of a damaged nation.

Doctors were at the forefront of efforts to reform tolerated prostitution, even as they constituted the core of the system itself. In contrast to charity workers and social reformers who intervened to assist the women caught up in the world of prostitution, doctors could affect the management of the system from within the belly of the beast. They worked to bring ever-widening categories of women under their control and defined the parameters of prostitution in increasingly broad terms. As the quotation above suggests, they set out to register women who had ostensibly slipped through police controls—including those who did not self-identify as prostitutes. Doctors imposed "objective" standards on suspected "prostitutes," applying the label to women of particular social classes and employment categories. Police physicians used the practice of registering "discreet" or "secret" prostitutes alongside those who practiced venal sex full time in the hopes of "guaranteeing the examination of *every* prostitute—especially those who avoid regulation." Some doctors even recommended entire categories of female workers be subjected to police inspection on the assumption they were selling sex in their off hours.

One function of medical confidence in conquering the venereal plague was a redoubled effort to impose experimental cures on recalcitrant public women. Venereologists coaxed their patients into accepting painful and often disfiguring procedures, even seeking government mandates to strengthen their authority over treatments. At the same time, doctors remained confident that "fallen women" could be assimilated back into healthy society once they left the public rolls. They expressed little doubt that a "cured" prostitute could return to "honest" work and even take a husband and raise healthy children. In contrast to some middle-class reformers who feared former prostitutes would be shunned from "normal" life, the medical community during the early years of regulation believed in the social reintegration of those who had turned to venal sex. Only in the early twentieth century, once new and frightening details about the effects of syphilis begin to emerge, did doctors become increasingly cynical about prostitutes as a primary vector of disease. In the years leading up to the outbreak of the First World War, a fresh panic arose over congenital syphilis, the syphilis of innocent wives, and the prevalence of venereal diseases among elite secondary and university students. Awareness that sexual diseases could neither be cured nor prevented through the regulation system prompted leading physicians to launch a campaign of purity and abstinence among Poland's youth. The physician-led purity initiative is the subject of chapter 9. This chapter examines the road to the Polish eugenics initiatives of the 1920s and the scientific despair that helped pave the way for them.

Polish Medicine between Empire and Nation

The evolution of the system of police-regulated prostitution represented part of a larger shift in the status of professional medicine across Europe.[1] The European medical community experienced unprecedented gains in social and political status during the long nineteenth century. From Britain to Russia, the growing prestige of rational science combined with increased public health concerns gave doctors newfound authority in the public sphere.[2] In Western Europe and the United States, governments took on heightened responsibility for protecting the health of the population, employing physicians in ever-wider social arenas.[3] For most of continental Europe, this expansion included the regulation of the female body through medically supervised prostitution.[4] In east-central Europe, where the medical community often comprised ethnic groups distinct from and subject to that of the ruling state, medicine maintained a more circumspect relationship to established sources of power. Yet here too across the German, Habsburg, and Russian empires, doctors managed to extend their professional authority by linking their services to imperial concerns about hygiene and sanitation, especially in the rapidly growing and overcrowded cities of eastern Europe.[5] Access to and control over prostitutes through the system of police regulation played a key role in expanding the social prestige of doctors.

In the Polish-speaking territories of east-central Europe, physicians faced greater challenges as they negotiated their status within government bureaucracies. Occupying authorities had crushed medical departments at most

---

1. For Europe, see W. F. Bynum, *Science and the Practice of Medicine in the Nineteenth Century* (Cambridge, UK, 1994).

2. Michel Foucault famously declared physicians to be the new "priests of the body" and linked the widening authority of medicine to the rise of the centralized state in the nineteenth century. Foucault, *Birth of the Clinic: An Archeology of Medical Perception* (New York, 1994), 36–37.

3. On the evolution of medical authority in the American context, see Paul Starr, *The Social Transformation of American Medicine: The Rise of a Sovereign Profession and the Making of a Vast Industry* (New York, 1982); and Charles E. Rosenberg, *The Care of Strangers: The Rise of America's Hospital System* (Baltimore, 1995).

4. See Oosterhuis, *Stepchildren of Nature*, on the link between the strong medical presence in the debate on sexual matters in nineteenth-century Europe and the enhanced scientific and social status of medicine.

5. Piotr Franaszek, *Zdrowie publiczne w Galicji w dobie autonomii (Wybrane problemy)* (Cracow, 2002), 7–10.

Polish universities after the late eighteenth century partitions, reducing their funding, staffing them with unskilled instructors, or curtailing their activities altogether.[6] The Polish medical profession thus experienced an extended crisis throughout the partitioned period. Aspiring physicians were forced to travel abroad for professional training and faced constrained employment opportunities on their return to Polish soil.[7] In both Prussian-occupied Poland and the Congress Kingdom, virtually all practitioners worked for the state; private initiative had a limited sphere of influence.[8] The situation was slightly more favorable in Galicia after the introduction of autonomy in 1867, but Polish-speaking physicians still struggled to gain a foothold in a foreign bureaucracy.[9]

One avenue for Polish doctors to acquire professional experience in this setting was through the machinery of regulated prostitution. As occupying authorities extended the mechanism of police-controlled prostitution to the newly acquired Polish lands, specialists in gynecology turned to the inspection system for employment opportunities.[10] In contrast to officials at higher levels in the judicial and law enforcement systems, the vice squads and police-medical commissions supervising prostitutes were staffed mainly with Polish speakers.[11] Impossible though their task would prove to be, supervision over prostitutes gave physicians increased access to infected female bodies. Regulation provided the specialized knowledge that helped define them as experts

---

6. The Department of Medicine (Wydział Lekarski) at Jagiellonian University in Cracow was the only continuously operating facility for training doctors in the Polish lands before 1918. The University of Vilnius Medical School operated from 1802 until 1832. The Department of Medicine at Warsaw University was closed after the November Uprising in 1830, reopened briefly as part of the Szkoła Główna from 1862 to 1869, and then converted to a much weaker Russified university after 1869. A Department of Medicine opened for the first time in Lwów in 1894. Because of the weakness of Polish educational facilities, most medical students from the Polish lands received some or all of their training in Berlin, Vienna, Geneva, Strasbourg, or other West European sites. Bronisław Sejda, *Dzieje medycyny w zarysie* (Warsaw, 1973), 460–94.

7. Franaszek, *Zdrowie publiczne*, 7–10; and Seyda, *Dzieje medycyny*, 460–94.

8. Deborah Brunton, *Medicine Transformed: Health, Disease, and Society in Europe, 1800–1930* (Manchester, UK, 2004), 125–26. The public-health efforts of Polish physicians were particularly restricted in Prussian Poland. See the complaints of the physician Adam Karkowski in his report on the progress of the Society for Combatting Contagious Sexual Diseases during the 1911 meeting of the organization. Karkowski, "Działalność Towarzystwa hygieniecznego w Wielkopolce," in *Księga pamiętkowa XI zjazdu lekarzy i przyrodników polskich w Krakowie, July 18–22, 1911* (Cracow, 1911), 622–24.

9. Sejda, *Dzieje medycyny*, 473–85.

10. On the evolution of regulationism among European doctors, see Peter Baldwin, *Contagion and the State, 1830–1930* (Cambridge, 1999), 355–523.

11. Even in the most repressive periods of Russian rule, police staff in Warsaw and other large cities remained Polish speaking and Catholic, partially because of a shortage of qualified Russian speakers. Andrzej Chwałba, *Polacy w służbie Moskali* (Warsaw, 1999).

and permitted them newfound punitive powers over their patients. In many respects, medicine in Poland became professionalized partially through the engine of regulated prostitution. Physicians in the Polish lands leveraged social anxieties over open prostitution to expand their own power and influence and used that heightened authority to impose their professional mark on a widening array of social problems. By the early years of the twentieth century, Polish doctors enjoyed the perception of specialized knowledge in matters of education, marriage, child rearing, alcohol consumption, public pornography, and workplace hygiene—an unprecedented expansion in the social reach of the medical profession. The physician's role as an inspector of prostitutes was part of a meteoric rise in medicine's social capital during the last quarter of the nineteenth century.

Medical Confidence and the Expansion of the Regulatory System

Doctors worked closely with police on inspection committees in most large and medium-sized cities across the Polish lands. The task of these medical commissions was daunting, yet physicians approached their work with a sense of faith in the effectiveness of the registration system.[12] In Warsaw alone, four police doctors and ten orderlies were responsible for checking some 1,400 registered prostitutes two times per week in 1869.[13] In addition to women examined on suspicion of prostitution or vagrancy, police doctors inspected some 16,000 criminals, military troops, and prison inmates each year.[14] Meanwhile, city hospitals were groaning under the strain of venereal patients. By 1871, 5,892 men and women were hospitalized annually for treatment of venereal diseases in one of two Warsaw-area army hospitals (Ujazdowski and Aleksandrowski), in the wards of the St. Lazarus police hospital, or in the Jewish facility, a total of some 2 percent of city's municipal population.[15] Police doctors struggled to accommodate small examination spaces, staffing shortages, and a limited supply of medical instruments and disinfectant. Complaints about workloads and scarce resources were

12. The police-medical committee in major cities of Congress Poland consisted of the commissioner of the medical division of the police department, two assistants, a moral official, four police doctors, and ten orderlies. In addition to this, in Warsaw, the doctor of the Warsaw district and an army doctor were on call to help serve the committee as needed. "Prostytucya w mieście Warszawy w latach 1867, 1868, 1869," *Gazeta Lekarska* 5, no. 30 (1871): 479–80.

13. "Prostytucya w mieście Warszawie," 508.

14. *Wykład chorób wenerycznych* (Warsaw, 1874), 409.

15. "Prostytucya w mieście Warszawie," 510–11.

endemic. In Galicia, the governor general's office revisited Habsburg regulations for inspecting prostitutes during the 1870s in response to grievances from crown land inspectors. The viceroy established a commission in 1874 to assign more doctors to the regulation system and to improve the resources at their disposal. Concerns about poor pay and enormous workloads continued, even as medical confidence rose. The Lwów physician Dr. Rieger expressed hope in 1877 that "the matter of organizing prostitution in [the crown land's] large cities will soon be resolved" by the government.[16]

The situation in industrial towns and military garrisons posed still greater challenges. Provincial inspectors worked in an atmosphere of extreme shortages, cramped examination facilities, primitive equipment, and scant supplies of disinfectant. One horrified sanitary inspector in Galicia discovered that examination rooms were so constrained in his district that a thorough checkup was nearly impossible. In the oil-refining town of Borysław, inspector Józef Barczycki described the examination room as a passageway that was "so small that each time an examination is conducted a heavy table must be brought in from another room." Barczycki suspected that "when I am not there the exam is conducted completely without an examination table," if it was conducted at all. The inspector found no speculum and no means of disinfectant on hand. The situation was even worse in the industrial town of Drohobycz in eastern Galicia, where the examination table had to be positioned partially outside the room with the door opened during inspections. Here, the inspector was appalled to note that the window of the exam room faced directly onto the street and was not covered up at the time of the inspection. Things were no better in the garrison town of Trembowla, where the town doctor, a surgeon, was responsible for inspecting prostitutes, again without the use of appropriate disinfectant. Medical examinations were conducted in the *gmina* (commune) district office where the "windows stood open for the curiosity of passersby, including . . . the eyes of schoolchildren."[17] The logistical impediments such reports reveal suggest local prostitutes were not subjected to routine semiweekly inspection, as police regulations required.

Despite these horrific scenes of medical malfeasance, doctors remained stubbornly committed to the notion that more and better examinations

---

16. A commission established by the Galician viceroy's office in 1874 increased the number of police doctors responsible for examining registered prostitutes in key crown-land cities, but failed to increase the salaries of the overtaxed physicians or produce instructions to guide their work. "Rzecz o uregulowaniu prostytucyi w Galicyi," *Dwutygodnik Medycyny Publicznej*, no. 6 (1877): 85–86.

17. "Nadzór nad prostytucyą u nas," *Świat Płciowy* 1, no. 5 (December 1905): 17–18.

represented the way forward in staunching the spread of venereal diseases. Indeed, inspectors proposed that the real problem lay in prostitutes who ostensibly remained beyond the reach of the regulation system—the secret prostitutes and those working in provincial towns untouched by police doctors. If only the influence of the imperial system could extend to these unsupervised women, the government would have a prayer of protecting the population's health.[18] As an 1874 medical textbook covering treatment for venereal disease noted, the primary cause of the spread of syphilis was seen to be "the irresponsible administration of [inspection] services" in police stations. Accordingly, "police authorities should endeavor to control all prostitution in Warsaw [because] only then will it be possible to eliminate its harmful effects." After 1864, a committee under the direction of the (Polish-speaking) police chief of Warsaw adopted "vigorous measures to pursue the work" of supervising prostitutes, effectively bringing a greater "number of prostitutes under police control." The more women under police supervision, the committee believed, the greater the "decrease in the number of sick civilians." Textbook authors expressed confidence that once police gained adequate authority and personnel, the inspection system in Warsaw would prove "good and beneficial much like regulations in . . . other great European cities."[19] The key to controlling venereal diseases lay in imposing police control over the greatest number of sexually active women.

Experts in sexually transmitted diseases encouraged police to arrest and examine any woman they suspected of engaging in venal sex, broadening the categories and grounds for suspicion. By the late 1860s, doctors in police stations across the Polish lands were engaged in a full-fledged campaign to force women selling sex "secretly" (using the vague definitions explored in chapter 2) to be inscribed on the prostitution registry. Police inspectors bragged that in the seven-year period from 1867 to 1874, secret prostitution was "cut in half" in Warsaw as the ranks of registered prostitutes now included far greater numbers of infected women. Authorities in Warsaw noted that whereas in 1842 some 267 infected women appeared on the public registry, an additional 800 women suffering from various venereal ailments were not yet listed as official prostitutes and thus were not subject to regular sanitary exams. By 1871, however, the numbers were reversed and 999 diseased women were already registered, whereas only 630 had to be arrested and checked for disease.[20] If the best hope for preventing contamination lay in

---

18. Ibid., 16.
19. *Wykład chorób wenerycznych*, 403–5.
20. Ibid., 407.

systematic medical inspections, then the category of those subject to supervision would have to be expanded. How police authorities could be confident women suffering from sexual diseases were in fact working as prostitutes is unclear. Contemporary officials assumed all women who contracted venereal diseases were prostitutes and thus that bringing more of them under medical control would effectively break the chain of contamination. In the 1870s, the Polish medical community had not yet discovered that wives and children could be innocent victims of their philandering husbands and fathers and, indeed, that a significant portion of the nonprostitute population had also contracted incurable sexual ailments. Moreover, the calculation that fully "half" the number of "secret" prostitutes on the streets of Warsaw had been brought under control by the mid-1870s begs the question of how many women were selling sex informally. Nonetheless, medical confidence was unabated as doctors sought to fulfill their professional agenda by imposing their civilizing mission on poor, young, working-class women.

From Brothels to Independent Living

Police doctors in the early years of regulation were particularly preoccupied with a shift in patterns of prostitution away from the use of licensed bordellos and toward greater reliance on selling sex out of private apartments. Statistics from major cities across Europe reflected a similarly dramatic change in practice. Paris, for example, was home to some 235 brothels in 1841 when it was a city of a mere 1.2 million inhabitants. By 1900, the Parisian population had tripled, yet the number of public houses fell to only 48 with a total of 504 prostitutes. Clearly this was not an "adequate" number of harlots for a city of three million, according to contemporary specialists.[21] Documentation on major cities across the Continent told a similar story. Brothels were closing at a rapid rate in Hamburg, where the number of public houses dropped 30 percent in the decade from 1859 to 1867, from 124 to 95. But the most dramatic decline was in St. Petersburg, where public houses decreased by almost 70 percent in the ten years between 1879 and 1888, from 206 to a mere 65 bordellos for a city of almost a million people.[22]

The trend toward declining brothel residence was reflected in Polish towns beginning in the late 1860s when police doctors noted a sharp climb

21. "Hygiena walka z prostytucyą i chorobami płciowymi," Review of E. Duhring, "W sprawie domów publicznych," *Zeitschrift fur Bekämpfung des Geschlechtskrank*, nos. 8 and 9 (1905), in *Zdrowie* 2, no. 22 (1906): 107–8.

22. "Hygiena walka z prostytucyą," 107.

in women either living alone and "tolerated" by police or "under supervision" because they "wander in certain areas" of town.[23] Although brothel residents remained constant in Warsaw, police began registering one to two hundred additional "independent" prostitutes each year beginning in the late 1860s, a trend that continued for the rest of the century. Doctors mostly applauded the drop in registered houses, believing them to be "harmful from the legal, social, and hygienic perspectives" because of their higher rates of syphilis infection and their disproportionate usage among the "inexperienced youth."[24] Nonetheless, the closing of urban bordellos created a new set of problems for police-medical personnel. How does one track, examine, and treat women working as prostitutes who were not safely ensconced in a licensed facility? The solution, in the short run, was to impose hyperregulation on the urban population in the hopes of casting the regulatory net wide enough to capture as many "informal" prostitutes as possible.

The shuttering of brothels placed doctors and police officials at odds with one another. Physicians in Lwów applauded the trend, claiming the presence of public houses in residential neighborhoods was "dangerous" for locals. Doctors feared the negative effects of bordellos in densely packed urban neighborhoods would "spread to the healthy portions of the population." A 1911 complaint addressed to the chief of police called attention to a particularly large bordello on one of the "most populated streets" in town, close to a hat shop, a school for girls, and a beautiful synagogue. Such a configuration revealed Lwów's status as a "coarse" town, less civilized than other European metropolises. "Only in Lemberg" were brothels permitted to operate in such close proximity to urban neighborhoods, claimed doctors (inaccurately). "The principle [of closing public houses] is observed everywhere," medical professionals claimed, but unfortunately not in the "primitive" Habsburg town of Lwów.[25]

In their defense, police officials insisted, "the supervision of prostitutes is extremely difficult" when streetwalkers conducted their trade out of private establishments. For this reason, the continued maintenance of public

---

23. Those officially registered by the police were checked twice a week, whereas those merely suspected of prostitution were required to be examined only two times a month. From Report of the Warsaw Police Medical Committee, in "Prostytucya w mieście Warszawie," 509–11.

24. It is important to note that *anyone,* male or female, arrested for any reason by municipal police in this period was subject to medical examination to detect venereal diseases. Vagrants, for example, who were diagnosed with syphilis remained under police supervision even after they were released from jail. "Prostytucya w mieście Warszawie," 509.

25. Interpellation from Drs. Baczyński, Lahodynshi, Straucher, Trylowski, Bartow, Bara, and others to Police Chief Łepkowski, July 5, 1912. Response dated August 21 and September 19, 2012, AGAD, CKMSW, sygn. 213.

houses was justified on the principle of social order. The majority of the 240 sex workers registered in Lwów during 1911 lived in apartments throughout the city; the remainder worked out of the dwindling number of some thirty official brothels. This proportion of private call girls, the police chief Łepkowski claimed, had a detrimental impact on the town's population, which was exposed daily to debauched women. The independent sex workers were forced to "roam the streets to entice men into hotels or hiding places." According to the police chief, this situation aroused even greater public hostility than the presence of brothels. In either setting, the habits of the prostitute were perceived to be catching—either through inner-city "miasmas" or through their bawdy demeanor rubbing off on their more virtuous neighbors. For police administrators, therefore, the supervision of prostitutes who lived in rented rooms was "extremely difficult" and control over bordellos was "much easier." Indeed, Łepkowski claimed, the number of prostitutes who were officially registered with police had dropped dramatically as a result of the decline of brothel residence, a slide from a high of over 1,000 inscribed women to only 250.[26]

Admittedly, expanding the scope of police regulation brought with it a host of challenges. Nonetheless, doctors remained confident of their ability to isolate infected girls from the healthy population and contain the spread of disease. Their efforts to bring soldiers under regulation also bore fruit, at least in the estimation of Austrian medical inspectors touring Galician garrisons. A new requirement mandating the examination of soldiers returning from a night out and subjecting them to a disinfectant shower reportedly led to plummeting rates of infection in the Galician military during the early twentieth century. Inspecting physicians believed requiring troops to report cankers immediately or face harsh penalties also contributed to the dramatic decline in syphilis rates among military personnel. Fully assured of the effectiveness of these techniques, inspectors testified that after finishing their three-year military service, soldiers could return home "completely healthy and will not contaminate their future wives with syphilis."[27] Again, doctors pursued the system of police inspection, medical treatment, and quarantining sick patients with the conviction that they were reducing the impact of venereal disorders while protecting the innocent population from moral degeneration. This faith in medical solutions would wane by the outbreak of the Great War. In the midst of the devastating conflict affecting the entirety of

---

26. Police Chief Łepkowski, response dated August 21 and September 19, 2012, AGAD, CKMSW, sygn. 213.

27. "Wenerya w wojsku," *Świat Płciowy* 1, no. 4 (November 1905): 11–13.

Polish territory, doctors worried about the spread of venereal diseases from returning troops to their wives and especially about the impact of syphilis on rural areas not covered by the medical regulatory net. Nevertheless, many physicians remained convinced that a rigorous system of mandatory inspection and treatment of unregistered prostitutes was key to gaining control over sexual diseases.

Scientific Experimentation and the Coercion of Female Patients

Already in the 1870s, confidence in their curative abilities prompted police doctors to seek coercive powers in treating public women. Despite creeping doubts about the effectiveness of medical solutions, physicians across Europe implemented programs for the treatment of a wide range of venereal diseases. The women whom police doctors sent to venereal wards would become targets of a medical preoccupation with experimentation and a search for cures. Legal authority over public women undergoing medical treatment was unclear. For example, in 1876 Dr. Edward Klink insisted he be given "permission to employ coercion in cases where the head doctor and the attending physician agree to the necessity of an operation for the patient."[28] Klink, a syphilologist at St. Lazarus Hospital in Warsaw, expressed frustration that hospital restrictions barred him from discharging patients while they were still ill and yet did not permit the imposition of treatments that might speed recovery from venereal diseases. "If patients do not want to agree to an operation that is crucial for their recovery," medical authorities were not permitted to mandate treatment. Similarly, district doctors in Galicia took a page from imperial military regulations and allowed "the state to enter city hospitals" and force venereal patients to "give themselves up entirely to a doctor's care."[29] Yet conflicting regulations remained: doctors could not impose cures but were forbidden to release patients with symptoms. The result was often an extended hospital stay and greater cost for the hospital. Despite repeated attempts to convince authorities to require treatment for such patients, civilian doctors never succeeded in gaining clear permission to impose unwelcome procedures.[30]

---

28. Edward Klink, "Sprawozdanie z czynności lekarskiej w oddziale kobiet publicznych w Szpitalu Św. Łazarza w Warszawie w r. 1876," *Medycyna* 5, no. 35 (October 1877): 552.

29. "Wenerya w wojsku," 13.

30. Klink, "Sprawozdanie," October 1877, 552.

FIGURE 8.1   St. Lazarus Hospital in Warsaw, which housed the town's police hospital and the largest VD clinic in the Polish territories.
Courtesy of Warsaw Medical Library (Główna Biblioteka Lekarska).

Dr. Klink voiced little sympathy for the hundreds of patients he treated each year in Warsaw's St. Lazarus hospital.[31] Indeed, he attributed many of their most severe symptoms not to the progress of the disease but to their dissolute lifestyle. One type of venereal canker observed in eight of his female patients, for example, was deemed the direct result of their unhealthy habits. "All of the cases" of this particular sore were found "among women from the public house of the lowest sort," Klink explained. He theorized that an "absence of good food and drunkenness [had] predisposed them to malignant canker sores."[32] For Klink, venereal diseases were not simply the result of deadly bacteria. Their symptoms were made more severe by immoral lifestyle choices.

Venereologists in public hospitals like St. Lazarus were overwhelmed with repeat offenders facing long hospital stays and complained of their inability to discharge their patients more quickly. As a result, they resorted to imposing

---

31. In 1876, a total of 1,328 patients were treated at St. Lazarus, 532 of whom were women on the public registry. Klink, "Sprawozdanie," *Medycyna* 5, no. 33 (August 1877): 517; and 5, no. 34 (September 1877): 534.

32. Klink, "Sprawozdanie," August 1877, 519.

experimental procedures on syphilitics, goading patients into accepting harsh forms of treatment. Some of Dr. Klink's patients put up determined resistance, relying on "weapons of the weak" to stave off uncomfortable cures. Nonetheless, over time doctors were able to prevail on their charges to accept experimental procedures. In one particularly telling example, Klink employed a painful surgical procedure to remove festering cankers from an eighteen-year-old registered prostitute named Eleanora B. The patient appeared at St. Lazarus Hospital the evening of November 14, 1875, presenting with "venereal sores" on her uterine lining. As the attending physician, Klink applied an undoubtedly uncomfortable "bandage with dressing of carbolic acid and poultice."[33] Two weeks later, he noted that the *bubo* (swollen lymph node) was still festering, as would be expected after the carbolic acid treatment. Klink expressed frustration that "the patient would not allow herself to be cut" in order to remove the sores.

Even without surgery, however, Eleanora's wounds appeared to be healing. Klink's report notes that "after six days, the bubo burst on its own, shrunk to the size of a hazelnut, and emitted a quantity of pus." Nonetheless, in Klink's view, the canker had not diminished enough to justify releasing the patient, so the hospital continued its interventions: "We administered sitz baths twice daily. The pus continued to be substantial, so we burned the skin around the sore. . . . It grew to the size of a walnut. . . . Again, the canker burst on January 20, 1876, on its own. By the end of January, we examined the sore more closely and found another chamber under the skin that was 4 cm. in length and another completely hidden inside that was almost the same length. Nothing seemed to help. We continued the twice-daily baths and the application of carbolic acid. Finally, at the end of March, another fresh chamber appeared at the internal end of the original canker." Throughout the treatment, Eleanora refused to be sedated for surgery, as was her right. Was she anxious about the effects of the procedure, which might have damaged her ability to work as a prostitute? Did she prefer to drag out the treatment and remain in the police hospital for as long as possible, where she could enjoy a warm bed and regular food in the midst of the harsh Polish winter? Or was it perhaps her fear of a demanding pimp or "boyfriend" that

---

33. Carbolic acid or phenol was discovered in 1834 by Friedlieb Ferdinand Runge, who extracted it from coal tar. Its antiseptic properties were made famous by Sir Joseph Lister in his 1867 publication of his pioneering technique of antiseptic surgery, which involved thoroughly cleaning wounds and then covering them with a rag or lint covered in carbolic acid. The severe skin irritation caused by continual exposure to phenol eventually led to the substitution of other aseptic techniques in surgery, but the method was still current throughout Europe at the time Dr. Klink performed his experiments on Eleanora.

bolstered her insistence on refusing surgery? She may simply have feared the pain of an unfamiliar procedure, not an uncommon view among patients in the period. It is difficult to trace the source of her resistance, but the effect was to keep her in the hospital from November 14 until May 20, a full six months of relative security, and the coldest and least profitable season for an independent prostitute.

Eleanora may well have been intent on extending her stay in the police hospital. Yet conditions were hardly luxurious in the venereal ward of this or other Polish medical facilities of the period. Warsaw hospitals were famously dark, overcrowded, and characterized by poor hygienic conditions. Long after Louise Pasteur demonstrated the importance of a sterile environment in preventing the spread of disease, Polish facilities still "made poor use of disinfectants such that epidemics raged" through them.[34] From what we know about life on the VD ward, prostitutes were permitted to socialize with one another and to visit with family and friends. At the same time, hospitalized sex workers were the subjects of various reforming efforts on the part of social activists, who treated them to educational lectures and stocked library shelves with uplifting literature. Despite the unsavory conditions of the hospital ward itself, visits took place in the "spacious vestibule where several dozen or even a hundred or more people" gathered in a festive atmosphere. As one medical reformer noted,

> Those visiting the prostitutes include their female associates from town, adorned in noisy colors and extravagant clothing, recognizable from far away: rouge, white wash, cosmetics, impertinent looks, and swinging movements. Alfonses also come to visit, seeking their circle of voluptuous eyes, abominable glances, their sensual and criminal appearance . . . these elegantly dressed brutes. They are protecting their victims so that they do not lose them through the hospital. Some Alfonses even bring their sick girls a few rubles per day, some sweets, food, and spend some time with the sick one purely in order to keep her in the trap . . . and in order that another pimp does not take her to a brothel once she leaves the hospital, or that she does not end up going to a shelter for fallen women. The madams from brothels also come to visit.[35]

Any of these diversions might have been more attractive than returning to the restrictions of a brothel or the vulnerability of independent sex work.

---

34. R. Wacław Męczkowski, *Stan i potrzeby szpitali Królestwa Polskiego* (Warsaw, 1905), 45–47.

35. Augustyn Wróblewski, "Dzieci w szpitalu św. Łazarza," *Czystość* 5, no. 25 (June 19, 1909): 385–86.

Hospitals could serve a variety of agendas, and those of the patient did not always correspond with the priorities of medical staff.

In Eleanora's case, Dr. Klink eventually wore down her resistance to surgical remedies. "At the end of April," he reports, "after many attempts, the patient agreed to chloroform treatment [as a general anesthetic], and we cut open the chambers and had to completely cut the lobes of the chamber into segments." Still, recovery was slow, and "the patient was [only] discharged from the hospital three weeks later as officially cured."[36] Such a regimen of cauterizing and cutting cankers was used regularly in hospitals throughout Europe in the early 1870s, often resulting in mutilated genitalia and extensive damage to internal organs.[37] Yet by the mid-1870s the procedure had been recognized as ineffective in preventing future outbreaks of syphilis symptoms. Medical textbooks determined that experiments with the technique were not advisable because "the drawbacks for patients outweighed the [possible] benefits" of the treatment in assuaging disease, according to a French medical encyclopedia published in 1884.[38] Even Alfred Fournier (1832–1914), the Parisian dermatologist who famously discovered congenital syphilis, balked at the notion of experimenting on unsuspecting prostitutes.[39] Nonetheless, the desire to create the appearance of a symptom-free patient (or perhaps to experiment with a novel procedure) overrode such cautionary impulses as Polish doctors applied everything in their professional kits to eliminate the venereal peril.

These physicians did so partly out of a persistent professional arrogance that insisted syphilis and other sexual diseases could be permanently cured. The prospect of declaring a prostitute free of disease was the crux on which the entire regulation system rested. If regular inspections could isolate illnesses and sick women sent to VD hospitals until they were pronounced cured and safe for their customers, the regulatory apparatus was justified. Once the possibility of eradicating contagious diseases from a prostitute's body was called into question, the premise on which the system was based would also be subject to challenge. Nonetheless, despite new information on the difficulties of treatment, most physicians remained confident in their ability to rid the prostitute's body of the syphilis bacterium. Even as late as 1914, Dr. Antoni Blumenfeld of Lwów insisted that despite new discoveries

36. Klink, "Sprawozdanie," August 1877, 517–23.

37. Quétel, *History of Syphilis*, 117–18.

38. "Syphilis," in *Dictionnaire encyclopedique des sciences medicales*, ed. Amedee Dechambre (Paris, 1884), cited in Quetel, *History of Syphilis*, 118.

39. Quétel, *History of Syphilis*, 142. Fournier, who is often considered the first professional syphilologist, was the first to describe congenital syphilis in 1883.

about the way the diseases spread to innocent sufferers, "syphilis [was] a disease that can be cured, and today thanks to wonderful measures and medical methods, we can nip it in the bud and free the organism forever from the effects of syphilis."[40] The key, doctors insisted, was keeping the sufferers under a doctor's care long enough to guarantee they were healthy when they reentered the population.

Everywhere, medical inspectors complained that prostitutes were released too early from hospitals before they were fully free of disease. In the central Galician town of Bochnia, for example, rates of syphilis infection among prostitutes were reported to be "exceptionally high," especially in comparison with Cracow or its suburb Podgórze. The imperial sanitary inspector theorized that the cause of this spike in disease might have been that prostitutes were "simply released too early from further treatment."[41] If only doctors could exert further control over the treatment of their patients, syphilis might be contained and the regulation system could do its work. Far from challenging the medical wisdom of assuming prostitutes were "clean" when they returned to their clients, authorities instead insisted that the sloppiness of district doctors, harlots' evasion of medical inspections, or the limited jurisdiction of the regulation system were the cause of the VD problem.

Curative Powers and the Social Reintegration of Prostitutes

Physicians persisted in employing such treatments partly in the hopes that some of their patients might return to a conventional life after leaving the public registry. Just as soldiers who had ostensibly been cured of their sexual diseases were expected to rejoin their families, so too were prostitutes under medical supervision seen as eligible to participate fully in lower-class life once their bodies had been purged of disease, at least in the early years of regulation. Police registries provide numerous examples to support this view. Medical records trace a pattern of women dropping off the prostitution rolls to take on salaried positions, to marry, or to return to their birth families in the countryside. Physician inspectors attached detailed annotations to case studies indicating that a particular patient had "changed her way of life" or

---

40. It is unclear what Blumenfeld means by a "cure" in this piece. By 1911, the German scientist Paul Erhlich had devised a method of eliminating some cases of syphilis through the use of an arsenic solution, which was sometimes fatal to the patient. Blumenfeld makes no mention of this or any other new methods. Antoni Blumenfeld, *Syfilis niewinnych* (Lwów, 1914), 23.

41. "Nadzór nad prostytucyą u nas," *Świat Płciowy* 1 (November 15, 1905): 17–18.

"stopped working as a prostitute" and should be removed from the rolls. Police documents reflect a dramatic rate of movement on and off the prostitution registry each year, with dozens of women in every major town taking up trades or transferring to positions as household servants.

These reports recognize the permeable boundaries between the world of prostitution and that of "normal" working-class Polish urban life. In 1868, for example, some thirty-seven women signed off the Warsaw registry to take up full-time work as household servants, two turned to some other type of trade, and nine married. Beyond this, hundreds of women left the registry each year for unnamed reasons and a new crop of several hundred practitioners signed on.[42] For physicians in this period, then, science had the potential to cure. Former prostitutes, like infected soldiers, could be rid of contaminates and resume a life unscarred by their exposure to venereal disease. Police doctors remained concerned that women with residual infections might harm the healthy portions of the population, but their belief in the possibility of socially reintegrating former prostitutes suggests an absence of clear stigmatization for those on the police list. Physicians such as Dr. Klink continued to view lower-class women as appropriate subjects for experimentation, and police doctors were obliged to regulate and restrict the activities of diseased women but not necessarily to brand them permanently.[43]

Medical confidence in the prospect of socially reintegrating registered prostitutes soon waned, however. Doctors grew concerned about the endless trail of diseased women choking city hospital wards. Despite the diligence of physicians like Dr. Klink, most doctors were unable to subscribe to the admonition to keep patients sequestered until they were asymptomatic. Instead, physicians complained incessantly about the shortage of hospital beds for all patients, but especially for those suffering from long-term illnesses like VD. Warsaw hospitals and clinics treated some forty-two thousand patients for sexual diseases in 1909 alone. The fraction of VD patients was climbing, reaching some 12 percent of the total patients, and the pressure

---

42. Like other towns under police-medical supervision, the prostitute population of Warsaw was never stable. It fluctuated dramatically as women left the registry to move to a new town, to marry, to take up salaried employment, or to return to their families. Women also were removed—at least temporarily—while they were pregnant. So, for example, 830 new women signed on to the Warsaw prostitution registry during the course of 1867, while 673 left the rolls. This net increase of 157 new entries on the registry was added to the 534 women who stayed on the registry into 1868. "Prostytucya w mieście Warsawie," 508–11.

43. Similarly, Mary Poovey argues that British prostitutes of the 1850s were perceived as innately moral and, indeed, sharing aspirations of bourgeois domesticity with middle-class women. "Speaking of the Body: Mid-Victorian Constructions of Female Desire," in *Body/Politics: Women and the Discourses of Science,* ed. Mary Jacobus, et al. (New York, 1990), 29–46.

on beds in VD wards was enormous.[44] In the first decade of the twentieth century, only 364 beds devoted to "venereal diseases of the skin" were available in civilian hospitals in the entire metropolitan area, 300 of them in the St. Lazarus police hospital, where Klink worked. How could thousands of syphilis patients be handled each year if each of them had to be kept in bed until they were "symptom free"? Klink's treatment of Eleanora could not have been conventional. The hospital would quickly have run out of beds to cater to its population of registered prostitutes. More likely, Klink was using Eleanora's case to support his argument for giving doctors coercive power over the public women in their care. If the state was required to keep women such as Eleanora sequestered until their diseases subsided, it was simply not practical to permit them the right to refuse treatment. Public women were the state's responsibility, and as such police doctors were obliged to cure them, even if it meant compromising their civil liberties. As definitions of the term "prostitution" expanded, medical officials would use this logic to press for curtailing the rights of still wider portions of the working-class female population.

Regional hospitals were equally burdened by the shipment of overflow patients from Warsaw's venereal wards. St. Józef Hospital in Lublin had only fifty dedicated beds to serve a town of fifty thousand people and these were constantly filled to capacity. St. Aleksy in Płock was in an even more challenged position with only twenty beds for its thirty thousand residents.[45] Here, conditions were still less conducive to recovery than in Warsaw's city hospitals. For the most part, provincial medical facilities throughout the Congress Kingdom were situated in old cloisters, schools, or private residences. Small-town hospitals were poorly ventilated and sometimes lacked baths for washing patients. As one medical inspector noted, "everything is as it was in the Middle Ages."[46] The pressure to cater to the needs of urban prostitutes strained the already challenged resources of Galician country hospitals. According to the imperial sanitary inspector Dr. Józef Barzycki, VD rates in garrison towns remained high partly because small-town medical facilities did not have space to keep patients in bed until they were fully cured. The hospital in Bochnia, for instance, was significantly expanded in 1901 in response to a spike in syphilis cases. Nonetheless, medical inspectors were appalled to discover that "the very same prostitute suffering from syphilis was admitted and released from the hospital three times inside of

---

44. Sokołowski, *Wielkie klęski społeczne*, 311–13.
45. Męczkowski, *Stan i potrzeby szpitali*, 32–37, 44.
46. Ibid., 48.

seven months," clearly never having been completely cured of her symptoms. Inspector Barzycki noted that the number of prostitutes infected with syphilis was exceptionally high in Bochnia in comparison with the rate in Cracow or nearby Podgórze, arguably the result of too many venereal patients released while still infectious.[47] Even well-managed hospitals could not hope to treat all the infected patients in their district. The regional hospitals of Rzeszów and Stanisławów were exceptionally well run, yet the number of patients infected with syphilis in neighboring towns (like Słocina, Drabinianka, and Staroniwa near Rzeszów and Knihynin near Stanisławów) had grown dramatically in recent years. Since smaller locales were not required to impose supervision over their prostitutes, they became major sites of "secret prostitution." Infected prostitutes were "able to flee inspection in other towns and seek protection" in such places. Extending the system of regulation to small towns and villages would resolve this problem, the inspector argued, though admittedly such a shift would impose an administrative nightmare on the Galician government.

In addition to lamenting the inadequate facilities in which they conducted inspections and treated patients, police doctors were frustrated with their powerlessness in other areas. Rampant, untreated venereal diseases led them to try to widen the net of patients on whom they could impose inspections, even recommending increased police control over women living outside registered brothels.[48] Police doctors set out to put more teeth in their enforcement machinery, believing that venereal diseases would only be brought under control if state power was employed to restrict the activities of public women. Taking a page from the Austrian military, they sought to impose penalties on civilian women who did not seek immediate treatment for obvious venereal symptoms.[49] Doctors complained bitterly that their efforts were hampered by civilian courts' reluctance to punish prostitutes for failure to appear at examinations. As one physician pointed out, "if a prostitute does not appear for inspection, the matter is sent to a civil judge, who either lets her go or at most fines her 25 kopeks."[50]

---

47. "Nadzór nad prostytucyą u nas," 17.

48. "Recently, the authorities have determined that the cause of such poor results [in reducing secret prostitution] has been the irresponsible administration of the inspection process, that is . . . that medical officials with the help of the police have been responsible for the task, whereas in fact the reverse should be the case and the police should manage the system primarily while medical authorities should assist them." *Wykład chorób wenerycznych*, 404.

49. "Wenerya w wojsku," 13–14.

50. Henryk Stankiewicz, "Kwestyja prostytucyi m. Warszawy pod względem administracyjnym i lekarskim," in *Pamiętnik Towarzystwa Lekarskiego Warszawskiego*, ed. Edward Klink (Warsaw, 1881), 590–92.

The Woes of Inherited Disease: Congenital Syphilis and Syphilis of the Innocents

Despite laws in all three partitions of divided Polish territory mandating police registration and medical inspection of prostitutes, specialists grew disheartened at the ineffectiveness of the police supervision system. The dissolute women lining elegant boulevards and loitering in city parks were becoming more than an eyesore. By the late 1880s medical discoveries had confirmed new and threatening insights about the effects of syphilis on unborn children and innocent wives. the Parisian syphilologist Alfred Fournier introduced the phenomena of "congenital syphilis" and the "syphilis of honest women" into medical literature in an 1887 report, estimating that some 5 percent of syphilitics were contaminated in nonsexual ways, including by means of wet nurses who infected newborns, glassblowers contaminated in the course of their work, and patients who contracted disease through unsterile medical instruments or via tattooing. Even more serious was the incidence of so-called innocent syphilis contracted by fiancées and wives of male clients who had visited prostitutes, a category Fournier estimated to comprise 20 percent of infected women.[51] Polish doctors quickly incorporated Fournier's findings into their own prognosis about the horrifying effects of congenital and hereditary syphilis. As Teodor Belke warned in 1881, "syphilis ruins the health and the strength not only of the infected man but also of his wife, and through his sperm also infects the fetus."[52] Calling syphilis "more deadly than the bloodiest war," Belke was one of the first Polish doctors to argue that sexually transmitted diseases were decimating the population by affecting a patient's "environment, his family, and even . . . children in the mothers' womb."[53]

Such laments were mainly restricted to the columns of professional journals during the waning years of the nineteenth century. But by the outbreak of the 1905 Revolution, anxiety within the medical community spread to the general population and demands for reform of the dysfunctional regulatory system grew more heated. Polish representatives to a 1905 meeting of the Society for Combatting Venereal Disease in Munich complained of the "cloak of false modesty" that had "until recently" prevented open

---

51. Corbin, *Women for Hire*, 248–50; and Quetel, *History of Syphilis*, 137.

52. Teodor Belke, "Kilka słów o sposobach tamujących szerzenie się chorób wenerycznch," *Medycyna* 9, no. 28 (1881): 443–45. Polish doctors reflected the common contemporary myth of "hereditary syphilis": the unborn child was infected through the sperm of the father, although this theory was later disproven.

53. Teodor Belke, "Kilka słów o nierządzie publicznym," *Medycyna* 19, no. 10 (1891): 158–59.

discussions of venereal disease in the Polish lands. In the aftermath of the May Alfonse Pogrom and the less restricted censorship of the revolutionary period, reformers stressed that "in the Polish lands, the first rank of prudery is held by Warsaw, whose publicists have long since pointed to the dire need for meetings about this incredibly important subject and for attempts to devise solutions to stop the spread of infection," yet the public had not followed suit in its effort to reform the regulation system. Experts recognized venereal diseases were "ruining the population materially, physically, and morally, causing multiple disabilities, and threatening the degeneration of future generations." Only after the liberalization of press censorship laws did the general public begin to participate in open discussions about the medical threats sexual diseases posed.[54] Middle-class Polish readers gained access in this period to works by Dr. Antoni Blumenfeld, a Lwów physician who warned of the dangers of VD to society at large. Summarizing the full range of dangers syphilis posed, Blumenfeld emphasized that "it cannot be a matter of indifference for society that a huge number of people are becoming blind, deaf, dumb, filling our insane asylums and homes for incurable diseases, and yet it continues to flower with still greater strength."[55] Medical experts cited the work of German and French specialists, complaining that "among us" in the Polish lands, too little was being done on this issue, despite the fact that "it is well known that venereal diseases are spreading and what terrible harm they cause."[56] Polish physicians passed on the discoveries of Fournier and Neisser, who had confirmed that venereal diseases were not subject to easy cures, but rather were "chronic and, especially in the third stage" of syphilis, had a "profound impact on the patient's health and the entire fate of the ill person."[57]

Symptoms resulting from these diseases were even more painful and long lasting than Polish medical experts had previously believed. The Berlin syphilologist Dr. Blaschko estimated that one-tenth of Europe's metropolitan inhabitants were infected and that prostitutes represented a huge fraction of total patients. "Every prostitute is prone to contracting the disease," Blaschko warned, and unlike earlier estimates, there was absolutely "no guarantee the symptoms will relapse." The disease was "often extremely painful and unpleasant" and left far more lasting damage on the human organism than

54. Janusz Bilewski, "Walka zarazą weneryczną," *Świat Płciowy* 1, no. 1 (May 31, 1905): 39–40.

55. Quoted in Emil Wyrobek, *Choroby a małżeństwo* (Cracow, 1906), 78.

56. Review of Professor Dr. Bunge, *Wystąpienie chorób Płciowych/Die Ausrottung der Geschlechtskrankheiten* (Leipzig, 1911), in *Zdrowie*, 27, no. 12 (December 1912): 47–49.

57. Władysław Chodecki, "O żadaniach lekarza w walce z chorobami werycznymi," *Zdrowie* 22, no. 8 (August 1906): 556–63.

had earlier been suspected. Blaschko described the specific effects syphilis wrought on the human organism, including damage to the arteries and the brain, and the attacks of "apoplexy with partial paralysis." He characterized a paralysis so severe that it affected much of the brain and caused "mental functions gradually to cease until death frees [the patient] from his soul-less body." Gonorrhea was even more widespread than syphilis, Blaschko reminded his readers, and although much less deadly, the side effects from untreated gonorrhea could be severe and often led to medical complications including inflammation of the testicles, bladder, or kidneys, rheumatoid arthritis, and life-threatening inflammation of the heart. Among women, the ailment was even more dangerous and could cause inflammation and infection of the uterus and ovaries, leading to infertility.[58] Polish doctors maintained case studies on the progress of diseases among prostitutes and were able to conclude "on the basis of [their own] research" that 80–85 percent of the women under police control became infected "during the course of their addiction to public sex."[59]

The threat of contaminating unborn children was the greatest source of anxiety. By the early years of the twentieth century, Fournier's findings about congenital syphilis had been widely circulated among Polish medical circles. The Lwów physician Jan Papée highlighted the danger of syphilitic men contaminating their wives and, in turn, their unborn children. "One of the most significant consequences of syphilis is its transfer to one's progeny," Papée wrote in 1906, citing Fournier's study of "hereditary syphilis" to demonstrate that mothers were typically already contaminated when they gave birth to infected babies.[60] Of the 28 pregnancies of syphilitic women Fournier attended, Papée reminded his Polish readers that 21 resulted in miscarriages, a rate of 75 percent.[61] Polish specialists also referenced a more comprehensive 1898 study published by the German dermatologist Hyde. Dr. Hyde studied 1,700 pregnancies among syphilitic women, 579 of which ended in miscarriages or stillborn children. Of those children who survived, an additional 956 died in their first year of life.[62] These horrific survival rates did not leave much room for hope among Polish medical experts.

---

58. Review of Professor Dr. Bunge, *Wystąpienie chorób,* 48–49.

59. Jan Papée, *Kiły u prostytutek we Lwowie* (Warsaw, 1908), 17.

60. Jan Papée, *Choroby weneryczne, ich rozszerzenie i zapobieganie* (Lwów, 1906), 5.

61. Alfred Fournier, *L'heredite syphilitique* (1891), 85, cited in Papée, *Choroby weneryczne,* 5–6. See also review of Dr. P. Good, *Hygiena i moralność,* and Dr. Lowenfeld, *Życie płciowe i system nerwowy,* in *Zdrowie* 22, no. 2 (1906): 571–74.

62. Cited in Papée, *Choroby weneryczne,* 6.

Reports of infant mortality rates as high as 95 percent among syphilitic mothers sent terror through the hearts of Polish commentators. By the early twentieth century, specialists were aware that most infants born with syphilis were "destined for an early grave." Those who did survive infancy tended to "die of convulsions, develop a weak mental capacity, [or become] idiots or cretins." Such children had less immunity from disease and suffered from "deviations in their digestive organs."[63] Syphilitic children were portrayed as a severe "burden on society." Women with gonorrhea, often thought to be a less serious ailment, were now reported to experience "extremely difficult pregnancies," only to deliver children who were "often blind." One report issued in 1912 noted that fully half of all children born blind were delivered to mothers suffering from gonorrhea.[64]

To make matters worse, many women giving birth to syphilitic babies were unaware they were carrying the disease. Leading Polish physicians were careful not to accuse their bourgeois patients of sexual indiscretions in contracting syphilis or passing it along to their wives and progeny. Instead, they painted a range of far-fetched scenarios to explain how the disease might make its way into the bourgeois bloodstream. Dr. Papée reminded his readers of the possibility innocent victims could be contaminated by working in a glass-blowing factory, through a midwife, a wet nurse, or by taking part in a Jewish circumcision ritual.[65] Dentists were even accused of infecting their patients as doctors campaigned to alert their patients to the heightened possibilities of infection. "In these epidemics," noted one practitioner, "only a minority of the cases are spread in the 'usual [sexual] way.' The rest are contaminated in other, [nonsexual] ways and from other sources."[66] Dr. Emil Wyrobek of Cracow proposed that syphilis might be passed from wet nurses who were exposed by nursing syphilitic children, and then back to healthy babies, who in turn infected their mothers. Wyrobek even described the fate of a "typical" Victorian woman, pure until her marriage, who unknowingly contracted syphilis or gonorrhea and then passed it on to her children. He takes as his example "an innocent daughter, protected from all that is dirty in society." The girl's "parents choose a good, clean man as a husband for her. Then, an impudent brother or cousin spreads the 'venom of syphilis' on some household objects and she is infected for life. All is ruined."[67] In this scenario, even the bourgeois husband remains blameless as a random male relative inadvertently spreads the disease.

63. Ibid., 5–7.
64. Review of Prof. Dr. Bunge, *Wytępienie chorób*, 49.
65. Papée, *Choroby weneryczne*, 4.
66. E. Sonnenberg, "Źródła i drogi pozapłciowego szerzenia syfilisu," *Zdrowie* (1897): 44–58.
67. Wyrobek, *Choroby a małżenstwo*, 70.

More likely than these complicated vignettes, medical personnel realized, was the incidence of husbands infected through their dalliance with prostitutes directly contaminating their "innocent" wives. Doctors suspected that syphilis remained in the body and could be contagious for "at least two to three years" after the initial infection. For this reason, doctors advised their patients to avoid marriage or contact with their wives for at least two years following their contamination. "If a man marries in the first two years after being infected he passes the disease onto his wife," noted one particularly candid report. Contamination was reportedly "less likely in the third year, and still less so later." Yet because most men violated this precautionary practice, "hundreds of thousands of innocent women carry the disease their entire life and pass it on to their offspring."[68] Some patients were aware of the principle of innocent contamination and strived to protect their wives from infection, not always successfully. One of Dr. Wyrobek's patients confessed he had contracted a venereal disease from a "grass widow" who was practicing prostitution. He informed Wyrobek that he carefully watched himself for signs of insanity (a common symptoms of syphilis in its tertiary stage). He kept his distance from his wife and children so he would not infect them, but then, when the symptoms began to subside, he relaxed, only to read with horror in a medical journal that this did not necessarily mean he was cured of the disease. The man mistakenly returned to sexual relations with his wife and was mortified that he might be infecting her and their unborn children.[69]

Classism and Venereal Disease: The Impact on Bourgeois Men

Such anecdotal evidence belied a creeping unease among Polish physicians that the flower of the Polish bourgeoisie was under threat from venereal diseases. Indeed, the very data doctors cited as evidence of the ravages of sexual disease was culled from case studies of upper-class patients. Dr. Fournier's observations about the nervous disorders common in third-stage syphilis, for example, drew directly on his experience with "patients who were from among the well-off portions of the bourgeoisie." Moreover, German Professor Erb argued that third-stage syphilis had a greater impact on the nervous system "of those who work as intellectuals." Polish authorities worried about the "huge implications" venereal diseases had for "the health of the nation

---

68. Review of Professor Dr. Bunge, *Wytępienie chorób*, 48.
69. Emily Wyrobek, *Śmiertelność i choroby jako skutek rozwiązłego życia* (Cracow, 1907), 21–22.

and for the viability of its development" because young men from the social elite—along with their unborn progeny—were being inflected at such high rates.[70] According to one turn-of-the century survey conducted in Warsaw, almost half the men suffering from venereal diseases were students, a statistic with enormous implications for the future Polish leadership class.[71]

News of the shockingly high rates of prostitution usage among university and high school students added fresh fuel to these concerns. A spate of surveys conducted in 1903 brought to light the degree to which prostitution and venereal diseases had become deeply embedded in upper-class Polish life, even among young men in their teenage years. A questionnaire circulated among high school students in Lwów surprised even the most cynical Polish commentators, revealing that the incidence of venereal disease had quadrupled over the previous three years among high school students alone.[72] Data from a similar survey in Cracow showed that out of every 1,000 students, an astounding 846 sought the services of a prostitute at least five times per year.[73] These numbers reflected an impending public-health crisis among elite youth in other towns as well: 20 percent of all Warsaw University students were infected with at least one venereal disease and over a quarter of all Austrian army troops were unfit for service because of symptoms resulting from sexual diseases.[74]

A similar survey of Warsaw youth soon sent a seismic shock through the Polish medical community. A young doctor named Robert Karol Bernhardt,[75] with the help of two university students, circulated an extensive questionnaire among 266 Warsaw University and Polytechnic students, asking for detailed information about their sexual lives.[76] The results were

---

70. Interestingly, Professor Erb's treatment for venereal diseases was a trip out to sea because "the ocean climate and swimming in the sea significantly improves matters." Chodecki, "O żądaniach lekarza," 56.

71. Sokołowski, *Wielkie klęski społeczne*, 313.

72. "Ankieta zdrowotna," *Przegląd Hygieniczny* 2, no. 5 (May 1903): 78; and "Ankieta w sprawie zwalczania—Chorób Płciowych u młodzieży szkół," *Przegląd hygieniczny* 2, no. 10 (October 1903): 158–59. The survey showed that Lwów high school students turned to outpatient clinics for treatment in increasing numbers, from 69 students in 1901 to 115 for the first half of 1903 alone.

73. Egeniusz Piasecki, "W sprawie hygieny płciowej młodzieży," *Przegląd Hygieniczny* 5, no. 5 (May 1906): 113–14.

74. Ibid.

75. Born in Kalisz in 1874, Bernhardt's professional training was limited to a year working in a medical clinic and four years running a laboratory. In 1906, Bernhardt would join the staff of St. Lazarus Hospital as a specialist in diseases of the skin and venereal diseases. He would later publish a magnum opus, *Choroby Skóry*, in 1922. "Idiopathic Multiple Hæmorrhagic Sarcoma (Kaposi): Trauma an Ætiological Factor," *Journal of Cutaneous Diseases* 27, no.11 (November 1909): 522-25. Republished in *Archives of Dermatology* 145, no. 11 (2009): 1222.

76. Survey questions can be found in Tadeusz J. Łazowski and Konrad Siwicki, "Życie płciowe warszawskiej młodzieży akademickiej według ankiety z roku 1903," *Zdrowie* 1, no. 2 (November

leveraged in support of a wide range of reform projects, from abolition of regulated prostitution to abstinence campaigns and the need for sex education in the schools.[77] All of the respondents were of middle-class intelligentsia background and the vast majority identified as Poles, a sample group that represented a cross section of future Polish leaders.[78] Of the students surveyed, most had been sexually active since between the ages of fifteen and twenty, and the majority had used prostitutes at least once. About one-third of the respondents (77 out of 266) confessed to having contracted a venereal disease, though only about half of these had availed themselves of medical attention. Commentators were shocked that "although treatment is quite accessible for students, some 39 of them simply wandered around knowing they were sick and continued to have sex."[79]

Back in Lwów, news of the far-reaching effects of sexual diseases prompted local physicians to take action. The academic senate of the Lwów Hygienic Society met to discuss the potential harm befalling elite Polish students. They encouraged the town's student population to find other pastimes such as ice-skating, gymnastics, or hiking in the nearby mountains to alleviate sexual frustration and avoid visits to prostitutes. The nation risked a disaster in the form of a venereal epidemic if sexual promiscuity continued among upper-class youth, doctors argued. As medical data poured in, specialists grew increasingly concerned about the side effects of syphilis and gonorrhea. Members of the Hygienic Society stressed, for example, that "the newest research and medical observations indicate that sexual and venereal diseases [sic] have much sadder implications than previously thought. Today there is no doubt that they often are accompanied by a whole range of serious secondary illnesses, that they are not infrequently the cause of long-lasting emaciation and premature death, as well as incalculable suffering to the individual, the family, the nation, and the society."[80] Leaders of the Hygienic Society stressed that venereal ailments threated the national body; their influence was no longer limited to the individual and his family. News that "these diseases befall university youth in disproportionate numbers" was heartrending, they emphasized. The cohort that represented Poland's

---

1905): 919–25. Łazowski and Siwicki were students at the Politechnik and the University of Warsaw, respectively.

77. See, for example, the controversial article by the feminist activist Izabela Moszczeńska, "Czego nie wiemy o naszych synach" (Warsaw,1904).

78. A few identified as "Pole of Lithuanian ancestry" or "Jew Pole," "Pole Jew," or "Pole of Jewish background." Łazowski and Siwicki, "Życie płciowe," 920.

79. "Życie płciowe," Zdrowie (March 1906): 152–53.

80. "Zwalczanie chorób płciowych," Przegląd Hygieniczny 8, no. 11 (November 1909): 316.

"promise of better hopes for its future" was instead leading the country on a path to "ruin and death."[81]

Reports of venereal contamination in imperial armies compounded popular anxiety about youth infection. Studies of Austrian Galician garrisons, in particular, showed embarrassing rates of infection among Polish troops. An imperial brochure published in 1905 depicted widespread venereal contamination in the Austro-Hungarian army as a whole, with Polish troops suffering far more sexual disease than soldiers in other parts of the monarchy. Out of eight large cities that housed military garrisons, Lwów and Cracow ranked at the top in levels of infection among the troops with 93 percent and 73 percent infection rates, respectively. Eleven of the fifteen smaller Austrian garrison towns with higher than average infection rates were in Galicia.[82] A staff physician in the Lwów garrison hospital claimed to have "heard from reliable sources that the Cracow garrison ranks among the worst . . . of the entire Austrian army."[83] As the local police inspector Dr. Jan Papée emphasized, army infections soon spread to the local population. Thus, it was no surprise that sexual diseases comprised some 17 percent of all patients treated for any diseases in Galician hospitals.[84] Clearly, the infection had spread dangerously beyond the ranks of registered prostitutes and enlisted troops into the population at large.

Worse yet, evidence suggested venereal diseases were creeping beyond urban centers and garrison towns and taking root in Poland's rural areas. A detailed report compiled by the Łódź chapter of the Warsaw Hygienic Society in 1904 found that the countryside was not nearly as sexually pure as contemporaries often assumed. Epidemics were particularly severe in villages near where soldiers were stationed. Enlisted men suffering from gonorrhea could contaminate an entire settlement. "Not long ago," for example, the report relayed, "there was a case in the village of Rawa Mazowiecka, in which a soldier infected a couple of girls upon his return from the army. They in turn passed the disease on to several boys. Everyone ended up in the hospital in Rawa."[85] The situation in the countryside was complicated by what one

---

81. "Zwalczanie chorób," 316.

82. Papée, *Choroby weneryczne, ich rozszerzenie i zapobieganie*, 14–15.

83. The author was a staff physician in the Lwów garrison hospital, which may have colored his view of the relative venereal devastation in the Cracow garrison. Review of Dr. A. Buraczyński, *Die venerische Erkranzungen und deren Prophylakse in der Armee* (1905), in *Cystość* 1, no. 9 (1905): 96.

84. Jan Papée, *Nadzór lekarski nad prostytucyą* (Lwów, 1907), 3–5.

85. The findings were presented at a 1904 meeting of the Hygienic Society but not published until 1906. They were published in the same edition of *Zdrowie* as Leon Wernic's call to arms to fight regulated prostitution in the name of ethics and abstinence. Stanisław Skalski, "Prostytucya w Guberni Piotrkowskiej," *Zdrowie* 22, no. 8 (August 1906): 552.

physician characterized as the frequency of sexual relations outside of marriage among rural people. Challenging the notion of peasant communities as the repository of moral innocence, Dr. Rodziewicz of Bełchatów posited that "village girls have sexual relations outside of marriage" regularly and "not necessarily to earn money." Such high rates of casual extramarital sex, the doctor argued, sent the rates of venereal infection skyrocketing.[86]

Sex outside of marriage was also said to be common in the small town of Aleksandrów, where municipal authorities reported no one was making a living directly from full-time prostitution, yet roughly "twenty girls working in local factories and workshops were 'easy to obtain.'" Elsewhere, girls coming in from the villages to work informally as prostitutes became known as "barefoot girls." Towns like Radomsk and Rawa usually featured a dozen or so such independent women.[87] But nowhere was the myth of peasant virtue shattered more effectively than in reports of widespread venereal ailments among the Hutsul people living in the Pokucie region of eastern Galicia. Heavily idealized for their craftsmanship, folk culture, and unique music, the Hutsul highlanders were in many ways the prototypical insulated peasant people.[88] Ethnographers like Oskar Kolberg had emphasized the uniqueness of their way of life and its distinctions from the more cosmopolitan urban culture in Polish cities. Yet reports circulating after 1905 showed that even "the finest and bravest of the Hutsul type are dying off because syphilis is raging through their settlements and devastating the population." The Hutsul mountain area was reportedly becoming a "danger zone for a larger outbreak of the disease in the country as a whole."[89] How could Polish culture maintain its assumptions about the moral innocence of country folk while at the same time painting village inhabitants with the brush of sexual licentiousness?[90] The implications for the nation's self-image were nothing short of damning.

---

86. Skalski, "Prostytucya w Guberni Piotrkowskiej," 553.

87. Ibid., 550–53.

88. On the rich history and Polish perceptions of Galician highlanders, see Dabrowski, "'Discovering' the Galician Borderlands: The Case of the Eastern Carpathians," *Slavic Review* 64, no. 2 (2005): 380–402.

89. Bilewski, "Walka zarazą weneryczną," 41.

90. David Kertzer traces a similar dynamic in late nineteenth-century Italian efforts to reduce the transmission of syphilis between rural wet nurses and urban foundlings. Authorities were reticent to accuse "morally pure" countrywomen of contaminating their charges. Similarly, Russian doctors refused to link syphilis with sexual activity in the late nineteenth century because of the implications this association might have for views of infected village women. David I. Kertzer, "Syphilis, Foundlings, and Wetnurses in Nineteenth-Century Italy," *Journal of Social History* 32, no. 3 (1999): 589–602; and Engelstein, *Keys to Happiness*, 165–211.

Redefining Prostitution: The Medical Expansion of Venal Sex

Evidence that bourgeois males and country folk were contracting venereal disease in unprecedented numbers prompted physicians to take drastic action. If prostitutes were the primary vectors of venereal diseases and the rates of venereal disease were on the rise, then clearly more women must be labeled as "prostitutes."[91] The futility of standard medical remedies and the long-range implications of sexual ailments sent police doctors into a frenzy of registration that dramatically expanded the pool of women required to undergo inspections. New categories of prostitution including "discreet prostitutes," "secret prostitutes," and "part-time" prostitutes cast the net of those subject to police supervision ever wider. Such regulations effectively linked particular combinations of gender, social class, and sexual activity as pathologies of their own and imposed the restraining powers of the police system on an entire subculture of urban women. The medical reach into lower-class communities—and the dramatic expansion of the categories of women brought under the police physician's speculum—effectively conflated poverty and disease with female sexual immorality, bracketing working women as less ethical and more contaminated than their bourgeois sisters.

One of the greatest sources of untreated venereal diseases, doctors argued, was the so-called unregulated prostitute. These sexually promiscuous women who avoided registration by concealing their activities behind a cloak of "honest work" were deemed the key to controlling the venereal plague. Everywhere, physicians established separate police registries for "clandestine" prostitutes, forcing women detained on mere suspicion of selling sex to register with the police. Doctors hoped in this way to bring under official medical control the legion of working-class women they suspected of leading dissolute lives. Already in the early 1880s, police examiners fought to expand their supervisory authority over additional categories of women, including female workers in breweries and other establishments employing migrants from the countryside. Warsaw physicians argued that authorities in Russian Poland should model their surveillance guidelines on regulations in Prussian Poland, where "no employee is permitted to work [in a factory] without an examination" and where all female waitresses and barmaids were subject to medical inspection.[92] They lobbied to include in the police registries "the

---

91. Mary Spongberg examines the transition in nineteenth-century medical science from the conception that all women were carriers of venereal disease to the isolation of prostitutes as the primary source of disease. *Feminizing Venereal Disease: The Body of the Prostitute in Nineteenth-Century Medical Discourse* (London, 1997).

92. Stankiewicz, "Kwestyja prostytucyi," 592.

huge number" of seamstresses, milliners, and governesses they believed were spreading contagion in large cities. Some police doctors even claimed that "secret prostitution was out of control" in the villages and smaller settlements, where "masses of sick girls . . . contaminate others with syphilis" because medical police did not have jurisdiction outside of large towns."[93] Once again, the Polish myth of peasant purity was under threat as potential agents of contamination were rooted out in country and city alike. As Dr. Teodor Belke asserted, since prostitution in all its manifestations was the primary cause of the venereal contamination, "doctors have a responsibility to prevent the spread of infection everywhere prostitutes are used—in factories, industrial plants . . . within families," and even in the village.[94]

All the state bureaucracies governing Polish territory employed legal mechanisms for labeling those suspected of entertaining multiple sex partners as "prostitutes," even against their will. Article 44 of the 1886 Russian criminal code authorized police to evaluate female morality using circumstantial evidence, including being observed walking "with someone who uses prostitutes" or loitering "in a particular location."[95] The court was also permitted to consider the neighborhood in which a suspect was detained as evidence that she was engaging in commercial sex activities. Efforts to track women suspected of selling sex also ratcheted up in Galicia after the results of the 1903 Lwów survey revealed high rates of prostitution use and syphilis among elite adolescents. The Lwów health commission responded to survey results by casting the regulatory net wider to include "even those who avoided regulation and who have been removed" from the registry.[96] Similar to Russian decrees of the time, these new guidelines permitted police doctors to register women who did not perceive themselves as prostitutes but whose public behavior, place of residence, or social milieu suggested they were sexually immoral and potentially diseased. The guidelines were formalized in 1906 when Lwów police established a separate registry of so-called discreet or clandestine prostitutes, recording the names of *all* women who were ostensibly "camouflaged" by their occupations as waitresses, cashiers, or shopkeepers. By 1908 police doctors also recommended household servants be placed under police control and required to undergo hygienic exams as a routine component of their employment.[97]

93. Belke, "Kilka słów o sposobach," 443–45.

94. Belke, "Kilka słów o nierządzie publicznym," 158–59.

95. J. Rogowicz, "Oględziny lekarskie kobiet w obliczu obowiązującego u nas prawa," *Medycyna* 24, no. 1 (1896): 19–21.

96. "Ankieta w sprawie zwalczania," 158–59.

97. Papée, *Kiły u prostytutek we Lwowie*, 5.

These expanded categories of supervision arose initially out of medical confidence in the possibilities of curing patients suffering from venereal disorders. The problem, according to police doctors, was that too few women supporting themselves through prostitution were under police supervision and therefore continued unknowingly to spread disease. In the view of Dr. Papée, the highest priority of police doctors should be to "search for sufficient means to compel [unregistered women] to accept treatment." Those who should be coaxed into submitting to medical examinations included older former prostitutes likely to be trading sex for room and board, household servants, female industrial workers, cashiers, and waitresses.[98] Doctors in Russian Poland agreed, arguing that especially in industrializing regions of the empire, industrial enterprises created the "ideal conditions for the spread" of disease. As S. Kogon, a factory doctor in Ekaterynoslav, noted at an assembly of industrial medical inspectors, "thanks to the lower cultural levels of the population" workers were extremely susceptible to contracting VD.[99] Much greater inspection and enforcement powers would be necessary if doctors were to bring contamination under control.

Physicians were also thrown off by the sheer variety of circumstances in which women turned to paid sex. The endemic poverty and rapid social change in newly constructed factory towns made it difficult to predict which women might rely on paid sex to supplement their incomes. Doctors felt besieged and overwhelmed by the problem. They began during the post-1905 period of revolution and popular uprisings to view poor women who resorted to venal sex as an enemy within—comprising a separate culture and moral compass from the intellectuals who commented on them. Doctors employed military language to depict their sense of embattlement against the forces of rampant venal sex, labeling sex workers an "army" that claimed ever more "victims" in their male clients. No longer seen to be poor, unfortunate, or misguided sisters, women working as prostitutes were now viewed with hostility and doctors confessed they simply did not have "accurate familiarity" to cope effectively with the phenomenon.[100] In a trend that contrasted sharply with the approach of many female reformers, physicians viewed their prostitute patients less as innocent victims of challenging circumstances than as malevolent threats to national well-being. Social welfare

---

98. Ibid., 3–5.

99. Ekaterynoslav, in southeastern Ukraine, experienced rapid industrial growth in the early years of the twentieth century as a result of the discovery of iron ore and the intense railroad construction in the area.

100. Skalski, "Prostytucya w Guberni Piotrkowskiej," 548.

activists and doctors agreed that the women who worked the nation's streets bore much of the responsibility for the country's medical and moral collapse. They agreed that reform of prostitution lay at the core of any program for national resurrection. Yet their professional affiliations led them to differ on the engine that would drive that reform. Charity workers increasingly saw their charges as reformable and capable of returning to "normal" life, whereas medical professionals insisted on sequestering sex workers from the healthy population in order to prevent further contamination.

Even more disturbing was the increase in informal prostitution in provincial areas, leading doctors to recommend expanding the regulatory net to include geographically remote regions. Since towns of fewer than ten thousand inhabitants were not required to maintain a system of supervised prostitution, sex work in those communities often went unreported and untreated. Municipal doctors in towns with easy access to Łódź, for example, emphasized that the absence of an inspection system "does not mean provincial prostitution does not exist." Instead, "barefoot girls" (bosówki) traveled from towns like Pabianice and Konstantynów into nearby Łódź and sold sex to factory youth. Young brides in these areas picked up diseases from their factory-worker husbands. Similarly, "barefoot girls" in the town of Rawa, which lacked a registered brothel, were recruited from among "former serving girls, factory workers, or the daughters of laborers." City administrators in Częstochowa reported similar conditions, with as many as fifteen to twenty secret prostitutes recruited among servants and factory workers loitering around hotel lobbies, according to the municipal physician Doctor Sękowski.[101] Clearly, the boundary separating sexually active working girls and professional prostitutes was thin and permeable. Regardless of whether the "barefoot girls" viewed their informal behavior as prostitution, police and medical officials were choosing to define their actions as subject to regulation.

A License to Brand: Doctors and the Stigmatization of Poor Women

Despite the enthusiasm with which many physicians pursued the steady expansion of medical authority over the bodies of working women, some professionals expressed quiet dissent at the social implications of their interventions. Doctors recognized that the police registration system resulted in

---

101. The vast majority of prostitutes working in the border town of Sosnowiec were also reportedly "factory girls." Skalski, "Prostytucya w Guberni Piotrkowskiej," 547–50.

the "branding" of many women as immoral, asocial, or sexually deviant. By the close of the nineteenth century, Polish public opinion increasingly understood police registration as constructing a permanent status, one from which a woman would be hard-pressed to return to the moral mainstream. In this sense, physicians would play a prominent role in permanently stigmatizing entire categories of women. As one Warsaw police doctor noted, "although the measures conducted against prostitution are necessary for maintaining the health and morality of society, they also have the effect of restricting individual freedom and imprinting a sort of moral stigma on her . . . and this can lead to her being inappropriately stigmatized as one of this category of people . . . and lead not only to shame for the person but also cause moral and material harm."[102]

Despite this professional unease, however, few doctors associated with the police regulation system accorded impoverished female detainees the benefit of doubt in registering them. Doctors maintained their distance even in the face of strident middle-class activists who came to the defense of poor single women being "pestered by the police." After registries for clandestine prostitutes were introduced in key cities across Polish territory, opponents of regulated prostitution voiced vigorous opposition to the use of circumstantial evidence to brand impoverished women as prostitutes. "The omnipotent powers of the police in this matter," complained one participant in an equal-rights meeting, "have reached the point that they can arrest a woman when they come across her alone, returning home late in the evening, or if she is in the apartment of a 'suspected' woman when it is searched."[103] Medical practitioners themselves lamented that the "honor of a woman could be permanently stained" simply by walking in the company of someone who used prostitutes or being spotted in a particular location known for prostitution transactions. Such identifiers could be "construed for evidence she is guilty" and cause her to be inappropriately labeled as a "prostitute."[104] All of these techniques were deemed perfectly legal. Indeed, law courts in the Congress Kingdom were authorized to consider the neighborhood in which a woman was arrested to determine her guilt if she refused to sign the prostitution registry voluntarily. This kind of guilt by association risked working-class women being judged guilty of sexual debauchery and officially branded with the stigma of prostitution for purely circumstantial reasons, activists argued. Since the institution of prostitution existed in a peculiar twilight status, being

---

102. Rogowicz, "Oględziny lekarskie," 18.
103. Stanisław Teodorczuk, "Zjazd kobiet polskich," *Czystość* 2, no. 10 (1906): 107.
104. Rogowicz, "Oględziny lekarskie," 19.

neither legal nor illegal, forced registration did not permit any appeal. Instead, the powerful police doctor and his accomplices could categorize a woman as sexually deviant, diseased, or degenerate with complete impunity.

Pressure to bring informal or part-time prostitutes under medical control by expanding the system of regulation continued despite recognition of the social effects registration entailed. Indeed, leading syphilis specialists warned that police inspectors were often distracted by the moral implications of placing women on the prostitution rolls and reticent to add them to the lists.[105] Dr. Jan Papée insisted that the regulation system in Galicia served an important function for the wider population in that it protected "public morality and the public order by limiting and prescribing the activities of prostitutes."[106] Papée encouraged police doctors to work harder to combat "secret prostitution" and bring as many practitioners as possible under the system of medical inspection. He was convinced that the small numbers entered on the "discreet" prostitution list did not reflect the breadth of women engaging in informal paid sex. Police headquarters in Lwów, he reported, successfully registered forty-three unwilling women in 1903, an additional forty-three in 1904, and only eleven new registrants in 1905, numbers comprising between 8 and 15 percent of the total number of registered women.[107] Police raids had evidently become less frequent after the Habsburg registration system was introduced in large cities in the 1870s and Papée was disappointed in the number of "secret prostitutes" brought under police control.[108]

Seeing Like a State: Prostitution as Pathology

Specialists like Papée were particularly concerned to widen the swath of women brought under their regulatory gaze for yet another, medically related reason. They hoped to take advantage of access to the prostitute's body to discover more about the progress of sexual diseases. Police inspections offered doctors a wealth of data on every aspect of venereal infection, allowing them to assemble detailed case histories using the conscripted bodies of female registrants. In an age when male doctors rarely touched the bodies of their

---

105. Papée complained the recordkeepers neglected their hygienic responsibilities out of concern with the "moral aspects" of their task. "O reformie prostytucyi," 4.

106. Papée, *Nadzór lekarski nad prostytucyą*, 174.

107. Papée, "Nadzór lekarski," *Lwowski Tygodnik Lekarski* 2, no. 17 (1907): 200.

108. The system of maintaining registration lists and requiring semiweekly health inspections and forced hospitalization on professional prostitutes was instituted first in Vienna in 1873 and then expanded to large cities in Galicia in 1876. The Imperial Council of Health established a commission to manage the system consisting of one official from the governor general's office, the director of

female patients and almost never examined bourgeois women unclothed, prostitutes provided invaluable information on the manifestations of venereal ailments.[109] Information about the long-term ramifications of syphilis and its failure to respond to medical treatment helped affirm the growing sentiment in favor of segregating diseased women from the rest of "clean" society. This preoccupation with labeling, documenting, and isolating replaced the earlier emphasis on treatment, cure, and reintegration of morally suspect women into the social mainstream. Medical confidence in a prostitute's return to "normal" life and "honest" work waned as evidence mounted about the lifelong impact of sexual diseases. At the same time, the system of tolerated prostitution made the public woman much more legible to the state than her less sexually active sisters. She was monitored and supervised in nearly every aspect of her life, from employment and marriage to health and reproduction. Part of nineteenth-century liberalism's encroachment into private life, the regulation system is one manifestation of bureaucrats' tendency to bring ever greater numbers of subjects under imperial oversight.

The process of registering public women took on a logic of its own for many physicians. Once police doctors assumed responsibility for documenting the medical histories of prostitutes, the very act of compiling statistical information became a predictor for how women of a certain social class would behave. As James Scott observes in *Seeing Like a State*, governmental collection of statistical material about a population encouraged state officials everywhere to characterize their populations in new ways. Labeling this changed state-society relationship "high modernism," Scott argues that statistical output came to be viewed as characteristic and even predictive of a people. "Statistical facts," he notes, were "elaborated into social laws," and it was "but a small step from a simplified description of society to the design and manipulation of society, with its improvement in mind."[110]

In the police examination room, the step from statistical measurement and documentation of disease to manipulation of the patient's body was

---

police, and one member of the Health Council. The commission was tasked with writing instructions for participating doctors and circulating regulations for the conduct of prostitutes. The police chief managed the registration system in Cracow and Lwów; in smaller towns, the process was operated out of the magistrate's office. The system was introduced in Brody, Przemyśl, Stanisławów, Tarnów, Tarnopol, Kołomyja, Jarosław, Stryj, Drohobycz, and Brzeżany in December 1876. In 1888, the governor general expanded it to include all towns with populations greater than ten thousand and any town with a military garrison. Papée, "Nadzór lekarski," 200.

109. On the evolution of the doctor-patient relationship in nineteenth-century Europe, see Bynum, *Science and the Practice of Medicine*, 33–34, 176–217.

110. James C. Scott, *Seeing Like a State: How Certain Schemes to Improve the Human Condition Have Failed* (New Haven, CT, 1998), 91–92.

particularly small. Evidence from disease-ravaged prostitutes would eventually form the core of medical knowledge about the progress of syphilis and other sexual disorders, as well as inform a wide range of advances in gynecological understanding.[111] Doctors soon learned they could take advantage of the sheer numbers of sexually active female patients in their care to collect statistical material that would help them analyze the types and stages of sexual diseases. Police records reportedly demonstrated differential rates of infection among particular demographic groups. Dr. Wysłouch reported, for example, that young women before the age of eighteen were more susceptible to the spread of venereal ailment and thus "the most active propagators of disease."[112] Such information, though perhaps not medically sound by modern standards, would have been nearly impossible to obtain in private practice. According to Dr. Papée, "prostitutes represent by far the best material on which we can repeatedly and without interruption in our observation chart the course of syphilis through a whole range of years, not only during the period of its appearance but also during periods when it is relapsing, which in private practice and in the hospital we have only very rare opportunities to observe." Taking advantage of the rare opportunity to chart the progress of disease in a subset of regulated women, Papée set out to compile case histories of each prostitute under his care. His daily experience examining infected women allowed him to establish an aggregate history of syphilis at each stage of its development. He collected information on such questions as "how many girls are infected with syphilis, in what category or stage has the disease developed, which are the most common changes between stages, and at what stages is it important to focus more attention."[113]

Papée's research helped push Polish medical understanding of syphilis to new levels of sophistication. Some of his findings were mere curiosities, such as the observation that "older prostitutes rarely contract the more severe form" of gonorrhea or that the disease "causes the uterus to change shape."[114] Other conclusions had more serious implications and fed a rising panic about the long-term dangers of venereal diseases. For example,

111. Understanding of the menstrual cycle and the process of ovulation came through discoveries in the late nineteenth century, partially based on studies with prostitutes. See Weeks, *Sex, Politics, and Society*, 42–44.

112. According to Dr. Fournier, young girls contracted venereal disease more easily than older women. In Paris, he reports, 63 percent of prostitutes contracted VD before they reached adulthood. Alfred Fournier, *Prophylaxie de la syphilis par le traitement* (Paris, 1900), cited in Wysłouch, *Prostytucja i jej skutki*, 28–29.

113. Papée, *Kiły u prostytutek we Lwowie*, 1–3.

114. Papée, *Choroby weneryczne, ich rószerzenie i zapobieganie*, 14–15.

Papée's disheartening discovery of neurosyphilis in two prostitutes whom he believed had long since been cured of the disease opened up the prospect that women suffering from syphilis might be permanently contagious. "I myself," he noted, "had the opportunity to observe two girls who had ceased to show symptoms of syphilis after five and seven years, respectively, but then presented with syphilis of the brain."[115] Papée's depiction challenged the belief among many contemporary practitioners that once symptoms subsided the syphilis infection was no longer present in the body. Even more worrisome to the broader public was Papée's definitive demonstration of what had long been suspected, that "in the course of her career nearly every prostitute becomes infected with gonorrhea and also with syphilis." Indeed, he explained, some public women contracted gonorrhea several times in the course of their careers, and most (80–85 percent) were infected with syphilis at some point during their professional lives. There was no escaping the conclusion that regulation of prostitutes had been a failure in preventing the spread of diseases. No matter how frequently or how carefully women's bodies were inspected, prostitutes could never be declared free of contamination. Papée's research showed that the police supervision system had been utterly ineffective in preventing the spread of syphilis. The most dangerous and contagious stages of the disease, he demonstrated, typically occurred either before women were officially registered by the police or during the first three most active years on the registry.

The documentation Papée compiled also had frightening implications for the future reproductive capacity of diseased women and consequently for the nation as a whole. Papée's statistics demonstrated, for example, that most public women first contracted syphilis at the height of their childbearing years, before the age of twenty-five.[116] Together with revelations about bourgeois males catching sexual ailments from prostitutes and passing them on to their wives, such medical discoveries poured fuel on the flames of public anxiety about prostitution. As a deeper understanding of the ravages of syphilis undercut medical confidence in the prospects of treatment, physicians turned from expanding the pool of women forced to undergo inspections to isolating potentially afflicted patients from the healthy population.

---

115. Papée, *Kiły u prostytutek we Lwowie,* 16. Alfred Fournier in Paris circulated his findings about tertiary syphilis and its manifestations in 1875, but his theories linking the initial outbreak of the disease to neurological damage years later were not universally accepted. Quetel, *History of Syphilis,* 134–36.

116. Some 37 percent of the prostitutes registered in Lwów contracted syphilis before the age of twenty, and 42 percent showed symptoms of the disease between the ages of twenty and twenty-five. Papée, *Kiły u prostytutek we Lwowie,* 17–18.

By the early years of the twentieth century, medical experts across Europe raised the specter of degeneration and the damage that inherited traits could have on the strength of the population. Medical sympathy for the young women who appeared in police examination rooms declined as doctors proclaimed inherited syphilis a "social disaster" whose victims were "becoming deaf, dumb, and blind, filling our insane asylums and homes for incurable diseases."[117] Frightened by the impending health crisis and liberated to speak more openly about nationalist aspirations during the 1905 Revolution, medical activists campaigned for changed sexual behavior as an element of national sacrifice. As we will see in chapter 9, belief in scientific progress gave way to a sense of professional futility as leading medical specialists helped inaugurate chapters of eugenics organizations throughout the Polish lands.

The Social Ascension of Polish Medicine

A central element in this broadening campaign to improve public morality was a dramatically expanded role for physicians in private and family life, a broadening purview that would boost the Polish medical community's authority as it introduced eugenics reforms during the early years of the twentieth century. Anxiety about the ravages of syphilis and the rise in prostitution use gave medical science a platform from which to develop new public-health programs. The expertise doctors gained in monitoring registered prostitutes garnered them the prestige necessary for maintaining hygiene in the home, the school, and the marital bed. Polish physicians increasingly functioned as mediators between science and the problems of everyday life, as well as mediators between imperial concerns for social hygiene and the medical profession's preoccupation with national vitality. The turn toward medical intervention in the private realm was, of course, part of a Europe-wide trend. As Harry Oosterhuit reminds us, physicians everywhere sanctioned "a hygienic role in the interventionist state" during the nineteenth century as they expanded their expertise into formerly nonmedical realms like alcoholism, crime, sexual perversion, and other social pathologies. By mediating between science and the vexing problems of everyday life, Oosterhuit points out, doctors "succeeded in convincing the public of the indispensability of their expertise." In this way, medical technicians "came to replace the clergy as authoritative personal consultants in the realm of sexuality" and beyond.[118]

---

117. Blumenfeld, *Prostytucya i hygiena płciowa*, quoted in Wyrobek, *Choroby a małżenstwo*, 70.

118. Oosterhuit, *Stepchildren of Nature*, 29–30. Oosterhuit takes issue with both Foucault and Jeffrey Weeks for not seeing the emergence of the science of sexuality as a deplorable medical

In the Polish setting, physicians were hampered in their ability to serve the public because of their strained relationship with ruling governments. As Ilana Lowy-Zelmanowicz has argued, Polish doctors were aware of the social aspects of medicine through their foreign training, but "the political circumstances in which they were obliged to work sharply reduced the scope of their activity in this domain."[119] Physicians lamented the inaccessibility of the lower classes to their public-health campaigns and the "great distance separating their professional aspirations from the practical possibilities of realizing" those goals. Such cultural and educational limitations might be corrected if Polish physicians had greater influence in the political sphere.[120] Although political exigencies hampered the success of professional medicine in the occupied Polish lands, research on public-health issues nevertheless made important strides in these years.[121] During the last decades of the nineteenth century, Polish medical experts became preoccupied with hygienic questions, establishing the influential Warsaw Hygienic Society (Warszawskie Towarzystwo Higieniczne) in 1898 with a broad public-health agenda. The society, with its branches in Łódź and elsewhere, sponsored shelters, provided medical care for children of poor families, worked to improve local hospital facilities, and set about establishing a program of public education about hygienic issues.[122] The group's membership soon climbed to over six hundred medical experts and its biweekly journal, *Zdrowie*, became the newspaper of record for public-health issues. Questions of sexual practice and morality preoccupied the society. Members had access to a burgeoning literature on sexual deviance from across Europe, including Krafft-Ebing's

colonization. He does not view the rise of medical authority as a "new form of moral tyranny," but rather as part of a process of labeling deviations that pre-dated the medical categorization of them (7–13).

119. Ilana Lowy-Zelmanowicz, *The Polish School of Philosophy of Medicine: From Tytus Chalubinski (1820–1889) to Ludwik Fleck (1896–1961)* (London, 1990), 4–5.

120. Transcription of speech by Dr. Mucha, "Zebrania i rozprawy: Sekcye szpitali i przytułków," *Słowo*, April 20, 1901, 2.

121. The Medical Section of the Cracow Scientific Society (renamed the Academy of Sciences in 1872), established in 1815, issued dozens of scientific papers that kept physicians informed of new developments in the field of medicine. Medical societies flourished briefly in the Congress Kingdom, including the Wilno Medical Association and the Medical Society of Warsaw (Towarzystwo Lekarskie Warszawskie), but were shut down following the November Uprising. Conditions for medical research were harsher in Poznań, where a medical society was sustained only between 1832 and 1840, producing a thin semiannual German-language pamphlet reflecting its research. Warsaw and Lwów continued to boast medical journals through the early decades of the twentieth century, including *Tygodnik Lekarski*, *Gazeta Lekarski*, and the weekly Warsaw journals *Medycyna* and *Krytyka Lekarska* from 1897 to 1907. *Wykład chorób wenerycznych*, 398–99; and Lowy, *Polish School of Medicine*, 5.

122. N., "W. Tow. Hygienicznym," *Kurier Warszawski*, April 23, 1900, 7–8.

Psychopathia sexualis, first published in Vienna in 1886, and the work of the British human sexuality specialist Havelock Ellis beginning in 1890 and the German dermatologist Iwan Bloch, who together with Magnum Hirschfeld founded the scientific field of "sexology," publishing a complete encyclopedia of the "sexual sciences" in 1906.[123]

Taking into account the work of Western scholars, Polish doctors launched a full-scale campaign to educate the public about sexually communicated diseases. They began with a pragmatic program to stem the tide of VD through treatment, prevention, and education. Polish specialists like Antoni Wysłouch and Witold Chodźko proposed opening outpatient clinics to dispense medicine free of charge, circulating educational brochures, and reorganizing hospital wards for more effective treatment.[124] Secondary-school education was the linchpin of this campaign, and the wagon to which the medical community hitched its ambitious agenda of expanded authority. Doctors proposed nothing short of a revolutionary transformation in the way information about sexual issues was communicated to children. Moving to place themselves in the forefront of sexual indoctrination, physicians explicitly advocated displacing both the family and the school from the sexual education of Polish youth. They recommended all secondary-school pupils be tutored in the risks of sexual activity. As Dr. P. S. Czajkowski warned in his 1904 lecture to the Warsaw Hygienic Society, leaving such instruction to parents or to "self-education" was no longer adequate.[125] Doctors, he insisted, had to insert themselves into everyday questions of adolescent behavior, seeking influence over what was once restricted to the private realm.

Supporters of a medical monopoly over sex education relied on campaigns similar to those waged in Western Europe to buttress their arguments. They cited 1907 German regulations giving physicians full responsibility to teach the "dangers of sexual relations." Modeling their proposals on German law, Warsaw Hygienic Society members recommended that Congress Kingdom schools add lessons on anatomy, sexual hygiene, and morality to

---

123. The editors of *Wykład chorób wenerycznych* noted in their 1874 introduction that "because of the severe shortage of textbooks in the Polish language treating the subject of venereal diseases," the authors found it necessary to tap the latest foreign sources to discuss this phenomenon. *Wykład chorób wenerycznych,* 1. On the confluence of publication on sexual matters, see also Oosterhuit, *Stepchildren of Nature,* 43–59.

124. Wysłouch and Chodźko's detailed plan for combating venereal diseases including a proposal to eliminate all brothels, construct VD wards in every general hospital, establish outpatient clinics to treat sexual diseases free of charge, and organize a special section of the Hygienic Society devoted purely to the problem of fighting VD.

125. "Odział Łódźki Warsz. Tow. Hygienicznego, Sekcya III—Pedagogiczna," May 3, 1904 session, in *Zdrowie* 21, no. 1 (January 1905): 81.

their curriculum. They advocated mandatory sex-education classes in trade schools, high schools, and post-secondary institutions, and argued that local communes should be required to offer comparable courses to all youth who opted not to attend a secondary school.[126] Drawing on discussions surrounding the new German law, Polish physicians appealed for a complete medical monopoly on all matters pertaining to sexual instruction. "It would be a brutal thing if parents and teachers spoke to the younger generation . . . about the phenomenon of childbirth," the society proclaimed.[127] Sexual education was "too important to be left up to parents," members warned, since "not all parents [were] capable" of imparting such instruction and many trained pedagogues were often not even "up to the task" of making lessons clear and accessible. "For teaching young people about matters of sexuality only a doctor is suitable," the society's leaders insisted.[128] Instruction by medical professionals was intended to eclipse completely the lessons parents might provide in matters of sexuality.[129]

Sex education would become a key weapon in the medical community's arsenal for rescuing Poland from its moral and physical decline. Attempts to mandate physician-led sex education in the schools soon expanded as doctors inserted themselves into other aspects of the educational mission. Medical experts weighed in with opinions on the matter of coeducation in secondary schools.[130] They led the charge in recommending all secondary schoolboys be subject to medical regulation and encouraged pupils to seek treatment for venereal ailments in order to not pass them on to others.[131] Doctors expressed concern about the protection of youth in all its manifestations, including the exposure of innocent children to syphilitics in hospital venereal wards. The problem of housing minors with their adult patients was particularly acute in the dermatology ward, where doctors pointed out the atmosphere was "erotic." As many as sixty children per year as young as ten or twelve passed through the St. Lazarus Hospital to be treated for scabies and other skin

---

126. Dr. Sarason, "W sprawie uświadamiania płciowego," *Zdrowie* 24, no. 3 (March 1908): 160–62. This is a summary from the journal *Zeitschrift fur Schulgesundheitspflege*, no. 12 (1907).

127. V. Digalski, "Stanowisko rodziców wobec płciowego uświadamiania ich dzieci," *Zdrowie* 25, no. 11 (November 1909): 746. Translated and reprinted from *Die Jüngenfursorge*, no. 10 (1909).

128. Theodor Altschul, "Płciowe uświadomienie młodzieży," *Zdrowie,* 25, no. 6 (June 1909): 427–28, summarized by W. D. in *Zeitschrift für Schulgesundheitspflege*, no. 12 (1908); and Heller, "Uwagi, dotyczące zagadnień seksualnych," *Zdrowie* 25, no. 12 (December 1909): 804, translated and summarized by Dr. T. K. in *Zeitschrift für Schulgesundheitspflege*, no. 9 (1908).

129. Sarason, "W sprawie uświadamiania płciowego," 161.

130. "Wydział hygieny wychowawczej posiedzenie d. 4 listopada 1903," *Zdrowie* (1904): 172–76.

131. "Ankieta w sprawie zwalczania chorób płciowych u młodzieży szkoł średnich," *Zdrowie* 20, no. 5 (May 1904): 292.

diseases. The "innocent, unspoiled children" shared rooms with the "huge mass of prostitutes" sentenced to hospital stays while recovering from syphilis and gonorrhea.[132] Such pure children were exposed to hardened prostitutes in what was described as a "demoralizing" atmosphere characterized by the "worst kind of licentiousness, debauchery, and sometimes even criminality."[133] As with the miasmas ostensibly emitted from urban bordellos to the healthier residents in town, hospitalized prostitutes exposed younger, uncorrupted patients to an alien but seductive way of life. "A young, honest, and humble girl is sick with scabies and starts a friendly conversation with her neighbor, an official or unofficial prostitute. What the two friends discuss among themselves, no one knows, but after checking out of the hospital the girl often visits the colleague she became acquainted with there, until she disappears from the home of her parents and moves with her into a wonderful apartment. Although she entered the hospital with scabies, the girl lost one hundred times more than she gained and the cause of this loss was the ward for skin disorders."[134] The impact of such a cohousing situation was more than just improper, according to medical experts; it was criminal. Innocent girls were also "frightened" by the prostitutes admitted with them to outpatient clinics for skin diseases. Such practices needed to be reformed in order to protect children from early corruption and irreparable harm. Who but physicians had the authority to impose such protection?[135]

Physicians also symbolically entered the bedrooms of their patients and began disseminating advice about everyday sexual practices as never before. Responding aggressively to the 1903 survey of Warsaw university youth, Warsaw doctors issued cautionary notes about habits that might cause lasting harm to children. They warned of physical damage when young men awakened their sexual interest too early, predicting impotence, memory loss, headaches, disorientation, listlessness, and severe fatigue from premature intimate relations. Doctors cited examples from survey respondents expressing anxiety about early sexual experiences, including one student who reportedly "lost his outstanding ability in math" after practicing masturbation and another who claimed to become so nervous that he "would lie in bed without pause for six hours at a time, not going to dinner, and ignore all [his] obligations." The respondent had the feeling that his "memory was starting to slip" and

---

132. Wróblewski, "Dzieci w szpitalu św. Łazarza," 385–86.
133. Lecture by Zygmunt Kramsztyk at meeting of Wydział Hygieny szpitali i przytułków Warsz. Tow. Hyg., December 20, 1901, printed in *Krytyka Lekarska* 6, no. 4 (March 19, 1902): 83.
134. Ibid.
135. "Z Warszawskiego Tow. Hygienicznego: Protokol posiedziena Rady z dnia 30 Marca 1904," *Zdrowie* 20, no. 3 (March 1904): 627–29.

that he "felt tired after the slightest bit of work." A third student was reported to have felt "disturbances in [his] body: a back pain that occurred during certain activities, especially when standing up, an unusually nervous condition and an inability to perform mental work." And a fourth spoke of "severe headaches, pustules on his entire body, and general overall weakness." The effects of nocturnal emission of semen went beyond physical ailments to include "nervousness, sensitivity to light, depression, irritability, apathy, and dark thoughts."[136] The message was clear. Early sexual arousal, even if it did not include sexual intercourse, was a gateway activity that could lead down the slippery slope of premarital sex and reliance on prostitutes. Polish youth should be prevented at all costs from engaging in such activities.

The medical community was in a difficult position, however, in gauging how to advise adolescents about early sexual experiences. A growing wing of Polish medical science promoted the view that the venereal threat could be contained only through sexual abstinence prior to marriage. In offering this advice, doctors challenged a long tradition of family physicians counseling unmarried men to "find a woman" with whom to have sexual relations as a cure for any number of medical maladies. Physicians writing for the Warsaw Hygienic Society journal *Zdrowie* viewed such advice with outright hostility. The practice of abstinence before marriage had absolutely no negative consequences, they insisted, and in most cases was the safer, healthier option compared with relying on prostitutes for sexual satisfaction. Advocates of abstinence for hygienic and moral reasons claimed they could not "find adequate words to express [their] contempt" for individuals who advised young men to "find a woman." This they claimed was bad advice that was ultimately harmful to the individual's health. Still, doctors supporting the abstinence campaign were faced with an uphill slog convincing their young clientele of their position. Student respondents to the Warsaw survey, doctors conceded, complained about the ill effects of abstaining from sex during their young adult years. Roughly equal numbers of respondents claimed abstinence had positively and negatively affected them. In particular, nine students complained of serious medical symptoms, including headaches, nervousness, and a "negative effect on [the respondent's] intellect" caused by sexual abstinence.[137]

Polish medical science was also conflicted about the question of when it was appropriate for a syphilitic to consummate a marriage. Physicians in Galicia were required to issue an *ubezpieczenie* or guarantee of health prior to

---

136. "Życie płciowe warszawskiej młodzieży," March 1906, 160–62.
137. Ibid., 160–63.

marriage, and were consequently required to determine when a VD patient was no longer contagious. The responsibility to provide such a certification prompted a heated discussion in the medical community about when an infected patient should be deemed free of the syphilis infection. By 1906, experts like the hygiene specialist Professor Emil Wyrobek of Jagiellonian University had come to the devastating conclusion that because of the way the disease progressed it was impossible to know whether a patient had been fully cured. Wyrobek confirmed that "a long period can pass when the disease lies dormant and the patient has no symptoms, yet he is not completely healthy and the disease can then suddenly crop up and threaten him."[138] Thus, Wyrobek wrote, "in truth the patient should never marry" because he might well continue to be contagious. The consequences of permitting such sufferers to marry and sire children were potentially calamitous, he warned. Syphilitic children, he reminded his readers, generally died soon after birth, and those who survived were destined for a life as idiots, cripples, or worse.

Wyrobek was one of the first doctors in the Polish lands to acknowledge publicly that no known treatment, including the expensive and painful ingestion of mercury, was effective in eradicating patients of syphilis. "I don't want to take an opposing viewpoint to the mercury cure," he noted, diplomatically, "but in today's circumstances, it is fundamentally inadequate." In fact, no matter what doctors tried, from salves to invasive surgical procedures, absolutely "no method of treating syphilis will cure it."[139] Syphilis had become, in Wyrobek's view, "a social disaster." Dr. Antoni Blumenfeld of Lwów agreed, lamenting that "it cannot be a matter of indifference for society that a huge number of people are becoming blind, deaf, dumb, and filling our insane asylums and homes for incurable diseases, and yet [syphilis] continues to flower with still greater strength."[140] Nonetheless, Wyrobek, as a professor concerned with public health, was forced to think practically. Given the widespread exposure most unmarried men had to venereal diseases through their relations with prostitutes, the medical community could hardly forbid them all from marrying. If, as experts had recently estimated, one in four men suffered from syphilis, it would be "absurd" to prohibit marriage among all those who had shown symptoms of the disease. In the end, Wyrobek settled for a compromise prescription, cautioning that "no syphilitic should marry as long as he continues to have symptoms" and that

138. Wyrobek, *Choroby a małżeństwo*, 79.

139. Ibid., 67–72.

140. Antoni Blumenfeld, *Choroby płciowe* (Lwów, 1905), quoted in Wyrobek, *Choroby a małżeństwo*, 78.

the longer he waits to marry, the less likely he will pass the disease onto his wife and offspring. Since it was typically assumed that syphilis disappeared three to five years after the original onset of the illness, Wyrobek recommended granting medical certification of good health for the purposes of marriage following two years without symptoms.[141] Yet even this prescription was given with little conviction since it could only really be regarded as a compromise with practical life.

The police doctor and venereologist Jan Papée approached the marriage question with similar caution, acknowledging the depth of disagreement among medical professionals. "Some say four, seven, or ten years," Papée reported, but really "no one knows for sure." Papée himself claimed he was "extremely careful giving permission for marriage especially in cases where the timing of the original infection is not known." Like Wyrobek, Papée compromised and indicated his willingness to allow men to marry providing they (claimed) they had been symptom free for at least three years.[142] Again, though, these were guesses and both men knew that the likelihood remained that the disease could resurface with devastating consequences for wives, families, and unborn children.

Alcohol and the Prostitute: Medicalization of Social Problems

Once Polish physicians had crossed the threshold into giving advice about childrearing and marriage, they found themselves monitoring other practices common to family life, from breast-feeding to alcohol consumption.[143] Rising rates of drunkenness, in particular, were a source of concern in the medical community for much the same reason that syphilis was a threat: it ruined marriages, caused inherited defects, and weakened the population's capacity for work. Alcohol dependency represented both an environmental harm within the family and a biological concern because of its effects on unborn children. For doctors occupied with issues of moral decline, drunkenness was closely tied to prostitution. Alcohol suffused nearly every stage

---

141. Wyrobek was a pragmatist and worried that banning marriage for all syphilitics would simply increase the number of informal marriages not protected by law and lead to an increased number of poor and sick foundling children in the care of cash-starved public institutions. Wyrobek, *Choroby a małżeństwo*, 79.

142. Papée, *Choroby weneryczne, ich rozszerzenie i zapobieganie*, 7.

143. The campaign to reintroduce breastfeeding among the social elite rather than giving infants over to wet nurses for care during their early months was led by the Polish literary giant Tadeusz Boy-Żeleński, who initiated his "kropla mleka" or "drop of milk" campaign in order help reduce infant mortality. See, for example, "Kropla mleka w Krakowie," *Nowe Słowo* 6, no. 7 (1907): 157–59.

of the prostitute's life, they argued, from the atmosphere in which she was raised to the conditions of her work. Alcohol was the poison that helped create the prostitute herself by producing girls with limited mental capacity who turned to prostitution for want of other ways to support themselves, and compromised the judgment of young men who famously sought the company of harlots when they were under its influence.

In tracing these linkages, Polish doctors reflected the findings of medical researchers across the Continent, placing themselves in line with expert opinion elsewhere in Europe. The Warsaw-based addiction specialist Dr. Władysław Chodecki demonstrated the dangerous consequences of drunks conceiving children. "The drunk rarely conceives normal offspring," he reported. Referencing the work of the French chemist Maurice Nicloux, he traced the route by which "alcohol moves very quickly to the testes, the seminal fluid, and then to the ovaries at the moment of relations," causing the infant to become an alcoholic and to display all the "developmental defects" associated with this disorder.[144] The use of alcohol at the time of conception, Chodecki asserted, was an "outstanding example of degeneration," causing the resulting offspring to present with the full range of "mental, physical, and moral impairments connected with nervous disorders and epilepsy; they are prone to crime, and among female members of the family—prostitution."[145] Polish studies linking alcoholic fathers and their prostitute daughters tapped into a wave of research on inherited disorders conducted by psychiatrists and anthropologists in Italy and Germany. According to such studies, antisocial tendencies could be passed on within a single family. The German psychiatrist Dr. Bonhoffer, for example, traced the family histories of 190 prostitutes in a Wrocław prison, discovering that nearly half of them were predisposed to alcoholism because of their parents. Only 32 percent of the prostitute prisoners in the study displayed no abnormal physical or psychological qualities.[146] Research among Italian and American scholars produced similar results. Twenty percent of prostitutes studied by Gurrieri and Fournasari, students of Cesare Lombroso, had alcoholic fathers; 48 percent of the two thousand prostitutes Dr. Sanger included in his 1863 study of New York prostitutes had alcoholic parents, and 69 percent of the criminals

---

144. Other French scientists reportedly corroborated these results by conducting experiments on dogs who had ingested alcohol, showing that the offspring of the intoxicated beasts were deficient in many ways. Władysław Chodecki, "Alkoholizm a prostytucya," *Zdrowie* 24, no. 5 (May 1908): 308–9.

145. Chodecki, "Alkoholizm a prostytucya," 302.

146. Ibid., 303.

and prostitutes Tarnovska examined in Russia were born into families of drunks.[147] Such research suggested a biological link between drunken fathers and their asocial, psychologically impaired, or prostitute daughters.

For Chodecki and other Polish specialists, the influence of alcohol was also environmental. Exposure to an alcoholic household reportedly encouraged resort to prostitution, not least because the poverty and physical abuse children in these households suffered prompted them to leave home early. According to societies for the care of abandoned children, "by far the largest percentage of homeless children had been forced onto the streets to beg for an alcoholic father."[148] Out of necessity, these children resorted to theft, prostitution, and a life on the streets. As always, the lines between poverty, vagrancy, and exchanging sex for money became blurred as women made their entrée into the world of paid sex. Chodecki himself studied the records of craftsmen associations and found numerous examples of "the children of habitual drunks" who "practiced prostitution on the streets of Warsaw." Other environmental factors played into the links between alcohol consumption and the construction of the prostitute as well. The poor prenatal care pregnant mothers received in alcoholic homes hampered their children's development. Homes of drunkards were also reportedly devoid of formal education since "the majority of children in a drunk's family do not attend school at all," giving them a complete lack of formal training and contributing to their need to resort to crime and prostitution.[149]

The day-to-day world of prostitution was also awash in spirits. Prostitutes reportedly were forced to drink in order to "tolerate the shame of their profession." "Prostitution without alcohol," Chodecki insisted, was simply inconceivable. Moreover, prostitutes sought to drink with their clients so that the latter would overcome their scruples, ignore their personal dignity, and be vulnerable to robbery in the end. In all of these ways, alcohol abuse and sexual degeneracy were wound up in a pattern of mutual dependency. Alcoholism, according to medical specialists, "produced individuals unable to work, enemies of the social order, in a word, antisocial elements, which includes also the fall of the prostitute."[150] To solve one social

---

147. These inherited effects of alcoholism found reflection in external signs of degeneration. Chodecki repeated Lombroso's famous research on the physiogamy of prostitutes, including reference to anomalies of teeth position, the so-called wolf jaw, and asymmetrical face. Chodecki, "Alkoholizm a prostytucya," 302–3.

148. Chodecki, "Alkoholizm a prostytucya," 304.

149. Chodecki claimed that almost 80 percent of prostitutes in the Congress Kingdom could neither read nor write, a figure not borne out by prostitution registries in the major cities of the period. Chodecki, "Alkoholizm a prostytucya," 305.

150. Ibid.

problem meant to tackle both, and Polish medical professionals meant to do exactly that.

The growing prestige of the medical profession across the Polish lands at the turn of the twentieth century placed doctors at the forefront of efforts to reform the system of regulated prostitution. As discoveries rolled in about the effects of congenital syphilis, the syphilis of the innocents, and the failure of medical science to eradicate VD, physicians began to despair of resolving the wider impact of sexual debauchery in Polish society. Even as their professional influence and authority over their patients climbed and they entered the bedrooms and living rooms of their clientele as never before, medical guidance failed to staunch the skyrocketing rates of syphilis, alcoholism, and prostitution. These would become the trifecta that drove degeneration theory in the first decades of the new century, prompting new and bolder solutions to the problem of commercial sex and its attendant medical disorders. United in their perception of the gravity of the prostitution problem, medical experts disputed solutions among themselves. The heightened power of medicine provided a new scientific basis for morality campaigns in the period leading up to the Great War and the rebirth of the Polish state. As we will see in chapter 9, purity and eugenics campaigns battled neoregulationists in a fight over who would govern health policy in the new Polish Republic. The heated debate would widen the divide between the impoverished practitioners of prostitution and those who decreed measures to remedy the institution and to purify the body of the nation itself.

CHAPTER 9

Purity and Danger

Prostitution Reform and the Birth of Polish Eugenics

> Defilement is never an isolated event. It cannot occur
> except in view of a systematic ordering of ideas. . . .
> The only way in which polluting ideas make sense
> is in reference to a total structure of thought whose
> keystone boundaries, margins and internal lines are
> held in relation by rituals of separation.
>
> —Mary Douglas, *Purity and Danger: An Analysis of
> Concepts of Pollution and Taboo*

> Society today is riddled with filth, rot, and hypocrisy.
> We need to have in our thoughts and in our action
> dynamite that will explode all the strongholds of
> today's civilization stink.
>
> —Andrzej Baumfeld, "O czystości kilka uwag"

Scientific anxiety over the potentially devastat-
ing consequences of venereal disease laid the foundation for a unique eugenics
initiative in the Polish lands. In contrast to eugenics agendas elsewhere, Polish experts focused their energies on improving social hygiene and preventing disease rather than purging the nation of ethnic and religious pollutants.
After a century of scientific optimism in which specialists embraced science
as a tool for social improvement, the early twentieth century inaugurated a
more cynical scientific milieu in Poland and across the European continent.
Reports surfaced about the unchecked spread of tuberculosis and venereal
disease, the harmful effects of life in filthy urban centers, and the seemingly
pathological explosion of alcohol abuse, gambling, pornography, and other
"deviant" practices. Doctors and other scientific experts trained their considerable authority on reform projects that extended their clinical powers into
new realms of human experience. In the years leading up to the outbreak of
World War I, physicians would combine their rising public stature with the
energies of bourgeois social reformers to construct new programs aimed at
eliminating the damaging impact of the public woman. Socially conscious
doctors agreed that the status quo could not persist; prostitution, they argued,

must either be eradicated completely or become subject to more effective regulation in order to protect the health of male clients.[1] In either case, the registration system so highly regarded during the latter years of the nineteenth century was in for a dramatic overhaul.

To address these new conditions, doctors devised two opposing programs for prostitution reform, both of which relied on scientific data to support their claims. The new strategies soon settled into sharply divergent camps: neoregulation, which called for strengthening the clinical aspects of the registration system, and abolition, which aimed to outlaw commercial sex and to eliminate the social conditions that necessitated it. For those who supported neoregulation, the curative powers of biological science mandated bringing increasing numbers of women under the speculum and permanently sequestering those who practiced venal sex. Neoregulationists such as the police inspector Jan Papée in Lwów insisted that unmarried males required the services of prostitutes as a "necessary evil" to satisfy their sexual needs. For Papée and others, the potential for exposure to venereal diseases could only be reduced through increasingly frequent and carefully scripted medical examinations of registered prostitutes. The dire conditions that characterized public health across the Polish lands, according to this perspective, made moralizing about sexually licentious behavior a luxury Polish society could ill afford. To ignore the problem of paid sex and sexual disease, they stressed, would be catastrophic for the Polish nation.

At the opposite end of the reform spectrum, the growing faction of Polish abolitionists issued equally dire warnings. Those who opposed the regulation system called for completely dismantling the police-medical registration apparatus and introducing measures to curb overall resort to prostitution. Abolitionists emphasized the horrific "defects of regulated prostitution."[2] Doctors such as Augustyn Wróblewski, Leon Wernic, Antoni Wysłouch, and Władysław Chodecki lobbied for sexual abstinence as an alternative to sex with prostitutes as "the only way to extend life."[3] They put forward an aggressive program of public education, free medical clinics for voluntary treatment of venereal diseases, and a sexual "purity" campaign aimed at high school and university students.[4] Abolitionists rejected the notion of "isolating" prostitutes as a practice that had outlived its utility. "The creation of

1. Papée, *Nadzór lekarski*, 3–5.

2. Leon Wernic, "Podstawowe drogi do walki z chorobami wenerycznymi," *Zdrowie* 6, no. 8 (January 1906): 517–20; and Karkowski, "Działalność Towarzystwa hygienicznego w Wielkopolsce," 622–24.

3. Wernic, "Podstawowe drogi," 517–20.

4. Karkowski, "Działalność Towarzystwa hygienicznego w Wielkopolsce," 622–24.

a ghetto for prostitutes," they argued, did "not comprise a solution" to the problem of sexual disease.[5] Only moral restraint could offer the possibility of equal rights for men and women and eliminate what they referred to as the "slave prostitute" population.

Yet the debate about reforming regulated prostitution represented far more than a discussion of VD control. In the atmosphere of public despair and searing self-criticism that characterized the prewar medical establishment, the image of the sexually licentious prostitute served as a lightning rod for attacks on the wider social disorder plaguing the Polish nation. The prostitute's disease-ridden body, with its ability to infect ever-wider circles of clients and their innocent families, became a symbol for the rot eating away at the national corpus. As Mary Douglas suggests in *Purity and Danger*, the human body often functions as "a model which can stand for any bounded system." In the Polish case, the image of the public woman became a foil for debating the hopes and anxieties implicit in the nation itself. Leading advocates for both reform initiatives took aggressive aim at public sex and transformed prostitution into a paradigmatic problem at the heart of national resurrection. The sex worker's status as an object of state regulation and public control helped reinforce the tacit correlation between her physical form and the health of the larger nation.

These sharply divergent directions in Polish thinking came about as a result of decades-long frustration with the problem of paid sex and the failed efforts to stem its tide. Medical experts throughout the Polish territories despaired of finding a solution to commercial sex and its related disorders. A half century after the introduction of regulated prostitution, the registries of tolerated women continued to grow and thousands of undocumented prostitutes plagued the public spaces of city and country alike. Sexual diseases raged out of control, their debilitating effects reflected in deformities and early mortality rates. Worse, the moral fabric of Polish society appeared irreparably torn. Alcohol abuse, pornography, and sexual debauchery were rampant. Pundits and muckrakers highlighted the sores on the Polish social body. As patriotic despair was inscribed onto medical frustration, a peculiar form of eugenics evolved that helped tell the story of the Polish nation at the dawn of the new century. In time, elements of the abolitionist approach to prostitution reform provided the foundations of what would become a eugenics conversation in the reborn Polish state. Social engineering in the Polish context would focus overwhelmingly on pathologies such as sexual

---

5. Wernic, "Podstawowe drogi," 517–20.

deviance, leaving issues of ethnic contamination and religious difference to the side. Despite aggressive efforts over the course of two decades of political independence, however, the abolitionist camp—now closely associated with the Polish eugenics movement—faced repeated disappointments in its effort to outlaw prostitution. Supporters of neoregulation would win the day after the rebirth of the Polish Republic in 1918. We turn to the abolitionists' postwar losses and the ascendance of the neoregulationists in chapter 10. The remainder of this chapter is devoted to charting the path of the Polish abolition movement and its peculiar links to eugenics.

Abolition: The Birth of the Purity Crusade

In the spring of 1905, the Jagiellonian University professor Augustyn Wróblewski made his way to Warsaw, where, in the midst of the revolutionary fervor, he launched *Czystość*, a biweekly newspaper devoted to fighting alcoholism, venereal diseases, and prostitution.[6] The chemist and social activist brought together dozens of leading medical minds behind a reform program centered on the ills of commercial sex. He took advantage of the wave of revolutionary activism in the former capital, observing that the spirit of the times in Warsaw offered more than just "idle talk." Rather, "words and appeals had turned into action." Across the Russian-occupied city "organizations had been founded to bring about the reform of society." The new journal, as he envisioned it, would position itself at the helm of this movement and would unite antiprostitution activists in common cause.[7] Wróblewski set about constructing a transpartition antiabolitionist campaign that would unite activists in support of improved medical hygiene, equal rights for women, and social purity. This powerful mix of cultural and scientific activism helped build a movement that dominated public discussions about prostitution in the years leading up to the war and the reemergence of the Polish state.

The new journal's editorial board drew together leaders of several important reform societies, each intent on overhauling the ineffective system of prostitution control. Among them were activists involved in the Warsaw

---

6. The new periodical was founded in partnership with the feminist publication *Nowe Słowo*, which produced the first six issues. Soon thereafter, the editorial staff relocated to Warsaw, while the paper was still physically produced in Cracow, probably to avoid more rigorous tsarist censorship. "Teodora Męczkowska," *Biographical Dictionary of Women's Movements and Feminisms in Central, Eastern, and Southeastern Europe: 19th and 20th Centuries*, ed. Francisca de Haan, Krasimira Daskalova, and Anna Loutfi (Budapest, 2006), 324–26.

7. "Nasz program," *Czystość* 1, no. 1 (June 20, 1905): 1.

Hygienic Society (Warszawskie Towarzystwo Higieniczne), the Society to Combat Prostitution and Venereal Disease (Towarzystwo Walki z Nierzą-dem i Chorobami Wenerycznymi), and the League of Equal Rights for Women.[8] In addition, the short-lived clandestine organization the Society of Abolitionists (Towarzystwo Abolicjonistyczne) established its own journal, *Ogniwo* (The Link), in 1902, but this was quickly shut down by tsarist agents fearful of losing the ability to spy on Polish rebels through the brothel system.[9] Each of these organizations had been active in combatting particular aspects of the prostitution nexus—the reduction of communicable diseases, restricting human trafficking, and eliminating the sexual double standard—and their membership overlapped.

Wróblewski's genius was to unite the energies of these camps behind a single campaign to abolish prostitution. The VD specialist Antoni Wysłouch, for example, stressed the dismal "hygienic implications" of the existing prostitution regime.[10] Polish feminists such as Teodora Męczkowska and Maria Turzyma decried the system's sexual inequality, pointing out that the failure to subject both males and females to medical exams perpetuated a sexual double standard. To their motto, "one law and one morality for both sexes," women's rights groups added a concern for protecting innocent wives and children. A "large portion of the younger generation," they complained, was "wasting away because of incurable and horrible diseases." Consequently, their own innocent daughters paid "throughout their entire lives for the sins they [themselves] did not commit" and invariably "give birth to weak infants . . . sick with congenital syphilis."[11]

By far the strongest impulse in Wróblewski's new program, however, was a purity initiative rooted in efforts to reorient and restrict private behavior. It is this wing of the movement that Wróblewski soon dominated. "Purity" advocates, who headed up ethical societies across the Polish landscape, argued

---

8. The Warsaw Hygiene Society, founded in 1898, included among its membership the anti-prostitution activist (and future founder of the Polish Eugenics Society) Leon Wernic and Antoni Wysłouch, who worked through the journal *Zdrowie* to circulate information about the dangers of prostitution.

9. *Ogniwo* was edited and published under the leadership of Stanisław Posner, head of the Circle of Polish Abolitionists. The paper became the center of activism around the young abolitionist movement and featured texts by leading Polish antiprostitution activists like the feminist Teodora Męczkowska, the antitrafficking expert Antoni Wysłouch, and the doctors Leon Wernic and Maurycy Bornstein. Wacław Wesołowski, "Walka z chorobami wenerycznymi a obrona rasy," *Zagadnienia Rasy* 1, no. 1 (July 1918): 11; and Ryszard Zabłotniak, "Dzieje Polskiego Towarzystwa Eugenicznego," *Kwartalnik Historii Nauki i Techniki* 16, no. 4 (1971): 770.

10. Wysłouch also stressed the "social injustice, moral monstrousness, and violations of individual rights" implicit in the system. Wysłouch, *Prostytucya i jej skutki*, 35

11. "Kroniki," *Nowe Słowo*, April 1, 1903, 155–56.

that syphilis and related sexual diseases could only be prevented through a nationwide campaign to change sexual norms. *Czystość* served as the press organ for disparate purity associations across the Congress Kingdom and Galicia, whose members used the newspapers' columns to publicize their own programs.[12] As one fourteen-year-old subscriber confided to his fellow readers, "the majority of our youth . . . is demoralized and a significant portion is sick with venereal diseases."[13] The newspaper helped turn such decentralized local activism into a nationwide movement, bringing together the voices of dozens of purity societies, many of which had been founded in direct response to the 1903 publication of the Warsaw Survey of Youth Sexual Practices.[14] As one enthusiastic reader commented, the new paper quickly became the voice of the "purity camp" (*obóz czystych*).[15] Members focused on maintaining physical and moral health, while encouraging those suffering from sexual diseases to seek medical attention. Ethical circles also sprung up in secondary schools across Galicia, technically violating Austrian law since many of them were politically affiliated, either with the National Democrats or with the Socialists.[16] All these associations worked to combat

---

12. Among these were the Ethos Society (Akademickie Towarzystwo Ethos) and the Society for the Defense of Youth (Ochrona Młodzieży) founded in Lwów in 1905, the Society for the Purity of Morals (Towarzystwo Czystości Obyczajów), and the Society for Combating Venereal Diseases and Promoting the Principles of Abolitionism (Towarzystwo dla Walki z Chorobami Wenerecznymi i Szerzenie Zasad Abolicjionizmu). Magdalena Gawin, "Progressivism and Eugenic Thinking in Poland, 1905–1939," in *Blood and Homeland: Eugenics and Racial Nationalism in Central and Southeast Europe, 1900–1940*, ed. Marius Turda and Paul J. Weindling (Budapest, 2007), 169–70; and "Towarzystwo 'Ochrona młodzieży,'" *Czystość* 1, no. 4 (August 1, 1905); 31–32. supplement to *Nowe Słowo*: 31–32.

13. Letter from Zygmunt Osterzetzer, a fourteen-year-old gymnasium student, to *Czystość* 1, no. 4 (August 1, 1905): 34.

14. Warsaw's Zdrowie Młodzieży, an organization intended to promote sexual purity among gymnasia pupils, and its parallel organization for university students, Zdrowie Młodzieży Akademickiej, opened their doors soon after the survey's publication. The Zdrowie society drew on the preexisting efforts of organizations such as the Kółka Etyczne founded in individual gymnazia, which largely folded their activities into those of Zdrowie after 1902. By 1905, some three hundred pupils had joined the citywide organization and participated in regular hikes and open-air outings. H. R., "Zdrowie młodzieży," *Czystość* 1, no. 5 (August 15, 1905): 43–45. "'Eleusis,' katolickie towarzystwo bezwzględnej poczwórnej wstrzemięźliwości," *Czystość* 1, no. 1 (June 20, 1905): 7; "Wyjątki ze statute akademickiego Tow. 'Ethos,'" *Czystość* 1, no. 1 (June 20, 1905): 6–7; "Powitanie Obyczajowego wiecu publicznego oraz Sekcji IV. Zjazdu kobiet polskich w Krakowie," *Czystość* 1, no. 9 (October 15, 1905): 81–82; "Wiadomości bieżące," *Czystość* 1, no. 8 (October 6, 1905): 79–80 and Wyrobek, *Śmiertelność i choroby,* 1–2.

15. Zdzisław Dębicki, "Obóz czystych," *Gazeta Polska,* in *Czystość* 1, no. 8 (October 1, 1905): 79–80.

16. Those affiliated with the Warsaw Zdrowie movement remained politically unaffiliated and aligned themselves with the "czyści ludzie" or purity movement "Wiadomości bieżące," *Czystość* 1, no. 7 (September 15, 1905): 63–64.

pornography and alcohol abuse, to encourage physical fitness, and to promote education about sexual danger in the schools. The postrevolutionary atmosphere in the Polish lands created space for an organized battle to transform public morals, including the abandonment of the entrenched system of regulated prostitution, a subject that had been virtually taboo in mainstream journals.

Czystość was a direct outgrowth of the "Ethos" Society Wróblewski helped found at Jagiellonian University in 1902.[17] The Cracow organization was established to draw attention to questions of juvenile sexual morality through regular lectures and the circulation of educational material. Wróblewski himself was a colorful personality who drew on his own vivid past to motivate his audiences. His speeches were spiked with reflections on the bawdy behavior of his youth, his "addiction" to alcohol and prostitution, and long periods mired in the red-light districts of Warsaw, Petersburg, and elsewhere.[18] By reprising his own moral exoneration, he modeled the possibility of recovery from the depths of debauchery. A teetotaling anarcho-syndicalist who contributed to socialist publications and societies, Wróblewski also espoused atheist and anticlerical views, an orientation that regularly incurred the displeasure of Habsburg authorities.[19] More than this, though, Wróblewski was a Polish patriot who hailed from a passionately nationalist political family in Vilnius. His father and older brother had both spent time in tsarist prisons and in Siberia for their underground activities and Wróblewski himself was dedicated to the resurrection of a healthy Polish state. He had learned as a young child to see the world through the eyes of the Siberian exiles with whom his father had shared his own youth.[20] Wróblewski's belief was that by encouraging those who "love the fatherland and wish to serve it" to reform their personal behavior he could bring about a national renaissance.[21]

The abolitionist strategy involved a program of social reform that was revolutionary in its scope. Rather than "merely highlighting the singular

---

17. The affiliation lay at the root of the editor's troubles with the Austrian government. Soon after the Ethos Society and its newspaper, *Eleusis,* were launched, Wróblewski was incarcerated in a psychiatric hospital in Cracow and accused of "chronic paranoia." He was not released until 1905, when he left Cracow for Warsaw. Ignacy Z. Siemion, "Sława i zniesławienie: O życiu i pracach Augustyna Wróblewskiego," *Analecta: Studia i Materiały z Dziejów Nauki* 11, nos. 1–2 (2002): 251–97.

18. "O moralności płcowej," *Czystość* 1, no. 25 (July 1, 1905): 12–15.

19. Wróblewski also briefly edited *Przyszłość*, an anti-alcohol journal, and made abstinence a centerpiece of his ethical campaign.

20. Siemion, "Sława i zniesławienie," 252–53.

21. Augustyn Wróblewski, "O moralności płciowej," *Czystość* 1, no. 4 (August 1, 1905): 33–34.

evil of prostitution and venereal diseases," leaders sought a complete transformation of morals, emphasizing improved ethical standards and sex habits for the "mass" of Polish people.[22] First, the abolitionists set out to eliminate the demand for prostitution by encouraging abstinence from sex outside of marriage. Abstinence for young men was a deeply unpopular stance, however. Popular belief maintained that refraining from sexual intercourse for long periods was harmful both physically and mentally for adult males. Yet abolitionists insisted sexual restraint was "recommended by progressive physicians" and was the only guaranteed way to avoid contamination. Experts at the 1902 Brussels Congress of Doctors, they explained, advised that "purity" (i.e., abstinence) was central to preventing venereal ailments.[23] Venereal ailments, they stressed, comprised a "grave social danger, against which [we] have an obligation to defend [ourselves]" in order to maintain a competitive labor force and healthy offspring.[24] The tradition of late marriage among upper-class males made restraining sexual desires until marriage all the more important. Men in certain socioeconomic strata were putting off marriage until age thirty-five, on average, often relying on prostitutes for close to twenty years. Wróblewski and others set out to convince Poles that abstinence before marriage was not harmful, even offering the example of leading experts who supported the policy, among them Alfred Fournier and Josephine Butler.[25]

Second, and related to the prohibition on sex outside of marriage, abolitionists supported the complete reconstitution of romantic relations between men and women. Courtship, they argued, should be approached on the basis of "pure brotherhood and sympathy," sentiments that would preclude sensual passions and build a purer form of romantic love. This type of association was "biologically proven" to "benefit the soul" and "elevate the spirit." Ethos leaders, for example, encouraged young men to pursue "spiritual work" during their young adult years, thereby delaying marriage until the age of thirty, when the "body and the mind are fully formed."[26] This new foundation for romantic love would help society move toward a "hygienic system that will

22. Andrzej Baumfeld, "O czystości kilka uwag," *Czystość* 1, no. 3 (July 15, 1905): 17–20.

23. Drs. Neisser in Wrocław and Strohmberg from Dorpat (Tartu) both argued for promoting abstinence as the key to VD prevention. See Wysłouch, *Prostytucja i jej skutki*, 24–26.

24. Review of Dr. Antoni Blumenfeld, *Prostycya i hygiena płciowa* (Lwów 1905) in *Czystość* 1, no. 9 (October 15, 1905): 91–93.

25. Among those who had lent their support to the Polish purity movement were Krafft-Ebing, the Austrian expert in sexual pathologies, and the Polish syphilologists Leon Wernic, Nusbaum, and Blumenfeld. Wróblewski, *O prostytucji*, 38.

26. Review of Professor Dr. Paul Christ, *Sinnlichkeit und Sittlichkeit* (Zurich, 1904), *in Czystość* 1, no. 9 (October 15, 1905): 91–93.

defend us from immorality."[27] Finally, purity advocates hoped to promote their crusade through schools and other health-educational programs. Both in the family and in the classroom, youth had to be taught about the dangers of sexual relations, about the implications of venereal diseases, and about the need for self-restraint to stem the spread of debauchery.

Enter the Nation

Although founded in opposition to prostitution use, the purity initiative comprised a much wider program of behavior modification that represented a new wing of nationalist activism. From its inception, the movement positioned itself as the embodiment of national revival and a step in the nationalist debate, one that addressed the campaign to regain Polish independence on a moral rather than a political level. By conducting the discussion about a prospective national renaissance in an ethical rather than a military idiom, educated Poles managed, for the most part, to voice their concerns about the nation's future and plot a course for national revival without risking the censure of the partitioning powers. Integral to this platform was the notion that the eighteenth-century leadership classes had failed the nation by indulging in sexual promiscuity, excessive alcohol consumption, and improprieties toward lower-class women, setting a low moral standard for the entire society and causing citizens to neglect their political obligations. Wróblewski mapped out these nationalist claims at a youth conference in Cracow. The Polish *szlachta* or gentry in the old eighteenth-century commonwealth (*rzeczpospolita*), he claimed, consistently abused its authority, "taking advantage of the charms of rural virgins." Polish kings themselves set a tragic example of unrelenting debauchery. From Augustus of Saxony to Stanisław Augustus Poniatowski, Poland's last king, the behavior of Polish monarchs helped support a "string of brothels" along the Vistula River and the dramatic expansion of prostitution usage among noblemen. Wild sexual liaisons and binge drinking, Wróblewski declared, were the main vices that led to the collapse of the Polish state. Such practices were confirmed under the partitions, he complained.[28]

Tolerated prostitution was "devouring our nation" through disease and immoral behavior, Wróblewski noted. "Why does such a system continue to exist among us? Why must we tolerate evil, destroying our nation's moral

27. Wróblewski, "O moralności płciowej," *Czystość* 1, no. 4 (August 1, 1905), 32–34.
28. Ibid., 20–22.

and physical strength? Why do we, who dream of the rebirth of our nation, not defend against the existence of these nests of corruption?"[29] Wróblewski's new ethics society set out to clean up sexual immorality as part of an explicitly nationalist campaign. The newspaper's banner boldly proclaimed that "immorality loses the nation," whereas "improving morality rescues the nation." The entire agenda of ethics reform was thus directed at the "interests of the . . . whole Polish nation" and the rebirth of that nation through its purification. Editors advised readers to bear in mind that "people who are more moral, people who are more abstemious, more pure, who are capable of taking care of themselves can also better fulfill every social and civic responsibility" within a reunited and resurrected national body.[30]

The most effective means of reforming the population's corrupt morals was to address the habits of elite youth who represented the future of the nation. Gymnasium and university students bore a disproportionate share of responsibility for ethical reform. "From the breast of the noble Polish youth," Wróblewski proclaimed, "should come the cry to the entire land: Down with prostitution! Polish youth ought to set an example, to lead their society toward a pure moral life; it should show that it despises the wretched institution that is ruining their health, their morality, the sublimity of their thought and the purity of their feelings."[31] Images of reformed adolescents served as a powerful metaphor for a reborn Poland in Wróblewski's conception. His depiction of moral collapse and salvation were told through the fall and rise of individual students, and especially of his own youthful indiscretions. Reflecting on his personal biography, the physician outlined the road to national salvation. "I myself have suffered through moral collapse," he confessed, noting how he faced "battles with temptation that overcame me." Wróblewski's experience of "deep collapse and a moral exoneration" was offered both as an inspirational example to his youthful audience and a powerful metaphor of national redemption. Despite being raised in a deeply religious and moral household, surrounded by the ideas of "patriotism and devotion," Wróblewski had been driven by his renegade schoolmates to the depths of debauchery. Nonetheless, he was eventually able to redeem himself and embark on the "road of purity" in order to commit himself fully to "our poor Fatherland." Nation, morality, reform—this was the message Wróblewski and his colleagues sought to convey to a new generation of

29. Wróblewski, "O moralności płciowej," *Czystość* 1, no. 3 (July 15, 1905): 20–22.

30. Wróblewski, "O moralności płciowej," part 1, *Czystość* 1, no. 1 (June 20, 1905): 2–3; and part 2, no. 2 (July 1, 1905): 12.

31. Wróblewski, "O moralności płciowej," July 15, 1905, 22.

Polish national leaders. Here, the personal became the political. Reform of one's individual habits was key to national revival.[32]

University students were the first line of defense in combating tolerated prostitution. Purity activists appealed to them to help rescue the nation from its moral downfall. "I see in the hall many university students," one lecturer noted. These youth called themselves the "head of the nation" and "future leaders of society." Yet this was the very cohort that was most complicit in maintaining the system of regulated prostitution across the Polish lands. Rates of sexual illness and prostitution usage were far higher among elite youth than working-class males. Unmarried young men of means comprised the chief clients of prostitutes. Over 85 percent of Warsaw university students used prostitutes, the speaker proclaimed. In Cracow, the number of infected university students grew steadily each year. "You are all sick with venereal diseases," remarked a professor of syphilology and dermatology gloomily at Jagiellonian University. In Lwów, experts claimed that prostitution usage and related sexual infections began as early as age fourteen among gymnasium students.[33] This was not the population the Poles could rely on to resurrect a strong national state. Poland's cultural vanguard had to reform its own practices to lead the society as a whole.[34] University youth had to become "those who are the most moral, who wear in their hearts the seed of the rebirth of society."[35]

A Challenge to the Empires

Discussion of the ills of prostitution offered a way to represent the ongoing damage rendered by foreign occupation of Polish soil. Underaged prostitution, trafficking in women, and levels of venereal contamination were far worse "*u nas*" than in the "West" or in "civilized Europe," partially because of Poland's status as an imperial subject.[36] Even in the context of the states

---

32. Wróblewski, "O moralności płciowej," July 1, 1905, 12–15.

33. Łazowski and Siwicki, "Życie płciowe warszawskiej młodzieży akademickiej," as cited in Wróblewski, *O prostytucji*, 33–35.

34. These statistics were taken from Blaschko's study of Berlin, where 25 percent of university students suffered from venereal diseases in the early 1900s, in contrast to only 8 percent of workers. Wróblewski, *O prostytucji*, 40.

35. Wróblewski, *O prostytucji*, 41.

36. See, for example, Antoni Wysłouch's rant on the public-health implications of tolerated prostitution in the Polish lands in contrast with the "civilized West." *Prostytucya i jej skutki*, 30–32. Similarly, the *Czystość* editorial in its inaugural issue notes that "in the West, we are seeing increasingly frequent opinions against" regulated prostitution. The hope is clearly that Poles might model their purity campaign after similar movements in Western Europe. "Precz z prostytucyą i nierządem," *Czystość* 1, no. 1 (June 20, 1905): 5–6.

controlling Polish territory, they complained, Polish-speaking provinces were underserved and rarely privy to educational programs that cautioned youth against the dangers of prostitution. Most West European universities offered education about sexual diseases upon matriculation, warning students about the risks entailed in turning to prostitutes. Matriculates to the University of Vienna received such information, but those at provincial Polish academies, such as Cracow and Lwów, did not and consequently resorted more cavalierly to venal sex.[37]

This imperial relationship between the Polish provinces and the foreign rulers that governed them provided the backdrop to discussions about Polish sexual mores. Bordellos were painted as explicit symbols of "slavery and despair," reflecting Poland's politically subject position.[38] How could Polish society hope to cleanse itself of immoral sexual practices if the country remained in a subservient relationship to the governing powers? Of what use was it to work to eliminate debilitating diseases and "purify" the Polish body politic when an impure foreign influence remained? As the *Czystość* contributor Andrzej Baumfeld summed up, "to abstain from prostitution in order to protect oneself and one's offspring from disease, and at the same time (as a Pole) to bow toward a foreign government . . . is like keeping one shoe clean and well brushed while leaving the other muddy and covered with dung. *This second shoe propagates the stink*" (emphasis in the original).[39] For activists like Baumfeld, personal chastity was directly tied to national salvation. Efforts to achieve greater social hygiene and reduce the impact of diseases could only strengthen the national body in the absence of the corrupting influence of foreign occupiers. Liberation from foreign rule was wound deeply into the goals of the movement for Polish purity activists. Prostitution reform had become a means to national revival, turning the movement for social purity into nothing short of a liberation campaign by other means.

Purity's Nemesis: *Świat Płciowy* and Neoregulation

Purity activists approached their campaign as a morality tale tied to the survival of the Polish nation. They played off reports circulated in an opposing Polish journal, this one produced some 300 kilometers to the east in the bawdy provincial capital of Lwów. *Świat Płciowy* (Sexual World) began publication at the same moment as *Czystość* and set about exposing the

---

37. "Kroniki," *Nowe Słowo* 2 (April 1, 1903): 155.
38. Wysłouch, *Prostytucya i jej skutki*, 32.
39. Baumfeld, "O czystości kilka uwag," 18.

gritty sexual underworld of urban life. Standing in almost complete opposition to its rival in Cracow, *Świat Płciowy*'s coverage explored the casual
sexual encounters of household servants, the drama of impoverished parents
forcing their daughters onto the street, and the unwritten code requiring
female industrial workers to have sex with their foremen. The paper ran
advertisements for birth control and reported on women who abandoned
or aborted their infants.[40] Editors of both journals shared a sense of crisis
rooted in the sexual ethics of the time. *Czystość* editors characterized the
contents of *Świat Płciowy* as "pornographic," pointing especially to stories
that addressed the colorful realities of prostitution or featured advertisements
for birth control.[41] In order to discredit the social reformers who managed
the competing journal, *Czystość* writers called for its boycott. The purity
camp accused *Świat Płciowy* of "masquerading in the clothing of science,"
circulating "demoralizing contents," and at the same time giving Poland's
younger generation "a lesson in pornography." The sexual detail splashed
across the pages of the new paper was represented as virtually treasonous.
Czystość editors accused *Świat Płciowy* of working against the national cause.
Attention to the more ribald aspects of life in the Galician capital city had
to be discouraged. "Is this not a shame on Galician society . . . is it not an
embarrassment for the Polish press?"[42]

Abolitionists also turned their critical eye to avant-garde artists such as
Felicien Rops, the Belgian Symbolist (1833–1898) whose semi-erotic work
was on display in Warsaw and Cracow in 1909, to demonstrate the limits
of Polish patriotic engagement. *Czystość* commentators struggled with the
painter's immense popularity, advising that "the most effective way to escape
from sexual imagery," such as that featured in many of Rops's paintings, was
"to avoid it altogether" and steer clear of the exhibits. They were clear that
such artistic decadence had "no place at the Polish table" and cautioned that
the presence of the works on Polish territory would "ruin" Polish gallery
visitors young and old. But they reserved their harshest judgment for the
work of Polish painters like the Symbolist and Matejko-trained member of

---

40. On Polish-language papers addressing issues of female sexuality, see Anna Pawłowska, "Kwestie
etyczno-obyczajowe"; and Bożena Urbanek, "Zagadnienia seksualności w polskich poradnikach
medycznych I poł. XX–do1939 r," *Medycyna Nowożytna: Studia nad Historią Medycyny* 12, nos. 1–2
(2005): 163–80. On the significance of *Czystość*, see Magdalena Gawin, *"Rasa i nowoczesność": Historia polskiego ruchu eugenicznego (1880–1952)* (Warsaw, 2003).

41. Interestingly, *Czystość* ran vivid descriptions of artwork it labeled pornographic, including
advice on how to overcome physical discomfort resulting from exposure to pornography. "Artyzm
a pornografia," *Czystość* 5, no. 3 (1909): 472–74.

42. "Świat Płciowy," *Czystość* 1, nos. 13–14 (1905): 171–72.

Young Poland Jacek Malczewski (1854–1929), whose work was the focus of sharp criticism by writers like Maria Konopnicka and Eliza Orzeszchowa. In the ribald atmosphere of prewar eastern Europe, sexual innuendo appeared omnipresent: on the boulevards, in the galleries, across the pages of the popular press—as well as in the doctors' offices and clinics, where the implications of sexual excesses played out on a daily basis. For purity activists like the contributors clustered around *Czystość* all of these improprieties had nationalist implications. The purity campaign was pitched at the level of individual practice, but its agenda encompassed the far larger horizon of national renewal and the rebirth of a cleaner, more moral Polish state.

In the end, *Czystość*'s appeal to moral suasion outlived the muckraking sensibilities of *Świat Płciowy*, which closed its doors in 1907 along with many other revolutionary-era publications. *Czystość* survived until 1913 and its contributors later found a home at the press organ for the new Polish eugenics association *Zagadnienia Rasy* (Race Issues). Indeed, it was in *Czystość* that some of the first proposals for combatting social pathologies through eugenics programs appeared.[43] These writers played on heightened public awareness of the long-term effects of sexual ribaldry to launch a new effort aimed at curbing sexual licentiousness and preventing genetic harm to future generations.

The Biological Basis of Sexual Deviance

Frustrated with their inability to eliminate the effects of venereal diseases through curative powers, the Polish scientific community borrowed a page from specialists in Western Europe and focused increasingly on prevention. Specifically, doctors and other scientists sought to limit further contamination by controlling the process of reproduction. Across Europe, members of a new field called criminal anthropology or forensic anthropology partnered with biologists to isolate the links between genetic inheritance and social deviance. Combining the study of inherited traits with an understanding of environmental influences, specialists researched techniques to strengthen the qualities of unborn children. Polish physicians were similarly preoccupied with the link between rampant prostitution and degenerative characteristics.

---

43. In addition to Gawin on Polish eugenics, see Zabotniak, "Dzieje Polskiego Towarzystwa Eugenicznego"; Krzysztof Kawalec, "Spór o eugenikę w Polsce w latach 1918–1939," *Medycyna Nowożytna: Studia nad Kulturą Medyczną* 7, no. 2 (2000): 87–102; and Michał Musielak, *Sterylizacja ludzi ze względów eugenicznych w Stanach Zjednoczonych, Niemczech i w Polsce (1899–1945): Wybrane problemy* (Poznań, 2008).

Abolitionists led the campaign for greater appreciation of the biological implications of sexual immorality. Antoni Wysłouch, a founding member of the *Czystość* group, stressed the medical implications of police-regulated prostitution in one of the journal's early issues, arguing that sexual debauchery led directly to "degeneration, the bastardization of the species and of the race." Dr. Wysłouch reminded his readers of innocent wives who contracted diseases through their profligate husbands and passed them onto their unborn children. The damaged infants who survived the early weeks of life, he pointed out, bore the physical marks of sexual dysfunction their entire lives, often passing these genetic abnormalities onto their own offspring.[44]

Such inherited deficiencies, Wysłouch cautioned, had a lasting impact on the overall decline of the human race. From deafness to mental retardation, syphilis and gonorrhea brought permanent deformities to the human organism. "Some [patients] wear the fatal mark of the disease on certain organs such as teeth, skull, nose, eyes, mouth, etc.," Wysłouch explained. "Others have their entire organism affected, such as infantile senility, infantilism among older adults, or the so-called *rachityzm*, which is a swelling of the head and curving of the legs. Finally, although rarely, the inherited trait may appear in a new generation born as monsters."[45] Along with these disorders, Wysłouch noted, venereal illnesses were implicated in a frightening number of other ailments, including psychopathy, neuropathy, hysteria, infertility, and epilepsy.[46] The epidemic of sexual diseases had unleashed a decline in fertility and damaged physical and mental capacities in those who survived.

Polish medical experts pushed their notion of "hereditary" ailments one step further. Taking a page from West European researchers, they argued that inherited deformities often *caused* resort to prostitution. In this sense, preventing mental and physical incapacity in newborn children might help curtail the turn to paid sex later in life. The physician and member of the Warsaw Hygienic Society Władysław Chodecki cited Italian and German scholarship to demonstrate that severe physical or mental degeneration was present in a disproportionate number of registered prostitutes. In addition, a Dr. Bonhoffer in Wrocław discovered signs of mental illness or deficiencies in the majority of prostitutes he studied. Out of a group of 190 prostitutes incarcerated at a prison in Wrocław, Bonhoffer reported, some 68 percent displayed signs of profound abnormalities. Twenty-eight percent were imbeciles, 3 percent idiots, 5 percent suffered from hysteria, 7 percent from

---

44. Wysłouch, *Prostytucya i jej skutki*, 12.
45. Ibid., 12–17.
46. Ibid., 16.

epilepsy, and another 21 percent were habitual alcoholics.[47] Preventing or curing mental illness, he concluded, could likely also reduce the number of practitioners in the sex trade.

Bonhoffer and Chodecki both drew on the work of the Italian scholar Cesare Lombroso, father of the concept of the "born criminal." Lombroso famously claimed to have discovered physiological connections linking prostitution with the "handicapped organization of the brain." According to Chodecki, Lombroso's data showed that prostitutes suffered from unusually small brain capacity and a whole string of other abnormalities, including "anomalous teeth, wolfish jaws, and asymmetrical facial features."[48] Such evidence would encourage Polish practitioners in the postwar period to promote legal restrictions on marriage between people displaying inherited anomalies.[49] Lombroso's theory that the turn to prostitution resulted from genetic disorders was influential in scholarly debates partly because it gave "the appearance of extreme scientific rigor" to explain the sharp increase in women resorting to paid sex.[50] His study of the "born prostitute," first published in 1893, argued that female criminality and most significantly prostitution were fundamentally biological in origin and that female "deviant" social behavior was rooted in sexuality. He portrayed prostitutes as closely related to the "primitive woman" with "atavistic" mental capacity and physical abilities.[51] The prostitute, Lombroso contended, was closer to the savage than the "honest woman" and possessed "weak cranial and orbital capacities." Women who worked as prostitutes typically were driven into the sex trade at a young age because of "moral insanity." According to this theory, prostitutes did not share the same feelings of modesty, family ties, or affection that "normal" women enjoyed.

The results of this research were circulated widely among European and North American academics, helping establish Lombroso as an important figure in the birth of the new field of criminal anthropology. At the same time, theories of biologically rooted social deviance also found their origin

---

47. Bonhoffer, cited in Chodecki, "Alkoholism a prostytucya," 302.
48. Chodecki, "Alkoholism a prostytucya," 302.
49. On the early years of the Polish eugenics movement, see Gawin, "Progressivism."
50. Corbin, *Women for Hire,* 300–301.
51. Lombroso published his theory in Italian under the title *La donna delinquent* (*Criminal Woman*). It is important that Lombroso's ideas about the biological roots of criminal deviance were circulated as early as 1876 in his study *Criminal Man* (*L'uomo delinquent*). Cesare Lombroso and Guglielmo Ferrero, *Criminal Woman, the Prostitute, and the Normal Woman,* trans. and with a new introduction by Nicole Hahn Rafter and Mary Gibson (Durham, NC, 2004); and Mary Gibson, *Born to Crime: Cesare Lombroso and the Origins of Biological Criminology* (Westport, CT, 2002).

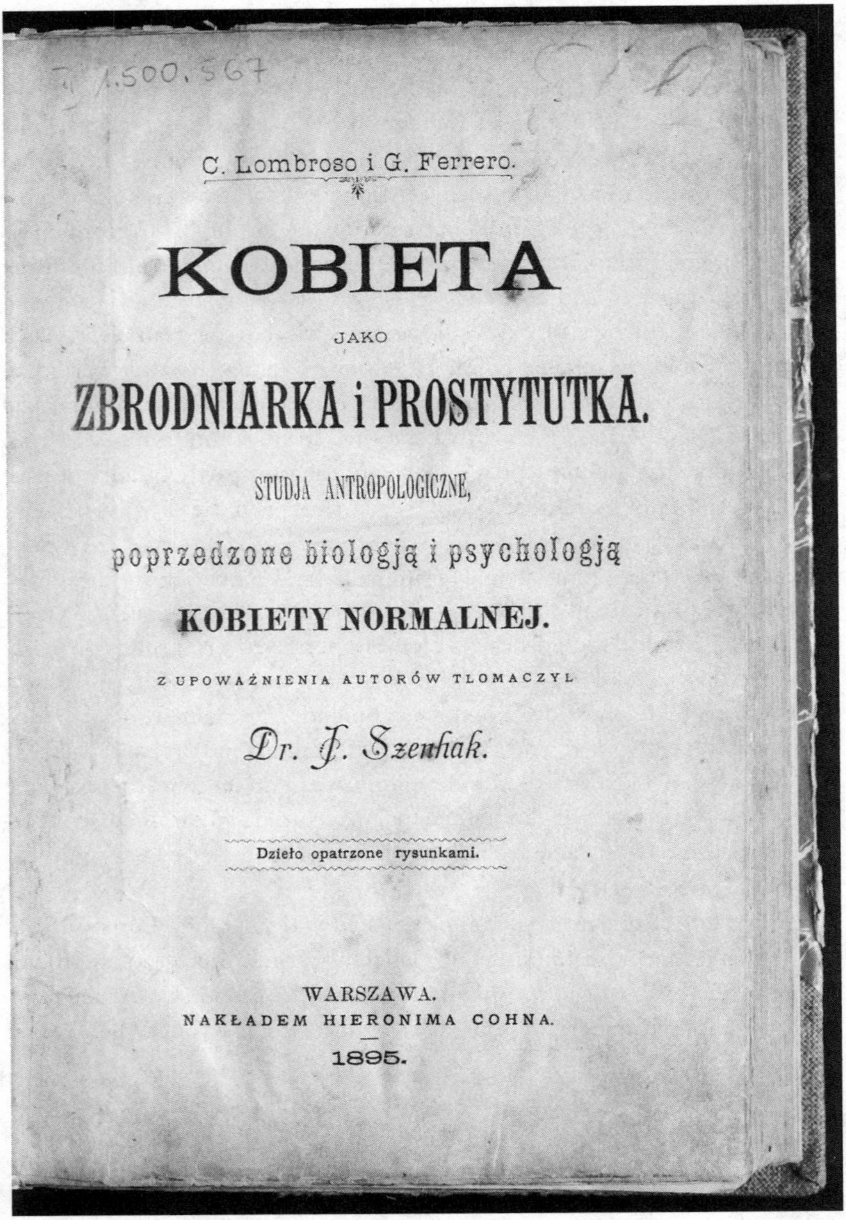

C. Lombroso i G. Ferrero.

KOBIETA

JAKO

ZBRODNIARKA i PROSTYTUTKA.

STUDJA ANTROPOLOGICZNE,

poprzedzone biologją i psychologją

KOBIETY NORMALNEJ.

Z UPOWAŻNIENIA AUTORÓW TLOMACZYL

Dr. J. Szenhak.

Dzieło opatrzone rysunkami.

WARSZAWA.
NAKŁADEM HIERONIMA COHNA.
1895.

FIGURE 9.1 Lombroso's *Criminal Woman, the Prostitute, and the Normal Woman* in its 1895 Polish translation. The book was translated into Polish almost immediately after its original 1893 Italian printing.

in Russian research, including that conducted by the Russian anthropologist Paulina Tarnovska (Tarnowsky), studies to which Polish scholars had easy access. Tarnovska collaborated closely with Lombroso, providing over one hundred case studies of Moscow prostitutes that helped shape his theories. She, however, published her Russian-language work before Lombroso's study was released.[52] For both Tarnovska and Lombroso, professional prostitutes bore signs of inherited personality disorders such as extreme lack of affection, violent jealousy, a wish for revenge, a weak sense of personal property and feeling of friendship, atrophy of maternal instinct, as well as a tendency to physical violence and to greed. The two scholars claimed that the intelligence of the prostitute was well below average, that she was voracious and had a predisposition for alcohol abuse, and that prostitutes had developed sexual frigidity as a "Darwinian adaptation." Sex workers could perform the sexual act easily because it was both morally and physically insignificant to them.[53] According to these theories, the inclination to perform sex work was an inherited tendency and scientists could help repair this degenerate inheritance if they were given greater control over at-risk women.

The theory of degeneration and the new "scientific" field of eugenics helped elevate medicine at a time when the profession was particularly bloated. A glut of medically trained professionals made physicians eager to expand their domain by claiming special expertise in new fields. Medical men were at the center of the debate about social dysfunction. As Robert Nye has emphasized, "the most powerful spokesmen for this unified way of viewing social deviance were doctors. Medical men had enough training in basic science to be credible as scientific mediators between the mysteries of the clinic and the vexing problems of everyday life. Doctors were also well organized, thoroughly secular and political in their outlook, and fierce defenders of their professional and social prerogatives."[54] In Germany the number of practicing doctors doubled in the last quarter of the nineteenth century, prompting young physicians to "colonize new areas for medicine, such as sexuality, mental illness, and deviant social behavior" in order to increase their clientele.[55] Physicians in France and Germany

---

52. Tarnovska published her own study of the biological characteristics of prostitutes in 1889. See Lombroso and Ferrarro, *Criminal Woman*, 37, 140, 264, n.11.

53. Corbin, *Women for Hire*, 303.

54. Robert A. Nye, *Crime, Madness, and Politics in Modern France: The Medical Concept of National Decline* (Princeton, NJ, 1984), xi.

55. The institution of national health insurance in 1883 prompted a rush to study medicine to profit from state-funded medical care, bringing about an enormous overpopulation of physicians in the German Reich. Paul Weindling, *Health, Race, and German Politics between National Unification*

began labeling social dysfunction as "disease." They took responsibility for diagnosing and treating everything from suicidal tendencies to insanity, alcoholism, homicide, and theft. By the end of the nineteenth century, even cleanliness became medicalized and health professionals were consulted about disinfecting homes, railway facilities, and factories. Ailments like venereal disease and alcoholism were increasingly treated as biological rather than behavioral as the medical profession increased its influence over wider aspects of patients' lives and hospitals expanded to accommodate the increased patient load.[56]

New discoveries in biology helped enhance the prestige of eugenics discourse. By the mid-1870s, biologists understood the process of fertilization and had experimented with manipulating cell nuclei and chromosomes to demonstrate techniques of selective breeding, adding scientific credibility to medical efforts to control the quality of human reproduction. Everywhere, politics partnered with science to prompt public-health campaigns addressing declining birth rates, genetically inferior offspring, and biological damage to the nation.[57] In Britain, social anxiety about dropping birth rates and class differentials in reproduction sparked a preoccupation with "race quality" and race suicide.[58] The British questioned the fitness of their military recruits in the aftermath of their spectacular defeat in the Boer War. France and Germany witnessed similar concerns about national strength and military preparedness, compounded with worry about dropping birth rates.[59] Cities now bore the brunt of overcrowding, disease, and the poverty of the laboring classes and became "the breeding ground of a subhuman class of permanently pauperized beings known as the residuum."[60] Crime, vagrancy, and sexual deviance appeared rampant on urban streets, a view enhanced by sensationalist trials of homosexuals.[61] Italy's government struggled to explain

and Nazism, 1870–1945 (Cambridge, 1989), 7. In 1876, immediately following German unification, 13,728 doctors were licensed to practice in the Reich. By 1900, that number had grown to 27,374. Many of these new practitioners were forced to search for new specialties to justify their practice.

56. Weindling, *Health, Race, and German Politics*, 18–20. German hospital expansion in the period following unification was fast paced. In 1876, the Reich had 140,900 hospital beds; by 1900, there were over 370,000.

57. Weindling, *Health, Race, and German Politics*, 16–17.

58. Richard A. Soloway, *Demography and Degeneration: Eugenics and the Declining Birthrate in Twentieth-Century Britain* (Chapel Hill, NC, 1995).

59. France's 1870 defeat in the Franco-Prussian War followed by the unification of the German Reich threw the population into a national frenzy, spiking anxiety over stymied national growth. The French led Europe in rates of alcohol consumption and faced a rising incidence of TB and syphilis and an aging population. Nye, *Crime, Madness, and Politics*, 133–41.

60. Nye, *Crime, Madness, and Politics*, 332.

61. Weindling, *Health, Race, and German Politics*, 8; and Nye, *Crime, Madness, and Politics*, 337.

north–south distinctions in crime, disease, insanity and syphilis.[62] In Switzerland, the Zurich-based psychiatrist Auguste Forel warned that criminals, prostitutes, alcoholics, and the mentally ill comprised the greatest threat to Swiss strength. The Swiss, he warned, needed to subject their "disorderly citizens" to the collective interest of the national community.[63]

As medical science focused on the nationalist implications of degeneration theory, physicians increasingly embraced eugenics concepts as an effective model to express the hygienic needs of the total population. Eugenics became popular well before the First World War as a component of nationalist competition and a reflection of competitive military preparedness. Yet eugenics-based thinking stressed varying emphases across the Continent. French scientists favored a neo-Lamarckian approach to degeneration theory in which nature and nurture were interdependent and acquired characteristics could be transmitted from parents to children.[64] Similarly, in the Netherlands, eugenics would become marginalized as popular resistance to the medical regulation of reproduction increased.[65] Elsewhere, "soft" approaches to eugenics, combining an emphasis on improving the larger environment with hereditary explanations, were widespread.[66] Variations in intellectual and cultural practices as well as in political context and institutional conditions affected the way the new turn to eugenics manifested.[67]

Polish abolitionists were similarly preoccupied with debates about Lombroso's theories, leaning on them to help justify their antiprostitution agenda. Most adopted a position that combined (biological) nature with (social) nurture and consequently allowed them to continue fighting for purity, abstinence, and temperance. Experts in the Polish lands agreed that biological inheritance alone did not account for the dramatic rates of prostitution growth. Poverty, alcohol abuse, and an unhealthy or immoral upbringing accounted for at least part of the rising numbers of public women. Drawing on the findings of German practitioners like the dermatologist and social

62. Gibson, *Prostitution and the State in Italy*, 170.

63. Leo Lucassen, "A Brave New World: The Left, Social Engineering, and Eugenics in Twentieth-Century Europe," *International Review of Social History* 55, no. 2 (2010): 278–80.

64. William H. Schneider, *Quality and Quantity: The Quest for Biological Regeneration in Twentieth-Century France* (Cambridge, UK, 1990).

65. Elazar Barkan, *The Retreat of Scientific Racism: Changing Concepts of Race in Britain and the United States between the Two World Wars* (Cambridge, UK, 1992).

66. Mark B. Adams, ed., *The Wellborn Science: Eugenics in Germany, France, Brazil, and Russia* (Oxford, UK, 1990).

67. See, for example, P. J. Bowler, *The Non-Darwinian Revolution: Reinterpreting a Historical Myth* (Baltimore, 1988); and Frank Dikotter, "Race Culture: Recent Perspectives on the History of Eugenics," *American Historical Review* (April 1998): 467–78.

reformer Alfred Blaschko, Polish specialists labeled the vast majority of prostitutes "completely normal" in their physical and psychological characteristics, arguing that biologically induced characteristics could not account for this high level of public women from a given social class, so economic need had to play a significant role.[68]

Nonetheless, Polish specialists did not reject biological determinism completely. Many agreed Lombroso's ideas contained at least a "grain of truth" and that "a small portion of prostitutes betray[ed] abnormal traits."[69] The Warsaw physician and purity activist Władysław Chodecki, for example, supported the notion of "born prostitutes," while acknowledging that environmental factors may also have been influential. Chodecki saw evidence of anomalous brain size and facial features among women working as prostitutes and argued that this "degenerate inheritance" accounted for the spread of prostitution among certain social groups. At the same time, Chodecki asserted that this degeneracy was not all biological. Some of the deviance he found in women who worked as prostitutes was rooted in the physical and moral environment in which they were reared. "In a certain number of cases," he explained, "prostitution flourishe[d] as part of the domain of alcoholism" and was "linked to mental and moral neglect." Chodecki and other Polish medical scholars believed an unhealthy, immoral, alcohol-soaked domestic environment could prompt the resort to theft and prostitution as careers.

Even more dangerous for society as a whole, however, the predilection for sex work could be reproduced as a biological trait in later offspring, according to Chodecki. Young men who sought refuge in Warsaw's homeless shelters and drunk tanks were typically children of habitual drunks themselves, as were their prostitute sisters. Such evidence suggested, he argued, that the "whole atmosphere in which a child is raised can influence her to turn to prostitution." Children in alcoholic families, moreover, become sexually active earlier and "in this way [also] prepared for a future career as a prostitute." Organizations caring for runaway children agreed that the majority of homeless children forced by their parents to prostitute themselves were children of alcoholic fathers. Offspring in dysfunctional households rarely received extensive education and consequently had little choice but to earn their living through crime or the sex trade.

---

68. A. Blaschko, *Hygiene der Prostitution* (Jena, 1901), cited in Rosset, *Prostytucja*, 6–7; see also Paul Weindling, "Sexually Transmitted Diseases between Imperial and Nazi Germany," *Genitourinary Medicine* 70, no. 4 (1994): 284–89.

69. Rosset, *Prostytucja*, 6–7.

Nevertheless, biological inheritance was not inconsequential for the way Polish scholars understood the turn to paid sex. Specialists cited the disproportionate number of prostitutes shown to have "early onset of the menses (16 percent)," a condition they linked with peculiar sexual proclivities later in life. And children conceived while their parents were drunk also "frequently developed mental and physical handicaps," prompting many of them to turn later to theft and prostitution. Thus, according to Polish specialists, the connection between inheritance and environment was far from simple. Unwilling to adopt either Lombroso's fatalistic notion of a "born prostitute" or the idea of environmental factors playing a decisive role in the creation of a criminal, Polish scholars instead relied on a complicated blending of the two theories in which the domestic environment shaped a child's biological inheritance and physical and mental defects could come about as a result of the parents' actions.[70] In this understanding of biological causality, "nervous mothers produced nervous children" and social pathologies such as prostitution could be passed down to unborn children.[71] An overall tendency toward deviant behavior could be inherited even if the fatalistic implications of Lombroso's original thesis were rejected.

Degeneration Theory and the Birth of Polish Eugenics

One result of the nature-nurture debate was thus the creation of a common ground between the proponents of inherited criminality and those who believed environment predisposed individuals to criminal behavior. Into this interpretive gap stepped the theory of degeneracy, the scientific notion that organisms adapted to accommodate short-term needs of their environment, but that when those adaptations were passed on, they often played a dysfunctional role in later generations. Specialists in social pathologies relied on the theory to explain inherited alcohol dependency, hysteria, and sexual dysfunction. Degeneracy theory tied in easily with national anxieties about low birth rates and the high incidence of infant deformity connected to congenital syphilis. It also became a diagnosis of medical provenance. Once doctors had assumed responsibility for social pathologies such as sexually deviant behavior, compulsive gambling, or alcohol abuse, it was an easy step

---

70. Chodecki, "Alkoholism a prostytucya," 298–305.

71. Prof. Dr. Gruber, *Wychowanie dziewcząt a hygiena rasy,* reviewed in *Przegląd hygieniczny* 13, nos. 7–8 (July–August, 1914): 198–99.

for them to diagnose these practices as "degenerative" because of their negative implications for future generations.[72]

Polish specialists toyed with the idea of "inherited" social diseases long before the debate about Lombroso caught hold of the medical profession. As early as the 1840s, Polish-speaking physicians in Poznań agreed that medical disorders like tuberculosis, apoplexy, and cancer could be passed directly from mother to child, but differed over how this transmission occurred. For these midcentury physicians, the moment of conception was key to determining the genetic makeup of the fetus. T. T. Matecki argued in 1848, for example, that "the moment of impregnation was important because it was then that the parents had influence over whether the child would reflect their love through its beautiful features." By contrast, if conception was the result of "lustful and lewd love, the child would be born slow, weak, and have a horrible appearance."[73] Similarly, Polish scientists in Galicia cited the work of the Viennese psychiatrist Krafft-Ebing from the 1860s to make the case that certain disorders like "moral insanity," prostitution, and criminality were congenital. Krafft-Ebing based his conclusions on the family trees of his patients, arguing that environmental factors such as the ills of "modern civilization," "unfavorable social conditions," "particular life phases," "bad habits," or social class could contribute to degeneration and hence mental illness.[74]

Like other central European psychiatrists, Krafft-Ebing was unclear about the relationship between social pathologies and heredity, often leaving causality ambiguous or unarticulated. Similarly, Polish scholars like Wróblewski were flexible in their understandings of the causes of degeneration among prostitutes. Citing the work of Paulina Tarnovska, Wróblewski identified degeneracy as a leading cause of prostitution, but claimed this predisposition was both inherited and originated from within the environment where the girls were raised. Tarnovska's research, Wróblewski showed, demonstrated that 83 percent of Moscow prostitutes showed "some signs of degeneracy" but not all of them were born with these traits. Wróblewski argued that these "degenerate individuals" had developed their conditions either via biological inheritance or a combination of poor upbringing, unsavory working conditions, and alcoholism in the household. For this reason Wróblewski

---

72. Nye, *Crime, Madness, and Politics*, 127–30.

73. T. T. Matecki, *Poradnik dla młodych matek czyli fizyczne wychowanie dzieci w pierwszych siedmiu latach* (Poznań, 1848), 62, in Katarzyna Jargiło, "Ciąża, poród i połóg kobiety dziewiętnastowiecznej" (MA thesis, Jagiellonian University, 2005), 12.

74. Oosterhuit, *Stepchildren of Nature*, 103–5.

treated prostitution as "a social disease" that might be "cured" through social intervention.[75]

The medical implications of embracing degeneration theory were enormous. European and North American physicians began advocating restrictions on marriage for individuals suffering from degenerative disorders. Regardless of how such traits were acquired, evidence that they could be passed on to offspring was enough to launch legislation restrictive of reproductive rights. Wróblewski and other purity activists proposed an educational campaign about the dangers of extramarital sex, disease, and prostitution usage. They initiated a conversation, along with their German and British colleagues, about banning marriage between infected partners. Their proposals drew on earlier campaigns in the Habsburg lands to "prevent tainted individuals from procreating" and thus restrict the spread of mental and nervous disorders to future generations. Already in 1873, Krafft-Ebing proposed legal regulations for marriage.[76] By the early 1900s, purity activists like Leon Wernic supported the prohibition of marriage between people who suffered from "serious diseases" and between "socially unacceptable" individuals.[77]

Biology and the Polish Nation

For the Poles, discussions of biological inheritance, social environment, and national degeneracy converged around perceptions of a national crisis caused by rising rates of prostitution usage and venereal disease. The Polish Eugenics Society was formally constituted in the waning months of World War I, but the movement traced its genesis to the wave of public action to combat the sex trade on Polish territory during the early years of the century.[78] Leading members, including doctors Leon Wernic, Augustyn Wróblewski, and Antoni Wysłouch, were active in Warsaw's Society for Practical Hygiene, the parent organization of the wartime Section to Combat Venereal Diseases and Prostitution. By 1916, this important subcommittee had broken away to become an independent society on its own, forming the core of a new,

75. Wróblewski, lecture at Zgromadzenie Ludowe, Jagiellonian University, Cracow (October 27, 1907), reprinted in Wróblewski, O prostytucji, 31. Elsewhere, syphilis was labeled a "social plague" and a "social scourge," in the same category as alcoholism and tuberculosis, all of which resulted in the "degeneration and stunting of the race." Wacław Wesołowski, "Syfilis w stosunku do społecznstwa," Zdrowie 20, no. 20 (February 1904): 446–47.

76. Oosterhuit, Stepchildren of Nature, 110.

77. For Wernic, the three major sources of racial degeneration were alcoholism, prostitution, and venereal disease. See Gawin, "Progressivism," 171–72.

78. Wesołowski, "Walka z chorobami wenerycznymi," 11–12.

formal Polish eugenics organization.[79] All of these initiatives focused directly on strengthening the Polish nation by improving the inherited traits of the population, or as the Eugenics Society journal noted in 1918, the organization had its roots "in the love of fatherland, emphasizing above all other feelings the influence of inherited traits and the physical as well as psychological peculiarities that make up the basis of our race."[80] The Polish Eugenics Society evolved directly from the Society for Combating Prostitution and Venereal Diseases, whose leadership and organizational priorities it shared. Activists applied their energies in both organizations specifically to combating the "racial poisons" of alcoholism, venereal diseases, and prostitution.[81]

The turn toward more scientific language to promote prostitution reform was part of a larger shift away from an understanding of sex work purely in moral terms and toward treating it within a scientific framework. An emphasis on heredity in passing on character traits meant that social reform had little place in eradicating the problem of venal sex; this was the work of scientists and established state organs.[82] Even though (or perhaps because) physicians had failed to contain the spread of venereal disease through regulation, doctors still controlled the conversation about reforming the existing system of police regulations. The fledgling eugenics association linked the moralistic perspective of the purity camp and the bourgeois reformers with the scientific approach of professional physicians.[83] Eugenics advocates set about abolishing the regulation system as a first step on their campaign to eliminate prostitution itself and with it the immorality of men and the double sexual standard for women. Eugenics became a lever to convince the Polish public that reform was essential if the nation was to survive.

Behind the establishment of a Polish eugenics society was the conviction that social reform in general and regulation in particular had failed. Charitable and welfare activity were simply inadequate to combat the ills facing Polish society. A firmer, more organized, "scientific" approach was the only route to resolving the deep ills plaguing Polish society. The two

---

79. A. R. "Sprawozdanie z działalności Polskiego towarzystwa walki z nierządem i chorobami wenerycznymi," *Zagadniena Rasy* 1, no. 1 (July 1918): 24; and Zabotniak, "Dzieje Polskiego Towarzystwa Eugenicznego."

80. Wesołowski, "Walka z chorobami wenerycznymi," 12.

81. Gawin, *Rasa i nowoczesność*, 12.

82. Jeffrey Weeks reminds us that behind the eugenics movement everywhere was the conviction that social reform had failed or was at least insufficient to protect the "race" from extinction. Weeks, *Sex, Politics, and Society*, 129.

83. Ruth Rosen discusses this transition from moral to scientific perspectives in the American fight against prostitution around the turn of the nineteenth and twentieth centuries. Rosen, *Lost Sisterhood*, 12–13.

concerns about biological inheritance and national degeneration soon converged in discussions about the future of the independent Polish state. By
the outbreak of the Great War, the idea that Poland might return to the map
of Europe was taken increasingly seriously across the European continent.
As the war effort dragged on, Polish intellectuals began considering the
makeup of an administrative apparatus staffed by Polish nationals, but they
grew increasingly wary of the venereal threat posed by the swelling ranks
of public women. Shifting sexual practices and gender relations prompted
a return to the panicked language of the 1890s. This time, however, rather
than moral critiques about the scandalous behavior of "fallen" women and
subsequent efforts to "save" those who had strayed off the path of upright
Victorian behavior, the panic was met with a harsher, more scientific tone.
Antisocial actions were now viewed increasingly as part of a wider set of
pathologies and treated with medicalized prescriptions. Social "diseases"
were to be remedied through incarceration, isolation, and sometimes forced
medical treatment. Meanwhile, physicians had climbed in social esteem and
could be found commenting on any number of public ills. It was in this
context of public fears about the unstaunched spread of horrifying diseases,
the seemingly rampant expansion of public immorality and skewed gender
relations, and the return of the Polish nation to the map of Europe that
Poland's eugenics turn should be understood. How could all of these forces
be brought together in the resurrection of the nation state? It is to these questions that we turn in chapter 10.

Let us return to the metaphor of the human body Mary Douglas proposes
as a site for positioning broader critiques. It is important to recognize that
everywhere the body of the prostitute is subject to social analysis. As a visible
spectacle reminding us of the ungovernable elements in human nature and
of society's failure to police these impulses, prostitutes are frequently objects
of derision. During the late nineteenth century when medical science and
social-reform programs were confident they could reorient her wayward
direction, the streetwalker was approached with pity. Confident that a rising
tide would lift everyone, charity workers sought to feed, house, and retrain
prostitutes in the hopes of reabsorbing them back into the social mainstream.
The early twentieth century saw a shift in attitudes about sex workers as
science realized its limitations and devised more militant, less sympathetic
solutions to commercial sex. Among these was the notion—supported by
Lombrosian anthropology—that prostitution could not be cured, it could
only be prevented. Drawing on the work of Lombroso himself, the link
between social class and criminality allowed Polish physicians to characterize
prostitutes as "morally insane" based on their physical traits. As elite actors

everywhere contemplated how to incorporate the masses into political and social life in the late nineteenth century, their concerns about lower-class violence and criminality became all the more prescient. The new clinical definition of prostitution and its "scientific" causes provided Polish intellectuals the vocabulary to navigate these social traumas and their potential impact on the national trajectory, a debate that grew heated with the reemergence of the Polish state in 1918.

CHAPTER 10

Sex in the New Republic

> The Polish Society for Combatting Prostitution and
> Venereal Diseases [is] of the deep conviction that the
> political, economic, and cultural development of the
> Polish nation depends closely upon the strength and
> resistance of the race. . . . [We] view as the highest
> priority the risk caused by prostitution and the spread
> of venereal diseases . . . which are the subject of a
> new science—eugenics.
>
> —Inaugural issue of *Zagadnienia Rasy*, July 1918

The outbreak of the First World War in the sum-
mer of 1914 gripped Polish society with particular fury. Young men mobilized
into the armies of Austria, Germany, and Russia set off to do battle on the vast
eastern front, often opposing their own countrymen along shifting lines of
military engagement. Within a year, most of divided Poland was engulfed in
war. Battles raged in Przemyśl and Łódź, Kalisz and Brześć, destroying the country's industrial infrastructure. Tsarist troops invaded Lwów, Germans occupied
Warsaw, and Habsburg forces controlled Lublin. Even as ethnic Poles celebrated
the prospect of a European-wide war ushering in the country's long-awaited
political rebirth, the conflict brought untold human suffering and deprivation.
Repeated occupations and evacuations combined with the scorched-earth policy of both armies left the countryside in ashes, millions of hectares of farmland
destroyed, and roads, bridges, and railway lines all flattened. Displaced civilians roamed the country in search of food and shelter, hiding in forests or
abandoned buildings. Thousands of them would die of hunger and disease.[1]

---

1. Approximately 800,000 Polish civilians were deported to the Russian East and several hun-
dred thousand were sent to labor camps in Germany. Civilian deaths totaled roughly 750,000. Robert
Bideleux and Ian Jeffries, *A History of Eastern Europe: Crisis and Change* (London, 1998), 186; and
Jerzy Holzer and Jan Molenda, *Polska w pierwszej wojnie światowej* (Warsaw, 1967), 64–70. See also Jan
Lewandowski, "Austro-Węgry wobec sprawy polskiej w czasie I wojny światowej: Początki zarządu
okupacyjnego w Królestwie," *Przegląd Historyczny* 66, no. 3 (1975): 383–408.

Meanwhile, some two million Polish recruits fought alongside imperial officers for whom they felt diminishing loyalty. Thousands did not return. Still others came home maimed and incapable of resuming normal life.[2] War also took its toll on the population's sexual behavior. Desperate women, many of them wives of recruits or workers displaced by the war economy, turned to paid sex in unprecedented numbers to feed starving, fatherless families. Rates of prostitution and sexual diseases skyrocketed as furloughed soldiers sought entertainment during military leaves, passing armies took advantage of female civilians, and desperation everywhere made sex a key unit of exchange.[3] Worse yet, rural communities previously untouched by venereal contamination now suffered frightening rates of infection.

More than anything, though, war brought the prospect of political independence and, with it, both excitement and anxiety about the fragile health of the country's population. News of shocking levels of wartime VD set off debates behind the front lines about how to contain the spread of disease. Swelling ranks of full- and part-time prostitutes prompted fresh proposals to reform the antiquated regulation systems inherited from Poland's imperial rulers. As the scientific community mapped out solutions to repair the hygienic damage of the war, the prostitute's body took on a new and more powerful significance. No longer an icon of imperial occupation and degradation to be sequestered from polite society, the prostitute was becoming an important—if still cloaked—symbol of Poland's future. The incidence of women from all social castes turning to the streets transformed sex workers from creatures to be ostracized to objects of pity and concern in the early years of the war. Still, public resentment about the spread of sexual diseases continued to run high. Resolving the problem of commercial sex and its attendant diseases and rescuing Poland's poorest citizens from a life of sex work quickly consumed the new postwar administration. The seven years between the 1914 assassination of Archduke Franz Ferdinand and the end of the Polish-Soviet War in 1921 were a time of almost constant warfare, material shortages, and disruption. The war years were also a period in which Polish leaders worked feverishly to establish the administrative machinery of independence and to begin the process of uniting a disparate people into a single political entity. As desperation bred crime and immorality, the Polish

---

2. Approximately 450,000 died on the battlefield and close to 1 million were wounded. Bideleux and Jeffries, *A History of Eastern Europe*, 186.

3. Nancy M. Wingfield, "The Enemy Within: Regulating Prostitution and Controlling Venereal Disease in Cisleithanian Austria during the Great War," *Central European History* 46, no. 3 (2013): 568–98.

administration struggled to bring the body politic in line with their hopes for Poland's future. Public women in many ways lay at the heart of the campaign for national regeneration. The hopes and fears for the new state played out in debates about the business of prostitution, the body of the prostitute, and the sexual diseases for which she was ostensibly responsible.

Three sets of shifting conditions in the world of commercial sex helped focus reformers' agendas during the war and in the early years of the new Republic. First, the sheer number of women turning to the sex trade and the broad range of social backgrounds from which they came, from soldiers' wives to village girls, elicited newfound sympathy for their plight in the early postwar years. Legislative reform of prostitution regulations touched a much broader swath of the population and could be treated as a commensurately higher priority. Second, the eugenics impact of the war prompted heightened concerns about depopulation and the overall vitality of the new state's citizenry. Polish scientists were part of a Europe-wide discussion about the "science" of eugenics during the 1920s, a discussion that focused first and foremost on eliminating prostitution and reducing the impact of venereal diseases. Third, the high cost of caring for venereal patients—many of them full-time or part-time prostitutes—was to be borne by the local municipality in the new state. As rates of VD infection climbed, hospital administrators begged local government for help in treating patients during their long periods of convalescence, putting greater pressure on the campaign for prostitution reform. Sympathy for prostitutes waned as the Second Republic faced other social problems, but the belief that women selling sex were not criminals remained at the foundation of police, medical, and social-welfare reform initiatives. This widely shared perception helped drive an almost continuous effort to reshape the administration of the regulation system.[4]

Taken together, these concerns about prostitution's pervasiveness, its biological impact on the wider population, and the rising costs of its treatment helped stimulate a broad range of initiatives to abolish existing regulations and introduce new statutes to resolve the dangers of the sex trade. In the process of negotiating political reform, prostitution became a central metaphor for the Polish national body, which had been neglected during decades of imperial rule. Prostitution in the 1920s and 1930s arose as one of many veiled means for engaging broader social issues in the new Polish Republic. The Jagiellonian University medical professor Emil Wyrobek underlined the elision between public bodies and the national corpus in his 1916 depiction

---

4. On the growing consensus in interwar Poland that prostitution should not be criminalized, see Lipska-Toumi, *Prawo polskie wobec zjawiska prostytucji*, 227.

of the "physical and moral misery that course[d] through the blood and bones of society," an image that engaged the diseased body of the prostitute and her client to depict the dangers faced by the new state.[5] If the damaged body of the prostitute could be healed, then so too might the dismembered Polish nation be made whole again, Wyrobek proposed. Yet social reformers often worked at cross-purposes in the period, focusing both on humanizing the registration and inspection process for prostitutes and on eventually abolishing the hated system they were forced to administer. In the end, despite energetic action by physicians, social activists, feminists, socialists, and others, the political chaos of interwar Poland prevented the implementation of significant reform initiatives prior to the country's collapse in 1939.

Rezerwistki, Unemployment, and Wartime Desperation

Seven years of near continuous warfare brought Polish society to its knees. Not only did the Poles experience first Russian then German occupations, but they also fought a series of border conflicts with Czechoslovakia, Ukraine, Lithuania, and the Bolshevik state. The social impact of these traumas cannot be underestimated. Commentators warned that hunger and desperation were so acute that the whole society was barely "hanging on." Within six months of the war's outbreak, the country's morals were in sharp decline. "Envy, hatred, dishonesty, exploitation in all its forms" characterized all levels of Polish society, observed Emil Wyrobek. Sexual immorality, in particular, became more pronounced. On city streets, one witnessed "shameless clothing, immorality in the theaters and movie houses." Worse yet, "marital infidelity among the soldiers in the field" was matched by the behavior of women at home. "With every moment in this endlessly protracted war," Dr. Wyrobek reported, moral turpitude worsened.[6] By war's end, some forty thousand women across the Polish territories had turned to open or secret prostitution, mainly out of poverty and financial desperation.[7] As the Great War played out and Poland drew closer to the possibility of independence, anxiety about the quality of the country's future citizenry and especially the impact of sexual diseases loomed large. Observers worried

---

5. Wyrobek, *Choroby weneryczne, ich rozszerzenie i zapobieganie*, 64–65.

6. Emil Wyrobek, *Z posiwu bogina wojny: Alkoholizm, prostytucya, choroby płciowe, nerwowe i umysłowe, gruźlica i samobójstwo*, part 1, *Alkoholizm i prostytucya* (Cracow, 1917), 45–46.

7. "Spis prostytutek zaregestrowanych w okupacji niemieckiej d. Kongresówki w lipcu 1918 roku," *Zagadnienia Rasy* 2, no. 7 (1920): 6–7; and Lipska-Toumi, *Prawo polskie wobec zjawiska prostytutcji*, 203, n.68.

that VD threatened to reduce the size of the nation through increasing steril-ity, while weakening the population qualitatively for generations to come.[8]

Hunger and privation caused by closing factories and loss of breadwin-ners to military recruitment helped swell the ranks of sex workers. Shopgirls and household servants lost their incomes as employers fled occupied cities. Women in Lwów reportedly quit positions as dressmakers, waitresses, and governesses to offer themselves to Russian officers, often claiming they were the abandoned wives of engineers, officials, or doctors.[9] Prostitution rates climbed in Warsaw after the 1915 German occupation provided an active clientele for willing practitioners. Over half the new registrants to Warsaw's prostitution rolls during the first year of the German occupation turned to the sex trade because the invading army brought them to financial ruin. A full quarter of these noted their misfortune was due specifically to the loss of their husband's income to the war. These so called *rezerwistki* or reservists' wives would become the focus of popular concern as the war dragged on. Otherwise upstanding lower-class women who resorted to sex work out of financial desperation, they grew symbolic of the moral turpitude financial privation caused in the era leading up to Poland's political independence.[10] All three imperial states provided modest stipends to soldiers' wives to make up for the loss of income. Nonetheless, public opinion initially blamed the spike in prostitution on the effects of widespread conscription in poor fami-lies and treated the new streetwalkers as objects of pity. "From the moment the reservists were mobilized," noted the Łódź statistician and demographer Dr. Edward Rosset, "flocks of women were left without support." Not the routine hunger of the ordinary urban underclass, but rather "the cataclysm of war reduced these women to poverty," he argued.[11] Across Polish territory, in every major city suffering an enemy occupation, women from all social ranks were turning to the sex trade to survive. "It is simply beyond belief," noted one contemporary report, "the number of women coming from the sphere of the intelligentsia and the wealthy who have out of hunger put in their lot with the mountain of Polish prostitutes." Not only wives, but also teenage daughters of military conscripts turned to the streets to help support

---

8. Stanisław Ciechanowski, "Niebezpieczeństwo społeczne chorób wenereycznych," *Przegląd Lekarski* 40, no. 6 (1916): 125.

9. Jan Papée, "Choroby weneryczne u prostytutek we Lwowie w czasie wojny 1914–1918," *Gazeta Lekarska*, no. 41 (1919): 500–501.

10. A total of 2,689 new registrants appeared on Warsaw's prostitution index for 1915–1916, of which some 1,058 were characterized as direct victims of the war, made desperate because of the loss of a breadwinner or the closing of a factory. Rząśnicki, *Prostytucja a proletarjat*, 7.

11. Rosset, *Prostytucja i choroby weneryczne w Łódzi*, 8.

their fatherless families. In Russian-occupied Czernowitz, in eastern Galicia, for example, "children, young girls barely past the age of a governess's care," were reportedly "sacrificing their bodies to maintain their entire families." Rates of teenage prostitution in this impoverished town had long been high, but these young girls were now depicted with unprecedented empathy, "their eyes filled with tears" as they recalled "the hell of their lives" and the "abominable memories" of the sex trade.[12] The very women whom popular opinion had represented as immoral hussies in search of meaningless trinkets were now depicted as victims of war and occupation. Not materialism but the desire to feed one's family now became the primary motive for the move to prostitution.

Although public opinion may have temporarily softened toward new recruits into the sex trade, the demographic background of registered prostitutes actually differed little from that of those who had signed on to police registries in preceding generations. Professional sex workers remained poor, largely illiterate, and unskilled. They suffered from venereal diseases long before they underwent police supervision. The Warsaw tuberculosis expert Dr. Alfred Sokołowski described the two thousand new registrants to Warsaw's 1915–1916 police rolls as typical inscribed women: only two had finished the sixth grade, 7 percent were completely illiterate, and the vast majority could barely read or write. All the women on the registry reportedly grew up in working-class families and most were the daughters of factory workers or laborers in port cities. Perhaps most significantly, the rates of venereal infection found in women joining the prostitution registry for the first time during the war were just as high as for a typical new crop of public women in any other setting, suggesting the registrants had engaged in sex with multiple partners well before the occupation began. Ninety percent of these initial registrants were already infected with some form of venereal ailment despite being so new to the registry.[13]

The link between wartime conscription, military occupation, and the mobilization of poor women into the ranks of Poland's prostitutes also helped cement another notion in the public's consciousness: the turn to sex work was increasingly understood in economic rather than moral terms. By the end of the Great War, Lombroso's theories of psychopathy or moral inheritance as the genesis for prostitution were all but dislodged in favor of economic privation as a driving force. In the waning days of the war and the founding years of the Second Republic, experts across Poland compiled statistical evidence

---

12. Wyrobek, *Z posiewu bogina wojny*, 177–79.
13. Sokołowski, *Wielkie klęski społeczne*, 313–20.

about economic conditions among the population's underclass, wage rates for poor women, and shifting levels of unemployment. Experts like the Cracow economist Dr. Zofia Daszyńska-Golińska, a supporter of the Polish Socialist Party and an early member of the Polish Eugenics Society, argued vigorously that Poland's "working class understands well the dependence of prostitution on scarcity." The correlation between industrial unemployment and growing resort to prostitution was corroborated in the "statystyki miasta Łodzi" for the period 1918–1920, which showed that the vast majority of women leaving the police registry found work in the resurgent Łódź industry. Such a connection was clearly in keeping with research underway in Western Europe and the United States. The American statistics expert Abraham Flexner, for example, demonstrated that decreased wages in industrialized countries were typically reflected in a similar rise in rates of prostitution wherever paid sex was officially tolerated.[14]

Country Maidens, City Vipers

Perhaps most distressing of all, the turn to prostitution and the spread of venereal diseases now encompassed city and country alike. The venereal contamination of Poland's village girls quickly became a generalizable symbol of the declining wartime morality. The vaunted sexual innocence of the Polish countryside crumbled as vacationing soldiers, returning conscripts, and members of occupying armies sought entertainment in previously remote rural communities. The mobilization of men from all regions of the country meant that returning soldiers spread VD at ever increasing rates to less densely populated towns and villages.[15] The Polish countryside, ostensibly governed before the war by a "general sense of morality and religious tradition," was now exposed to visitors whose sexual conduct threatened to contaminate entire *gminas* (communes). In several districts in the former Russian partition, specialists reported, the venereal infection rate approached 95 percent of the population.[16] Anecdotal observations about country girls working Cracow's city streets prompted Wyrobek to lament the loss of female peasant virtue. "Naïve village girls" caught up in the world of prostitution represented for him a visible sign of the decline of Polish morality. The recent war, he reported, had brought increased rates of alcoholism, nervous disorders, orphaned children, and prostitution to the Polish countryside. These "once

14. Rosset, *Prostytucja i choroby weneryczne*, 19.
15. Papée, *Choroby weneryczne, ich rozszerzenie i zapobieganie*, 3.
16. Sokołowski, *Wielkie klęski społeczne*, 297–301.

beautiful village daughters" who had lost their "honor [and] their health" were but one poignant symptom of the social malaise Poland faced at the end of the war.[17] Such observations became part of the widespread recognition that prostitution and its related disorders were now integral to Polish society at all levels.

Yet Polish observers were so intent on maintaining the image of the pure village girl that many seem to have willfully obscured the sources of this contagion, failing to acknowledge that sexual diseases were widespread in the countryside long before the outbreak of wartime hostilities. Rural leaders complained of country girls' exposure to venereal disorders via visiting soldiers of the Russian Army, but in reality, as army doctors confirmed, soldiers were *contracting* sexual diseases from the civilian population of remote villages where recruits vacationed. A 1917 report on the health of Polish legionnaires, for example, compared rates of VD contamination in two separate regiments. For those stationed where civilians had previously been evacuated and the army had little contact with local people, "one rarely sees venereal infection," the study found. By contrast, the regiment encamped near a population center was "riddled with venereal infection." Indeed, significantly higher rates of infection prevailed among those behind the lines on leave than among those who had not been granted furlough. In other words, far from spreading venereal contamination to the rural population, Polish soldiers in 1917 appear to have been contracting these illnesses directly from the country folk. This contamination was no longer limited to the corrupt big cities on Polish territory. Rather, the report affirmed that "legionnaires experience[d] the greatest rate of venereal infection deep in the countryside." It was here, in the previously isolated, "pure," and traditional villages, "where soldiers become infected during leaves."[18]

Polish medical personnel acknowledged the impact of looser wartime sexual mores on the spread of sexual diseases. More "relaxed" marital relations came about when men left their home fires to serve in the war, experts argued, a situation physicians agreed created prime conditions for the spread of sexual diseases.[19] But vague complaints about "marital infidelity among

---

17. Emil Wyrobek, *W pętach rozpusty i pijaństwa: Obrazki z codziennego życia* (Cracow, 1920), 3–5.

18. Jan Stopczański, "Choroby weneryczne w Legionach," *Przegląd Lekarski* 56, no. 39 (September 30, 1917): 308–10. Lecture from the First Conference of Warsaw Medicine held on February 2, 1917 in Warsaw. Stopczański compares the differential rates of infection between the two halves of the Polish Legions during the first two years of the war.

19. Jan Papée, *Choroby weneryczne i ich zwalczanie w czasie wojny (1915–1918)* (Cracow, 1919), 4. Lecture to the National Health Council (Krajowa Rada Zdrowia), January 11, 1919.

soldiers in the field and women at home" rarely took account of the actual aberrant sexual behavior of military wives and enlisted men.[20] The turn to informal prostitution accounted for much of the rise in disease. Statistics spoke for themselves. The longtime Lwów police medical inspector Jan Papée compiled a detailed analysis showing wartime rates of sexual infection in the former Galician province for the Polish National Health Council (Krajowa Rada Zdrowia) in January 1919. Papée stressed the disproportionate rates of infection among males and females in occupied Poland, noting that diagnosed cases of venereal disease among women had increased more than threefold during the war years. Lwów hospital records indicated that approximately 700 women had been diagnosed in the city in 1913; by 1917 the number had climbed to over 2,200.[21] The eighty-six-bed clinic dedicated to treating VD in this city of close to a quarter million was overwhelmed with 250 female patients applying for treatment every day during 1915 and 1916.[22] The greatest spike in infection rates came with the arrival of female refugees from across the border with the Congress Kingdom in 1915–1916, women who had worked as prostitutes in Russia and who charged lower rates than local girls. Above all, though, Lwów became the transfer point of masses of foreign troops as they crossed through east Galician territory. Like other major cities on former Polish soil, the city was a destination for soldiers on military leave or vacationing from the front, a situation that meant "even more infections than towns with military installations."[23]

Venereal Care as Financial Disaster

The potential costs of dealing with the venereal crisis were as daunting as the physical effects of the disease itself. Civilian and military hospitals faced overwhelming numbers of venereal patients during the war years and medical experts worried about the limited resources available to care for them. Rates of VD contamination in the Polish territories were already on the rise before the war, comprising almost 20 percent of all patients in civilian hospitals and a whopping 64 percent of those in army facilities, figures that far exceeded the overall contamination rate in other European countries.

---

20. Wyrobek, *Z posiewu bogina wojny*, 46.

21. Papée, *Choroby weneryczne i ich zwalczanie*, 8.

22. J. Lenartowicz, "Stan szpitalnictwa i środków walki z chorobami wenerycznemi we wschodniej części Galicji," *Zagadnienia Rasy* 2, no. 5 (August 1919): 3.

23. Papée's data indicate that rates of diagnosed female infection in Lwów jumped by more than 50 percent from 405 infected women before the war to 693 in 1916. Papée, *Choroby weneryczne i ich zwalczanie*, 3–9.

Even more embarrassing, Polish specialists were hard-pressed to blame these rates of infection on occupying armies. By far the greatest percentage of the population suffering from sexual diseases before the war was in the self-governing province of Galicia, especially in the ancient capital of Cracow and the administrative center of Lwów. The situation was still worse in smaller garrison towns across Galicia where VD patients in local hospitals comprised 60–80 percent of the overall patient population.[24] In the Polish divisions of the Habsburg army stationed in Galicia, rates of infection had climbed to nearly 100 percent by the end of the war, hardly an auspicious statistic for a newly founded country establishing its own independent military.[25]

Galician officials were well aware of the dangers venereal contamination posed and were vocal in the need to combat its spread. Yet wartime shortages and the costs of large-scale mobilization meant resources to diagnose and isolate sexual infections were stretched. City fathers in Cracow fought vigorously to control contamination rates among registered prostitutes but were limited in their personnel, clinical space, and access to medical equipment. Cracow's mayor complained formally to the governor general's office in Biała during the German occupation that his city lacked qualified medical examiners for inspecting prostitutes and did not even have a dedicated examination room or proper chemicals for processing test results. Instead, the single police doctor tasked with inspecting registered prostitutes was expected to examine all 180 registered prostitutes in the city of Cracow on a daily basis (increased from the twice-weekly rate of prewar times presumably to deal with wartime dangers of increased contamination) in addition to the roughly 70 secret prostitutes brought in routinely on police roundups. Even devoting five minutes apiece to each inspection would have required the inspector to work around the clock.[26] How could the effects of venereal disease be stemmed when the province lacked basic resources for even identifying those in need of treatment? Hospital staffs were further constrained by a Galician law that prevented women from leaving the hospital or VD clinic until they were declared cured, a requirement nearly impossible to enforce even in the best of times, but which meant turning away hundreds of infected patients for want of bed space.[27]

---

24. Papée was chagrined to learn that only about 40 percent of soldiers in the German, French, and Russian armies were infected with VD, whereas the Polish rate was closer to 65 percent. Papée, *Choroby weneryczne i ich zwalczanie*, 3.

25. Leon Wernic, "W sprawie walki z chorobami wenerycznemi," *Zagadnienia Rasy* 3, no. 11 (August 1921): 14–16.

26. "Magistrat stol. Krol. Miasta Krakowa do c. k. Namiestnictwa w Białej," July 24, 1916, APKr, DPKr 110, 1043–44.

27. F. Krzyształowicz, "Metody walki z chorobami wenerycznymi," *Zagadnienie Rasy* 2, no. 4 (May 1919): 4–5.

Physicians in Warsaw complained similarly that after the Bolshevik invasion of 1920, prostitutes traveling with the Russian Army became a threat
to public order. According to the military doctor Józef Geisler, Bolshevik
officials typically failed to register or examine prostitutes traveling with their
armies. Polish authorities imposed a system of twice weekly medical checks
on women serving the troops stationed at Brześć, in eastern Poland, but the
numbers of contaminated patients quickly overran the military hospital. The
overflow had to be transferred to Warsaw, further straining the resources of
the besieged capital.[28] Meanwhile, medical personnel in Russian-occupied
Lwów claimed that "despite the dissolution of its administrative apparatus"
the Bureau of Sanitation nonetheless continued to fulfill its responsibilities.
Yet the execution of those duties, according to the chief medical inspector,
"was rather circumscribed," being limited by the shortage of personnel and
conducted in "unpleasant circumstances, full of surprises, and without the
support of the [occupying Russian] authorities," who were reportedly unin-
terested in monitoring prostitutes.[29]

Disease as National Threat

Polish venereologists expressed distress at the widespread appearance of VD
across Polish terrain and increasingly framed their frustration about lethal
infections in nationalist and postimperial terms.[30] According to Dr. Wyrobek,
the wartime spread of venereal diseases would claim as many victims as
had been killed and wounded on the battlefield. "Venereal damage might
well haunt the populace for generations to come," he worried. "Among
the wounds and shots that are consuming tens of thousands of victims," he
cautioned, "the unfortunate individuals, the unfortunate families, who are
invaded by venereal disease may appear to be only a trifle, but in reality this
is not the case. Individuals and families make up society, and when a lot of
these individuals are affected, the very existence of society can be ruined."[31]

---

28. Józef Geisler, "Krótkie sprawozdanie z działności szpitala wojsk: Dla prostytutek i ambulatorjum wenerycznego w Brześciu," *Lekarz Wojskowy* 2, no. 8 (1921): 234–35.

29. Jan Papée, "Choroby weneryczne u prostytutek we Lwowie," *Gazeta Lekarska*, nos. 41–42
(1919): 500.

30. The tone of these reports suggests the Austro-Hungarian administrators viewed their own
efforts to battle sexual diseases as far superior to those of the Russian occupiers. Jan Papée, "Choroby
weneryczne u prostytutek we Lwowie," *Gazeta Lekarska*, nos. 43–44 (1919): 513.

31. Emil Wyrobek, Zposiewu bogina wojny: alkoholizm, prostytucya, choroby płciowe, nerwowe i umysłowe, grużlica i samobójstwo. Part I: Alkoholizm i prostytucya (Cracow, n.d.), 45–48.

Already during the second year of war, Dr. Stanisław Ciechanowski calculated that the losses from the conflict included "those who fight with weapons in hand, those who fell defenseless because they found themselves in the line of battle, hundreds of thousands of exiles, hundreds of thousands of victims of poverty, hunger, and suffering, and finally those losses that come from the decreasing number of births, these are losses that will affect the nation for dozens of years in the damage to its physical and moral health."[32] Ciechanowski warned that the venereal diseases riddling both the army and civilian populations would effectively "inhibit the rebirth of the nation." Gonorrhea would "ruin thousands of men" and syphilis would "make thousands of women sterile, causing them to suffer miscarriages or to give birth only to misery." The "pitiful existence" of syphilitic children would, he argued, "leave future generations with weak and fragile constitutions."[33]

For the time being, Wyrobek acknowledged in 1916, "we have war," and the eyes of the public were focused on the unspeakable horrors of battle. But, he stressed, "the war will end" and with it the period of preoccupation about great matters, leaving the Polish family "weak, miserable, and powerless." Venereal disease, he emphasized, meant that "many, many affected bodies will be damaged and their souls will be still worse." Wyrobek cautioned his countrymen that "when the time comes," they had to "do battle with this enemy [the VD epidemic] because neither our silence nor our contempt frighten it away."[34] He urged his fellow citizens to bring the battle with VD to the schoolhouse, to the newspaper, and to political institutions once the independent Polish state was established. Wyrobek would be among the leaders of the new Eugenics Society that sought to address these population issues after 1918.

Professor Wyrobek's appeal was greeted with an outpouring of support from academic physicians and military medical inspectors, all of whom agreed that the incidence of sexual diseases threatened the future of the nation at the very moment of its rebirth. Wyrobek's perspective helped turn VD into a measure of the country's overall health. His hope was to "awaken the sleeping leaders of the nation" from their "apathy and idleness" with depictions of the unspeakable harm caused by sexual diseases.[35] Dr. Alfred Sokołowski agreed, predicting that more than the war wounds of Poland's enlisted men, the sexual diseases they bore presented a deeper and more

---

32. Ciechanowski, "Niebezpieczeństwo społeczne chorób wenerycznych," 125.

33. Ibid., 126.

34. Wyrobek, *Choroby weneryczne: Ich skutki i znaczenie w życiu jednostki i społeczeństwa, tudzież osoby leczenia i zapogiegania* (Cracow, 1916), 64–65.

35. Reviews of Wyrobek's earlier work are included in Wyrobek, *Z posiewu bogina wojny*, ii.

lasting danger to the nation's future, placing Polish society "on the verge of a new and dangerous calamity." The loss of life from venereal infections would soon outpace deaths from military engagements, he worried, leading to a depopulation crisis. Roughly forty to fifty thousand births per year would be lost because a "whole generation of Poles ha[d] been infected with these diseases," Sokołowski warned. The battle with sexual diseases was held up as "one of the most important topics" for Polish experts as they contemplated the birth of political independence.[36]

Disease and Recovery: Implications for the Postwar Order

As the First World War wound down and talk of Polish independence consumed public life, anxiety about sexual disease consumed the medical community. Returning soldiers and refugees rejoined their families, infecting wives and children in ever-growing numbers. Experts predicted VD rates would jump again once these decommissioned men were no longer under medical supervision and scientists predicted catastrophic implications for the postwar family.[37] Doctors felt the responsibility of monitoring the eugenic qualities of the new state's population and regulating these deadly disorders. "The future of the Polish nation," physicians contended, lay in the hands of medical experts more than ever before. "Doctors," declared one speaker at a 1916 Cracow meeting of the Society of Physicians, "are best equipped to take on foundational activity [and] it is our obligation to make sure that today's sanitary needs are on the national agenda. Poland will become that which we ourselves create."[38] Others agreed, noting that "today in Poland, venereal diseases have become a social-national threat throughout the country." Illnesses such as VD were approached as more than mere wartime calamities, but rather a phenomenon that "touched all of society." Deadly venereal disorders had the potential to "reduce the size of the nation" by causing sterility in diseased couples and "worsening its quality, squandering future generations" with weak and deformed children who were incapable of shouldering the responsibilities of citizenship.[39]

---

36. Sokołowski, *Wielkie klęski*, 297–301.

37. Krzyształowicz, "Metody walk z chorobami wenerycznymi," 5; and Wyrobek, *Z posiewu bogina wojny*, 47.

38. Wyrobek, *Z posiewu bogina wojny*, 186–87.

39. Ciechanowski, "Niebezpieczeństwo społeczne chorób wenerycznych," 125. Published in a special issue devoted to combatting venereal diseases.

Rates of VD infection continued to climb even after the November armistice. The 1919–1921 Polish-Soviet War brought a fresh wave of venereal disease, prompting heightened concern about contamination. The Warsaw doctor and eugenics activist Leon Wernic nonetheless continued to attribute responsibility for the diseases Polish civilians suffered to the various imperial occupations of Polish territory, arguing that high syphilis rates among Russian soldiers and rapes of Polish women by Bolshevik infantrymen sent infection rates up to near 80 percent in the eastern section of the country.[40] Moreover, state resources devoted to fighting the Bolshevik war had detracted from efforts to combat VD in this period, placing even more responsibility for the contagion on the shoulders of Russia. Studies conducted in 1918 and 1919 indicated that over a million citizens—some 4 percent of the total population of the new Polish Republic—were under a doctor's care for some form of venereal disease at the end of the war, a rate roughly fourteen times higher than the official prewar incidence of disease.[41]

Depopulation, Biological Damage, and the Eugenics Option

Public concern about the venereal epidemic combined with preparation for the rebirth of the independent state gave eugenics ideas a burst of renewed support. Polish eugenicists reached the crest of their professional success after the end of the Great War. Eugenics advocates led nearly every effort to reform the system of police regulation for prostitutes during the interwar years, and the Polish Ministry of Health would be directed by a member of the Eugenics Society every year until the Ministry's dissolution in 1924. The quest to strengthen and purify the postwar citizenry was part of a larger wave of efforts to establish the new state on stable ground after more than a century of foreign rule. Early discussions among eugenicists sprung from efforts to calculate the implications of wartime losses on the biological makeup of the nation. Not unlike public debate in Britain and France in the aftermath of the Great War, Polish scholars circulated detailed studies depicting the declining birthrate and the threats to the quality of children born after the war.

---

40. Wernic claimed that by the fall of 1922, infection rates had already begun to decline in Poland's major cities thanks to placing contaminated women under doctors' care. Leon Wernic, "O Zwalczaniu chorób wenerycznych w Państwie Polskim," *Biuletynie Ministerstwa Zdrowia Publicznego*, no. 1 (1921): 1.

41. Rosset, *Prostytucja i choroby weneryczne*, 26; and Leon Wernic, "Sprawa ludności w Polsce, a choroby weneryczne," *Zagadnienia Rasy* 2, no. 4 (May 1919): 14–15.

Specialists such as Professor Karaffa-Korbutt of the University of Vilnius emphasized the specific eugenics effects of removing adult men from reproduction during their military service. Across Europe, Karaffa-Korbutt noted, approximately 4 percent of all twenty-to-twenty-two-year-old males were in the army at any given moment during the war, taking them out of procreative life for the period of their enlistment. War losses meant that many of these soldiers did not return and start families, prompting a gender imbalance in the lands out of which the Polish state was carved. Women outnumbered men in Russia by war's end by 152 to 100. In Austria-Hungary, the figure was lower but still significant at 123 women for every 100 males.[42] Even those who survived wartime battles were not always fit for fatherhood. The trauma of military engagement, of extended exposure to death and violence, rendered many of the returnees "unfit" for family life. As Karaffa-Korbutt noted, "the war caused various nervous disorders, many of which led to suicide. [It] reduced the number of talented people and at the same time increased the number of people with negative psychological characteristics. This is the eugenic effect of the war."[43] Equally important for Polish eugenicists, the majority of the soldiers returning from the front were infected with some form of venereal disease, which they promptly passed on to their wives and families.

Under such circumstances, concern about the production of healthy offspring in the new state remained a grave public issue well into the interwar period. The medical community agreed that venereal diseases comprised "one of the [chief] links in the long chain of causes" leading to Poland's declining birthrate and lay at the root of the new country's problem with decreasing fertility in the postwar decade.[44] Children born to syphilitic parents or those infected with gonorrhea were deemed "inferior in terms of their physical as well as their spiritual value." They were described as "defective in every way" and poor citizens of the new state. Dr. Jan Lenartowicz, chief dermatologist at Lwów University, reminded his audiences that syphilitic children were "monstrous" in their appearance, with faces "pale, miserable, and wrinkled." Such "damaged" infants, he noted, often failed to thrive in their early months because they lacked the strength to suckle, were sensitive to physical strain, and became sick easily. More subjectively, if they survived, they displayed "inferior spiritual traits" later in life, including "a weak intellect" and evidence of being "dull, thick witted, and apathetic."

42. K. Karaffa-Korbutt, *Eugenika służba wojskowa a wojna* (Warsaw, 1926), 12–17.
43. Ibid., 20.
44. Rosset, *Prostytucja i choroby weneryczne*, 29.

These "spiritual disorders" also presented as physical characteristics. Syphilitic youth became "nervous, grew sick with epilepsy," or even "turned into complete idiots."[45] Such offspring were, in a word, "of less worth" than the children of healthy parents.[46] Taken as a whole, these characteristics would effectively reduce the quality of the new state's population, a dangerous situation for the foundling country. Overall, the wages of commercial sex and rampant sexual diseases risked endangering the new country even before it was officially founded. The dire situation called for urgent action.

Administering Prostitution in the New Poland

The hardships Poland endured during the extended wartime period paled beside the monumental struggles the new country faced as four disparate geographic regions were welded together into a single administrative entity. Poland was officially reborn on November 11, 1918 with the exodus of German troops from Warsaw and Marshall Piłsudski's appointment as military chief and temporary head of state. Yet Polish sovereignty, later confirmed by Allied leaders at Versailles, would be hard fought. The expulsion of German and Russian troops from Polish territory represented only the first step as the infant country sought to secure its borders. Conflicts swiftly followed with Ukraine, Czechoslovakia, and Lithuania in 1918–1920, and an all-out war with Soviet Russia that drained the fledgling country's resources until 1921. Polish citizens continued to experience economic distress and political instability as government representatives struggled to rebuild the ruined state. Hyperinflation, brought on partly by food scarcities, continued well into the 1920s, peaking on the eve of Marshall Piłsudski's 1926 coup. The Polish mark (later the złoty) was subject to volatile swings in value, exploding from an exchange rate of 8 marks to US$1 in 1918 to 9.3 million marks to US$1 in June 1924.[47] Prices of consumer goods increased some 250 percent between 1914 and 1920; by 1923 they had climbed almost one-million-fold, with prices on average doubling every nineteen days.[48]

---

45. Jan Lenartowicz, *Czym są i czym grożą choroby weneryczne* (Warsaw, 1927), quoted in Rosset, *Prostytucja i choroby weneryczne*, 31.

46. Rosset concludes, "the offspring of parents infected with syphilis are of less worth in terms of their physical and spiritual capacity." *Prostytucja i choroby weneryczne*, 30.

47. Peter Mathius and Sidney Pollard, eds., *The Cambridge Economic History of Poland*, vol. 8, *The Industrial Economies: The Development of Economic and Social Policies* (Cambridge, 1989), 930; and E. Dana Durand, *Supplement to Commerce Reports, Trade Information Bulletin nr. 32: Public Finance of Poland* (Washington, DC, June 19, 1922), 1–9.

48. A currency reform introduced in January 1924 established the worth of one new Polish zloty as 1.8 million Polish marks, eventually helping to bring hyperinflation under control. T. J.

Economic malaise increased anxiety about the country's health, making prostitution reform a top priority for the young state. Regional health departments lodged regular complaints about the enormous burden they were asked to shoulder caring for local prostitutes. State law required ill citizens to return to their native *gminas* for treatment, yet prostitutes were notorious for traveling without proper documentation, compelling the city where they plied their trade to foot the bill for their care.[49] Health officials expressed outrage at the high cost of treating the "whores" (*ladacznica*) flooding Poland's key cities, taking "hundreds of thousands of złoty from [municipal] budgets."[50] Hospital administrators in Poznań, for example, complained in 1920 that care for sick prostitutes, most of whom were not even natives of the city, was consuming their health-care facilities.[51] Poznań's municipal hospital had treated only thirty-two prostitutes in 1913, but by 1920 over five hundred sex workers were hospitalized for a total of over twenty-eight thousand days, an average of fifty-three days for each illness.[52] The potential for greater expenditures increased as Poland's economic crisis deepened. By 1924, Poznań counted close to two thousand full-time and part-time sex workers, the majority of them selling sex as a second job to supplement their primary employment.[53]

Postimperial tensions played into these local resentments. Not only did hospital administrators protest that they were forced to treat women from out of town, but they also complained they were monitoring prostitutes from prewar partitions that had maintained much lower hygienic standards than their own residents. Officials in Poznań were irked, for example, that their city was "flooded with muck from the former Congress Kingdom and Lesser Poland (Małopolska)." Even the small coterie of prostitutes in prewar Poznań had been "mostly Germans from Berlin," officials claimed. Since then, several hundred additional prostitutes had migrated from Russian

---

Sargent, "The Ends of Four Big Inflations," *Working Paper* (Minneapolis, 1981), 158. See also Elmus Wicker, "Terminating Hyperinflation in the Dismembered Habsburg Monarchy," *The American Economic Review* 76, no. 3 (June 1986): 351–54.

49. Complaint from the Poznań Section of Social Care and Hospitals to the Commissioner of the Department of Public Health, Warsaw, February 1927, APP, AMP, 4140.

50. Appeal from Poznań city officials to Warsaw Department of Public Health, March 16, 1926, APP, AMP, 4140.

51. Poznań District Public Health Office to all doctors in the Poznań province, February 4, 1920, APP, AMP, 4216.

52. Bureau of City Hospitals from the Bureau of the Poor, Poznań, June 3, 1922, APP AMP, 4140; Minister of Health in Poznan to Ministry of Public Health in Warsaw, October 28, 1922, APP AMP, 4140.

53. Table of registered and part-time "dorabiające" prostitutes in the city of Poznań, 1914–1926. City Police Commission, March 26, 1927, APP, AMP, 4140.

Poland and Galicia and begun "practicing their sleazy business without any medical supervision" since these "less civilized" practitioners were ostensibly unaccustomed to registering with the police in their native districts. The medical care of transient harlots, who were breeding infection among the city's soldiers and students, fell unfairly on the municipal government, according to local authorities.[54]

The genesis for change had been laid long before the outbreak of war in the establishment of three important reform groups: the Warsaw Hygienic Society, the Polish Society to Combat Prostitution and Venereal Diseases and the League of Equal Rights for Women, all based in Warsaw. Each of these organizations had been active in combatting separate aspects of the prostitution nexus—fighting to reduce communicable diseases, restricting human trafficking, and opposing the sexual double standard that encouraged resort to prostitution. The groups first came together officially to address the prostitution problem in 1916 during the German occupation of Warsaw.[55] Already in 1915 responsibility for monitoring the system of police regulated prostitution had passed into the hands of the Polish Society to Combat Prostitution and Venereal Diseases, under the leadership of Leon Wernic and Teodora Męczkowska. Wartime proposals mapped out a new set of emphases that stressed the economic causes of prostitution, shifting the basis on which regulation would be administered. The Warsaw Hygienic Society confirmed the economic roots of commercial sex and recommended dismantling the machinery of regulation once Poland obtained its independence. The society called for greater government expenditures on programs to assist poor women and advocated professional training for unskilled female workers. Medical attention, according to this view, would be dispensed free of charge to VD patients and only those who knowingly had sex while infected should be subject to prosecution.[56]

Experienced abolitionists from prewar societies dominated the postwar conversation on prostitution reform. Yet despite their placement in high-level administrative positions, antiprostitution leaders fell short in their efforts to dismantle the machinery of regulation and had to settle for a mere administrative restructuring of the registration apparatus, removing it from the

54. Petition from the Poznań magistrate's office to the city doctor of the Poznań Police Commission, requesting that all unregistered prostitutes be punished and sent to forced labor, as was German policy prior to the world war (APP, AMP, 4140).

55. Leon Wernic, "Polski project ustawy walki z chorobami wenerycznemi i nierząd," *Nowiny Lekarskie* 40, no. 20 (1928): 710–11.

56. Sokołowski, *Wielki klęski społeczne*.

primary jurisdiction of the police and placing it in the hands of the medical community. Supporters of abolition faced persistent opposition in their efforts to dismantle the centuries-old regulation apparatus from a faction of the medical community that feared the impact of potentially deadly venereal diseases. Instead, as an intermediate measure while the Polish Sejm considered new legislation, the Hygienic Society recommended registration of prostitutes be transferred from police jurisdiction to specialized sections of municipal hospitals, a switch designed to focus increasingly on disease control rather than punitive measures. By removing primary supervision from the jurisdiction of police and placing it under the sanitation-vice department of local hospitals, the hope was to deemphasize the criminal aspects of paid sex and address instead its more dangerous public-health implications.[57] These suggestions quickly passed into law after the founding of the Polish Second Republic. The Ministry of Public Health passed regulations in December 1918 "temporarily" transferring responsibility for the inspection of prostitutes from police to medical facilities.[58]

In January 1919 the new Ministry of Public Health was tasked with the responsibility for managing the problems of VD and prostitution, and the Polish eugenics head Dr. Leon Wernic became director of the Section to Combat Venereal Diseases.[59] At the same time, the Ministry of Internal Affairs officially subsumed the vice police under the jurisdiction of the Ministry of Public Health, eliminating forever the monopoly of the police over prostitution regulation and transferring governance of the vast network of testing and treatment facilities to state medical authorities. From this moment on, a somewhat watered-down system of regulated prostitution was firmly in the hands of those who wished it to be abolished.[60] Thus the mechanics of police-medical regulation over prostitutes was superseded by so-called neoregulation, in which the medical community bore primary responsibility for inspecting sex workers. Unfortunately for the abolitionist camp, this is where prostitution reform in the new Republic would stop.

---

57. The former Lwów police medical examiner Jan Papée made this argument in "Choroby weneryczne u prostytutek we Lwowie," 516.

58. This hastily passed legislation was designed as a stopgap while the Ministry of the Public Health and Hospitals devised a more comprehensive set of regulations to govern prostitutes after the machinery of police regulation was dismantled. Maks Muszkat, "Walka z nierządem," *Głos prawda,* nos. 1–2 (1939): 13–14.

59. Gawin, "Progressivism and Eugenic Thinking," 173.

60. Chodźko, *Prostytucji i choroby weneryczne,* 7–8; and Lipska-Toumi, *Prawo polskie wobec zjawiska prostytucji,* 203–4.

Figure 10.1 Leon Wernic, specialist in venereal diseases and founding member of the Polish Eugenics Society.
Courtesy of the Warsaw Medical Library (Główna Biblioteka Lekarska).

From this early initiative, leaders of the Hygienic Society, the Polish Committee for Combatting Traffic in Women and Children, and the newfound Eugenic Society worked closely for two decades with Polish government officials to introduce what they called a system of "positive abolition" to replace the prewar regulation requirements.[61] Under Wernic's leadership, the Sejm passed legislation in 1919 reorganizing the administration of prostitution, closing all public houses and forbidding new ones to open.[62] Almost immediately after the law was passed, however, opposition arose from members of the medical community who supported continued police control over public sex. These so-called neoregulationists successfully introduced provisions to ensure that supervision over registered prostitutes continued to be the purview of a combined medical-police commission in each municipality.[63] The emphasis in the administration of prostitutes and sexual disease had shifted, however. New regulations permitted the local sanitation-vice departments to establish institutions where patients could receive medical treatment without disclosing their names, where care was dispensed free to indigent patients, and where treatment was under the supervision of local state-supported physicians. Nonetheless, at least one representative of the local police was always present at examinations—after 1925 this representative was a member of the newly founded Polish Women Police, one of the first such feminized forces in Europe.[64] In many respects this new branch of the police represented the outgrowth of decades-long activity among women's charity organizations focused on improving conditions among less privileged members of society. Early efforts to reduce the power of the police in regulating prostitutes thus did not imply the complete removal of the state from the lives of Poland's sex workers. Instead, the intervention of the police and the courts were necessary on occasions when women refused to comport with the schedule for medical checkups.[65]

---

61. "Memorial Polskiego Komitetu Walki z Handlem Kobietami i Dziećmi," *Lekarz Polski* 15, no. 4 (April 1938): 93–94.

62. The Basic Sanitation Law (Zasadniczej Ustawy Sanitarnej) of July 1919 initially applied only to the territory of the previous Russian partition. Its provisions were officially valid for the entire Polish Republic as of 1922. Sources note that the prohibition on brothels was routinely violated and that some four hundred secret houses of assignation continued to operate quite openly in Warsaw alone. Zaleski, *Prostytucja powojenna,* 119; and Lipska-Toumi, *Prawo Polskie wobec zjawiska prostytucji,* 209, n.78.

63. Paleolog, *Women Police of Poland,* 10–11; and Bogusław Zając, "Sprzedajność niewiast na ziemiach polskich," *Polityka* (November 4, 2009), 2.

64. Paleolog, *Women Police of Poland,* 15.

65. Jan Backiewicz and Henryk Gromadzki, *Pamiętnik II-ego Zjazdu Hygieniestów Polskich* (Warsaw, 1918), 138.

This new and unstable system of controlling professional prostitution focused on preventing the spread of disease but avoiding harsh disciplinary techniques. The system gradually eroded at the impulse of ever-eager abolitionist advocates. In practice, supporters of abolition worked at cross-purposes with neoregulationist advocates for most of the life of the interwar Second Republic. Oversight of women working as prostitutes was split between representatives of the Ministry of the Interior and the Ministry of Work and Social Welfare, the latter of which continued to sponsor the shelters for "fallen women" and Magdalene homes that pre-dated the war. In many respects, activists whose experience was honed during imperial times rose to find niches in state and private institutions and to perform increasingly professional tasks in independent Poland. The shadow state of doctors and female aid workers fed government institutions and welfare programs in the united Polish care network.

With public anxiety about sexual diseases at its zenith, support for the abolition of registered prostitution waned. Fears that without police sanctions compulsory examination and treatment of diseased women would not be enforced kept the practice in a legal twilight zone for the duration of the Second Republic. Meanwhile, activists devised proposals to address the economic aspects of the move to prostitution. These initiatives were tied to concerns about the health of the Polish national body as an organic whole. The Lublin dermatologist and venereal expert Dr. Kazimerz Jaczewski stressed the need for the new Polish state to focus its resources on the creation of honest jobs for poor women. Reflecting his eugenics sympathies, Jaczewski noted that this was the only way to "rescue the nation from degeneration and extinction."[66] Public sex clearly lay at the center of debates on the nation's future vitality, with the primary effort focused on curing, educating, and reintegrating women who sold sex rather than punishing or socially ostracizing them.

Concerns about scientific progress continued to suffuse these efforts. Even as the Polish medical community fought a losing battle with the legislature to wrest total control over the supervision of sex workers away from criminal courts and police inspectors, doctors addressed the primitive conditions prevailing in the infrastructure devoted to medical inspection of prostitutes. Municipal medical authorities touted modern testing equipment, expanded facilities, and better-equipped examination rooms. Despite dire economic conditions in the early years of the new state, medical personnel sought to

---

66. Ibid., 139.

distinguish their own scientific practices from those that prevailed under the three empires previously governing Polish territory. Jan Papée, now Lwów's sanitary vice commissioner, boasted for example that his offices featured all that was necessary for modern bacteriological research: two microscopes, a sterilizer, and materials for disinfecting medical instruments.[67] Everywhere medical examinations of registered prostitutes required blood tests conducted using state-of-the-art microscopes.[68] At the same time, medical experts worked with the legislative system to propose severe penalties for prostitutes who avoided medical exams, who refused to be sent to hospital, or who knowingly engaged in sexual relations while sick. To implement these controls, social reformers envisioned an expanded state bureaucracy with access to mechanisms of enforcement. A strong state was key to improving the Polish national body.

The Eugenics Solution: A Retrospective

Poland was reborn as a sovereign state at the crest of eugenics popularity among medical circles and other intellectuals across the Continent. The Polish preoccupation with the "damage" wrought to the population through the impact of venereal diseases made prostitution a core concern of the eugenics movement. As eugenics experts were drawn into the service of the new state, their credo took hold on the very formation of the Department of Health and was reflected in some of the agency's early goals.[69] Eugenics provided the language of biological integration and the vocabulary for mapping out a road to national strength and unity, focusing most centrally on the problem of prostitution in the new state. In contrast to eugenics movements in Western Europe and the United States, however, which addressed the results of massive waves of immigration, racial segregation, or depopulation following World War I, activists in eastern Europe focused more on the prevention and cure of diseases they believed weakened the social fiber of their new states.

---

67. Papée was so preoccupied boasting about his new equipment that his report focuses almost entirely on the instruments used for the examination and their storage (tables for microscopes, a shelf for tools, and examination chair) and omitted any information on the women under the speculum. Papée, "Choroby weneryczne u prostytutek we Lwowie," 500.

68. Z. Horbowski, "Organizacja i działalność Urzędu Sanitarno-Obyczajowego w Warszawie," *Zagadnienia Rasy* 4, no. 3 (1922): 11–16; and Lipska-Toumi, *Prawo polskie wobec zjawiska prostytucji,* 190.

69. The Polish Eugenics Society founder and longtime activist for prostitution reform Dr. Leon Wernic was appointed head of the VD section of the new ministry and used his position to introduce a number of prostitution reform initiatives to the Sejm.

Polish activists stressed issues of social class over those of race, expressing ongoing anxiety over the sexual habits of poor, urban women selling sex as a supplement to their day jobs. Polish eugenicists also refrained from using anti-Semitic or racist terminology in their writings. Indeed, the membership included many physicians and social activists of Jewish origin.[70]

Though Polish eugenics advocates often employed the vocabulary of "race" (*rasa*), the term was used to denote society as a whole rather than to refer to a particular ethnic group. After years of planning and strategizing, eugenics activists were eager both to express their "patriotism" and to "purify" society of pollutants like "adverse working conditions, a poor upbringing, etc."[71] The Polish national "race" included, for eugenicists, the lower-class women who sold sex. However degenerate they may have been, prostitutes were nonetheless conceived as an integral part of the Polish national "race." No longer could they be held at arm's length, exoticized, demonized, or otherwise displaced as belonging to some "other" outside group. Women practicing prostitution on Polish territory were Poles, regardless of their social status, ethnicity, or religion. Interwar reformers accepted this even while trying to isolate and eliminate the diseases they bore. As a class-based rather than an ethnically grounded program, eugenics wrote the female outsider back into the nation, though admittedly not yet as a full citizen.[72]

Polish eugenics matured and became politically active with the birth of the new state. As the Polish Eugenics Society founder and longtime activist Leon Wernic observed in a retrospective on the society's accomplishments, the Polish Hygienic Society (a precursor of Polish eugenics) arose "in the workshop of the rising state." Only through state power could the initiatives of these scientific-social reformers be realized.[73] Wernic boasted in 1928 that "the conditions of the [eugenicists'] work improved as they received material and moral support from the [Polish] Health Department, the institutions of self-government, and the Institute of State Hygiene."[74] Nonetheless, as Wernic himself acknowledged, the eugenicists' influence in the nation's public health peaked in the mid-1920s. The increasingly "anemic" legislation to

---

70. Kamila Uzarczyk, "'Moses als Eugeniker'?: The Reception of Eugenic Ideas in Jewish Medical Circles in Interwar Poland," in Turda and Weindling, *Blood and Homeland*, 283–97.

71. Opening statement of the Polish Eugenics Society, *Zagadnienia Rasy*, 1, no. 1 (July 15, 1918): 1.

72. Registered prostitutes were forbidden to appear in public in certain social settings. They could neither sit in the front section of theaters, movie houses, or the circus nor ride in open carriages or automobiles on public streets or squares. They were banned from all museums, exhibits, and even the public library. Lipska-Toumi, *Prawo Polskie wobec zjawiska prostytucji*, 191.

73. Wernic, *Polskie Towarzystwo Walki z Nierządem i Chorobami Wenerycznemi* (Warsaw, 1916), 2.

74. Leon Wernic, "Ruch eugeniczny w Polsce," *Nowiny Lekarskie*, no. 21 (1928): 13.

combat VD and prostitution continued to frustrate eugenics activists, social reformers, and medical specialists.[75] Proposed legislation to shore up existing practices and tighten legal requirements for reporting illness was regularly rejected in the Sejm.

By the eve of the country's descent into a new and more bloody international conflict, reformers were still waiting for passage of two additional bills, one to strengthen medical efforts to combat the spread of VD and the other to introduce government assistance to help curtail resort to prostitution. As late as November 30, 1937, the Polish Council of Ministers approved a project to tighten control over sexual diseases and hoped the Sejm would adopt it during its 1938 session. The intended legislation, which never made it to the floor of the Sejm, was designed to reflect the belief that neither traditional regulation nor neoregulation were effective in reducing prostitution or in controlling venereal disease. Prostitution, proponents argued, had to be formally outlawed and the state had to do everything in its power to discourage poor women from taking economic refuge in sex work. As one frustrated legal specialist noted, "the classic system of regulation as well as the [current] system of neoregulation have succeeded in creating an overall male population that is infected with venereal diseases and a legion of secret prostitutes who convince the population of the safety of prostitution usage." Moreover, the outdated system had effectively "hidden from the eyes of the authorities the contamination caused by wandering prostitutes who are not easily available for policing." Perhaps worst of all, the new system of regulating prostitution reflected an ongoing double standard of morality in which "administrative authorities are [viewed as] tolerant of registering prostitutes and, on the other hand, are intolerant of prostitutes, as indicated by their attempts to purify the parks, streets, entertainment sites, restaurants, hotels, and furnished rooms of prostitutes."[76]

Diseases, immorality, and the sexual double standard continued to plague interwar Polish life even as reformers sought every possible means to abolish or update the antiquated system of dealing with commercial sex. The Polish government's failure to implement a coherent new approach to prostitution can be attributed to political dysfunction and to the wide spectrum of

---

75. The Polish Eugenics Society's influence in public affairs declined sharply after the early years of the state's founding. A member of the society headed the Ministry of Public Health continually from 1918 on (Tomasz Janiszewski was the first), but the ministry's dissolution in 1924 eliminated this access point. After 1926, Pilsudski's government consistently rejected the society's efforts to introduce legislation to force sterilization on "unfit" citizens of the Republic. Gawin, "Progressivism and Eugenic Thinking," 174.

76. Muszkat, "Walka z nierządem," 14–15.

interest groups competing to address the problem. Nonetheless, the conditions of the debate, the tone in which it was conducted, and the vocabulary it employed reflected a new status for the body of the commercial sex worker in modern Polish imaginings. No longer ostracized or shunned, the prostitute had become a sad reflection of Poland's economic status and of its failure to modernize adequately in her two short decades of political independence. Efforts to eliminate regulation may well have been the final salvo in a long-term campaign to remove the stain of inherited lower-class immorality that had followed poor women from country to city and into the brothels and red-light districts of growing towns. The reform campaign was but one of many unrealized programs of the interwar Second Republic.

Conclusion

Prostitution and the Shaping of the National Community

> A sex trafficking trial began Tuesday at the Warsaw
> District Court. The defendants are three Bulgarians.
> The victims are Ukrainian women forced into
> prostitution on the roads leading out of the capital.
>
> —Bogdan Wróblewski, "Proces o handel kobietami"

In the spring of 2002, Poland's leading daily newspaper, *Gazeta Wyborcza*, published the story of a Bulgarian trafficking ring accused of smuggling women into Poland on the promise of landing them prestigious engagements as dancers. In reality, the article revealed, the women were put to work as escorts servicing Polish truck drivers on routes between major cities.[1] The piece was but one in a stream of reports characterizing pimps, procurers, and prostitutes in postcommunist Poland as illicit invaders making their way into the country from the former Soviet Republics and other states on the periphery of the European Union.[2] Interviews with young Poles reflected the common belief that most prostitutes working in the country were citizens of Ukraine, Romania, or Moldova and that pimps and traffickers were mainly Bulgarian or Russian. In the popular culture of postcommunism, the women who sold sex in Polish hotels and nightclubs and who stalked the country's main roadways existed outside the Polish community of obligation. Marked as moral outsiders by their behavior, sex workers had become a lightning rod for criticism about ethnic

---

1. "Zmuszali do prostytucji kobiety z Ukrainy," *Gazeta Wyborcza*, March 8, 2012.
2. About Bulgarian traffickers, for example, see "Zmuszał do prostytucji 19-latkę: Pracowała jako tirówka," *Gazeta Wyborcza*, August 24, 2010; and Bogdan Wróblewski, "Proces o handel kobietami," *Gazeta Wyborcza*, March 20, 2002.

"others." More scholarly studies demonstrating that the vast majority of East European prostitutes were native to the countries in which they worked had little impact on public opinion.[3] Casual observers continued to see sex workers as not "nasze" and therefore not a focus of concern for the Polish state or charitable organizations.

As the preceding chapters have suggested, the process of "othering" women who sold sex is a long-established pattern in Polish society. Critiques of female sexuality in general and the behavior of public women in particular have been fundamental to assessing how the Polish community policed its own borders. The concept of "community" is key to understanding how the sex trade was interpreted and internalized in the Polish lands. The women who lined the streets of nineteenth-century Cracow or Łódź, who occupied Saski Park in central Warsaw, or who wandered the military encampments of Stanisławów or Lwów were depicted as distinctly un-Polish, just as were their twentieth-century counterparts. These earlier shadowy figures were excluded from national concern on different grounds. Despite bearing all the cultural markings of Polish national membership, their social origins branded them as outside the world of Poland's elite actors. The underclass that staffed Poland's nineteenth-century bordellos and red-light districts was treated as an object of scorn and derision. Whether loathed or pitied, evidence shows that women working as prostitutes were held at arms' length from the social commentators who formed the conscience of the nation. Indeed, the moral code of Polish values was in many respects measured against the demeanor of public women. Prostitutes were characterized variously as aggressive, selfish, garish, lacking in communal values, materialistic, and unwomanly. Their brazen, overly sexualized manner marked them as the very antithesis of the *Matka Polka*, the idealized image of Polish womanhood according to which nineteenth-century observers evaluated female behavior.[4] The prostitute's symbolic violation of the sanctity of the bourgeois family established her as an iconic boundary violator, a transgressor of the sacred private realm and a polluter of the "pure" space of the home.

As views of postcommunist prostitutes suggest, popular attitudes toward sex workers have tended to be closely tied to perceptions of national boundaries.

---

3. Gail Kligman and Stephanie Limoncelli, "Trafficking Women after Socialism: From, To, and Through Eastern Europe," *Social Politics: International Studies in Gender, State and Society* 12, no. 1 (2005): 118–40.

4. On the *Matka Polka* imagery and its power, see Brian Porter-Szucs, *Faith and Fatherland: Catholicism, Modernity, and Poland* (Oxford, 2011); and Keely Stauter-Halsted, "Policing the Borders of Belonging: Gender, Sexuality, and the Polish Nation," *Rocznik Antropologii Historii* 4, no. 2 (2014): 37–54.

During the prostitution panic of the 1880s and 1890s, reactions to the visibility of paid sex were pitched in moral terms. Profligate women were made to stand in for the deep shame the country had experienced as imperial powers possessed and dominated the weakened state. Commentators portrayed the prostitute's fate using biblical metaphors, characterizing those who entered the ranks of registered women as having "fallen from grace." A single moment of sexual weakness, like Eve's original sin, could sentence a woman to a lifetime in the muck of paid sex. Prostitutes could never marry, hold honest jobs, or become responsible mothers. Their initial brush with immorality sentenced them to a life behind the closed doors of the bordello, sequestered from prying eyes in discrete neighborhoods. Such a scenario imagined no turning back, no forgiveness for the initial moral slip. Meanwhile, state apparatuses worked to bring poor women into their lens through the machinery of regulation, charting their physical movements, incidence of disease, family circumstances, educational background, and employment history. Public women were made legible through the regulation system and imperial authorities monitored their every move. Police registration was established as a netherworld of shamed women, controlled through institutionalized medical inspections, police hospitals, and the court system.

But half a century of exposure to the problem of paid sex brought fresh understandings of its meanings. Polish commentators turned from moral judgment to rational reform, reassessing their anxiety about commercial sex and establishing programs of reeducation to incorporate public women into mainstream national culture. This book has told the story of how such a transition occurred and why it is significant. Over time, prostitution was increasingly understood as a byproduct of modern industrial development in the Polish context. Polish observers came to recognize the migration of young women from village to city and their vulnerable economic circumstances in their transplanted homes as an essential pretext for the turn to commercial sex. Although social critics were by no means unanimous in their perceptions of the causality behind prostitution, many saw that the factory employment cycle and the humiliations of domestic service helped drive female workers to the streets. Emigration abroad brought still greater risks and experts acknowledged that the challenges of leaving home prompted some female migrants to slip into the sex trade and still others to be wrongly characterized as doing so. At the same time, critics noted that the limited opportunities for Jewish families to advance in the imperial economies of eastern Europe brought resort to trafficking and procuring from this quarter. A mobile, fractured, and often desperate population made use of paid sex as a tool to ease the transition to new economic circumstances.

Just as a modernizing female population approached prostitution as a pragmatic solution to the trauma of social dislocation, so too did social activists construct reasoned responses to the problem of commercial sex itself. Expert opinion varied about the most effective arena for resolving the prostitution crisis, but critics agreed that systemic change, not moral condemnation, was key. Feminists attacked the double sexual standard of the Victorian era and encouraged job training and education for poor women. Jewish activists critiqued the customary practices of their coreligionists. Medical experts redoubled their efforts to bring public women under their gaze, using scientific measures to cure the diseases prostitutes bore and prevent their spread. Purity proponents called for curbing licentious behavior and preached new ascetic standards for all social classes. And eugenics advocates prescribed preventative measures to improve the biological makeup of the Polish population. No longer was prostitution seen as a moral transgression from which a woman could never return. It was now a rational, scientific, measurable problem. As such, its effects could be evaluated, assessed, and conceivably repaired. This process of analyzing and correcting the damage prostitution wrought soon became a national project.

This book has argued that the country's new specialists took on the work of revolutionizing the way the wider public viewed prostitution. Polish biologists, dermatologists, psychologists, gynecologists, and venerealogists—the new scientific elite—found their voice in the last decades of imperial rule and communicated their findings to the wider public. They were joined by a phalanx of journalists, legal scholars, charity workers, and women's activists who set out to introduce middle-class values to the urban poor. These scientific professionals researched the world of the prostitute from every angle, examining her home life, her family background, her education, and her work environment. In the process of depicting and evaluating conditions among the lower classes, Polish pundits not only critiqued the choices of their less fortunate sisters but they also familiarized themselves with the environment in which these choices were made. Educated Polish speakers researched alcoholism and tuberculosis, malnutrition and child labor. They grew acquainted with the harsh personal circumstances and the dysfunctional family settings that drove women to the streets. The turn to prostitution shifted for these social reformers to reflect the effects of economic necessity, social dislocation, and familial instability. After half a century of observing, studying, inspecting, and conducting humanitarian work among them, Polish social activists came to see sex workers as part of a larger national community shaped by shared language and culture. If only because of the possibility that their potentially life-threatening contaminants might infect their upper-class clients, prostitutes had to be treated as a constitutive part of the national corpus. Their fate was bound up with the fate of the nation itself; their health risks were a danger to the broader society. This book has relayed the story of how that happened.

Fighting the Empires by Battling Prostitution

All of these were phenomena that could be improved, but not necessarily within the context of imperial domination. Polish actors increasingly supported state intervention for solving social need, but they despaired of working through the imperial bureaucracies they so profoundly distrusted. Instead, the conversation about social reform became part of a larger debate in partitioned Poland about national independence. During the long transition from imperial subjects to masters of their own nation-state, Polish observers conceptually integrated the women who worked as prostitutes into their vision of a national community. Experts in law, medicine, charity, education, and women's rights approached the problems of lower-class females as issues with a direct impact on the nation's fortunes. They did so as a result of several overlapping patterns in which the Polish elite came in direct contact with poor women and increasingly viewed them as sharing the same cultural universe.

The first of these was, of course, the bourgeois household. Our examination of the exodus of girls and young women from the postemancipation countryside to cities across Polish territory showed that this demographic shift made the services of household servants affordable for even the lowliest craftsman or shopkeeper. The glut of available serving girls fleeing the poverty and isolation of the family farm kept wages low or virtually nonexistent as families found they could exchange a cot in the kitchen and the remains of the family's dinner for live-in service. But for the ambitious young women who made their way to the region's burgeoning cities, domestic service was not enough. Instead, they had sex with delivery boys in exchange for trinkets and clothing, and eventually quit service to turn to more prestigious jobs as industrial laborers, shopgirls, or waitresses, employment that permitted them some modicum of independence. Even here, however, young women were subject to unwelcome advances from customers, clients, and shop foremen. The informal exchange of sex for privilege continued to characterize these relationships, and contemporary Polish observers began to recognize the extent to which sexual encounters were part of the fabric of urban life. The universal assumption that "all serving girls were prostitutes" underlined the lived reality that the sale of sex had penetrated the bourgeois economy and, more important, that the dangers of disease had made their appearance in the intimate setting of the middle-class family.

The increasingly permeable boundary between "legitimate" transactions within the urban household, the metropolitan café, or the theater, on the one hand, and the world of the part-time or short-term prostitute, on the other, helped raise questions about the rigid divisions separating social classes in partitioned Poland. If the trusted housekeeper, nanny, waitress, or salesgirl also sold sex on the side, then the prostitute was no longer a stranger to polite society. Rather, sex work had crawled out of urban bordellos and red-light districts into the bourgeois living room. Moreover, the use of prostitutes, middle-class Poles soon realized, was built into the sexual initiation of adolescent males. It was central to the socialization of university students and crucial to allowing middle- and upper-class males to marry late without risking the perceived health hazards of sexual abstinence. The awareness of this link between commercial sex and bourgeois masculinity made the prostitution question increasingly prescient.

At the same time, we have seen that questions about prostitution were tied into other concerns about lower-class behavior, including anxiety about massive overseas migration and the position of Jews as mediators and jobbers. By the 1890s, Polish leaders had come to fear the enormous outflow of young people—especially women of childbearing age—to foreign shores. Commentators saw the exodus damaging Poland's demographic future, reducing her potential military might and displacing future laborers. And yet the casual elision of single female migrants with sex workers was too much even for the Polish elite to accept unquestioningly. Instead, yellow journalists and charity workers attributed the "disappearance" of young women from Polish soil to the work of Jewish gangsters who, confusingly, could rarely be convicted on trafficking charges. Migrating women refused to testify against accused traffickers, highlighting the murky issue of agency in sex-worker relationships with their handlers. As whole villages emptied out and inhabitants made their way to transatlantic ports, emigration grew into a panic on a scale reminiscent of the anxiety surrounding visible prostitution. The chain of women turning to sex in foreign lands became so achingly familiar that those who opted for this path could hardly be reviled. Rather than judging her, Polish observers increasingly empathized with the prostitute's plight and sought to assist her, usually by attempting to bring her home. Again, the Polish public viewed prostitution and the prostitute with increasing familiarity and diminishing revulsion. Women who sold sex had problems like anyone else; it was the task of charitable organs and state institutions to help remedy the causes that drove them to the street.

Similarly, middle-class female charity activists discovered prostitution as a cause that liberated them from the routine of their households and provided a socially legitimate focus for their organizational energies. Aid workers first approached poor women and especially prostitutes with condescension, offering them biblical lessons and morality tales as remedies for their plight. But as their shelters remained empty and their portside warnings went unheeded, social workers too began advocating practical alternatives to sex work. Feminists pushed for a reevaluation of the sexual double standard that made prostitution a social necessity. They researched and critiqued the meager wages and horrific working conditions unskilled women experienced, emphasizing the challenges of single females alone in the city. Yet as with their male counterparts, bourgeois women's organizations faced constant impediments in their efforts to restructure the lives of poor women. The priorities of Poland's ruling empires made significant reform a near impossibility. Poles had neither the fiscal nor the administrative authority to affect transformative change.

Perhaps no profession balked at imperial restrictions more than medical practitioners. Driven to universities outside Polish territory for their training, physicians, biologists, chemists, and other scientific specialists developed a harshly critical eye toward public-health conditions back home. Doctors were in the forefront of research on the implications of and potential cures for venereal diseases. Though they did not always agree as a profession on remedies for the venereal epidemic, they were united in their conviction that public sex lay at the root of the contagion. These increasingly powerful medical men (and a few women) were counted among the new leaders of the nation. Along with charity workers and journalists, doctors helped constitute a shadow state of reformers intent on reordering Polish society from the ground up in keeping with modern standards of health, hygiene, and intimate relations. Our study has shown that collective efforts to solve the dilemma of prostitution allowed Polish specialists the opportunity to reshape the nation along more inclusive lines. The health of the weakest link in the population was vital to the country's collective future, and the prostitute and her client lay at the center of these concerns.

In the end, the rise of eugenics thinking among Polish experts was a logical extension of public-health anxiety surrounding the growth of incurable pathologies. Eugenics advocates focused especially on the question of assuring a strong and healthy citizenry in a reborn Polish state. Scientific research on born prostitutes and inherited predisposition to criminality were part of a larger agenda shaping and improving the biological strength on which the new Poland would be built. After a century of fracture, weakness, and foreign domination, these forward-thinking experts sought at all costs to guarantee the health of future citizens. Again, as our narrative has shown, questions surrounding the regulation of paid sex were very much at the core of their thinking about the modern nation.

Reform and Social Integration

A certain sense of the stigma of the nineteenth-century streetwalker had abated by the 1920s. She remained a source of fear within the medical community for the diseases she bore and their stubborn resistance to treatment, but resolving these ailments was increasingly approached from a scientific rather than a moral perspective. She was no longer targeted for discriminatory treatment primarily because of her social background. Instead, the Polish prostitute (who may well have been ethnically Jewish, Ukrainian, German, or Lithuanian) came home under the Second Republic, and with her a whole cohort of previously ostracized lower-class women were grudgingly incorporated into the community of concern that was the business of the new national government. By the birth of the Second Republic, the women who were inscribed onto police registries were sometimes family members of the military heroes who had sacrificed for the country's independence or "innocent" country girls who resorted to paid sex when their villages suffered enemy occupation. The sheer number of women turning to sex work to feed their families in these difficult times helped soften public opinion about them. Moreover, after Poland gained political independence, its leaders could no longer blame imperial powers for the outdated and ineffective registration system. They had to reform the regulation system if only to avoid the syphilis crisis that threatened to destroy the nation at the very moment of its rebirth. The result was the "normalization" of medical checkups for registered prostitutes, which were now conducted in the private and hygienic setting of the local hospital. Admittedly, postwar reforms did not go as far as abolitionist activists hoped, but in the context of the economic instability and political dysfunction of the new state, the transfer of the registration system from police station to clinic reflected a profound shift in public thinking about women who sold sex.

Part of a longer-term change in perceptions of the lower classes, in definitions of deviant behavior, and in attitudes about female sexuality, the decision to house the machinery of regulation in hospitals reflected an expansion of Polish national inclusivity. The late nineteenth-century registration system had permitted greater freedom for sex workers by allowing brothels to close and their residents to move about the city freely. Yet police-regulated prostitution continued to censure public women by branding them with the stigma of the passbook. Only when primary jurisdiction over prostitutes was turned over to the medical sector did the monitoring of sex work become fundamentally a health concern rather than a moral preoccupation. Polish society, like most modern communities, continued to render judgments on the practice of paid sex, but no longer was the behavior of prostitutes seen as emblematic of an entire class of permanent outcasts. Instead, half a century of contact between sex workers and nearly every segment of Polish society had finally bred familiarity. Scientific reason had supplanted moral condemnation and condescension as the primary register for assessing their behavior. The initial melodramatic representation of the "fall" of vulnerable young women into a life of prostitution had edged over into a professional conversation about the failures of the regulation system and finally emerged as a debate about how a democratic state should treat its less fortunate members. The meanings of prostitution shifted in this process to reflect multiple voices, among them the voice of possible reform. This transition from pariah to member of the larger community of obligation makes the study of prostitutes an important barometer of broader cultural change in modern Poland.

BIBLIOGRAPHY

Archives and Libraries

Archiwum Państwowe w Krakowie (APKr)—National Archive in Cracow

Prezydyum C. K. Namiestnictwa, Dyrekcja Policji we Lwowie i Krakowie, APKr, DPKr 110, Akta Przydialne 1916, 1904–1916
Dyrekcja Policji w Krakowie, Prostitution Registry for Cracow, DPKr 436–443, 1879–1911

Biblioteka Jagiellońska—Jagiellonian University Library (Cracow)

Polski Akademia Nauk, Krakow (PAN KR)—Polish Academy of Sciences (Cracow)

Oddział Specjalnych Zbiór, "Polskie Towarzystwe Emigracyne, 'Canadian Pacific'" Rps. 4094, "Materiały Zygmunta Łasockiego dot. Emigracji Polaków do Kanady"

Archiwum Państwowe w Poznaniu (APP)—National Archive in Poznań

Akta Miasta Poznania (AMP)
Prezydium Policji w Poznaniu (PPwP)
Starostwo Powiatowe Poznań-Wschód (StPP)

Archiv der Bundespolizeidirektion Wien (BPdWA)—Vienna Central Police Department Archive

Bestand Prostitution und Mädchenhandel, 1885–1917

Archiv der Republik (AdR)—Austrian State Archives, Vienna

Ministerium des Inneren:
1/7 Mdl 2121 Mädchenhandel 1900–1918
1/7 Mdl 2122 Mädchenhandel 1907; 1908–1918, 1900–1918

Archiwum Główne Akt Dawnych (AGAD)—Central Archives of Historical Records, Warsaw

Rada Głowna Opiekuńcza Szpitali (RGOSz)
C. K. Ministerstwo Spraw Wewnętrznych (CKMSW)

Biblioteka Lekarska Warszawska—Warsaw Medical Library
Biblioteka Narodowa—National Library of Poland (Warsaw)
Biblioteka Uniwersytecka w Warszawie—University of Warsaw Library (Warsaw)

Periodicals

Arbeiterzeitung
Biblioteka Warszawska
Bluszcz
Bulletin Continental
Czystość
Dzien (1913, 1914)
Gazeta Codzienna
Gazeta Lekarska
Gazeta Narodowa
Gazeta Polska
Głos
Głos Narodu
Humanistika Polski
Ilustrowany Kurier Codzienny
Izraelita
Kraj
Królowej Korony Polskiej
Kronika Lekarska
Krytyka
Kurier Codzienny
Kurier Poranny
Kurier Warszawski
Kurjer Polski
Medycyna
Naprzód
Neue Freie Presse
Niwa
Nowa Reforma
Nowe Słowo
Nowiny
Nowiny dla Wszystkich
Ogniwo
Pamiętnik Towarzystwa Lekarskiego Warszawskiego
Posłaniec Bractwa Najświęszej Marii Panny Pracownica Katolicka
Pracownica Polska
Prawda
Przedświt
Przegląd Hygieniczny

Przegląd Lekarski
Przegląd Powszechny
Przegląd Tygodniowy
Przyjaciel Sług (monthly suplement to *Grzmot*)
Przyszłość: Organ Towarzystwa Abstynentów
Robotnica (supplement to *Nowe Słowo*)
Słowo
Społeczeństwo
Ster
Świat Płciowy
Tygodnik Lekarski
Wiedza
Wiek
Zdrowie

Published Primary Sources

Aleichem, Sholem. "The Man from Buenos Aires." In *Tevye the Dairyman and the Railroad* Stories. New York, 1987.

Altschul, Theodor. "Płciowe uświadomienie młodzieży." *Zdrowie* 25, no. 6 (June 1909): 427–28.

Annański, St. [S. Auerbach]. "Zagadnienie prostytucji w świetle higjeny społecznej." *Wiedza* 1, no. 3 (1910): 80–87.

——. "Krytyka i sprawozdania: Dr. Aug. Wróblewski, 'O prostytucji i handlu kobietami,' Warsaw 1909." *Społeczeństwo* 35 (1909): 418–19.

Backiewicz, Jan, and Henryk Gromadzki. *Pamiętnik II-ego Zjazdu Hygieniestów Polskich.* Warsaw, 1918.

Asch, Sholem. *God of Vengeance.* Trans. Joseph C. Landis, *The Dybbuk and other Great Yiddish Plays.* New York: Bantam Books, 1966.

Bartkiewicz, Z. *Złe miasto: Obrazy z 1907 roku.* Warsaw: Jan Czempiński, 1911.

Baumfeld, Andrzej. "O czystości kilka uwag." *Czystość* 1, no. 3 (July 15, 1905): 17–20.

Belke, Teodor. "Kilka słów o nierządzie publicznym." *Medycyna* 19, no. 10 (1891): 158–59.

——. "Kilka słów o sposobach tamujących szerzenie się chorób wenerycznych." *Medycyna* 9, no. 28 (1881): 443–45.

Belmont, Leo. *Małżeństwo i prostytucja: O upadłej kobiecie.* Warsaw, 1910.

Bilewski, Janusz. "Służące a prostytucya." *Świat Płciowy* 1, no. 3 (October, 1905): 33–39.

——. "Walka zarazą weneryczną." *Świat Płciowy* 1, no. 1 (May 31, 1905): 39–40.

Billington-Greig, Teresa. "The Truth about White Slavery." *English Review* 14 (June 1913): 428–46.

Blaschko, Alfred. "Prostytucya w XIX wieku." *Nowe Słowo* 2 (November 1, 1903): 490–92.

Blay, Dr. Julja. "O czym kobiety nie mówią." *Ster* 7, no. 1 (January 10, 1913): 4.

Bloch, Iwan. *Die Prostitution*. Berlin: Louis Marcus, 1912.

———. *Das Sexualleben unserer Zeit in seinen Beziehungen zur modernen Kultur*. Berlin: Louis Marcus, 1908.

Blumenfeld, Antoni. *Prostytucya i hygiena płciowa*. Lwow, 1906.

———. *Syfilis niewinnych*. Lwów: Drukarnia Narodowa w Krakowie, 1914.

Boy-Żeleński, Tadeusz. "Kropla mleka w Krakowie." *Nowe Słowo* 6, no. 7 (1907): 157–59.

Buczyński, Roman. *Zarys stanu moralnego naszego społeczeństwa*. Warsaw: S. Orgelbrand i synów, 1885.

Bujwidowa, Kazimiera. "Idea demokratyczna w wychowaniu." *Nowe Słowo* 6, no. 8 (1907): 180.

Butler, Josephine E. *An Autobiographical Memoir*. Edited by George W. Johnson and Lucy A. Johnson. Bristol: J.W. Arrowsmith, 1909.

———. *A Letter to the Members of the Ladies National Association*. Liverpool: T. Brakell, 1875.

———. *Personal Reminiscences of a Great Crusade*. London: Horace Marshall, 1896.

Caro, Leopold. *Emigracya i polityka emigracyjna ze szczególnym uwzględnieniem stosunków polskich*. Translated by Karol Englisch. Poznań: Drukarnia św. Wojciecha, 1914.

Carpenter, Edward. "Małżeństwo: Rzut oka na przyszłość." *Nowe Słowo* 2 (July 15, 1903): 315–19.

Chodecki, Władysław. "Alkoholizm a prostytucya." *Zdrowie* 24, no. 5 (May 1908): 298–311.

———. "Co pchna służące w objęcia prostytucyi." *Zdrowie* 22, no. 8 (August 1906): 563–66.

———. "O żadaniach lekarza w walce z chorobami wenerycznymi." *Zdrowie* 22, no. 8 (August 1906): 556–63.

———. "Walka z prostytycją." *Zdrowie* 19, no. 5 (1903): 261–62.

Chodźko, Witold. *Prostytucja i choroby weneryczne jako zjawiska społeczne*. Warsaw: Drukarnia Miejska, 1939.

Ciechanowski, Stanisław. "Niebezpieczeństwo społeczne chorób wenerycznych." *Przegląd Lekarski* 40, no. 6 (1916): 125.

Cykalska, Stefanja Rygier. "Samoobrona społeczeństwa w walce z nierządem." *Zagadnienie Rasy* 2, no. 8 (July 1920): 7.

Digalski, V. "Stanowisko rodziców wobec płciowego uświadamiania ich dzieci." *Zdrowie* 25, no. 11 (November 1909): 746.

Dulębianka, Marja. "Polityczne stanowisko kobiety." *Ster* 1, no. 7 (1907): 255–65.

Durand, E. Dana. *Supplement to Commerce Reports, Trade Information Bulletin nr. 32: Public Finance of Poland*. Washington, DC: Government Printing Office, 1922.

Dyer, Alfred S. *The European Slave Trade in English Girls*. London: Dyer Brothers, 1880.

Ellis, Havelock. *Man and Woman: A Study of Human Secondary Sexual Characters.* London: W. Scott, 1897.

——. *Sexual Inversion* (with John Addington Symonds). London: Wilson and MacMillan, 1897.

——. *Studies in the Psychology of Sex.* London: The University Press, 1901.

Evans-Gordon, Major W. *The Alien Immigrant.* London: William Heinemann; New York: Charles Scribner's Sons, 1903.

Flexner, Abraham. *The Regulation of Prostitution in Europe.* New York: The American Social Hygiene Association, 1914.

Gagatnicki, A. "Skrzynka do listów: Opieka nad kobietami." *Kurier Warszawski,* April 8, 1900, 6.

Geisler, Józef. "Krótkie sprawozdanie z działności szpitala wojsk: Dla prostytutek i ambulatorjum wenerycznego w Brześciu." *Lekarz Wojskowy* 2, no. 8 (1921): 234–35.

Giedroyć, Franciszek. *"Domy wilczkowania" (Projekt organizacji wewnętrznej zamtuzów w Polsce.* Warsaw: Drukarnia Kowalewskiego, 1912.

——. *Nauka o chorobach wenerycznych w piśmiennictwie lekarskiem polskiem.* Warsaw: E. Nicz, 1909.

——. *Prostytutki jako źródła chorób wenerycznych w Warszawie (w ciągu ostatnich lat kilku).* Warsaw: Marya Ziemkiewiczowa, 1892.

——. *Rada Lekarska Księstwa Warszawskieto i Królestwa Polskiego (1909–1867).* Warsaw: Władysław Łazarski, 1913.

——. *Rys historyczny szpitała św. Lazarza w Warszawie.* Warsaw: Drukarnia Kowalewskiego, 1897.

Godlewski, Father Marceli. "Kilka uwag z powodu listu robotnicy fabrycznej w Łódźi." *Niwa* 16, no. 9 (1897): 161–62.

Gottliebówna, Róża. "Wywiady nad położeniem robotnic w Krakowie: Swaczki." *Nowe Słowo* 3, no. 10 (May 15, 1904): 217–19.

Grabski, Władysław. "Listy z Krakowskiego Przedmieścia." *Kurier Warszawski,* April 1, 1900, 2–4.

Grotowski, Z. *Rozwój zakładów dobrocznnych w Warszawie.* Warsaw: Drukarnia "Gazeta Handlowa," 1910.

Gruber, Max. *Hygiena życia płciowego.* Lwów: Drukarnia Uniwersytetu Jagiellońskiego, 1907.

——. *Die Prostitution vom Standpunkte der Sozialhygiene.* Vienna, 1905.

Heller. "Uwagi, dotyczące zagadnień seksualnych." *Zdrowie* 25, no. 12 (December 1909): 804.

Horbowski, Z. "Organizacja i działalność Urzędu Sanitarno-Obyczajowego w Warszawie." *Zagadnienia Rasy* 4, no. 3 (1922): 11–16.

H. R. "Zdrowie młodzieży." *Czystość* 1, no. 5 (August 15, 1905): 43–45.

In the Grip of the White Slave Trader. London: Offices of the M.A. P, 1911.

Instrukcya dla magistratów miast o 10.000 lub więcej ludności, i miast posiadających załogi wojskowe, względem wykonywania nadzoru nad publicznemi nierządnicam. Lwów, 1852.

Jewish Association for the Protection of Girls and Women. *Official Report of the Jewish International Conference.* London: Wertheimer, Lea, 1910.

——. *Special Report on the Traffic in Girls and Women*. London: printed privately, 1910.

Kamieński, Stanisław. "Warszawski Dom Wychowawczy w świetle statystyki porównawczej (z powodu artykułu 'Niwy Polskiej')." *Gazeta Lekarska* 16, no. 7 (1901): 177–82.

Kamiński, Jan Maurycy. *O prostytucji*. Warsaw: A. Pajewski, 1875.

Karaffa-Korbutt, K. "Eugenika służba wojskowa a wojna." *Lekarz Wojskowy* no. 2 (1926).

Karkowski, Adam. "Działalność Towarzystwa hygieniecznego w Wielkopolce." In *Księga pamiętkowa XI zjazdu lekarzy i przyrodników polskich w Krakowie, July 18–22, 1911,* edited by Adam Karkowski, 622–24. Cracow: Komitet Gospodarczy, 1911.

——. "O seksualnem wychowaniu młodzieży." *Przegląd Hygieniczny* 7, no. 5 (May 1908): 129–33; no. 6 (June 1908): 161–65.

Kelles-Krauz, Kazimierz. *Listy, 1890–97*. vol. 1. Edited by Feliks Tych. Warsaw-Wrocław: Zakład Narodowy im. Ossolińskich, 1984.

——. "Półśrodki." *Nowe Słowo* 1, no. 19 (1902): 455–58.

Klink, Edward. "Sprawozdanie z czynności lekarskiej w oddziale kobiet publicznych w Szpitalu św. Łazarza w Warszawie w r. 1876." *Medycyna* 5, nos. 33–35 (August–October 1877): 517–552.

Konczyński, Józef. *Stan moralny społeczeństwa polskiego na podstawie danych statystyki kryminalnej*. Warsaw: Skład główny w księgarni Gebethnera i Wolffa, 1911.

Korczak, Janusz. "Przeciw rospuscie." *Głos* 20, no. 22, May 21, 1905, 322–23.

Koreywo, Bolesław. *Dwie moralności i walka z nierządem*. Poznań: Nakładem Spółki Pedagogicznej Tow. Akc. Poznań, 1925.

Koszutski, Stanisław. "Na mównicy: Walka z prostytucją," *Głos* 15, no. 25 (June 23, 1900): 386–68.

Krafft-Ebing, Richard von. *Lehrbuch der gerichtlichen Psychopathologie, mit Berucksichtigung der Gesetzbegung von Österreich, Deutschland und Frankreich*. Stuttgart: Verlag von Ferdinand Enke, 1886.

——. *Psychopathia sexualis, mit besonderer Berucksichtigung der contraren Sexualempfindung: Eine klinisch-forensische Studie*. Stuttgart: Verlag von Ferdinand Enke, 1886.

Krzyształowicz, F. "Metody walki z chorobami wenerycznymi." *Zagadnienie Rasy* 2, no. 4 (May 1919): 4–5.

Kuczalska-Reinschmit, Paulina. "Reglamentacja prostytucji jako środek zapobiegawczy zarazie chorowenerycznych." In *Pamiętnik Wystawy Walka z Chorobami Zakaznemi, Maj 1915 roku*, 68–73. Warsaw: n.p., 1915.

Kumaniecki, Kazimierz. *Tymczasowe wyniki spisu ludności w Krakowie z 31 grudnia 1910 roku*. Cracow: Drukarnia Związkowa, 1912.

L., Józef. "Policja obyczajów." *Głos* 5, no. 30 (1900): 476–77.

Łazowski, Tadeusz J., and Konrad Siwicki. "Życie płciowe warszawskiej młodzieży akademickiej według ankiety z roku 1903." *Zdrowie* 1, no. 2 (November 1905): 919–31; 22, no. 4 (February 1906): 75–97; and no. 5 (March 1906): 143–77.

Lenartowicz, J. "Stan szpitalnictwa i środków walki z chorobami wenerycznemi we wschodniej części Galicji." *Zagadnienia Rasy* 2, no. 5 (August 1919): 3.

Limanowski, Bolesław. "Regulamentacyja występu." *Głos* 3, no. 31 (1888): 363–64.

Lombroso, Cesare, and Guglielmo Ferrero. *Criminal Woman, the Prostitute, and the Normal Woman.* Translated and with a new introduction by Nicole Hahn Rafter and Mary Gibson. Durham, NC: Duke University Press, 2004.

Lubińska, Teresa. "Handel żywym towarem i prostytucja." *Ster* 2, no. 6 (1908): 220–24.

Lubowidzki, Antoni. *Wielomęstwo w ustroju współczesnym i w przyszłości.* Cracow: Drukarnia Aleksandra Rippera, 1909.

Lutomski, B. "Upadłe samobójczyznie," *Głos* 5, no. 7 (1890): 76–77.

M. "W sprawie służących." *Ogniwo* 1, no. 50 (November 22, 1903): 195–96.

Macko, Jozef. *Nierząd jako choroba społeczna.* Warsaw: Nakład Polskiego Komitetu Walki z Handlem Kobietami i Dziećmi, 1938.

———. *Prostytucja.* Warsaw: Nakład Polskiego Komitetu Walki z Handlem Kobietami i Dziećmi, 1927.

Margulies, B. "Prostytucja w Łodzi." *Zdrowie* 22, no. 8 (August 1906): 539–47.

Martineau, L. *Prostytucja potajemna.* Warsaw: M. Filipowska, 1892.

Męczkowska, K. "Ze statystyki prostytucyi i nieprawych dzieci." *Świat Płciowy* 1, no. 1 (May 31, 1905): 37–41.

Męczkowska, Teodora. *Służące a prostytucja.* Warsaw: n.p., 1906.

Męczkowski, R. Wacław. *Stan i potrzeby szpitali Królestwa Polskiego.* Warsaw: Druk Aleksandra Ginsa, 1905.

Moriconi, Ludwika. "Przyczynek do sprawy prostytucyi u nas." *Przegląd chorób skórnych i werenycznych,* nos. 4–5 (1907): 168–73.

Moszczeńska, Izabela. "Czego nie wiemy o naszych synach." Warsaw: Nakład Naszej Księgarni, 1904.

———. "O służbie domowej." *Głos* 5, no. 25 (1900): 395–96.

———. "Podwójna moralność." *Nowe Słowo* 2 (March 1, 1903): 97–101.

———. "Prostytucya i praca kobiet." *Nowe Słowo* 1 (December 15, 1902): 370–75.

Muszkat, Maks. "Walka z nierządem." *Głos Prawa,* nos. 1–2 (1939): 1–25.

N. "W. Tow. Hygienicznym." *Kurier Warszawski,* April 23, 1900, 7–8.

National Vigilance Association. *Congress of the White Slave Traffic.* London: National Vigilance Association, 1899.

Okolski, Antoni. "O domach podrzutków." *Biblioteka Warszawska* 193 (January 1889): 12–40; (February 1889): 187–209.

Orion. "Echa prawdy: Z tajemnic Warszawy." *Prawda* 35 (1913): 2.

Papée, Jan. "Choroby weneryczne, ich rozszerzenie i zapobieganie." *Przegląd Hygieniczny* 5, no. 6 (June 1906): 137–43; no. 7 (July 1906): 165–69; nos. 8–9 (September 1906): 200–204; no. 11 (November 1906): 236–39; 6, no. 1 (January 1907): 10–17.

———. *Choroby weneryczne, ich rozszerzenie i zapobieganie.* Lwów: Drukarnia Związkowa.

———. *Choroby weneryczne i ich zwalczanie w czasie wojny (1915–1918).* Cracow: Drukarnia Uniwersytetu Jagiellońskiego, 1919.

———. "Choroby weneryczne u prostytutek we Lwowie w czasie wojny 1914–1918." *Gazeta Lekarska,* nos. 41–42 (1919): 498–502; nos. 43–44 (1919): 513–516.

———. *Kiły u prostytutek we Lwowie.* Warsaw: Odbitka z *Przeglądu Chorób Skórnych i Wenerycznych,* 1908.

——. "Nadzór lekarski nad prostytucyą." *Lwowski Tygodnik Lekarski* 2, no. 14 (1907): 159–61; no. 15 (1907): 173–76; no. 16 (1907): 186–88; no. 17 (1907): 199–202; no. 18 (1907): 211–214.

——. "O reformie prostytucyi." *Lwowski Tygodnik Lekarski*, no. 8 (1908): 3–4.

Pappenheim, Bertha. *Sisyphus Arbeit: Reisebriefe aus den Jahren 1911 und 1912.* Leipzig: Lindner, 1924.

——. *Sisyphus: Gegen den Mädchenhandel-Galizien.* Freiburg: Kore, 1992.

——. *Zur Jüdenfrage in Galizien.* Frankfurt: 1900.

Pappenheim, Bertha, and Sara Rabinowitsch. *Zur Lage der Jüdischen Bevölkerung in Galizien.* Frankfurt am Main: Neuer Frankfurter Verlag, 1904.

Paprocki, L. "Dom podrzutków przy Szpitalu Dzieciątka Jezus w Warsyawie." *Ekonomista* no. 8 (1871): 473.

Pawlikowski, Karol, J. Kosiński, B. Gepner, and H. Stankiewicz, eds. *Wykład chorób wenerycznych.* Warsaw: Drukarnia Józefa Bergera, 1874.

Perlmutter, Salomea. "Położenie lwowskich robotnic chrześcinjańskich." *Nowe Słowo* 2 (December 1, 1903): 535–41.

Piasecki, Egeniusz. "W sprawie hygieny płciowej młodzieży." *Przegląd Hygieniczny* 5, no. 5 (May 1906): 113–21.

Podgorska-Klawe, Zofia. "Warszawski dom podrzutków (1732–1901)." *Rocznik Warszawski* 12 (1974): 139–40.

Polańska, H. "Handel dziewczętami." *Świat Płciowy* 1, no. 3 (October 1905): 20–25.

P. [Poplawski?], J. "Warszawski towar." *Humanista Polski,"* no. 12 (1913): 6–7.

Poraj, St. "Dusza prostytutki i środki służące do jej odrodzenia. *Ster* 1, no. 9 (December 1907): 375–78.

Posner, Stanisław. *Nad otchłania.* Warsaw: Księgarnia. Naukowa, 1903.

Prus, Bolesław. "Doraźna kara." *Kurier Warszawski,* March 3, 1888, 3.

——, ed. *Kroniki.* 20 vols. Warsaw: Państwowy Instytut Wydawniczy, 1953–70.

——. "Nim słońce wejdzie." *Kurier Codzienny*, January 11, 1883, 3.

——. "Rozpusta czy bieda." *Kurier Codzienny*, October 28, 1900, 3.

——. "Znowu donzuaneria." *Kurier Warszawski*, March 6, 1888, 3.

"Przystań dla kobiet." *Słowo*, May 31, 1905, 2.

"Przytułek św. Antoniego w Lublinie dla upadłych dziewcząt." *Czystość* 1, no. 7 (September 1905): 61–62.

Raczyński, Kazimierz. *Kobieta niewolnica w wieku XX.* Poznań: Drukarnia Mieszczańska, 1933.

——. *Pierwsza pomoc w nieszczęśliwych wypadkach z dodatkiem najważniejszych ustaw sanitarnych, i.t.d. dla użytku funkcjonarjuszy policji państwowej, i.t.d.* Poznań: Drukarnia "Poradnika Gospodarskiego," 1925.

——. *Upadła kobieta.* Poznań: Drukarnia Przemysłowa, 1926.

Radek, Karol. "Prostytucya w naszej prasie." *Nowe Słowo* 3, nos. 17–18 (September 15, 1904): 407–11.

——. "Z badań nad prostytucyą." *Nowe Słowo* 3, no. 23 (December 1, 1904): 536–41.

Rygier, Marya. "Walka z prostytucyą." *Nowe Słowo* 2, no. 17 (August 1, 1903): 394.

Rogowicz, J. "Oględziny lekarskie kobiet w obliczu obowiązującego u nas prawa." *Medycyna* 24, no. 1 (1896): 19–21.

Rolle, Józef A. "Choroby weneryczne (1854–1864)." *Pamiątnik Towarzystwa Lekarskiego Warszawskiego* 8 (1865): 162–63.

———. "Materiały do topografii lekarskiej i hygieny Podola: Prostytucja." *Przegląd Lekarski* 8, nos. 38, 39, 40 (1869): 305–7, 313–15, 321.

———. "Spostrzeżenia z dziedziny chorób sifilitycznych." *Przegląd Lekarski* 3, nos. 1–2 (1864).

Rosset, Edward. *Prostytucja i choroby weneryczne w Łodzi.* Łódź: Nakład Wydziału Zdrowotności Publicznej Magistratu m. Łodzi, 1931.

Royal Commission on Alien Immigration. *Minutes of Evidence.* London, 1903.

Rząśnicki, Adolf. *Hygiena robotnicza.* Warsaw: Druk Wasława Maślankiewicza, 1922.

———. *Prostytucja a proletarjat.* Warsaw: Druk L. Bogusławskiego, 1920.

———. "Sprawozdanie z działalność Polskiego towarzystwa walki z nierządem i chorobami wenerycznymi." *Zagadniena Rasy* 1, no. 1 (July 1918): 24.

———. *W sprawie prostytucji.* Vilnius: Nakład "Wiedzy," 1911.

———. "W sprawie walki z handlem żywym towarem." *Społeczeństwo* 3, no. 44 (1909): 530–31.

Sarason. "W sprawie uświadamiania płciowego." *Zdrowie* 24, no. 3 (March 1908): 160–62.

S.-I, Wł. "Prostytucya ze szczególnem uwzględniem stosunków Lwowskich." *Świat Płciowy* 1, no. 3 (October 1905): 11–15.

Schrank, Josef. *Der Mädchenhandel und seine Bekämpfung.* Vienna: Selbstverlag, 1904.

———. *Die Prostitution in Wien in historischer, administrativer und hygieniescher Beziehung.* 2 vols. Vienna: Selbstverlage, 1886.

Sempołowska, Stefania. *Z dna nędzy.* Warsaw: Drukarnia K. Kowalewskiego, 1909.

Singer, Isaac Beshevis. *Scum* (1991). New York: Macmillan, 2003.

Skalski, Stanisław. "Prostytucja w Gubernii Piotrkowskiej." *Zdrowie* 22, no. 8 (August 1906): 547–56.

Sokołowski, Alfred. *Wielkie klęski społeczne i walka z niemi.* Warsaw: Gebethner i Wolf, 1917.

Sonnenberg, E. "Źródła i drogi pozapłciowego szerzenia syfilisu." *Zdrowie* vol. 13 (1897): 43–61.

Stankiewicz, Henryk. "Kwestyja prostytucyi m. Warszawy pod względem administracyjnym i lekarskim." In *Pamiętnik Towarzystwa Lekarskiego Warszawskiego,* edited by Edward Klink, 590–92. Warsaw: n.p., 1881.

Stopczański, Jan. "Choroby weneryczne w Legionach." *Przegląd Lekarski* 56, no. 39 (September 30, 1917): 308–10.

Sułkowski, W. A. *Z dziejów dobroczynności publicznej 1870–1884.* Warsaw: n.p., 1886.

Swiętochowski, Aleksander. "Liberum veto." *Prawda* 2, no. 11 (1882): 5.

———. *Wspomnienia.* Wrocław: Ossolineum, 1966.

Szczygielski, Bronisław-Topór. *Kobieta-Ciało: Odysseja kobiety upadłej.* Warsaw: A. Borsuk, 1914.

Szymański, Jan. *Z Ruchu etycznego wśród młodzieży.* Cracow: Ethos, 1906.

Tarnowsky [Tarnovskii], Venjamin. *Prostitution und Abolitionismus.* Hamburg: Verlag von Leopold Voss, 1890.

———. "Z badań nad prostytucya." *Nowe Słowo* 3, no. 23 (December 1, 1904): 536.

Teodorczuk, Stanisław. "Zjazd kobiet polskich." *Czystość* 2, no. 10 (1906): 107.

Turzyma, Marya. "Ekonomiczne przyczyny prostytucyi." *Nowe Słowo* 4 (December 15, 1905): 458–60.

———. "Handel kobietami." *Głos Kobiet* (1905): 143–62.

Wagener, Major D. H. *Der Mädchenhandel*. Berlin: Lichterfelde, 1911.

Weininger. *Sex and Character*. Vienna: Wilhelm Braumüller, 1904.

Wernic, Leon. "O Zwalczaniu chorób wenerycznych w Państwie Polskim." *Biuletynie Ministerstwa Zdrowia Publicznego*, no. 1 (1921): 1.

———. "Podstawowe drogi do walki z chorobami wenerycznymi." *Zdrowie* 6, no. 8 (January 1906): 517–20.

———. "Polski project ustawy walki z chorobami wenerycznemi i nierząd." *Nowiny Lekarskie* 40, no. 20 (1928): 710–11.

———. *Polskie Towarzystwo Walki z Nierządem i Chorobami Wenerycznemi*. Warsaw, 1916

———. *Ruch eugeniczny w Polsce i jego zagadnienia aktualne*. Poznań: Nakład Dr. J. Jagielskiego, 1928.

———. "Sprawa ludności w Polsce, a choroby weneryczne." *Zagadnienia Rasy* 2, no. 4 (May 1919): 14–15.

Wernic, Leon. "W sprawie walki z chorobami wenerycznemi." *Zagadnienia Rasy* 3, no. 11 (August 1921): 14–16.

———. *Walka z chorobami wenerycznemi i nierządem*. Warsaw: W. Pekarniak, 1917.

Wertensteinowa, W. "Z tragizmów życia." *Prawda* 37, no. 13 (1917): 3.

Wesołowski, Wacław. "Syfilis w stosunku do społeczeństwa." *Zdrowie* 20, no. 20 (February 1904): 446–47.

———. "Walka z chorobami wenerycznymi a obrona rasy." *Zagadnienia Rasy* 1, no. 1 (July 1918): 11.

Weychertowna, Wł. "Żródła społeczne i etyczne handlu żywym towarem." *Ster* 2, no. 6 (1908): 212–16.

Wojnarowa, Marya. "Zbudźcie się kobiety." *Czystość* 1, no. 4 (August 1, 1905): 41–42.

Wolski, N. E. *Obrona rodziny*. Warsaw: Piotr Laskauer, 1907.

Wróblewski, Augustyn. "Dzieci w szpitalu św. Łazarza." *Czystość* 5, no. 25 (June 19, 1909): 385–86.

———. "Handel kobietami," *Czystość* 5, no. 23 (May 14, 1909): 354–56.

———. "O moralności płciowej." *Czystość* 1, no. 1 (June 20, 1905): 2–3; no. 2 (July 1, 1905): 12–15; no. 3 (July 15, 1905): 20–22; no. 4 (August 1, 1905): 32–34.

———. *O prostytucji i handlu kobietami*. Warsaw: Piotr Laskauer, 1909.

———. "Przytułki dla upadłych kobiet." *Czystość* 5, no. 2 (June 26, 1909): 414.

———. *Ruch Etyczny*. Warsaw: Piotr Laskauer, 1908.

Wróblewski, Bogdan. "Proces o handel kobietami." *Gazeta Wyborcza*, March 20, 2002.

Wyrobek, Emil. *Alkohol i prostytucja a choroby weneryczne: Gruźlica i samobójstwo*. Cracow: Główny Skład w Księgarni G. Gebethnera i Spółki, 1910.

———. *Choroby a małżeństwo*. Cracow: Drukarnia A. Koziańskiego, 1906.

———. *Choroby weneryczne: Ich skutki i znaczenie w życiu jednostki i społeczeństwa, tudzież osoby leczenia i zapogiegania*. Cracow: Nakładem Księgarni sz. Taffeta, 1916.

———. *Śmiertelność i choroby jako skutek rozwiązłego życia*. Cracow: Wydawnictwo Towarzystwa Młodzieży "Ethos" w Krakowie, 1907.

———. *W pętach rozpusty i pijaństwa: Obrazki z codziennego życia*. Cracow: Drukarnia Przemysłowa, 1920.

———. *Z Otchłani chorób nędzy i upadku*. Cracow: Nakład Księgarnia "Wiedza i Sztuka," 1925.

———. *Z posiewu bogini wojny: Alkoholizm prostytucya, choroby płciowe, nerwowe, i umysłowe, gruźlica i samobójstwo.* Cracow: Nakładem Księgarni sz. Taffeta, 1917.

Wysłouch, Antoni. *Ohyda wieku.* Warsaw: Skład Główny w Księgarni E. Wende i S-ka., 1904.

———. *Prostytucya i jej skutki.* Poznań: Drukarnia św. Wojciecha, 1905.

Zaleski, Wacław. *Prostytucja powojenna w Warszawie.* Warsaw: R. Olesiński, W. Merkel, 1927.

———. *Z dziejów prostytucji w Warszawie.* Warsaw: Druk Policyna, 1923.

Zeromski, Stefan. *Dzienniki.* Warsaw: "Czytelnik," 1961.

Secondary Sources

Adams, Mark B., ed. *The Wellborn Science: Eugenics in Germany, France, Brazil, and Russia.* Oxford: Oxford University Press, 1990.

Agustin, Laura Maria. "The Disappearing of a Migration Category: Migrants Who Sell Sex." *Journal of Ethnic and Migration Studies* 32, no. 1 (2006): 29–47.

———. *Sex at the Margins: Migration, Labour Markets, and the Rescue Industry.* London: Zed Books, 2007.

Alpes, Maybritt Jill. "The Traffic in Voices: Reconciling Experiences of Migrant Women in Prostitution with Paradigms of 'Human Trafficking.'" *Human Security Journal* 6 (Spring 2008): 34–45.

Baczkowski, Michał. "Prostytucja w Krakowie na przełomie XIX i XX w." *Studia historyczne* 43, no. 4 (2000): 593–607.

Baldwin, Peter. *Contagion and the State, 1830–1930.* Cambridge: Cambridge University Press, 1999.

Barkan, Elazar. *The Retreat of Scientific Racism: Changing Concepts of Race in Britain and the United States between the Two World Wars.* Cambridge: Cambridge University Press, 1992.

Barry, Kathleen. *Female Sexual Slavery.* New York: New York University Press, 1984.

Bartal, Israel. *The Jews of Eastern Europe, 1772–1881.* Translated by Chaya Naor. Philadelphia: University of Pennsylvania Press, 2005.

Bell, Daniel. "The Myth of Crime Waves." In *The End of Ideology: On the Exhaustion of Political Ideas in the Fifties*, 151–74. Cambridge, MA: Harvard University Press, 1962.

Ben-Sasson, H. H., ed. *A History of the Jewish People.* Cambridge, MA: Harvard University Press, 1994.

Bernstein, Laurie. *Sonia's Daughters: Prostitutes and Their Regulations in Imperial Russia.* Berkeley: University of California Press, 1995.

Bideleux, Robert, and Ian Jeffries. *A History of Eastern Europe: Crisis and Change.* London: Psychology Press, 1998.

Blank, Inge. "From Serfdom to Citizenship: Polish Folk Culture from the Era of the Partitions to World War I." In *Roots of the Transplanted: Plebian Culture, Class, and Politics in the Life of Labor Migrants*, edited by Dirk Hoerder and Inge Blank, 111–73. Boulder, CO: East European Monographs, 1994.

Blejwas, Stanislaus. *Realism in Polish Politics: Warsaw Positivism and National Survival in Nineteenth-Century Poland.* New Haven, CT: Yale University Press, 1984.

Bliss, Katherine. *Compromised Position: Prostitution, Public Health, and Gender Politics in Revolutionary Mexico City.* University Park: Pennsylvania State University Press, 2001.

Blobaum, Robert. "The Revolution of 1905–7 and the Crisis of Polish Catholicism." *Slavic Review* 47, no. 4 (1988): 667–86.

——. *Rewolucja: Russian Poland, 1904–1907.* Ithaca, NY: Cornell University Press, 1995.

——. "The 'Woman Question' in Russian Poland, 1900–1914." *Journal of Social History* 35, no. 4 (2002): 799–824.

Bowler, P. J. *The Non-Darwinian Revolution: Reinterpreting a Historical Myth.* Baltimore: Johns Hopkins University Press, 1988.

Brinkmann, Tobias. "Why Paul Nathan Attacked Albert Ballin: The Transatlantic Mass Migration and the Privatization of Prussia's Eastern Border Inspection, 1886–1914." *Central European History* 43 (2010): 47–83.

Bristow, Edward J. "The German-Jewish Fight against White Slavery." *Leo Baeck Yearbook* 28 (1983): 301–28.

——. *Prostitution and Prejudice: The Jewish Fight against White Slavery, 1870–1939.* Oxford: Clarendon Press, 1983.

——. *Vice and Vigilance: Purity Movements in Britain since 1700.* Dublin: Gill and Macmillan, 1977.

Brubaker, Rogers. *Ethnicity without Groups.* Cambridge, MA: Harvard University Press, 2004.

Brunton, Deborah. *Medicine Transformed: Health, Disease, and Society in Europe, 1800–1930.* Manchester: Manchester University Press, 2004.

Bullough, Vern L. *The History of Prostitution.* New York: University Books, 1964.

——. "Problems and Methods for Research in Prostitution and the Behavioral Sciences." In *Studies in Human Sexual Behavior: The American Scene*, edited by Ailon Shiloh, 14–23. Springfield, IL: Thomas, 1970.

Bullough, Vern L., Margaret Deacon, Barrett Elcano, and Bonnie Bullough, eds. *A Bibliography of Prostitution.* New York: Garland, 1977.

Bunzl, Matti. "Desiderata for a History of Austrian Sexualities." *Austrian History Yearbook* 38 (2007): 48–57.

Bynum, W. F. *Science and the Practice of Medicine in the Nineteenth Century.* Cambridge: Cambridge University Press, 1994.

Choroby przenoszone droga płciowa. Edited by Tomasz F. Mroczkowsk. Warsaw: Wydawnictwo Lekarskie PZWL, 1998.

Chwałba, Andrzej. *Polacy w służbie Moskali.* Warsaw: Wydawnictwo Naukowe, 1999.

Cohen, Stanley. *Folk Devils and Moral Panics: The Creation of the Mods and Rockers.* London: MacGibbon & Kee, 1972.

Connelly, Mark. *The Response to Prostitution in the Progressive Era.* Chapel Hill: University of North Carolina Press, 1980.

Corbin, Alain. "Commercial Sexuality in Nineteenth-Century France: A System of Images and Regulations." *Representations* 14 (Spring 1986): 209–19.

——. *Women for Hire: Prostitution and Sexuality in France after 1850.* Translated by Alan Sheridan. Cambridge, MA: Harvard University Press, 1990.

Dabrowski, Patrice M. "Constructing a Polish Landscape: The Example of the Carpathian Frontier." *Austrian History Yearbook* 39 (2008): 45–65.

———. "'Discovering' the Galician Borderlands: The Case of the Eastern Carpathians." *Slavic Review* 64, no. 2 (2005): 380–402.

Data, Jan, ed. *Miasto-kultura-literatura, wiek XIX: Materiały sesji naukowej.* Gdańsk: Wydawn. Gdańskie Towarzystwo Naukowe, 1993.

Davies, Norman. *God's Playground: A History of Poland,* vol. 2, *1795 to the Present.* New York: Columbia University Press, 1982.

D'Emilio, John, and Estelle B. Freedman. *Intimate Matters: A History of Sexuality in America.* New York: Harper and Row, 1988.

de Vries, Petra. "'White Slaves' in a Colonial Nation: The Dutch Campaign against the Traffic in Women in the Early Twentieth Century." *Social and Legal Studies* 14, no. 1 (2005): 39–60.

Dikotter, Frank. "Race Culture: Recent Perspectives on the History of Eugenics." *American Historical Review* (April 1998): 467–78.

Doezema, Jo. "Loose Women or Lost Women?: The Re-emergence of the Myth of 'White Slavery' in Contemporary Discourses of 'Trafficking in Women.'" *Gender Issues* 18, no. 1 (2000): 23–50.

———. *Sex Slaves and Discourse Masters: The Construction of Trafficking.* London: Zed Books, 2010.

Douglas, Mary. *Purity and Danger: An Analysis of Concepts of Pollution and Taboo.* London: Routledge, 1966.

Dubnow, Simon. *History of the Jews.* 5 vols. South Brunswick, NJ: T. Yoseloff, 1973.

Engelstein, Laura. *The Keys to Happiness: Sex and the Search for Modernity in Fin-de-Siècle Russia.* Ithaca: Cornell University Press, 1992.

Evans, Richard J. *The Feminist Movement in Germany, 1894–1933.* London: Sage, 1976.

———. "Prostitution, State, and Society in Imperial Germany." *Past and Present* 70 (February 1976): 106–29.

———. "The Life and Death of a Lost Woman." In *Tales from the German Underworld,* edited by Richard J. Evans, 166–212. New Haven: Yale University Press, 1998.

Feldman, Egal. "Prostitution: The Alien Woman and the Progressive Imagination." *American Quarterly* 19 (1967): 192–206.

Finnegan, Frances. *Poverty and Prostitution: A Study of Victorian Prostitutes in York.* Cambridge: Cambridge University Press, 1979.

Foucault, Michel. *Birth of the Clinic: An Archeology of Medical Perception.* New York: Vintage, 1994.

Franaszek, Piotr. *Zdrowie publiczne w Galicji w dobie autonomii (Wybrane problemy).* Cracow: Wydawnictwo Uniwersytetu Jagiellońskiego, 2002.

Frank, Alison. "The Children of the Desert and the Laws of the Sea: Austria, Great Britain, the Ottoman Empire, and the Mediterranean Slave Trade in the Nineteenth Century." *The American Historical Review* 117, no. 2 (2012): 410–44.

Franke, Jerzy. *Prasa kobieca w latach 1820–1918: W kręgu ofiary i poświęcenia.* Warsaw: Wydawnictwo SBP, 1999.

Frankel, Jonathan. "The Crisis of 1881–82 as 'Turning-Point in Modern Jewish History.'" In *The Legacy of Jewish Migration: 1881 and Its Impact,* edited by David Berger, 9–22. New York: East European Monographs, 1983.

French, William E. "Prostitutes and Guardian Angels: Women, Work, and the Family in Porfirian Mexico." *Hispanic American Historical Review* 72, no. 4 (1992): 529–54.

Fuchs, Rachel. *Poor and Pregnant in Paris: Strategies for Survival in the Nineteenth Century.* New Brunswick, NJ: Rutgers University Press, 1992.

Gabaccia, Donna. *From the Other Side: Women, Gender, and Immigrant Life in the U.S., 1820–1990.* Bloomington: Indiana University Press, 1994.

——. "Women of the Mass Migrations: From Minority to Majority, 1820–1930." In *European Migrants: Global and Local Perspectives,* edited by Dirk Hoerder and Leslie Page Moch, 90–111. Boston: Northeastern University Press, 1996.

Gabaccia, Donna, and Franca Iacovetta, eds. *Women, Gender, and Transnational Lives: Italian Workers of the World.* Toronto: University of Toronto Press, 2003.

Gąsowski, Tomasz. "Urbanizacja Galicji w dobie autonomicznej." *Studia historyczne* 28, no. 2 (1985): 223–43.

Gawin, Magdalena. "Progressivism and Eugenic Thinking in Poland, 1905–1939." In Turda and Weindling, *Blood and Homeland,* 167–83.

——. *Rasa i nowoczesność: Historia polskiego ruchu eugenicznego (1880–1952).* Warsaw: Wydawnictwo Neriton, Instytut Historii PAN, 2003.

Geertz, Clifford. "Local Knowledge: Fact and Law in Comparative Perspective." In *Local Knowledge: Further Essays in Interpretive Anthropology,* 215–234. New York: Basic Books, 1983.

Gibson, Mary. *Born to Crime: Cesare Lombroso and the Origins of Biological Criminology.* Westport, CT: Praeger Publishers, 2002.

——. *Prostitution and the State in Italy, 1860–1915.* Columbus: The Ohio State University Press, 1999.

Gilfoyle, T. J. *City of Eros: New York City, Prostitution, and the Commercialization of Sex, 1790–1920.* New York: W.W. Norton and Company.

——. "Prostitutes in the Archives: Problems and Possibilities in Documenting the History of Sexuality." *American Archivist* 57, no. 3 (1994): 514–27.

Gitelman, Zvi. *A Century of Ambivalence: The Jews of Russia and the Soviet Union, 1881 to the Present.* Bloomington: Indiana University Press, 2001.

Glickman, Nora. "The Jewish White Slave Trade in Latin American Writings." *American Jewish Archives* 34, no. 2 (1982): 178–89.

Gorham, Deborah. "The 'Maiden Tribute of Modern Babylon' Re-examined: Child Prostitution and the Idea of Childhood in Late Victorian England." *Victorian Studies* 21, no. 3 (1978): 353–79.

Grittner, Frederick K. *Myth, Ideology, and American Law.* New York: Garland, 1990.

——. "White Slavery: Myth, Ideology, and American Law." PhD diss., University of Minnesota, 1986.

Gubernat, I. "Miasto Zapolskiej." In Data, *Miasto-kultura-literatura, wiek XIX,* 213–25.

Guy, Donna J. "Lower-Class Families, Women, and the Law in Nineteenth-Century Argentina." *Journal of Family History* 10, no. 3 (1985): 318–31.

——. *Sex and Danger in Buenos Aires: Prostitution, Family, and Nation in Argentina.* Lincoln: University of Nebraska Press, 1991.

——. "White Slavery, Public Health, and the Socialist Position on Legalized Prostitution in Argentina, 1913–1936." *Latin American Research Review* 23, no. 3 (1988): 60–80.

Hamann, Brigette. *Hitler's Vienna: A Dictator's Apprenticeship*. New York: Oxford University Press, 1999.

Harris, Ruth. *Murders and Madness: Medicine, Law, and Society in the Fin de Siècle*. Oxford: Clarendon Press, 1989.

Harsin, Jill. *Policing Prostitution in Nineteenth-Century Paris*. Princeton, NJ: Princeton University Press, 1985.

Healy, Maureen. *Vienna and the Fall of the Habsburg Empire: Total War and Everyday Life in World War I*. Cambridge: Cambridge University Press, 2004.

Hershatter, Gail. *Dangerous Pleasures: Prostitution and Modernity in Twentieth-Century Shanghai*. Berkeley: University of California Press, 1997.

Hoerder, Dirk, ed. *Labor Migration in the Atlantic Economies: The European and North American Working Classes during the Period of Industrialization*. Westport, CT, 1985.

Holzer, Jerzy, and Jan Molenda. *Polska w pierwszej wojnie światowej*. Warsaw: Wiedza Powszechna, 1967.

Hondagneu-Sotelo, Pierrette. *Gendered Transitions*. Berkeley: University of California Press, 1994.

Hüchtker, Dietlind. "Enlightenment—Education—Social Reform: Concepts of Sociopolitical Activities in the Habsburg Province of Galicia." In *History of Social Work in Europe (1990–1960): Female Pioneers and Their Influence on the Development of International Social Organizations*, edited by Berteke Waaldijk and Sabine Hering, 161–69. Wiesbaden: VS Verlag für Sozialwissenschaften, 2003.

Ihnatowicz, E. "Miasto kryminalne." In Data, *Miasto-kultura-literatura, wiek XIX*, 111–24.

Inglot, Stefan. *Historia chłopów polskich*. Warsaw: Ludowa Spółdzielnia Wydawnicza, 1972.

Irwin, Mary Ann. "'White Slavery' as Metaphor: Anatomy of a Moral Panic," *Ex Post Facto: The History Journal* 5 (1996): 1–22.

Jargiło, Katarzyna. "Ciąża, poród i połóg kobiety dziewiętnastowiecznej." MA thesis, Jagiellonian University, 2005.

Jarowiecki, Jerzy. *Dzieje prasy polskiej we Lwowie do 1945 roku*. Cracow: Księgarnia Akademicka, 2008.

Kaczyńska, Elżbieta. *Człowiek przed sądem. Społeczne aspekty przestępczości w Królestwie Polskim (1815–1914)*. Warsaw: Wydawnictwo Uniwersytetu Warszawskiego, 1994.

Kaplan, Marion A. *The Jewish Feminist Movement in Germany: The Campaigns of the Jüdischer Frauenbund, 1904–1938*. Westport, CT: Greenwoood Press, 1979.

——. *The Making of the Jewish Middle Class: Women, Family, and Identity in Imperial Germany*. New York: Oxford University Press, 1991.

——. "Prostitution, Morality Crusades, and Feminism: German-Jewish Feminists and the Campaign against White Slavery." *Women's Studies International Forum* 5, no. 6 (1982): 619–27.

Karpińska, Małgorzata. *Złodzieje, agenci, policyjni strażnicy . . . Przestępstwa pospolite Warszawie 1815–1830*. Warsaw: Wydawnictwo DiG, 1999.

Kawalec, Krzysztof. "Spór o eugenikę w Polsce w latach 1918–1939." *Medycyna Nowożytna: Studia nad Kulturą Medyczną* 7, no. 2 (2000): 87–102.

Keire, Mara L. "The Vice Trust: A Reinterpretation of the White Slavery Scare in the United States, 1907–1917." *Journal of Social History* 35, no. 1 (2001): 5–41.

Kemadoo, Kamala, and Jo Doezema, eds. *Global Sex Workers: Rights, Resistance, and Redefinition*. New York: Routledge, 1998.

Kępski, Czesław. "Łódzkie Zydowskie Towarzystwo Dobroczynności w latach 1899–1918." *Biuletyn Zydowskiego Instytutu Historycznego w Polsce*, nos. 3–4 (1990): 93–100.

——. *Towarzystwa dobroczynności w Królestwie Polskim 1815–1914*. Lublin: Wydawnictwo Uniwersytetu Marii Curie-Skłodowskiej, 1993.

Kertzer, David I. *Sacrificed for Honor: Italian Infant Abandonment and the Politics of Reproductive Control*. Boston: Beacon Press, 1993.

——. "Syphilis, Foundlings, and Wetnurses in Nineteenth-Century Italy." *Journal of Social History* 32, no. 3 (1999): 589–602.

Kieniewicz, Stefan. *The Emancipation of the Polish Peasantry*. Chicago: The University of Chicago Press, 1969.

Kieval, Hillel. "Middleman Minorities and Blood." In *Essential Outsiders: Chinese and Jews in the Modern Transformation of Southeast Asia and Central Europe*, edited by Daniel Chirot and Anthony Reid, 208–33. Seattle: University of Washington Press, 1997.

——. "Neighbors, Strangers, Readers: The Village and the City in Jewish-Gentile Conflicts at the Turn of the Nineteenth Century." *Jewish Studies Quarterly* 12, no. 1 (2005): 61–79.

——. "The Rules of the Game: Forensic Medicine and the Language of Science in the Structuring of Modern Ritual Murder Trials." *Jewish History* 26, nos. 3–4 (December 2012): 287–307.

Klier, John D. "Emigration Mania in Late-Imperial Russia: Legend and Reality." In *Patterns of Migration, 1850–1914*, edited by Aubrey Newman and Stephen W. Massil, 21–30. London: Jewish Historical Society of England, 1996.

——. *Russians, Jews, and the Pogroms of 1881–82*. Cambridge: Cambridge University Press, 2011.

Kligman, Gail, and Stephanie Limoncelli. "Trafficking Women after Socialism: From, To, and Through Eastern Europe." *Social Politics: International Studies in Gender, State and Society* 12, no. 1 (2005): 118–40.

Kmiecik, Zenon. *Prasa warszawska w latach 1886–1904*. Wrocław: Zakład Narodowy imienia Ossolińskich Wydawnictwo, 1989.

Kofman, Elinor. "Female 'Bird of Passage' a Decade Later: Gender and Immigration in the European Union." *International Migration Review* 33 (1999): 269–99.

Kołodziej, Edward. "Emigracja z ziem polskich od końca XIX wieku do czasów współczesnych i tworzenie się skupisk polonijnych." In *Emigracja z ziem polskich w XX wieku*, edited by A. Koseski, 11–24. Pułtusk, Poland: Wyższa Szkoła Humanistyczna, 1998.

Konarski, K. "Ruch stowarzyszeniowy w Warszawie w latach 1905–1915 (w świetle akt kancelarii gubernatora warszawskiego)." In *Z dziejów książki i bibliotek w Warszawie*, edited by S. Tazbir. Warsaw: Państwowy Instytut Wydawniczy, 1961.

Kowalski, Gregorz Maria. *Przestępstwa emigracyjne w Galicji, 1897–1918*. Cracow: Wydawnictwo Uniwersyteta Jagiellońskiego, 2003.

Kozłowska-Sabatowska, Halina. *Ideologia pozytywizmu galicyjskiego: 1864–1881*. Wrocław: Zakład Narodowy im. Ossolińskich, 1978.

Kurkowska, Marta. "Birth Control in the Industrial Age: Cracow 1878–1939." *Polish Population Review*, no. 10 (1997): 161–84.

Largent, Mark A. *Breeding Contempt: The History of Coerced Sterilization in the United States.* New Brunswick, NJ: Rutgers University Press, 2011.

Lennartsson, Rebecka. *Malaria Urbana: The Registergirl Anna Johannesdotter and Prostitution in Stockholm around Nineteen Hundred.* PhD diss., Department of Cultural Anthropology and Ethnology, Uppsala University. Stockholm: Stockholm Public Library, 2001.

Levine, Phillipa. *Prostitution, Race, and Politics: Policing Venereal Disease in the British Empire.* New York: Routledge, 2003.

Lewandowski, Jan. "Austro-Węgry wobec sprawy polskiej w czasie I wojny światowej: Początki zarządu okupacyjnego w Królestwie." *Przegląd Historyczny* 66, no. 3 (1975): 383–408.

Limoncelli, Stephanie A. *The Politics of Trafficking: The First International Movement to Combat the Sexual Exploitation of Women.* Stanford, CA: Stanford University Press, 2010.

Lindenmeyr, Adele. *Poverty Is Not a Vice: Charity, Society, and the State in Imperial Russia.* Princeton, NJ: Princeton University Press, 1996.

Lipska-Toumi, Marzena. *Prawo polskie wobec zjawiska prostytucji w latach 1918–1939.* Lublin: Wydawnictwo KUL, 2014.

Loentz, Elizabeth. *Let Me Continue to Speak the Truth: Bertha Pappenheim as Author and Activist.* Cincinnati, OH: Hebrew Union College Press, 2007.

Łojek, Jerzy, ed. *Prasa polska w latach 1864–1918.* Warsaw: Państwowe Wydawnictwo Naukowe, 1976.

Lowy-Zelmanowicz, Ilana. *The Polish School of Philosophy of Medicine: From Tytus Chalubinski (1820–1889) to Ludwik Fleck (1896–1961).* London: Kluwer Academic, 1990.

Lucassen, Leo. "A Brave New World: The Left, Social Engineering, and Eugenics in Twentieth-Century Europe." *International Review of Social History* 55, no. 2 (2010): 265–96.

Luddy, Maria. *Prostitution and Irish Society, 1800–1940.* Cambridge: Cambridge University Press, 2007.

Magocsi, Paul Robert. *Historical Atlas of Central Europe.* Toronto: University of Toronto Press, 2002.

Mahler, Sarah, and Patricia Pessar. "Gender Matters: Ethnographers Bring Gender from the Periphery toward the Core of Migration Studies." *International Migration Review* 40, no. 1 (2006): 27–63.

Mahood, Linda. *The Magdalenes: Prostitution in the Nineteenth Century.* New York: Routledge, 1990.

Markiewicz, Henryk. *Pozytywizm.* Wrocław: Państwowe Wydawnictwo Naukowe, 1950.

Markiewiczowa, Hanna. *Działalność opiekuńczo-wychowawcza Warszawksiego Towarzystwa Dobroczynności 1814–1914.* Warsaw: Wydawnictwo Akademii Pedagogiki Specjalnej im. Marii Grzegorzewskiej, 2002.

Mathius, Peter, and Sidney Pollard, eds. *The Cambridge Economic History of Poland,* vol. 8, *The Industrial Economies: The Development of Economic and Social Policies.* Cambridge: Cambridge University Press, 1989.

Mazur, Elżbieta, ed. *Od narodzin do wieku dojrzałego: Dzieci i młodzież w Polsce,* Part 2, *Stulecie XIX i XX.* Warsaw: Instytut Arceologii i Etnologii Polskiej Akademii Nauk, 2003.

Mazur, Elżbieta. *Dobroczynność w Warszawie XIX wieku.* Warsaw: Instytut Archeologii i Etnologii Polskiej Akademii Nauk, 1999.

———. "Opieka nad sierotami w dziewiętnastowiecznej Warszawie." In *Od narodzin do wieku dojrzałego: Dzieci i młodzież w Polsce,* Part 2, *Stulecie XIX i XX,* edited by Elżbieta Mazur, 39–50. Warsaw: Instytut Archeologii i Etnologii Polskiej Akademii Nauk, 2003.

Meyerowitz, Joanne J. *Women Adrift: Independent Wage Earners in Chicago, 1880–1930.* Chicago: University of Chicago Press, 1988.

Milewski, Stanisław. *Ciemne sprawy dawnych warszawiaków.* Warsaw: Państwowy Instytut Wydawniczy, 1982.

Morawska, Ewa. "Labor Migrations of Poles in the Atlantic World Economy, 1880–1914." *Comparative Studies in Society and History* 31, no. 2 (1989): 237–72.

Mosse, George L. *Nationalism and Sexuality. Respectability and Abnormal Sexuality in Modern Europe.* New York: Howard Fertig, 1985.

Murdzek, Benjamin P. *Emigration in Polish Social-Political Thought, 1870–1914.* Boulder, CO: East European Monographs, 1977.

Musielak, Michał. *Sterylizacja ludzi ze względów eugenicznych w Stanach Zjednoczonych, Niemczech i w Polsce (1899–1945): Wybrane problemy.* Poznań: Wydawnictwo Poznańskie, 2008.

Musil, Robert. *The Man without Qualities.* vol. 2. London: David and Charles, 1979.

Myśliński, Jerzy. *Studia nad polską prasą społeczno-polityczną w zachodniej Galicji, 1905–1914.* Łódź: Państwowe Wydawnictwo Naukowe, 1970.

Najdus, Walentyna. *Rodzina i domownicy rzemieślnika polskiego w latach 1772–1918 na podstawie materiałów małopolskich.* Warsaw: Państwowe Wydawnictwo Naukowe, 1991.

Narkiewicz, Olga. *The Green Flag: Polish Populist Politics, 1867–1970.* London: Croom Helm, 1976.

Nautz, Jürgen. "The Effort to Combat the Traffic in Women in Austria before the First World War." *Journal for Police Science and Practice* 2 (2012): 82–95.

Nawyn, Stephanie, A. Reosti, and L. Gjokaj. "Gender in Motion: How Gender Precipitates International Migration." In *Advances in Gender Research* 13 (2009): 175–202.

Nemes, Robert. *The Once and Future Budapest.* DeKalb, IL: Northern Illinois University Press, 2005.

Nietyksza, Maria. *Ludność Warszawy na przełomie XIX i XX wieku.* Warsaw: Państwowe Wydawnictwo Naukowe, 1971.

———. *Rozwój miast i aglomeracji miejsko przymysłowej w Królestwie Polskim, 1865–1914.* Warsaw: Państwowe Wydawnictwo Naukowe, 1986.

Nye, Robert A. *Crime, Madness, and Politics in Modern France: The Medical Concept of National Decline.* Princeton, NJ: Princeton University Press, 1984.

Obrębski, Joseph. *The Changing Peasantry of Eastern Europe.* Cambridge, MA: Schenkman Publishing Company, 1976.

Od narodzin do wieku dojrzałego: Dzieci i młodzież w Polsce. Part 1: Maria Dąbrowska and Andrzej Konder, eds. *Od średniowicza do wieku XVIII.* Part 2: Elżbieta

Mazur, ed. *Stulecie XIX i XX.* Warsaw: Instytut Archeologii i Etnologii Polskiej Akademii Nauk, 2002–2003.

Oosterhuis, Harry. *Stepchildren of Nature: Krafft-Ebing, Psychiatry, and the Making of Sexual Identity.* Chicago: The University of Chicago Press, 2000.

Paleolog, Stanisława. *The Women Police of Poland.* London: Association of Moral and Social Hygiene, 1957.

Pawlowska, Anna. "Kwestie etyczno-obyczajowe w prasie kobiecej przelomu XIX i XX wieku (na łamach 'Steru' i 'Nowego Slowa')." *Studia historyczny* 30, no. 4 (1987): 571–88.

Peiss, Kathy Lee. *Cheap Amusements: Working Women and Leisure in Turn-of-the-Century New York.* Philadelphia: Temple University Press, 1986.

Pick, Daniel. *Faces of Degeneration: A European Disorder, 1848–1918.* Cambridge: Cambridge University Press, 1989.

Pivar, David J. *Purity Crusade: Sexual Morality, and Social Control, 1868–1900.* Westport, CT: Greenwood Press, 1973.

Plach, Eva. *The Clash of Moral Nations: Cultural Politics in Piłsudski's Poland, 1926–1935.* Athens, OH: Ohio University Press, 2006.

Podgorska-Klawe, Zofia. "Warszawski dom podrzutków (1732–1901)." *Rocznik Warszawski* 12 (1974): 111–45.

Polonsky, Antony. *The Jews in Poland and Russia,* vol. 2, *1881–1914.* Oxford: Oxford University Press, 2010.

Poovey, Mary. "Speaking of the Body: Mid-Victorian Constructions of Female Desire." In *Body/Politics: Women and the Discourses of Science,* edited by Mary Jacobus, et al., 29–46. New York: Psychology Press, 1990.

Porter-Szucs, Brian. *Faith and Fatherland: Catholicism, Modernity, and Poland.* Oxford: Oxford University Press, 2011.

Quataert, Jean H. *Staging Philanthropy: Patriotic Women and the National Imagination in Dynastic Germany, 1813–1916.* Ann Arbor: University of Michigan Press, 2001.

Quétel, Claude. *History of Syphilis.* Cambridge: Polity Press, 1990

Ransel, David. *Mothers of Misery: Child Abandonment in Russia.* Princeton, NJ: Princeton University Press, 1988.

Rogger, Hans. "Government Policy on Jewish Emigration." In *Jewish Policies and Right-Wing Politics in Imperial Russia,* edited by Hans Rogger, 176–87. Berkeley: University of California Press, 1996.

Rosen, Ruth. *The Lost Sisterhood: Prostitution in America, 1900–1918.* Baltimore: The Johns Hopkins University Press, 1982.

Rosenberg, Charles E. *The Care of Strangers: The Rise of America's Hospital System.* Baltimore: Johns Hopkins University Press, 1995.

Rudzki, Jerzy. *Aleksander Świętochowski i Pozytywizm Warszawski.* Warsaw: Państwowe Wydawnictwo Naukowe, 1968.

Sargent, T. J. "The Ends of Four Big Inflations." Working Paper. Chicago: University of Chicago Press, 1982.

Schneider, William H. *Quality and Quantity: The Quest for Biological Regeneration in Twentieth-Century France.* Cambridge: Cambridge University Press, 1990.

Scott, James C. *Seeing Like a State: How Certain Schemes to Improve the Human Condition Have Failed.* New Haven, NJ: Yale University Press, 1998.

——. *Weapons of the Weak: Everyday Forms of Peasant Resistance.* New Haven, CT: Yale University Press, 2008.

Scott, Joan Wallach. *Gender and the Politics of History.* Revised ed. New York: Columbia University Press, 1999.

Sejda, Bronisław. *Dzieje medycyny w zarysie.* Warsaw: Państwowy Zakład Wydawnictw Lekarskich, 1973.

Siemion, Ignacy Z. "Sława i zniesławienie: O życiu i pracach Augustyna Wróblewskiego." *Analecta: Studia i Materiały z Dziejów Nauki* 11, nos. 1–2 (2002): 251–97.

Sikorska-Kowalska, Marta. *Wizerunek kobiety Łódźkiej prełomu XIX i XX wieku.* Łódź: Wydawnictwo Ibidem, 2001.

Sikorska-Kulesza, Jolanta. "Miasto-przestrzeń niebezpieczna dla kobiet (prostytucja w Królestwie Polskim w drugiej połowie xix wieku)." *Polskie Towarzystwo Historyczne przełomy w historii. XVI Powszechny Zjazd historyków Polskich: Pamiętniki* 3, no. 4 (1999): 341–49.

——. "Prostitution in Congress Poland." *Acta Poloniae Historica* 83 (2001): 123–33.

——. "Prostytucja w XIX wieku na podolu w świetle badań Józef Apolinarego Rolle." *Przegląd Wschodni* 5, no. 3 (1998): 435–42.

——. "Sądy doraźne nad prostytucją w Warszawie w maju 1905 roku w świetle prasy." *Rocznik Warszawski* 45 (2007): 111–27.

——. *Zło tolerowane: Prostytucja w Królestwie Polskim w XIX wieku.* Warsaw: Mada, 2004.

Smith, Helmut. *The Butcher's Tale: Murder and Anti-Semitism in a German Town.* New York: W. W. Norton, 2002.

Soares, L. C. *Prostitution in Nineteenth-Century Rio de Janeiro.* London: ISA Occasional Papers, no. 17, 1988.

Soloway, Richard A. *Demography and Degeneration: Eugenics and the Declining Birthrate in Twentieth-Century Britain.* Chapel Hill: University of North Carolina Press, 1995.

Spector, Scott. "Where Personal Fate Turns to Public Affair: Homosexual Scandal and Social Order in Vienna, 1900–1910." *Austrian History Yearbook* 38 (2007): 15–24.

Spongberg, Mary. *Feminizing Venereal Disease: The Body of the Prostitute in Nineteenth-Century Medical Discourse.* London: Macmillan, 1997.

Stansell, Christine. *City of Women: Sex and Class in New York, 1789–1860.* Urbana: University of Illinois Press, 1987.

Stapiński, A. *Zwalczanie kiły i rzeżaczki w Polsce.* Warsaw: Państwowy Zakład Wydawnictw Lekarskich, 1979.

Starr, Paul. *The Social Transformation of American Medicine: The Rise of a Sovereign Profession and the Making of a Vast Industry.* New York: Basic Books, 1982

Stauter-Halsted, Keely. "'A Generation of Monsters:' Jews, Prostitution, and Racial Purity in the 1892 L'viv White Slavery Trial." *Austrian History Yearbook* 38 (2007): 25–35.

——. "Jews as Middleman Minorities in Rural Poland: Understanding the Galician Pogroms of 1898." In *Antisemitism and Its Opponents in Modern Poland,* edited by Robert Blobaum, 39–59. Ithaca, NY: Cornell University Press, 2005.

———. *The Nation in the Village: The Genesis of Peasant National Identity in Austrian Poland, 1848–1914.* Ithaca, NY: Cornell University Press, 2001.

———. "The Physician and the Fallen Woman: Medicalizing Prostitution in the Polish Lands." *Journal of the History of Sexuality* 20, no. 2 (2011): 270–90.

———. "Policing the Borders of Belonging: Gender, Sexuality, and the Polish Nation." *Rocznik Antropologii Historii* 5, no. 1 (2015): 37–54.

Steidl, Annemarie, Engelbert Stockhammer, and Hermann Zeitlhofer. "Relations among Internal, Continental, and Transatlantic Migration in Late Imperial Austria." *Social Science History* 31, no. 1 (2007): 61–92.

Stoler, Ann Laura. *Carnal Knowledge and Imperial Power: Race and the Intimate in Colonial Rule.* Berkeley: University of California Press, 2002.

Surdacki, Marian. "Dzieci porzucone w społeczeństwach dawnej Europy i Polski." In *Od narodzin do wieku dojrzałego: Dzieci i młodzież w Polsce,* Part 1, *Od średniowiecza do wieku XVIII,* edited by Maria Dąbrowski and Andrzej Klonder, 169–91. Warsaw: Instytut Archeologii i Etnologii Polskiej Akademii Nauk, 2002.

Sylvester, Roshanna. *Tales of Old Odessa: Crime and Civility in a City of Thieves.* DeKalb: Northern Illinois University Press, 2005.

Szajkowski, Zosa. "How the Mass Migration to America Began." *Jewish Social Studies* 4, no. 4 (1942): 291–310.

Thomas, William, and Florian Znaniecki. *The Polish Peasant in Europe and America.* 3 vols. Chicago: University of Chicago Press, 1919.

Tobera, Marek. *"Wesołe gazetki": Prasa satyryczno-humorystyczna w krolestwie polskim w latach 1905–1914.* Warsaw: Państwowe Wydawnictwo Naukowe, 1988.

Turda, Marius, and Paul J. Weindling, eds. *Blood and Homeland: Eugenics and Racial Nationalism in Central and Southeast Europe, 1900–1940.* Budapest: Central European University Press, 2007.

Urbanek, Bożena. "Zagadnienia seksualności w polskich poradnikach medycznych I poł. XX–do1939 r." *Medycyna Nowożytna: Studia nad Historią Medycyny* 12, nos. 1–2 (2005): 163–80.

Uzarczyk, Kamila. "'Moses als Eugeniker'?: The Reception of Eugenic Ideas in Jewish Medical Circles in Interwar Poland." In Turda and Weindling, *Blood and Homeland,* 283–97.

———. *Podstawy ideologiczne higieny ras i ich realizacja na przykladzie slaska w latach 1924–1944.* Torun: Wydawnictwo Adam Marszałek, 2003.

Van Heyningen, Elizabeth B. "The Social Evil in the Cape Colony, 1868–1902: Prostitution and the Contagious Diseases Acts." *Journal of Southern African Studies* 10 (April 1984): 170–97.

Vincent, Isabel. *Bodies and Souls: The Tragic Plight of Three Jewish Women Forced into Prostitution in the Americas, 1860 to 1939.* New York: HarperCollins Publishers, 2005.

Vital, David. *A People Apart: The Jews of Europe, 1789–1939.* Oxford: Oxford University Press, 1999.

Vyleta, Daniel M. *Crime, Jews, and News: Vienna, 1890–1914.* New York: Berghahn Books, 2007.

Wahab, Stephanie. "'For Their Own Good?': Sex Work, Social Control, and Social Workers, a Historical Perspective." *Journal of Sociology and Social Welfare* 29, no. 4 (2002): 39–57.

Walaszek, Adam. "Wychodżcy, Emigrants, or Poles: Fears and Hopes about Emigration in Poland, 1870–1939." *Association of European Migration Institutions Journal* 1 (2002): 78–84.

Walkowitz, Judith R. *City of Dreadful Delight: Narratives of Sexual Danger in Late-Victorian London.* Chicago: University of Chicago Press, 1992.

——. *Prostitution and Victorian Society: Women, Class, and the State.* New York: Cambridge University Press, 1980.

Wandycz, Piotr. *The Lands of Partitioned Poland, 1795–1918.* Seattle: University of Washington Press, 1974.

Weeks, Jeffrey. *Sex, Politics, and Society: The Regulation of Sexuality since 1800.* : Leymann, 1981.

——. *Sexuality and Its Discontents: Meanings, Myths, and Modern Sexualities.* London: Routledge and Kegan Paul, 1985.

Weindling, Paul. *Health, Race, and German Politics between National Unification and Nazism, 1870–1945.* Cambridge: Cambridge University Press, 1989.

——. "Sexually Transmitted Diseases between Imperial and Nazi Germany." *Genitourinary Medicine* 70, no. 4 (1994): 284–89.

White, Luise. *The Comforts of Home: Prostitution in Colonial Nairobi.* Chicago: University of Chicago Press, 1990.

Wicker, Elmus. "Terminating Hyperinflation in the Dismembered Habsburg Monarchy." *The American Economic Review* 76, no. 3 (June 1986): 351–54.

Wingfield, Nancy M. "Destination: Alexandria, Buenos Aires, Constantinople; 'White Slavers' in Late Imperial Austria." *Journal of the History of Sexuality* 20, no. 2 (2011): 291–311.

——. "The Enemy Within: Regulating Prostitution and Controlling Venereal Disease in Cisleithanian Austria during the Great War." *Central European History* 46, no. 3 (2013): 568–98.

Wolfgang, Marvin E. "Cesare Lombroso." In *Pioneers in Criminology*, edited by Hermann Mannheim, 232–91. Montclair, NJ: Patterson Smith, 1972.

Wood, Nathaniel D. "Becoming a 'Great City': Metropolitan Imaginations and Apprehensions in Cracow's Popular Press, 1900–1914." *Austrian History Yearbook* 33 (2002): 105–29.

——. *Becoming Metropolitan: Urban Selfhood and the Making of Modern Cracow.* DeKalb: Northern Illinois University Press, 2010.

——. "Sex Scandals, Sexual Violence, and the Word on the Street: The Kołasówna Lustmord in Cracow's Popular Press, 1905–1906." *Journal of the History of Sexuality* 20, no. 2 (2011): 243–69.

——. "Urban Self-Identification in East Central Europe before the Great War: The Case of Cracow." *East Central Europe* 33, nos. 1–2 (2006): 9–30.

Yuval-Davis, Nira. *Gender and Nation.* London: Sage, 1997.

Zabotniak, Ryszard. "Dzieje Polskiego Towarzystwa Eugenicznego." *Kwartalnik Historii i Nauk Techniki* 16, no. 4 (1971): 769–87.

Zahra, Tara. "Travel Agents on Trial: Policing Mobility in East-Central Europe, 1889–1989." *Past and Present* 223, no. 1 (2014): 161–93.

Zając, Bogusław. "Sprzedajność niewiast na ziemiach polskich." *Polityka*, November 4, 2009, 2.

Żblikowski, Andrzej. *Żydzi krakowscy i ich gmina w latach 1869–1919.* Warsaw: Żydowski Instytut Historyczny w Polsce, Instytut Naukowo-Badawczy, 1994.

Zielecki, A. "Społeczeństwo Sanok u progu XX wieku." In *Sanok: dzieje miasta praca zbiorowa,* edited by Feliks Kiryka. Cracow: Wydawnictwo "Secesja," 1995.

Zipperstein, Steven J. *The Jews of Odessa: A Cultural History, 1794–1881.* Stanford, CA: Stanford University Press, 1986.

Zyblikiewicz, Lidia. *Kobieta w Krakowie w 1880 r.: Studium demograficzne.* Cracow: Historia Jagiellońska, 1999.

Index